ENCOUNTERING the LIVING GOD ... BECOME A BIBLE LOVER

by

Dean F. Kimball and Virginia M. Kimball

Joy in God Press
Westford, MA 01886
2019

ACKNOWLEDGMENTS

The first words to be written as part of the New Testament are: **"We always give thanks to God**." (1 Thessalonians 1:2) In this spirit, the authors want to give thanks to God for inspiring and embracing us in faith throughout our marriage. We both had the opportunity to study God's word and now we bring together our talents to write this book so that others may feel comfortable to begin a journey in reading, studying, and finding God's presence in the Bible. As God's gift, we both had the privilege of biblical education; however, both of us pursued this education adapting it to our own particular life journey as all bible readers must do.

For us and for our family, God has been with us throughout life's most joyful moments and also in critical moments as we raised our children and when we faced serious illnesses. We know that God has been with us throughout it all as a loving and caring Presence. For this reason, we strived to live faithfully and raise our children to know God as a life-giving Being. We want to give special thanks to Richard Clifford S.J. and Daniel Harrington S.J., members of the faculty at Weston Jesuit School of Theology; William Holiday, formerly professor at Andover Newton Theological School; and Bertrand Buby S.M., professor at the International Marian Research Institute [IMRI] at the University of Dayton. Also, we express our gratitude to all our professors who taught us to read the biblical text in theology and ministerial classes. Virginia Kimball holds a doctorate in Sacred Theology (STD) from the International Marian Research Institute (IMRI) at the University of Dayton, a pontifical academy associated with the Marianum Seminary in Rome, a License in Sacred Theology (STL) from IMRI, and a Master's Degree from Andover Newton Theological School. Dean Kimball holds a Masters of Divinity Degree from the Weston Jesuit School of Theology and a Master's Degree in Physics from Johns Hopkins University.

The authors especially want to thank Susan Lillian Fall – Longtime friend and inspiring assistant for all her help with this book, reading & reviewing content and providing useful edits. Her response to the material was positive and always encouraged us.

Finally, this publication would have never reached completion without the help of our son Thomas Kimball. He oversaw production of the on-line elements, as well as creating the graphics required for the cover and the chart on the inside.

WHAT THIS BIBLE STUDY IS ALL ABOUT!

An Observation

At the present time, there is a tremendous quantity of material available concerning all aspects pertaining to the Holy Bible. There are millions of books available about every possible topic concerning biblical matters – some of them are old and some of them are new; some of them are long and some of them are short; many of them are good but some of them are not so good. There are a very large number of internet sites devoted to things biblical – one can call up a copy of most of the bibles in print today for free online (although many times they do not include the study material available in the hard copy edition) and copies of most of the articles that have appeared in the scholarly journals as well as essays or sermons about every book of the Bible (if one consults a database at a library). In addition, many magazines, sermons and talks are available concerning biblical topics.

This staggering amount of material is a mixed blessing. On the one hand, an individual can obtain a considerable knowledge about all aspects of the Bible. On the other hand, a sincere individual wishing to become knowledgeable of the Bible and the inspired writings that it contains can be overwhelmed by it all and flounder around without ever achieving a solid understanding of the Bible and its message. Such an individual can have his or her desire weakened and ultimately give up the quest for knowledge entirely. Such an individual needs a helping hand.

The motivation for writing this book was just that – to give the serious learner of the Bible a helping hand. The material can be read and studied by an individual on his or her own or in a bible study group.

The Book

This book begins by putting forward the question: **What is the Bible?**

In answering this question, first it can be said that the word "bible" is derived from the Latin word "*biblia*" meaning "books." We discover that, in reality, "the Bible" does not exist. In actuality, "the Bible" is many different books under the same title and, therefore, one must speak of reading "a Bible." The phrase "you should read a Bible" is not really accurate either. Nobody actually reads a whole bible like one does other "books." The meaning intended by this phrase is that an individual should read the Scriptures (the inspired writings contained in a Bible). This book then goes on to help one become a faithful reader of the Scriptures. The word "holy scriptures" infers "holy writings."

ENCOUNTERING the LIVING GOD ... BECOME A BIBLE LOVER

I. THE TRUE NATURE OF THE BIBLE

II. KNOWLEDGE ESSENTIAL FOR READING THE SCRIPTURES WITH UNDERSTANDING

PART 1
THE SCRIPTURES: WRITINGS INSPIRED BY GOD

PART 2
THE TEXTS OF THE WRITINGS THAT ARE HOLY SCRIPTURE

PART 3
MORE INFORMATION NECESSARY FOR READING THE SCRIPTURES WITH UNDERSTANDING

III. EXPLORING THE CANONICAL WRITINGS WRITTEN BEFORE THE BIRTH OF JESUS

PART 1
THE ISRAELITE PERIOD

PART 2
THE EXILE AND THE RETURN

PART 3
THE WRITINGS OF THE HELLENISTIC PERIOD

PART 4
THE WISDOM WRITINGS

W4 Mark ch 11-6
Matthew ch 5
Luke ch 1-2
John ch.11
W4
Luke ch 24
Acts ch 1

PART 5
THE HEART OF THE OLD TESTAMENT

IV. EXPLORING THE CANONICAL WRITINGS WRITTEN AFTER THE BIRTH OF JESUS

PART 1
JESUS AND THE APOSTOLIC PERIOD

W4

PART 2
PAUL AND THE LETTERS OF PAUL

PART 3
THE REMAINING WRITINGS OF THE NEW TESTAMENT

PART 4
THE HEART OF THE NEW TESTAMENT

PART 5

THE HEART OF ALL THE SCRIPTURES

Thought to keep in mind …
the Old Testament and the New Testament form a unity of God's revelation.

The Transfiguration of Christ: "Six days later, Jesus took with him Peter and James and John, and led them up a high mountain apart by themselves. And he was transfigured before them, and his clothes became dazzling white, such as no one on earth could bleach them. And there appeared to them Elijah with Moses, who were talking with Jesus." (Mark 9: 2-8) Harper Collins Study Bible, New Revised Standard Edition, 1989).

CHAPTER ONE

The Bible - inspired texts and "study stuff"

Introduction

For us today, living active lives in the world of the 21st century, A Bible comes to us as a book. Every bible printed in the United States is identified by an ISBN number and it is also available electronically on devices like the Kindle, and publicly free and available on websites. Its great popularity is attested to by its being the bestselling book of all time. We see its importance when we observe that it is a featured section of its own in almost every library and book store. Further attestation to its popularity is provided by its having been featured in both movies and television programs.

A Bible, however, did not always exist in book form. The earliest of these writings began as oral traditions and only later came to be written down. The later ones began their existence written with a stylus and ink on papyrus or parchment (vellum) scrolls, or on single sheets if they were sufficiently brief. The writings did not appear bound in book form (known as a codex) until the middle of the 2nd century C.E. The codex form was well suited for the letters of Paul, which were written in the 1st century. Because being personal letters, they were suitably short in length. Many of these were written on scrolls and treasured and preserved in special clay jars.

Today, we have these sacred writings available in all kinds of print and digital forms. On first sight, a Bible does not immediately beg to be read. First of all, it is clearly a very long book as is evidenced by its large volume – over 1,500 pages. The very thin pages and the almost complete lack of illustrations also act to deter the aspiring reader. At the present time, many people prefer to read short books, like popular paperback romance novels. If one attempts to read the Bible, it is quickly found that the book contains writings about people who lived long, long ago in places that are foreign to us, who had a lifestyle with which we are unfamiliar and who participated in events about which most of us today know very little if anything at all. In addition, it does not seem to be composed with a continuous developing plot, but rather it is a collection of writings having many different literary types and styles including both narrative and poetical forms. Why, therefore, would anyone undertake, in this the 21st century, to undertake the apparently daunting task of reading this book?

Opposed to these reasons for not reading a Bible, however, are four facts that strongly suggest that this book is a must read! Fact #1: The Bible was the first book to be printed. When Gutenberg developed the first printing press with movable type in the 1450s, he chose a Bible as the very first book to print on his new invention. This suggests that the Bible held great significance not only to Gutenberg but to many people in the 15th century. Fact #2: The Bible is the bestselling of all the books that have ever been printed. Such great popularity is certainly an indication that it was believed to possess great significance. It continues to be listed as the most published book to this day. Fact: #3: The Bible has been printed in more languages than any other book. Surely, it must be of considerable significance if people took the time to translate it into a myriad of languages so that people living all over the world would be able to read it in their own language! Fact #4: Parts of the Bible are included in university courses on classic world literature. These are all clear indicators that a Bible must be important and is an inspirational read!

A person seeking to read the Bible can go to a bookstore, or to a library, or pop on internet bookstore web pages to obtain a copy. What happens in this actual quest to obtain a copy of the Bible? One quickly finds that the Bible comes in a wide range of sizes from reasonably thin to very thick and heavy. Also, it comes with a variety of cover types ranging from traditional hardcover to standard paperback. It becomes apparent that bibles come in various editions: there are simple bibles, known as Reader's Editions, that contain the writings and little else. There are bibles, known as Study Bibles that contain many pages of supporting scholarly articles and information. Today, there is even a "Green Bible" which is environmentally friendly because it has a cotton/linen cover, is printed on recycled paper, and is printed using a soy-based ink.

A very significant question now presents itself. It is the following: What is the source of the great popularity that is enjoyed by a Bible? The bibles that were printed in the, now, distant past on paper having gold edges provide a clue to a Bible's great popularity. The purpose of the gold edges was to symbolize that a Bible possessed very significant spiritual value.

Here is what seven individual people, living around the world, had to say about the importance of a Bible for themselves:[1]

1. *Strabonni, Bangledesh (South Asia)*
   Strabonni and others are finding a new life through the power of Scripture. "I want to thank those people who gave me this precious Holy Bible that brought me to the right path." Strabonni says. "I read my Bible in the morning and night."   January 2015

2. *Thon Bunnen, Cambodia*
   Thon discovered that God loves him by reading the Bible stories. He found courage in God's word. "I am so grateful to God," Thon says. "I always read the books I received after school and before I go to bed. I don't have any fear and bad dreams anymore. I read about David as a child when he defeated a big man because he prayed and trusted God. I believe that when I pray and trust God, I become like King David, able to overcome all troubles."   June 2015

3. *Returning Veterans, United States*
   Then there is the stress our veterans face after returning home. Physically and emotionally wounded, God's word helps these brave but battered veterans rebuild their lives. One veteran who struggled with despair says the Bible turned his life around. "My attitude about life in general has improved. I'm reading the Bible almost daily now. I feel more alive."   July 2015

---

[1] The seven quotations cited here are from The Bible-A-Month Partner's Report that is published monthly by the Bible-A-Month Partners of the American Bible Society [101 North Independence Mall East FLB, Philadelphia, PA 19106-2155].

4. *Pria, India (Asia)*
   She says, "The Bible means everything to me. I read the Bible in the
   morning and in the evening. It helps me to understand about God and
   live a holy life."   January 2017

5. *A young Christian from Cuba (Caribbean)*
   "A Bible means to me a divine gift from God Himself. It is his word,
   His guide for our life and conduct."   February 2017

6. *Wilma, South Sudan (East Africa)*
   "The Bible helped me a lot. I feel happy about having a Bible," she
   explains. "I read my Bible three times a day! It gives me the
   importance of being loved by God, despite the loss of my mother."
                                                             March 2017

7. *Wang, China (Asia)*
   "I am a bachelor and God's word is everything I have," he says. "When
   I have free time, I read. The Bible is my daily life. I receive energy
   from reading. I must read to know God's will."   April 2017

What is the spiritual value of a Bible? The answer to this question cannot be found by continuing to look at a Bible from the outside. So let us turn our attention from the outside to what is contained inside the Bible – **Let's Open it!**

Rachael Carson, in her book titled *Silent Spring* made the following statement:

The biologist George Wald [*A Pigment of the Eye*] once compared his work on an exceedingly specialized subject, the visual pigment of the eye, to a very narrow window through which at a distance one can see only a crack of light. As one comes closer the view grows wider and wider, until finally through this same narrow window one is looking at the universe. [2]

Beginning to read a Bible is much the same experience as looking through a narrow window. The more often and more deeply your reading of the Bible becomes, like approaching the narrow crack ever more closely, the more clearly your vision of the Creator of the universe becomes.

---

[2] Rachel Carson, *Silent Spring* (Boston: Houghton Mifflin, 2002), 199.

Part One … The Scriptures: Writings Inspired by God:
Inspiration – a Fundamental Mystery
Coming to Belief in Inspiration
Some Thoughts about Reading Inspired Texts
The Concepts of canon and the Four Principal Canons

CHAPTER TWO

INSPIRATION – A FUNDAMENTAL MYSTERY

The inspiration of the Scriptures is truly a mystery of God. On the one hand, the people who believe in the Scripture's inspiration have no way to **definitively** prove this to those who do not hold this view. On the other hand, those people who do not believe in the inspiration of the holy Scriptures have no way to definitively disprove the position of the believers. It is truly a mystery and all mysteries cannot be proven!

The claim that the Scriptures are divinely inspired is expressed in the Scriptures themselves. This is plainly stated in 2 Tim 3:16-17: "All Scripture is inspired by God and is useful for teaching, for refutation, for correction, and training in righteousness, so that one who belongs to God may be competent, equipped for every good work" But this statement does not constitute a definitive proof – it will not convince people who doubt the truth of this claim.

Therefore, this is the situation. On the planet earth, there are two groups of people. One group composed of Jews and Christians who fervently profess that the Scriptures are inspired by God. At the same time, there is a second group of people who just as fervently deny that the Scriptures are inspired by God. However, the first group states that people have to come by faith to belief in the mystery of inspiration of the Scriptures.

The "how" of inspiration

There are two ways to approach answering this question:

❑ We can take an **"approach from above."** We can first seek to determine who God is. Then working from that point, we can use deductive reasoning to rationally try and reach an understanding of "how" the Scriptures are inspired.

❑ We can take an **"approach from below."** Working with what the inspired text reveals, we can seek to determine how it is revealed within the writings themselves to see that the Scriptures were indeed inspired by God.

The first of these approaches is based upon the presupposition that we "understand" God well enough to be able to deduce the manner in which the Scriptures were inspired. There, however, is a problem here. God is both "totally other" and yet "always present to us." God is not a human to be analyzed. (A technical way to say this is that God is not "anthropomorphic.") God is a Being, a Source of Life, a holy One who is relational and loving, always giving care and mercy, and offering a bond of love. We find that Scripture itself states that God's ways are not our ways. This suggests that we really do not know God well enough, or ever will, to be able to claim an adequate answer by means of the first approach. In some ways, this calls to mind the mistake that Adam and Eve made in their relationship with God. They desired to obtain and be able to claim for themselves all the knowledge that is God's ("eat of the tree of the knowledge of good and evil.)" (Gen 2:9)

The second of these two approaches in understanding the "how" of inspiration, first of all, is to be familiar all of the Scriptures. Throughout the Scriptures, there appears, as one can sense, a consistent voice of God known as the *sensus plenior*. One has to be aware of God's voice throughout the writings, a miracle of God's revelation that was slowly uncovered over many centuries. As we progress through the study of all the writings, always try and be aware of God's voice. Overall, this is mystery and cannot be proven in a human or scientific way. And, yet, the concept that the Scriptures are inspired by God has been accepted and maintained over many centuries.

Revelation comes to mankind in cooperation with select human agents

We see from the writings of Scripture that God's word is communicated to mankind through the hands and minds of human beings. God is portrayed as speaking directly to Adam (**Gen 3:9**) and Moses (**Ex 3:4**). God speaks through dreams to Samuel (**1 Sam 3:1-15**), to Mary of Galilee by an angel (**Luke 1: 26-38**), and in visions to the author of the book of Revelation (**Rev 4:1**). The word comes to us in the Deuteronomistic History (DH) through its various writers and editors and in the wisdom books through the tradition of the community. In the letters of the apostle Paul, God's word comes to us through Paul himself. And finally, the ultimate revelation of the word comes to us through God's Son, the life, continued presence, and sayings of Jesus Christ. It also comes through all those people who remembered what Jesus said and wrote things down and passed this knowledge on orally as well. We acknowledge all this in the writings of who it was who wrote and redacted the Gospels.

In the case of the prophets, they knew that they were speaking a word that came from God. The books of the prophets abound with phrases like: "Thus says the Lord" (**Amos3:12**) and "hear the word of the Lord." (**Is 28:14**) The prophet Amos expresses this awareness as follows: "The Lord God has spoken; who can but prophesy?" (**Amos 3:8**)

Awareness on the part of the inspired speaker or writer, however, is not always essential. It is the case that many times the writer was unaware that God was working through him or her. Consider the following examples which appear to present the authors with more practical purposes:

❑ In the prologue to the Book of Sirach (Ecclesiasticus), the grandson of the man who wrote the book speaks of the task he undertook in translating the book from its original Hebrew into the Greek language: "During that time I have applied my skill day and night to complete and publish the book for those living abroad …." (NRSV) *It seems his immediate purpose was mainly translation.*

14

- ❑ In **1 Cor 7: 10, 12**
  In these verses, Paul distinguishes between what he says and what is said by the Lord. *Here in chapter seven of 1 Cor, Paul is pointing out that these particular words are from God.*

- ❑ In **John 20:31** John states that he has selected his material but he gives no indication that his selection was made by other than human means.

- ❑ In the prologue to his Gospel (**Lk 1:1-4**), Luke states that he has tried to write an orderly account. *Luke claims to be putting a record of the "events" concerning Jesus, and their fulfillment, into an orderly fashion as he knew them.*

The True Nature of the Holy Scriptures

Christians strongly believe that God is author of the Scriptures because it has been the belief of the Christian community since its beginning. This was the reason behind making a list of inspired books in the canon. But the faithful also strongly desire to believe in the freedom of the human authors because, as we study Scripture, we never encounter anything that compels us to believe that the human authors acted other than in a fully human way –the prophets being an exception because they were aware that they were speaking God's message directly to the people.

There is an avenue of escape from this dilemma concerning the manner of inspiration of the Scriptures. The solution is not to be found by seeking to find unassailable arguments in support of one side against the other. **The answer to this dilemma is to fully accept both sides at the same time!** The writings that make up the Holy Scriptures are the word of God **_and_** the word of mankind. The Holy Scriptures truly have God for their author **_and_** truly are the work of human authors at one and the same time!

We have arrived at a fundamental truth concerning the Holy Scriptures. The Scriptures participate in the great Christian mystery: the inter-penetration of the human and the divine. We see this in Jesus Christ, fully God and fully man at the same time. We see this in the Church, the body of Christ and a human institution at the same time. We see this in the Christian believer, divinized by the indwelling of the Trinity and human at the same time. How the Divine One can coexist, so to speak, with the human without destroying the independence and freedom of the human is the greatest and most fundamental mystery of all. We must remember that in the Bible's creation narrative, God said: "Let us make man in our image, after our likeness … God created man in his image, in the divine image he created him; male and female he created them." (Genesis 1: 26-27 NAB) The reality of this incarnational aspect of God is, however, experienced by the Christian faithful. Christ is both human AND divine, God has incarnated in the human world to communicate with us. Jesus said: "Whoever has seen me has seen the Father …. Do you not believe that I am in the Father and the Father is in me? The words that I speak to you I do not speak on my own. The Father who dwells in me is doing his works. Believe me that I am in the Father and the Father is in me." (John 14: 9- 11 NAB)

15

A Most Significant Consequence

The most significant consequence of the truth of Christian faith that the authorship of the Scriptures is, at the same time, **both human and divine**, is that when one reads the Holy Scriptures the reader experiences an engagement with the living God. Jews have always believed this. Almost all Christians – Catholic, Orthodox, Protestant and Independent Christian churches will attest to this truth. For Catholics, this is expressed in The Dogmatic Constitution on Divine Revelation *Dei Verbum*:

> For in the sacred books, the Father who is in heaven meets his children in great love and speaks with them....[3]

Official Statements of the Churches

Another important teaching of the Roman Catholic Church about the Bible is found in the Vatican II document, *Dogmatic Constitution on Divine Revelation*:

> For holy mother Church, relying on the belief of the Apostles (see John 20:31; 2 Tim 3:16; 2 Peter 1:19-20, 3:15-16), holds that the books of both the Old and New Testaments in their entirety, with all their parts, are sacred and canonical because written under the inspiration of the Holy Spirit, they have God as their author and have been handed on as such to the Church herself. In composing the sacred books, God chose men and while employed by Him they made use of their powers and abilities, so that with Him acting in them and through them, they, as true authors, consigned to writing everything and only those things which He wanted. [4]

This statement is referenced in the Roman Catholic ***Catechism of the Catholic Church*** (Article 3: Sacred Scripture, §105 and §106). This same belief is plainly stated in the recent document of the Pontifical Biblical Commission: *The Interpretation of the Bible in the Church,* 1993 (excerpt taken from section IIID3):

> The Word of God finds expression in the work of human authors. The thought and the words belong at one and the same time both to God and to human beings, in such a way that the whole Bible comes at once from God and from the inspired human author.[5]

The Eastern Orthodox Church and the Anglicans take the same position. In a joint statement issued at the Moscow Conference held in 1976, biblical scholars included the

---

[3] *Dogmatic Constitution on Divine Revelation (Dei Verbum)*, promulgated Nov 18, 1965, § 21.

[4] *Dogmatic Constitution on Divine Revelation (Dei Verbum)*, § 11.

[5] *The Interpretation of the Bible in the Church,* 1993 (excerpt taken from § III D 3):

statement: The Scriptures constitute a coherent whole. They are at once divinely inspired and humanly expressed. [6]

Here is a challenge. Can the reader think of any test that can be applied to the writings of Scripture that will prove that they have God for their author? Is the following idea of one person's experience a possible acceptable response to this challenge?

> The Bible is like a cathedral. The architect is God, the craftsmen and laborers are the sacred writers, and the materials are the different elements of the writings. If we wish to truly understand this divine monument which is the bible, we must never lose sight of its vital unity. To this end we must spare no effort, examine the triforia as well as the nave, climb up to the tribunes and the roof, study each element in the place it occupies where alone it takes on its true worth. It is only after such minute study and long years of familiarity that we will be able fully to grasp the meaning of the whole as well as of each detail. Then we will no longer be surprised at anything; we will, on the contrary, perceive such a splendor of order as could be attributed only to the hand of God. [7]

Three Theories of Inspiration That Have Been Rejected by Councils

Here are three positions concerning inspiration that have been proposed in the past but which were then subsequently rejected by scholars:

> a. **The dictation theory**
> This theory is built upon the position that God dictated the Scriptures to the human authors. But this theory clearly does not allow for the freedom of the human authors and must be rejected. Although you could hold that God dictated to each author in that author's own style so that the freedom of the human authors, as we see it, is only apparent. There is no way to disprove this position, but it is not a very satisfying position to hold.
> b. **The theory of subsequent approbation**
> This theory holds that the human writers wrote entirely on their own, NOT aided by God in any way. The finished writings were later approved by God. This theory preserves the freedom of the human authors but it certainly does not allow for the belief that the Scriptures have God for their author. This theory was condemned by the Roman Catholic Ecumenical Council of Vatican I, begun in 1868.
> c. **The theory of external and negative assistance**
> This theory holds that God only assisted the human authors by preventing them from making errors in their writing or saying things which God did not want them to say. This theory does not allow the human authors their full freedom nor does it allow God to be the true author of the Scriptures either. It was condemned by the Roman Catholic Council of Vatican I.

---

[6] Bishop Kallistos of Diokleia, "How to read the Bible" in *The Orthodox Study Bible* (Nashville, TN: Thomas Nelson Publishers, 1993), 762.

[7] Paul Synave and Pierre Benoit, *Prophecy and Inspiration* (New York, NY: Desclee Company, 1961), 130.

CHAPTER THREE

COMING TO BELIEF IN INSPIRATION

One cold, rainy morning, two bible teachers were sitting with a very close friend in *Dunkin Donuts*. The cool, rainy weather created a thoughtful frame of mind. One of the teachers, also familiar with geology, began commenting that he observed that the rain drops falling on the window glass followed a very crooked path down to the bottom of the window frame. This observation prompted him to ponder why, on a geological scale, water flowing over a flat floodplain gives birth to a meandering stream. The other teacher began musing about how often in scriptures that water is a symbol of life and is a mystical reference to the life-giving God.

You must know who these two teachers are! (Virginia and Dean) … Then, our friend broke the silence by asking a startling question. Obviously pondering in his own way, but perhaps because he was in the presence of two bible teachers, the friend asked: "I have heard that the Bible is the bestselling book of all time. *The Guinness Book of Records* in 2017 reported that the Bible Society concluded that recent copies of the Bible were estimated about five billion copies. But, why is that the case when I have observed many churchgoers these days don't seem to be reading it much? Do they still believe it is the word of God? Seeing this has convinced me that the idea of the Bible's inspiration is just an old-fashioned idea, a kind of fairy tale." One of the teachers responded to the friend's question almost without giving it a second thought: "It is true, though, that there are folks who in some way know the Bible contains scriptures which are writings that are holy and inspired by God. There's got to be a reason why the Bible is still the world's number one publication!" And with the friend's questions, a deep discussion had begun!

The raindrops continued to impact the window glass with an audible sound and the wind continued to blow. Seizing upon the moment, the friend asked a second question. "Although at one time I believed in the Bible, and read it from time to time, I have since fallen away from believing that it is inspired. Can you prove to me that the Scriptures are inspired by God?" Pausing for a moment, both teachers then responded to this question saying that the inspiration of the Scriptures is a mystery. There is, therefore, no way that it can be **proved** that Scriptures are inspired by God.

"What do you mean by mystery?" he inquired. "The word 'mystery,'" one teacher replied, "derives from the New Testament Greek word *mysterion*. This word essentially means: that which is hidden or incomprehensible. In the sense that God is wholly other and totally incomprehensible, God is a mystery."

The friend then persisted, asking, "If the Scriptures are truly inspired by God, then how can I come to belief in this reality if you cannot prove it to me?" One of the teachers came forth with an explanation. Some theologians hold that there is one way to establish that the Scriptures are inspired by God. These bible specialists argue that if you start with an understanding of who God is, then through the use of reason you can argue logically to the position that the Scriptures are inspired by God.

"This will not do," said the friend, in a friendly manner but not accepting the theory, "and for two reasons. First, by using this approach one can only arrive at the position that God **could** have produced the Scriptures, if God happened to be so inclined. But this approach cannot tell us that God **actually did do** this. Secondly, since it is most likely that arriving at who God is was accomplished on the basis of the Scriptures, it appears to be, at least at first glance, a case of circular reasoning."

"Alright then," the other teacher said, "if you will not accept this argument from reason, then we will present for you another argument based on authority. We will lay out before you a number of statements made by the official leaders of the churches testifying to the belief of their churches in the inspiration of the Scriptures. Here are a few such statements, beginning with the Catholic Church." It so happened the teachers were reviewing this material in their notes that day and it was handy to pull out! … One wonders what people around slowly sipping their coffee were thinking of all this?

The General Council of Florence – Decree for the Copts (1442)

[The Holy Roman Church] professes that one and the same God is the author of the Old and the New Testaments, i.e., of the Law, the Prophets and the Gospel, because by inspiration of one and the same Holy Spirit, the saints of both covenants have spoken.[8]

The General Council of Trent – Fourth Session (8 April 1546) [Roman Catholic Church]

Following, then, the example of the orthodox Fathers, it [the church] receives and venerates with the same sense of loyalty and reverence all the books of the Old and New Testament – for the one God is author of both […][9]

The First Vatican General Council, Third Session – Dogmatic Constitution *Dei Filius* On The Catholic Faith (1870) [Roman Catholic Church]

These [the books of the Old and the New Testaments] the Church holds to be sacred and canonical, not because, having been carefully composed by mere human industry, they were afterwards approved by her authority, nor merely because they contain revelation with no admixture of error, but because, having been written by the inspiration of the Holy Spirit, they have God for their author and have been delivered as such to the Church herself.[10]

---

[8] Decree for the Copts (1442), The General Council of Florence in *The Christian Faith in the Doctrinal Documents of the Catholic Church*, edited by Jacques Dupuis (New York: Alba House, 2001), §208, 100.
[9] Decree of Reception Of The Sacred Books and Apostolic Traditions, Fourth Session (8 April 1546), The General Council of Trent, in Dupuis, §210, 102.
[10] Dogmatic Constitution *Dei Filius* On The Catholic Faith, Chapter II: On Revelation, Third Session, The First Vatican General Council in Dupuis, §216, 104.

The Second Vatican General Council – Dogmatic Constitution Dei Verbum (1965) [Roman Catholic Church]

> [...] For the composing of these sacred books God chose human beings, and while he employed them, they made use of their own powers and abilities, so that with God acting in them and through them, they – as true authors – committed to writing all those things and only those things he wanted.[11]

The Catechism of the Catholic Church

> For Holy Mother Church, relying on the faith of the apostolic age, accepts as sacred and canonical the books of the Old and the New Testaments, whole and entire, with all their parts, on the grounds that, written under the inspiration of the Holy Spirit, they have God for their author and have been handed on as such to the Church herself.[12]

The teachers were careful to point out that this statement in the *Catechism* is only a quotation from the *Dogmatic Constitution on Divine Revelation* (*Dei Verbum*). It is, therefore, not an independent statement. But, they included it in this list because the *Catechism* has become such a popular document.

The friend seemed rather unimpressed with all these quotations. The teachers continued their effort to substantiate how the churches believe in inspiration. They decided to present one or two official statements from the other major Christian churches. These other churches, not being as highly hierarchically organized as the Catholic Church, usually don't generate such numerous official documents, they noted. And, they did add that this does not in any way indicate that these other churches reverence the Scriptures less than does the Catholic Church. In fact, often the lay members of these other churches usually make a greater use of the Scriptures than do the lay members of the Catholic Church. Here, then, the three friends were beginning to get into a serious conversation, without knowing that they may have been getting "looks" from others at coffee tables near them. But the two teachers continued and offered two more official statements, one representing the Eastern Orthodox Church and one representing the Lutheran Church.

The Eastern Orthodox Church taken from the *Agreed Statement of Moscow (1976)*

> The Scriptures constitute a coherent whole. They are at once divinely inspired and humanly expressed. They bear authoritative witness to God's revelation of himself in creation, in the Incarnation of the Word and in the whole history of salvation, and as such express the Word of God in human language. [13]

---

[11] Dogmatic Constitution *Dei Verbum* (1965), Chapter III: The Divine Inspiration of Sacred Scripture and Its Interpretation, The Second Vatican General Council, in Dupuis, §249, 120.

[12] Promulgated by Pope John Paul II, *Catechism of the Catholic Church*, Second Edition, (Liberia Editrice Vaticana, 1997), 31.

[13] Anglican-Eastern Orthodox Dialogue, *Agreed Statement* 1976, in "How to Read the Bible," Right Reverend Kallistos, *The Orthodox Study Bible*, Academic Community of St. Athanasius Academy, (Nashville, Thomas Nelson: 2008), 1757.

The Commission on Theology and Church Relations of the Lutheran Church – Missouri Synod (March 1975)

> The term "inspiration" denotes the guidance of the Holy Spirit under which the Biblical authors recorded what God had revealed to them about the mysteries of His being and the meaning of His mighty acts in human history for man's salvation and under which they wrote concerning any other subject, even if it was about a matter of which they had knowledge apart from revelation (e.g., that Josiah was killed at Megiddo, that Demas deserted Paul, that Eutychus fell out of a window).[14]

Feeling confident now, one teacher said, "There you have a number of official statements testifying to the reality of the inspiration of the Scriptures. Do you now have faith that this is in fact a reality?" The friend responded by saying: "You certainly have set before me a fair number of official statements testifying to a belief in the inspiration of the Scriptures from the Catholic, Protestant and Orthodox churches. They do not, however, convince me of the reality of this. No number of statements by the leaders of churches will ever bring me to a living faith in the inspiration of the Scriptures!" There were smiles at nearby tables.

"Okay," one of teachers said. "Well, here is some more information." (Not that many people wander into *Dunkin Donuts* with a pile of papers and books alongside their laptops.) "If no multiplicity of official statements will serve to bring you to belief then consider the testimony of believing people. There is a veritable 'cloud' (an expression from Heb 12:1) of witnesses who profess a belief in the inspiration of the Scriptures." The teachers explained that under the present circumstances, they could only consider here two or three of the members of this "cloud" but the testimony of such a small sample might perhaps be convincing. "Listen then to these representative people. Let's begin with St. Basil, who lived in the fourth century."

> The best way to find what is fitting [for one's life] is the meditation of the divinely inspired Scriptures. For in these are found counsels for our actions, and the lives of blessed men, though transmitted in writing, are put before us, like living images of a godly life, for our imitation of their good works.[15]

"Now consider St. Tikhon of Zadonsk," described by The Right Reverend Kallistos, Bishop of Diokleia:

> If an earthly king, our emperor," says Saint Tikhon of Zadonsk(1724-83), "wrote you a letter, would you not read it with joy? Certainly, with great rejoicing and careful attention." But what, he asks, is our attitude towards the letter that has been addressed to us by no one less than God Himself? "You have been sent a letter, not by any earthly emperor, but by the King of Heaven. And yet you almost

---

[14] A Report of the Commission on Theology and Church Relations of the Lutheran Church – Missouri Synod, March 1975, The Inspiration of Scripture, I. Inspiration and the Writers of Scripture.

[15] Quoted in, Theodore Stylianopoulos *Bread for Life*, (Brookline Department of Religious Education, Greek Orthodox Archdiocese of North and South America, 1980), 16.

despise such a gift, so priceless a treasure." To open and read this letter, St Tikhon adds, is to enter into a personal conversation face to face with the living God. "Whenever you read the Gospel, Christ himself is speaking to you. And while you read, you are praying and talking to Him."[16]

Finally, feeling a little exasperated, the teachers suggested the following statement from two professors: Dr. Fee who is at Regent College in Vancouver, British Columbia in Canada, and Dr. Stuart who is at Gordon-Conwell Theological Seminary in Massachusetts. (This just happened to pop up in the notes they had with them.) They explained how these scholars speak of the necessity for interpreting the Bible as significant for Christian life:

> A more significant reason for the need to interpret lies in the nature of Scripture itself. Historically the church has understood the nature of Scripture much the same as it has understood the person of Christ – the Bible is at the same time both human and divine. "The Bible," it has been correctly said, "is the word of God given in human words in history." […] He chose to speak his eternal truths within the particular circumstances and events of human history.[17]

"Does that testimony help you at all?" they asked.

The friend, starting to feel a little uncomfortable, commented: "I do not find this procedure helpful to me. Let me explain, when my daughter was attending a Catholic High School, I had occasion to go to one of the Father-Daughter nights. For entertainment, the nuns had hired a hypnotist. Never mind that I have heard that Catholics are not supposed to participate in hypnosis for entertainment! Anyway, there were three or four people in the crowd who were easily hypnotized and did anything they were asked to do. I feel that in a similar manner there will always be people who will believe anything, and testify to their belief – just like the hypnotized persons. If you ask a large group of random people to vote, I think you will find that a vast majority testify to their lack of belief in the inspiration of the Scriptures. Those individuals who do believe in the inspiration of the Scriptures are only a very small part of all people and hence they appear to me like individuals who were easily hypnotized. This method of private testimonies, therefore, does not work for me."

At this point, the teachers thought of a completely different approach. "If all those official statements and quotations from saints and scholars do not bring you to faith in the reality of the inspiration of the Scriptures, consider the following proposition. We suggest that if the Scriptures are really inspired by God, then people who read them should experience something that would touch them deeply. In support of this position, we want to offer you one example of the effect reading the Scriptures can have on one particular person. We could, of course, offer you many more examples, but for the moment one will have to suffice.

---

[16] Right Reverend Kallistos, "How to read the Bible," in *The Orthodox Study Bible*, (Nashville, TN: Thomas Nelson, 2008), 1757.

[17] Gordon D. Fee and Douglas Stuart, *How to Read the Bible for All It's Worth*, Third Edition, (New York:Zondervan, 2003), 21 and 22.

"Consider the following passage from a book written by a man who is an assistant professor in historical theology at Multnomah Biblical Seminary in Portland, Oregon. He recounts a story about a conversation similar to the one we have been having. In the story, an individual named Dave describes a friend who began reading the Bible. Let me quote this story," said one of the teachers. "It goes like this:

'After that, Dave shared, [that] the man started up yet another Bible read-through this time on his own. Dave reiterated how much the man was growing, even though the man himself wasn't particularly aware of the changes taking place in his life. In fact the man was able, offhand, to summarize the landscape of the entire Bible, but didn't think much about it.

'Dave asked him, "Would you have been able to do that a year ago?" Only then did it dawn on the man that the Bible was now much more alive to him – a part of his life in a way it had never been before. He had grown and changed, but it wasn't something he noticed as it happened. But from what Dave shared, it was pretty obvious to others.

'That's the way Bible reading works; it feeds our souls, drawing the "eyes of our hearts" upward as we open ourselves to the mind of Christ in a bolder way than ever before. We begin to grow in the process, and others see it even if we don't see it ourselves. That's the way real growth works isn't it?'" [18]

The friend seemed intrigued with this story. One teacher asked: "This is an interesting account, don't you think?"

Sensing that the friend was reflecting more on this idea, one more quotation was pulled out from the notes, a statement by an Eastern Orthodox priest:

So the faithful reader of the Bible is gradually transformed by God's grace into a spiritual person. Through devoted reading of the Bible this dialogue between the reader and God becomes a process of the reader's renewal of heart and mind, and leads him to the exhilarating discovery of the One Who speaks to the Christian through the Bible. [19]

"What do you think of this approach?" they again asked their friend.

The friend replied: "This is certainly interesting but it does not move me to come to faith. If you will remember, back in our younger years, there was a very popular book titled *The Power of Positive Thinking* by Norman Vincent Peale. The book had a positive effect on many people but no claim was ever made to the effect that it was inspired by God. Unfortunately, this approach does not do it for me! But let me add that I really like the concept that if the Scriptures are really inspired, then continued reading of them could cause a gradual transformation."

---

[18] R.N. Frost, *Discover the Power of the Bible*, (Oregon: Harvest House Publishers, 2000), 87.
[19] Theodore Stylianopoulas, *Bread for Life*, (Department of Religious Education, Greek Orthodox Archdiocese of North and South America, 1980), 23.

"Well, there is one more thought to consider," one of the teachers said. "We still have what we consider to be a very good argument for coming to faith in inspiration of the Scriptures. Would you consider the evidence provided by Scripture itself? The Scriptures speak of belief in the inspired character of the Scriptures." The friend smiled, knowing that he was bound to hear more. "Proceed," he said, "I will listen. It will be interesting to see what you can find in the Scriptures themselves."

"A good place to begin is with the prophet Amos," one teacher said. "Amos was a prophet of the 8th century BCE. If you look at the writing in the Scriptures under his name you will find a number of statements attached to what Amos said that say 'Thus says the Lord.' This indicates that Amos believed that what he said came to him from God. In fact, Amos makes this statement himself in 3:8: 'The lion has roared, who would not fear? The Lord God has spoken, who would not prophesy?' The Jewish people believed that the prophets all spoke what God revealed to them to speak. This is evidenced in the New Testament by the following statement from the Second Letter of Peter.

> 'Know this first of all, that there is no prophecy of Scripture that is a matter of personal interpretation, for no prophecy ever came through human will; but rather human beings moved by the Holy Spirit spoke under the influence of God.' (2 Peter 1:20-21)

"Similarly, Paul, in his first letter to the Thessalonians tells them that the Gospel which they received was not a human word:

> 'And for this reason we too give thanks to God unceasingly, that, in receiving the word of God from hearing us, you received not a human word but, as it truly is, the word of God, which is now at work in you who believe.' (Thessalonians 2:13)

"In the Old Testament, in the Foreword to Sirach, the grandson who is translating his grandfather's book makes mention of a three part canon. He first refers to 'the Law, the prophets, and the authors who followed them' and the second time he refers to 'the Law itself, the prophecies, and the rest of the books.' These are early references (ca. 175 BCE) to a three part canon, which are the Scriptures of the early Christians. Note, by the way, that the only reference to Christian Scriptures in the New Testament is 2 Pt 3:15-16. The Jews and Christians in the 1st century believed that all of the Scriptures were inspired, demonstrated in the following passage from 2 Timothy (3:14-17):

> 'But you, remain faithful to what you have learned and believed, because you know from whom you have learned it, and that from infancy you have known [the] sacred scriptures, which are capable of giving you wisdom for salvation through faith in Christ Jesus. All Scripture is inspired by God and is useful for teaching, for refutation, for correction, and for training in righteousness, so that one who belongs to God may be competent, equipped for every good work.'

"One final bit of evidence for belief in the inspired nature of the Scriptures is provided by the use of the phrase 'it is written' by the writers of the NT compositions. This phrase was their way of

24

indicating that they were making a quotation from the Holy Scriptures. Examples of this are found in: Mt 2:5-6; 4:4, 6, and 10."

A big sigh of relief came when these examples were completed. No one said anything for a minute or two. The one teacher dared to ask in a quiet tone: "Have we succeeded in winning you over to having faith in the inspiration of the Scriptures?"

The friend did pause but then he confided: "This was a very impressive presentation. It certainly established that the Jews and Christians of the 1st century had a real belief in the inspiration of the Scriptures. This testimony, however, is over two thousand years old. You know that in those days people believed many of the unexplained happenings of every day, such as the idea that weather and earthquakes were of divine acts and even gods themselves. I, therefore, do not find that this evidence completely provides a sufficient basis for coming to belief."

One of the teachers then said, "We have one additional argument for coming to faith in the inspiration of the Scriptures. Consider, if you will, the evidence provided by Jesus himself. Jesus does not come right out and say that the Scriptures are inspired but he does refer to the Scriptures in ways that indicate that he does know them and gives them authority. First of all, Jesus refers to the Scriptures by making use of the usual term 'it is written.' This establishes without doubt that Jesus shared in the belief of his followers in the inspired character of the Scriptures (e.g.: Mk 12:10; Lk 4:21; 22:37, Jn 13:18). Secondly, Jesus refers to the Scriptures in such a way that is clear that he believes that they have a special authority. Observe that he makes use of the phrase: 'Have you never read in the Scriptures …?' (Mt 21:42; see also Mt 22:29 for a different phraseology)."

"Unfortunately," the friend said, but in an honest way, "this is not convincing. Have you not heard of the Jesus Seminar? They studied all of the sayings of Jesus in the Scriptures in the 1980s and 1990s and came to the conclusion that only one of them can be held to be authentic. All of the others, they declared, were possibly the invention of the 1st century Christian communities and most likely not attributable to Jesus himself. I remain, therefore, unconvinced." Then, unexpectedly, the teachers got animated! They nearly jumped out of their chairs stating, "The work of the Jesus Seminar is not accepted as being correct by most of today's scholars." Of course, their friend didn't know that.

Without permission, the teachers continued and offered one more possibility: "There is one remaining procedure that you can follow." It was yet another biblical passage. "Read the account of the healing of the boy with a demon in the Gospel of Mark (Mk 9:14-29). The boy is possessed by a demon and the apostles tried but could not free the boy from the spirit. They asked Jesus why they couldn't make the spirit leave the boy and Jesus replied that 'this kind can only come out by prayer (v.29).' All we can say now is that if you wish to believe in the inspiration of the Scriptures that you take up a program of prayer and fasting!"

"And what kind of prayer?" the friend asked quietly. They suggested it can be either when one prays words out loud, usually in a community giving praise and petitions to God. But, importantly, it can be a quiet activity when one reflects, reads God's words, speaking honestly from one's own heart, and lifting one's inner being to God in thoughts and words of one's very own. Fasting is not necessarily just avoiding eating certain foods. It really means "self-discipline." To fast, for example, one can stop watching television and spend the time reading the Scriptures. Since the beginning of Christianity, fasting in its central meaning meant to direct everything in one's life to Christ and to not waste frivolous time or actions on just pleasing oneself.

At that point, the three friends all observed that it had stopped raining, the sun had come out, and there was a beautiful double rainbow in the sky across the street. The teacher who was also a scientist at heart mentioned: "If you look closely, you will see that the red is on the top in the primary bow and on the bottom of the secondary bow. Isn't that amazing, but there is a scientific explanation." Not asking for this explanation, the other teacher gazed at the spectacle and reflected, "God employed the rainbow as a sign of the covenant, made with Noah and also offered to all humanity. Why does a rainbow represent the covenant? God's life-giving is offered to all humanity in a loving bond, a sign of universal peace that comes after the terrible rupture of mankind from God in the Fall, much like the beauty of the rainbow appears after the darkness of a storm."

Did all of this conversation lead to the understanding that the recognition of God as the one who inspired the Holy Scriptures comes from openness to God, with a willingness to spend time with the writings and study them, while praying and practicing self-discipline? The thought was planted: that is when it may become obvious that the Scriptures are inspired writings and as one reads, they come alive.

The mood had changed. The friend smiled and gave both of his friends a warm hug. "Can we meet like this again? I think I have lots to think about."

CHAPTER FOUR

SOME THOUGHTS ABOUT READING INSPIRED TEXTS

How does someone approach reading an inspired text? To answer this question it is necessary to return to what it means for a text to be inspired. We know that inspiration is a mystery. Consequently, no simple definition of what this includes is possible. But this mystery concerns how God and a human being interact to produce a text that is both divine and written in human language! God is present in the particular human words that make up the inspired writings.

It was stated above that an inspired writing is, at the same time, both fully the word of God and fully the words of humankind. If we accept this as truly representing the reality of the matter, then there are two ways that one can read the holy texts.

First of all, an individual can read it just as one reads a writing that is not inspired. It is fully the word of humankind, so it can be read as any writing that is truly the word of humankind. Just sit down and read it! In this manner the reader will get the benefit of all of the qualities that the composition possesses as a word of humankind, such as the beauty of the poetry or the interesting aspect of human history that it records. The reader will, however, risk not obtaining the full benefit available from its being an inspired writing.

How should an individual approach a composition which is known to have been inspired by God in order to take advantage of the divine aspect of the writing? We can take a lesson from the Divine Liturgy of the Orthodox Church. In the liturgy of the Orthodox Church, at the time of Holy Communion, when the people are told to come up for Communion, the Eucharist, the priest or deacon makes the invitation as follows: "Approach with fear of God, faith and love." What does he mean by the expression "fear of God?"

In this expression, the word "fear" does not mean to be afraid of God like one would be afraid if he or she were approaching a mountain lion. As used in this application the word "fear" (as it comes from the original biblical language) specifies an attitude of awe and reverence; it is the proper response of an individual to God. If this is the proper response of an individual coming to receive Communion then it is also the proper attitude of a person coming to read an inspired text! It is significant for the individual seeking to read an inspired text to begin with the proper attitude of mind and heart.

Furthermore, the expression "fear of God," or as it is sometimes translated "fear of the Lord," is entirely biblical. In fact, it appears over one hundred times throughout the biblical text, in both the Old Testament and the New Testament. The following are a few examples (taken from *The Catholic Study Bible*, 3rd Edition):

"Now, therefore, Israel, what does the LORD, your God, ask of you but to fear the LORD, your God, to follow in all his ways, to love and serve the LORD, your God, with your whole heart and with your whole being, to keep the commandments and the statutes of the Lord that I am commanding you today for your own well- being." (Deut 10:12-13)

"Let all the earth fear the LORD;
    Let all who dwell in the world show him reverence.
For he spoke, and it came to be,
    Commanded and it stood in place." (Ps 33:8-9)

"Seized with great fear of the LORD, the men offered sacrifice to the LORD, his God, and made vows." (Jonah 1:16)

"The Church throughout all Judea, Galilee, and Samaria was at peace. It was being built up and walked in the fear of the Lord, and with the consolation of the Holy Spirit it grew in numbers." (Acts 9:31)

` The liturgy of the Orthodox Church offers us another lesson about dealing with inspired texts. In the Divine Liturgy, immediately before the reading the Gospel, the priest reads the following prayer:

Shine within our hearts, loving Master, the pure light of your divine knowledge and open the eyes of our minds that we may comprehend the message of Your Gospel. Instill in us also reverence for your blessed commandments, so that having conquered all sinful desires, we may pursue a spiritual life, thinking and doing all those things that are pleasing to You. For You, Christ our God, are the light of our souls and bodies, and to You we give glory together with Your Father who is without beginning and Your all holy good, and life giving Spirit, now and forever and to the ages of ages. Amen.[20]

The lesson learned in this case is to pray a prayer before beginning to read a text of this nature. (Another lesson learned after quoting this prayer is to pray that God will enlighten our hearts to truly understand and be able to share with others who have discerned the same meaning.)

So there you have it. The way to read an inspired text is to approach it with an attitude of reverence and awe of God and with many prayers asking the Lord for help in understanding the text that you are going to read.

There is one more thought. It is clear from the parable of the Ten Lepers (Lk 17:11-19) that Jesus liked to be thanked for the works that he performed in God's name. In this parable ten lepers are healed but only one of them returns to thank Jesus for the healing and Jesus asks about where are the other nine. On the basis of this parable, it is apparent that we should offer a prayer of thanksgiving at the completion of our reading of the Holy Scriptures.

It is apparent, then, that study of the Scriptures involves a considerable amount of looking for specific verses within the writings. The ability to find a verse quickly, therefore, enables an

---

[20] Fr. Emmanuel Hatzidakis, *The Heavenly Banquet* (Columbia, Missouri: Orthodox Witness, 2008),142.

individual to conserve a lot of time. The lack of this ability will be enhanced by becoming familiar with the locations of various "books of Scripture." One helpful hint is to remember that the NT occupies only about 20% of the volume of the Scriptures and is, therefore, located nearer to the end than would be expected on a 50-50 division between OT and NT.

Study stuff (footnotes, articles, and brief commentaries, maps, charts, and glossaries) attached to each passage in a Study Bible will direct us to related passages and provide very useful background information. In some bible the books of the deuteronomical canon (the second list) of inspired writings are placed in the middle of the book or at the end.

CHAPTER FIVE

THE CONCEPT OF CANON AND THE FOUR PRINCIPAL CANONS

The concept of canon

What is a "canon?" First of all, let's consider what a biblical "canon" is not. It is not a "cannon." A cannon is a military weapon that causes great destruction, a means of saluting when the flag is being lowered, and a musical instrument that is played at the end of *Tchaikovsky's War of 1812 Overture*. The word that is of interest here is distinguished from the word "cannon" by having a single "n" – canon.

The word "canon," comes from the Greek word meaning "measuring stick" and came into use among Christian believers during the first three centuries CE. Clement of Alexandria exhorted the Christians of his time to live in adherence with the "rule of faith." Thus, for these early Christians the word had the meaning of a rule or norm of faith.

In the early part of the 4th century CE, the word began to be applied more generally to the Christian writings in the Bible with the meaning of "list." The canon was the list of writings that were believed to have been inspired by God and, therefore, served as the rule of faith. A writing that was on the list was said to be "canonical." Writings that were not on that list, i.e. that were held not to have been inspired by God, were termed "non-canonical." This terminology has been widely accepted since the time of the 4th century.

If you take the time to look at The *TANAKH* (Jewish Scriptures), The *New American Bible* (Roman Catholic), *The Orthodox Study Bible* (Eastern Orthodox), and *The New Revised Standard Version* (Protestant), you will discover that each of these Bibles contains a specific list of inspired writings. If you take a closer look you will discover that these four lists all have quite a number of writings in common but that no two of them are exactly the same! In reality, these canons are four different canons!

Why are there different canons?

What does the existence of four different canons signify? First of all, the fact that they exist at all signifies that the Jewish and Christian traditions share in believing that God has revealed Himself through certain particular writings. The belief that God inspired writings came to the Christians through their belief in the holiness of the Scriptures of the Old Testament. They simply extended this belief to include certain writings written in the first 125 years of the Christian era.

The canons of the Jewish, Orthodox, Protestant and Catholic traditions that are today accepted as identifying the writings inspired by God are the result of lengthy and complex processes of historical development. These historical processes did not result in complete agreement between the four traditions.

Old Testament (OT) and New Testament (NT)

A Christian Bible is traditionally divided into two parts called: The Old Testament and the New Testament. There is a biblical basis for the use of these terms. The word "testament" refers to the covenant God made with the people of God. God made a covenant with Moses and the Israelites at the time of the Exodus. Jeremiah speaks prophetically of a "new covenant" (Jeremiah 31:31ff) and the early Christians saw the fulfillment of this prophecy in the life of Christ (see 2 Corinthians 3:6-18). The language of the old and new covenants is clearly referenced in Hebrews (8:13).

In the present age, in an attempt to avoid anything that can be construed to be anti-Semitic or in any way could be offensive to the Jewish people, an effort is being made to designate the writings of the Old Testament by some other title. For example, a recent edition of *The New Oxford Annotated Bible* refers to these writings as "The Hebrew Scriptures." This title, however, while it is correct for the Protestant OT, is not appropriate to Catholic and Eastern Orthodox OT canons because they contain writings which are not included in the Jewish canon. Also, some of the OT writings for Christians were originally written in Greek. This title is also unsatisfactory because it obscures the fact that the writings are Scripture for Christians as well.

The use of the title "The Hebrew Scriptures" will surely result in influencing many Christian people to think that they do not need to read these writings. The first individual to propose abandoning the OT was Marcion, in the latter half of the 2nd century AD. Marcion was a heretic. He wanted to reject the whole collection of the Old Testament and even parts of the New Testament.

In the present age, the desire to abandon the OT is made a reality by the practice by many Christians of simply ignoring its presence. This practice, however, is misguided. The OT is important to Christians, first of all, because **the OT is as much the word of God as is the NT**. When Jesus quotes from "the Scriptures" he is referring to the so-called OT. Consequently, the OT should be studied for its own sake. Secondly, the OT is very important for anyone wishing to understand the NT because the OT is fundamental to our understanding of Second Temple Judaism from which early Christianity grew. However, even from the earliest primeval accounts in Genesis there appear prophetic statements that refer to Christ (understood, of course, once Christ came). Thirdly, it is important because the OT is the primary literary source for the authors of the NT writings. There is hardly a verse in the NT that does not either directly quote the OT or refer to passages in the OT. And, lastly, in a mystical sense if Christ has always existed, then Christ's voice as God is present in the OT.

For convenience, we will use the terms "Old Testament" and "New Testament," usually abbreviated as OT and NT, because no alternative terminology has been proposed that adequately represents the two collections of writings and has also achieved wide acceptance.

Use of the term Deuterocanonical

In times past, Roman Catholic scholars distinguished between the canonical writings shared with the Jews and the canonical writings which are contained in the Apocrypha. Consequently, they adopted the terms **"protocanonical"** and **"deuterocanonical"** (meaning "first canon" and "second canon") for the former and the latter groups respectively. The intention for the use of this terminology was to indicate a writing that supposedly originated at a later time than the proto-canonical books. Modern studies of the historical process of the development of the canon, however, have shown that some of the deuterocanonical books were accepted as being canonical prior to the time of acceptance of some of the proto-canonical books. This distinction, therefore, was not valid and this terminology, which dates to Sixtus of Sienna in 1566, has now fallen into disuse. One should bear in mind, however, that the distinction was merely one of historical time. A belief that there was a difference in the inspired nature of the writings never existed.

The Term: "intertestamental period"

In reading scholarly commentaries on the Bible, one frequently encounters the expression **"the intertestamental period."** This phrase is meant to refer to that period between the last composition contained in the OT and the time when the first composition of the NT was written. In the case of the Protestant canon, this is a period of some 300 to 400 years. In the case of the Roman Catholic and Eastern Orthodox canons, however, this is a period of not more than about 100 years since the last book of the OT, Wisdom, was written about 50 years before the birth of Christ and the first book of the NT, 1 Thessalonians, was written in 50 or 51 CE, about 20 years after the death of Christ.

The Four Canons
Introduction

It was mentioned earlier that if you take the time to look at the *TANAKH* (The Jewish Scriptures), the *New American Bible* (Roman Catholic) and *the New Revised Standard Version* or *New International Version* (both Protestant), you will discover that each of these Bibles contains a specific list of writings. If you take a closer look, you also will discover that these three lists all have some books in common but no two of the lists are the same.

It was also stated earlier that the list of writings that is today accepted as canonical is the result of a lengthy period of historical development. The details of this process need not concern us here; knowledge of all those details will not help us to read the Bible with greater understanding. It is sufficient for us to recognize that as a result of historical processes there are, at the present time, four major canons:

Jewish
Eastern Orthodox
Roman Catholic
Protestant

It is both appropriate and useful, however, to now consider the specific writings that are included in each of these canons. In doing this, it is easiest to consider the four canons in their historical order, taking the Jewish canon first, then treating the Eastern Orthodox and Roman Catholic canons, and then finally looking at the Protestant canon.

The Jewish Canon

The canon of the Jewish Scriptures is traditionally divided into three parts: the **Torah** ("teachings or instruction"), **Nevi'im** ("prophets"), and **Kethuvim** ("writings"). This three-part division is set forth in the Foreword to the Book of Sirach which dates to the period 200-180 BCE. [The book of Sirach is not contained in the Jewish or Protestant canons but it is included, however, as part of the Eastern Orthodox and Roman Catholic canons.]

The term **Torah** designates the first five books of the Bible:

Genesis
Exodus
Leviticus
Numbers
Deuteronomy

The word "Torah" is a Hebrew word which means teaching or instruction, but it can also have a wider meaning such as God's law (Ex 12:49) or the wisdom of a single word of scripture. It can even stand for a reflection on the mystical meaning of one Hebrew letter. "Doing Torah" is the art of entering into the meaning and teaching of each and every word of Scripture and, at some times, of each and every letter. To let your eyes see each letter and each word, and to touch each letter and word with your finger and your mind, is to "do Torah," which in reality is understood to be an encounter with God.

Another word that is frequently used to designate the first five books of the Bible is **Pentateuch,** meaning "five jars (or scrolls)." Often, the ancient scrolls of the Bible were stored in very large clay jars which were known in Hebrew as *teuch.* The Greek prefix *penta* (a Latin prefix) designates "five," namely the first five books of the Bible.

The second part of the Jewish canon, *Nevi'im* (the prophets) designates the following twenty-one books:

Joshua	**Amos**
Judges	**Obadiah**
First Samuel	**Jonah**
Second Samuel	**Micah**
First Kings	**Nahum**
Second Kings	**Habakkuk**
Isaiah	**Zephaniah**
Jeremiah	**Haggai**
Ezekiel	**Zechariah**
Hosea	**Malachi**
Joel	

In regard to the books included in this division of the Jewish canon, the following three factors are important:

- The books Joshua-2 Kings appear to be books of history rather than books of the prophets. They were probably included here because the activity of prophets plays a prominent role in each of them.
- Isaiah, Jeremiah and Ezekiel are known as the major prophets. The other twelve books are known, collectively, as the minor prophets.
- The terms "major" and "minor" have nothing to do with the concept of importance. These terms are used in the sense of "long" and "short." The books of

the major prophets are very long – Jeremiah is 52 chapters. The books of the minor prophets are short – Obadiah is only 21 verses.

The third part of the Jewish canon, **Kethuvim** (the writings) includes the following 13 books:

Psalms	
Proverbs	**Esther**
Job	**Daniel**
Song of Songs	**Ezra**
Ruth	**Nehemiah**
Lamentations	**First Chronicles**
Ecclesiastes	**Second Chronicles**

This third section contains quite a variety of literary types: history (Ezra, Nehemiah, 1 and 2 Chronicles), wisdom (Proverbs, Job, Song of Songs, Ecclesiastes), apocalyptic (Daniel 7-12), prayers (Psalms and Lamentations), and folk literature (Ruth and Esther).

The five books – of the Song of Songs (or sometimes called the Song of Solomon) through Esther – are called the "five scrolls" (*hamesh megillot*). These books were most likely copied together on a single scroll and are arranged here in the order in which they are read during the Jewish liturgical year: Song of Songs (Passover in the early Spring), Ruth (Shavuot in the late spring), Lamentations (the feast of the ninth of Av in the summer), Ecclesiastes (Sukkot in the Fall), and Esther (the feast of Purim in the late winter).[21]

The Apocrypha

If one goes to a bookstore and looks at the bibles that are for sale, one will notice that some of the Bibles contain the phrase "with the Apocrypha" in their titles. What is meant by the term "apocrypha"?

In the 3rd and 2nd centuries BC/BCE, the Hebrew Scriptures were translated into Greek for the benefit of the Jews living in the **Diaspora** (i.e. the area where Jews were living outside Palestine). These Jewish people were more fluent in the Greek language than in Hebrew. This Greek translation of the Hebrew Scriptures is known as the Septuagint (or LXX for short). The name **Septuagint**, which means "70" in Greek, stems from a legend that seventy (actually 72) rabbis translated the Hebrew Scriptures entirely independently and, when the resulting manuscripts were compared, it was found that they were word for word the same! Or so the legend goes. Careful analysis of the text has revealed that the translation was actually carried out by a number of scribes of varying abilities over a rather lengthy period of time.

Over the next two centuries it became the practice of the Greek-speaking Jews to include other compositions in editions of the Septuagint written in Greek which they believed were of great value. It has become the custom to group these writings, which are not part of the Jewish canon, but which are contained in the Greek manuscripts of the Septuagint and in the Old Latin and Vulgate translations of it, under the name **"the Apocrypha."**

---

[21] Marc Zvi Brettler, "Kethuvim," in *The Jewish Study Bible*, Adele Berlin and Marc Zvi Brettler, Editors (New York: Oxford University Press, 2004), 1275.

It is not important right now to know about all of the writings of the Apocrypha. What is important to know is that both the Roman Catholic and the Eastern Orthodox traditions, over a long period of time, have come to recognize that a number of these writings are inspired and are to be included in the canon on an equal footing with the all the other writings contained in the biblical canon of their traditions.

The Roman Catholic and Eastern Orthodox Canons of the OT

In this section let us focus our attention on the OT portion of the canon. The Roman Catholic and the Eastern Orthodox traditions recognize all of the writings of the Jewish canon to be inspired. The canon of these traditions, therefore, includes all of the writings of the Jewish Scriptures. In addition, the Roman Catholic and Orthodox traditions recognize many of the writings of the **Apocrypha** as being inspired; and therefore, these writings, are included in their respective canon of the OT.

The Roman Catholic tradition recognizes the following writings of the Apocrypha as being inspired and, consequently, part of its canon:

Tobit	**Letter of Jeremiah**
Judith	**Additions to Esther**
Wisdom	**Prayer of Azariah**
Sirach	**Song of the Three Jews**
1 Maccabees	**Susanna**
2 Maccabees	**Bel and the Dragon**
Baruch	

The first seven on this list are individual books. Sirach is one of the longest books in the Bible. In addition, it is interesting to note that this entire list of seven writings is not insignificant as regards length because they constitute almost one-third of the OT of the Catholic and Eastern Orthodox bibles. The Letter of Jeremiah, Additions to Esther, the Prayer of Azariah, the Song of the Three Jews, Susanna, and Bel and the Dragon are all included as part of other writings in the Old Testament.

Where are the writings of the Apocrypha that came to be included in the Roman Catholic canon found in the Catholic Bible? (In other bibles, they may be found in other locations in the OT.) They are located in the following positions:

Tobit and Judith follow Nehemiah
1 and 2 Maccabees come after Esther
Wisdom and Sirach come after Song of Songs
Baruch follows Lamentations
Letter of Jeremiah is Chapter 6 of Baruch
Additions to Esther - These are extensive and the *New American Bible*
    (NAB) designates them as Chapters A through F as follows:
        Chapter A comes before Chap 1

Chapter B comes after Chap 3
Chapters C and D come after Chap 4
Chapter E comes after Chap 8
Chapter F comes after Chap 10
The Prayer of Azariah is 3:25-45 of Daniel
The Song of the Three Jews is 3:46-90 of Daniel
Susanna is Chapter 13 of Daniel
Bel and the Dragon is Chapter 14 of Daniel

The Eastern Orthodox tradition recognizes, along with the writings listed above from the apocrypha, a number of additional writings included in The Apocrypha as being inspired. Thus, the Orthodox Christian canon includes all of the above as well as the following:

1 Esdras
Psalm 151
Prayer of Manasseh
3 Maccabees

It is **very important to the reader**, if Roman Catholic or Orthodox, to make sure when buying a Bible that it contains the complete Catholic or Orthodox canon. Or, if selecting a Protestant Bible for purchase (because it is an excellent and scholarly translation), make sure that it states "with the Apocrypha" on the cover or on the title page. Some Protestant Bibles will say "Catholic Edition" when it contains the books from the apocrypha.

The Protestant Canon of the OT

The **Protestant OT** differs from the Roman Catholic OT and the Eastern Orthodox OT in that it contains only the same 39 books that make up the Jewish canon. This difference came about at the time of the Reformation (16th century AD/CE). For theological reasons, Luther turned against several of the writings in the accepted Christian canon. Ultimately, the Protestant traditions came to accept only those books of the OT that were originally written in Hebrew or Aramaic. They rejected the book of Sirach as not being canonical, which was originally written in Hebrew as stated in the Prologue to the book, but comes down to the present only in a Greek translation. To put it another way, the Protestants took the position that none of the writings of the Apocrypha were inspired.

Comparing canons

The Table below compares the canon as included in four recent major bible publications representing the **Jewish, Protestant, Roman Catholic and Orthodox canons**. It is easily seen that the Protestant OT canon contains the same books as the Jewish canon but has them arranged in the same order as does the Roman Catholic canon. The chart that follows compares four bibles … Jewish, Protestant, Roman Catholic and Orthodox. Notice the difference in order of some of the books.

A Jewish Bible *Jewish Study Bible*	A Protestant Bible *The Learning Bible*	A Roman Catholic Bible *Catholic Study Bible*	An Orthodox Study Bible *Orthodox Study Bible*

TORAH
The Old Testament
Genesis
Exodus
Leviticus
Numbers
Deuteronomy
 	
NEVI'IM
Joshua
Judges
First Samuel
Second Samuel
First Kings
Second Kings
Isaiah
Jeremiah
Ezekiel
Hosea
Joel
Amos
Obadiah
Jonah
Micah
Nahum
Habakkuk
Zephaniah
Haggai
Zechariah
Malachi
 	
KETHUVIM
Psalms
Proverbs
Job
The Scrolls
  Song of Songs
  Ruth
  Lamentations
  Ecclesiastes
  Esther
Daniel
Ezra
Nehemiah
First Chronicles
Second Chronicles
	The Pentateuch
	Genesis
	Exodus
	Leviticus
	Numbers
	Deuteronomy
	Historical Books
	Joshua
	Judges
	Ruth
	1 Samuel
	2 Samuel
	1 Kings
	2 Kings
	1 Chronicles
	2 Chronicles
	Ezra
	Nehemiah
	Esther
	Wisdom and Poetry
	Job
	Psalms
	Proverbs
	Ecclesiastes
	Song of Songs
	Prophetic Books
	Isaiah
	Jeremiah
	Lamentations
	Ezekiel
	Daniel
	Hosea
	Joel
	Amos
	Obadiah
		The Pentateuch
		The Book of Genesis
		The Book of Exodus
		The Book of Leviticus
		The Book of Numbers
		The Book of Deuteronomy
		The Historical Books
		The Book of Joshua
		The Book of Judges
		The Book of Ruth
		The First Book of Samuel
		The Second Book of Samuel
		The First Book of Kings
		The Second Book of Kings
		The First Book of Chronicles
		The Second Book Chronicles
		The Book of Ezra
		The Book of Nehemiah
		Biblical Novellas
		The Book of Tobit
		The Book of Judith
		The Book of Esther
		The First Book of Maccabees
		The Wisdom Books
		The Book of Job
		The Book of Psalms
		The Book of Proverbs
		The Prophetic Books
		The Book of Isaiah
		The Book of Jeremiah
		The Book of Lamentations
		The Book of Baruch
		The Book of Ezekiel
			Genesis
			Exodus
			Leviticus
			Numbers
			Deuteronomy
			Joshua
			Judges
			Ruth
			1 Kingdoms (1 Samuel)
			2 Kingdoms (2 Samuel)
			3 Kingdoms (1 Kings)
			4 Kingdoms (2 Kings)
			1 Chronicles
			2 Chronicles
			1 Ezra (2 Esdras)
			2 Ezra (Ezra / 2 Esdras)
			Nehemiah
			Tobit
			Judith
			Esther
			1 Maccabees
			2 Maccabees
			3 Maccabees
			Psalms
			Job
			Proverbs of Solomon
			Ecclesiasts
			Song of Songs
			Wisdom of Solomon
			Wisdom of Sirach
			Hosea
			Amos
			Micah
			Joel
			Obadiah
			Jonah
			Nahum
			Habbakkuk
			Zephaniah

Adele Berlin and Marc Zvi Brettler, eds., *The Jewish Sudsy Bible* (New York: Oxford University Press, 2004), the Jewish Publication Society TANAKH Translation.	Howard Clark Kee, et al, eds., *The Learning Bible, New International Version* (New York: American Bible Society, 2003).	Donald Senior, John J. Collins, Mary Ann Getty, eds., *The Catholic Study Bible, Third Edition* (New York: Oxford University Press, 2010).	Metropolitan Maximos, et al, eds., *The Orthodox Study Bible* (Nashville, TN: Thomas Nelson, 2008), prepared under the auspices of the Academic Community of St. Athanasius Academy of Orthodox Theology, Elk Grove, California.

The Canon of the NT

The Roman Catholic, Protestant and Orthodox traditions all share the same position concerning the identity of the writings that make up the canon of the New Testament. Furthermore, they all adhere to the same ordering of the 27 books that make up the NT. The canon of the NT is as follows

Matthew
Mark
Luke
John
Acts
Romans
1 Corinthians
2 Corinthians
Galatians
Ephesians
Philippians
Colossians
1 Thessalonians
2 Thessalonians
1 Timothy
2 Timothy
Titus
Philemon
Hebrews
James
1 Peter
2 Peter
1 John
2 John
3 John
Jude
Revelation

This **order of the books in the New Testament** is a traditional one. The four gospels come first followed by the Acts of the Apostles. Then we find the letters attributed to Paul divided into two groups: the letters addressed to churches followed by the letters addressed to individuals. The letters within each group are arranged in order of **decreasing** length. After the writings of Paul comes Hebrews. Then comes the seven writings addressed to Christian communities, sometimes referred to as the seven universal letters (despite the fact that they are addressed to the churches in a particular region and not to all the churches everywhere). The New Testament canon concludes with Revelation, a writing that contains seven letters (chapters 1-3) and an apocalyptic writing (chapters 3-22) that speaks of the end of time. This is an appropriate balance to the book of Genesis, at the beginning of the Scriptures, describing as it does the creation of all things and the completion of God's plan.

For Further Reading

Harrington, Daniel J., S.J. "Introduction to the Canon," in *The New Interpreter's Bible*, Vol. I, Edited by Neil M. Alexander. Nashville, TN: Abingdon Press, 1994), 7-21. This is a very readable introduction to the canon and contains a great deal of valuable information.

Harrington, *Invitation to the Apocrypha*. Grand Rapids, MI: William B. Eerdmans Publishing Company, 1999.

Newsom, Carol A. "Introduction to the Apocryphal/Deuterocanonical Books." In *The New Oxford Annotated Bible*, Third Edition, Michael D. Coogan, Editor, 3-383. New York: Oxford University Press, 2001. Do not be deterred by the number of pages stated here. You only need to read Pages 3-10, which presents a very clear introduction to the books of the Apocrypha. This short section is well worth reading.

Part Two … The Texts of the Writings that are Holy Scripture
Regenerating the ancient texts
Translating the ancient texts
Interpreting an ancient text

CHAPTER SIX

REGENERATING THE ANCIENT TEXTS

Introduction

When you start to read the Scriptures, they read like any other writings except that these writings contain a large number of unfamiliar names, places and events. You will read names like Jehoshaphat (1 Kgs 22:41) and Athaliah (2 Kgs 11:1). In fact, the first eight chapters of 1 Chronicles consist of nothing but a long list of such names! The Scriptures also mention some names that may be more familiar: like Abraham (18ᵗʰ or 19ᵗʰ century BC/BCE) and David (10ᵗʰ century BC/BCE) and Paul (1ˢᵗ century AD). But these are all names of **very** ancient people. The Scriptures also mention places that existed a very long time ago like Sodom and Gomorrah. Some places that existed a long time ago still exist today like Jerusalem, Thessalonica and Ephesus. In addition, the Bible mentions events which took place a long time ago, like the **Exodus** in the 13ᵗʰ century BC/BCE (Ex chapters 12-15), the **Babylonian Exile** in the 6ᵗʰ century BC (2 Kgs 19), and the **crucifixion of Jesus** in 30/33 AD (Mk 15:22-41). The events also carry deeper meaning in their spiritual interrelationship across the centuries. For example: the Passover ritual represents the Exodus which gives meaning to the Last Supper of Jesus. The Babylonian Exile represents the fact that earthly nations and kings do not last forever and that people must put their trust in God. And the gift of absolute love for us by God is found in the crucifixion.

What is the significance of the fact that the Scriptures deal with people, places and events of so long ago? There are many contemporary historical novels which portray people and events of the historical past. Are the Scriptures really writings of this sort? Can it be that they are truly ancient works? How can we reliably determine which of these two possibilities is actually the case? Are the Scriptures authentic works of ancient times or just cleverly written modern works of fiction?

For one thing, there are a large number of manuscripts (handwritten copies) of the Scriptures. Also, there are a number of nearly complete copies of the Scriptures that have been dated to the fourth century AD. There are fragments of the writings of the Scriptures that have been dated to as early as the second century AD. In 1947, a complete scroll of Isaiah and parts of all of the other books of the Jewish Scriptures, except Esther, were discovered in caves at Qumran in Palestine, called the Dead Sea Scrolls. These manuscripts date to the first century BC! This is amazing … these scrolls are older than 2,000 years! Further evidence concerning the existence of the biblical writings in ancient times is supplied by the quotations which are found in the writings of non-biblical authors of the first and second centuries AD and also by the longer biblical quotations that are found in the early manuscripts of liturgical books. The writings of Scripture, therefore, are truly ancient writings.

The generation of texts in the 1ˢᵗ century AD

In ancient times a number of different surfaces were used for writing: among these were clay tablets, stone, leather, various metals, potsherds (*ostraca*), papyrus and parchment. In the case of the biblical writings dating to the 1ˢᵗ AD, the materials of papyrus and parchment are of greatest interest.

The following description of the making of papyrus and parchment manuscripts is from Bruce Metzger:

> The manufacture of **papyrus** was a flourishing business in Egypt, for the papyrus plant grew plentifully in the shallow waters of the Nile at the delta (cf. Job viii.11, 'Can papyrus grow where there is no marsh?'). About 12 or 15 feet in height, the stem of the plant, which was triangular in cross-section and as thick as a man's wrist, was cut into sections about a foot long. Each section was split open lengthwise and the pith cut into thin strips. A layer of these was placed on a flat surface, all the fibers running in the same direction, and on top another layer was laid, with the fibers running at right angles to the lower layer. The two layers were then pressed together until they formed one fabric - a fabric which, though now so brittle that it can sometimes be crumbled into powder, once had a strength nearly equal to that of good paper.
>
> **Parchment or vellum** (often used interchangeably; more precisely the word *vellum* is used to describe a finer, superior quality of parchment) was made from the skins of cattle, sheep, goats, and antelopes; especially from the young of those animals. After the animal's hair had been removed by scraping, the skins were washed, smoothed with pumice, and dressed with chalk.[22]

Manuscripts of literary works were written in a style of handwriting called **uncials.** This style of handwriting consisted of large, carefully executed individual letters (much like our capital letters). This style of handwriting was replaced in the 9th century AD by a style having smaller, connected letters called **minuscules.** Within each of these periods, there were also different styles of making the letters. Analysis of handwriting is one way that scholars can date manuscripts.

Ancient scrolls were made of papyrus, utilizing reeds that grew along wet river areas like along the Nile in Egypt and the Tigris and Euphrates rivers in Mesopotamia. The reeds were cut, split and then beaten together on a flat surface and dried to make a writing material. This created a writing surface that had lines which were used for hanging the letters down from the line above, much like writing papers that are made for kindergarten students today (although they

---

[22]Bruce M. Metzger, *The Text of the New Testament*, 2ⁿᵈ Edition (New York, NY: Oxford University Press, 1968), 3-4.

learn to build the letters up from a lower line.) It is common opinion that papyrus is not a durable material. But that is not the truth. Papyrus is quite durable under the right conditions. It does become brittle and is subject to disintegration when it undergoes repeated wet and dry periods. It will, however, survive very well if protected from moisture (being put in a clay jar for example) or being kept in a dry climate (like Egypt or the desert near Qumran). It does not survive for long periods in regions that have high humidity (like Greece) One reason that many scholars give for doubting the validity of the spurious *Gospel of Judas* is that it was written on papyrus and not found in Egypt.

Parchment scrolls, known also as vellum, were made from various animal skins, including sheep, oxen, and deer. The animal hides were cleaned, stretched on frames and dried, sometimes with pieces later sewn together. Just like the papyrus material, after a scroll was written it was wound on wooden poles. With the modern knowledge of DNA, scholars today are now able to piece together hundreds of fragments of manuscripts found by identifying the very animal from which the parchment was taken.

The literary works in the Greco-Roman world were usually put in the form of a scroll. This scroll was made by gluing together the individual sheets of papyrus or parchment and then winding the long strip onto a stick. The length of a normal scroll was usually not more than 35 feet in length as that length was about the longest that could be handled conveniently. The books of Luke and Acts in the NT would each have occupied a scroll some 30 feet in length.

In the 2nd century AD, Christians adopted the **codex;** it was a book form made by binding, on one side, a number of papyrus or parchment sheets, sewn together on one side to make something like a modern book. The codex form for saving treasured biblical writings developed quickly because they found it was much easier to use and to carry around.

Transmission of texts

We have considered how texts for the NT were generated in the 1st century AD. Now let us consider how manuscripts, once generated, were transmitted. There are two senses of the term "transmitted." There is the sense of transmission from the place of origin to the place of an individual or group to whom the document was written. There is also the sense of how a written communication gets to places other than to the place for which it was originally intended, or comeS down to other historical times at much later dates.

There is a manuscript of the Bible at the Vatican Library in Rome that dates to the 4th century AD. What is of interest to us here is understanding the way that a letter written by Paul in the middle of the 1st century AD came to be part of a manuscript that dates to the 4th century.

The Letter of Paul in the Vatican manuscript is not the original letter. It is a copy of the letter. To be more precise: it is a copy of a copy of a copy of a copy of the autograph, the original letter. Why is this so? First, constant use of a manuscript written on parchment or papyrus caused it to deteriorate and become unreadable. Such documents, therefore, had to be copied periodically in order to preserve their clarity. Secondly, as the number of Christians grew and their geographic distribution increased, a demand was generated for additional copies to satisfy the increased and more widespread readership.

By the fourth century AD, it was the common practice for copies of manuscripts to be produced in a **scriptorium.** However, there is a strong argument by archaeologists that the stone foundation discovered at Qumran near the Dead Sea, much older than the 4th century AD, was actually a scriptorium and there certainly an individual leading an ascetic life evidently copied and studied scrolls. They even have found ink wells! However, as the monastic tradition of Christianity developed – at first in the desert of Egypt and later through the Near East, monks took up the task of scroll work. In a typical scriptorium a number of scribes sat at writing tables or desks in a room. Each scribe was equipped with papyrus or parchment, pens and ink. A reader slowly read aloud the text that was to be reproduced and, as he read, the scribes would write down what they heard. The number of copies produced obviously depended on how many individual scribes were available to be working in the room. The copying of scriptural and liturgical manuscripts became one of the major works in monasteries beginning as early as the 3rd century AD when monasticism emerged in the desert of Egypt. Recall the story of St. Anthony who gave away all his possessions and went to live an ascetic life in a cave in the desert.

The production of copies was no easy task. We can learn about how hard this task may have been by noticing the colophons (notes) which the scribes frequently put at the end of their manuscripts. Here are three examples:

1. "He who does not know how to write supposes it to be no labor; but though only three fingers write, the whole body labors."[23]

2. "Writing bows one's back, thrusts the ribs into one's stomach, and fosters a general debility of the body."[24]

3. In an Armenian manuscript of the Gospels a colophon complains that a heavy snowstorm was raging outside and that the scribe's ink froze, his hand became numb, and the pen fell from his fingers.[25]

It goes without saying that the scribes must have believed that the task of copying the scriptures was of such importance that it was worth suffering extreme discomforts and enduring long hours of tedious writing. It is because of the efforts of these dedicated individuals that we have the scriptures to read today!

Manuscripts transmitted in this manner are subject to the introduction of certain types of unintentional errors and intentional changes of various sorts. Unintentional errors include: confusing Greek letters that resemble one another; omission of a line or passage; omitting a line or phrase not heard; confusing two words that sound the same; and incorporation of words or notes written in the margin of a page into the text itself. Intentional changes include: changes

---

[23] Metzger, 17.
[24] Metzger, 17-18
[25] Metzger, 18.

43

resulting from a strong desire to harmonize discordant parallels; clearing up historical and geographical difficulties; conflation of passages; alterations made for doctrinal reasons; and addition of miscellaneous information and markings.

It is not important at this point that you understand the details of these types of unintentional errors and intentional changes. What is important is be aware that because of errors and changes, there are a large number of variant readings in the manuscripts that have survived to our time. It can be said, however, that these variant readings are only rarely of significant importance to the meaning or interpretation of the verse and, in fact, an intentional change can even result in a better understanding of the verse.

These unintentional errors and intentional changes are a mixed blessing. On the one hand, they are undesirable because they degrade the accuracy of the manuscripts in which they occur. On the other hand, however, they are highly useful in that they provide the means by which the manuscripts can be grouped into families and the history of the text tradition determined!

The Manuscript Evidence for the NT

During the years of transmission many copies of the manuscripts ended up being destroyed or succumbing to fire or natural causes. A few, however, ended up being put in libraries and private homes or stored in caves and then left there forgotten.

Now turn the clock ahead to the 18th, 19th, and 20th centuries. These centuries were a period of discovery! It was the period of finding many ancient manuscripts. A small number of those found were complete: for example, the Isaiah Scroll found in a cave at Qumran. The majority of manuscripts were only partially complete. The earliest consisted of only small fragments of once complete texts. The sum total of all of the manuscript evidence enables the text critics to reconstruct the ancient texts with a considerable degree of confidence.

Most often biblical manuscripts have been found in the course of excavations at various archaeological sites. Occasionally, however, important manuscripts were found in unusual circumstances. In 1844, Tischendorf was traveling through the Near East looking for manuscripts of the Holy Scriptures. While visiting the monastery of St. Catherine on Mount Sinai, he happened to notice some leaves of parchment in a waste basket full of papers that were about to be used to light the oven in the kitchen. When he examined them he found that they were part of a copy of the Septuagint version of the OT. This manuscript contained most of the OT, all of the NT and several additional writings. It is now known as the *Codex Sinaiticus*, dating to the 4th century AD.[26]

The manuscript evidence for the NT text which we now possess consists of over 5,000 Greek manuscripts (abbreviation: mss), some complete or nearly so and many only fragmentary. These manuscripts consist of the following four types:[27]

---

[26] Metzger, 42-44.
[27] Eldon Jay Epp, "Textual Criticism (NT) in "*The Anchor Bible Dictionary*, Vol. 6 (New York, NY: Doubleday, 1992), 419-430.

44

1. **Papyrus mss** – there are 94 of them dating from the 2nd century to the 8th century AD.

2. **Uncial mss** – these are continuous-text manuscripts written on parchment in uncial characters; there are some 270 of these. The most important of these are the following:
   a. **Codex Sinaiticus** – complete NT; dating to the 4th century
   b. **Codex Alexandrinus** – nearly complete; dating to 5th century
   c. **Codex Vaticanus** – all of NT except for an extensive portion of Heb through Rev, dating to 4th century
   d. **Codex Bezae Cantabrigiensis** – only 4 gospels (in the order of Mt, Jn, Lk and Mk), most of Acts and a small portion of 3 Jn, dating to late 4th to 5th century
   e. **Codex Washingtonianus** – the four gospels nearly complete (in the order of Mt, Jn, Lk, Mk), dating to early 5th century

3. **Minuscule mss** – there are several thousand of these; they all date to the 9th century or later.

4. **Lectionaries** – there are about 2,200 of these liturgical texts; they contain the readings for the Church liturgical year.

In addition to these four types of manuscripts, evidence for the early NT text is obtained from patristic quotations, passages of the NT quoted by early Christian writers, and from various versions -- translations of the Greek text into other languages, principally Syriac, Latin, Coptic, and Ethiopic.

The oldest manuscript fragment of the NT found to date is a 2 ½ inch by 3 ½ inch piece of papyrus containing a small portion of the Gospel of John. It dates to the 1st half of the second century AD. The most important manuscripts of the NT as a whole are the *Codex Sinaiticus* and *Codex Vaticanus,* both of which date to the fourth century as we have seen above.

What does a text of the Scriptures look like? You can explore one of the oldest (middle 4th century AD) and best texts of parts of the OT and the entire NT: it is called the Codex Sinaiticus. Just go to the following website entitled "codexsomaotocis.org."

The Science of Text Criticism

The term "text criticism" is the name given to the critical study of ancient manuscripts. **It is the basic assumption of those practicing this discipline of text criticism that the original texts of the NT writings are to be found within the manuscript evidence which is currently possessed.** The task of text critici sm is to determine, on the basis of all of the manuscript evidence, the original text (called the "autograph") of each of the NT writings. This task requires an enormous amount of effort and a scholarly and detailed knowledge of the textual evidence.

A small group of highly skilled people have made the tremendous effort required to work through all of the manuscript evidence. Through their dedication and skill there is available, for our reading today, a text of the writings in the NT that is the closest to the original texts that has been available to Christian believers since the 1st century AD!

The Text Underlying Our Modern Translations of the New Testament

Look in the Preface to the NT in your Bible. Look for where it tells you what Greek text was used for the translation. For example, in *The Catholic Study Bible*, Second Edition with the Revised New Testament, it first reprints the Preface to the New Testament from the first edition which reads as follows:

> In general, Nestle-Aland's *Novem Testamentum Graece* (25th edition, 1963) was followed. Additional help was derived from *The Greek New Testament* (Aland, Black, Metzger, Wikgren) produced for the use of translators by the United Bible Societies in 1966.[28]

Then it prints the Preface to the Revised Edition of the New Testament which reads as follows:

> The Greek text followed in this translation is that of the third edition The Greek New Testament, edited by Kurt Aland, Matthew Black, Carlo Martini, Bruce Metzger and Allen Wikgren, and published by the United Bible Societies in 1975. The same text, with a different critical apparatus and variations in punctuation and topography, was published as the twenty-sixth edition of the Nestle-Aland *Novum Testamentum Graece* in 1979 by the Deutsche Bibelstiftung, Stuttgart.[29]

What does all this mean? This means, first of all, that Kurt Aland and the others have done a great deal of work to bring us what they believe to be the best reconstruction of the original text of the NT. We owe a large debt of gratitude to this group of scholars! Secondly, it means that the *New American Bible*, Revised New Testament is not a translation of the same text as the first edition New Testament of the *New American Bible*. Thirdly, it means that if you read the *New American Bible*, Revised New Testament you are benefiting from 12 additional years of work by Aland and his coworkers on the text of the New Testament.

For those of you who can read Greek or plan to learn to read it, the result of the work of Aland *et al* is readily available in many religious bookstores or from some book distributors (e.g. the Christian Book Distributors). Keep in mind that the original language of the NT was Greek.

---

[28] Donald Senior, Editor, *The Catholic Study Bible*, Preface To The New American Bible, First Edition Of The New Testament (New York: Oxford University Press, 1990), *iib*.

[29] Donald Senior, Editor, *The Catholic Study Bible*, Preface to The Revised Edition (New York: Oxford University Press, 1990), ivb.

At this point, it is important to remind ourselves also that the original language of the Old Testament was Hebrew with some Aramaic included (a dialect of Hebrew) and later translated into the Greek Septuagint; and that the New Testament was originally written in Greek. Some OT scholars even tell us that there are a few Babylonian and Egyptian words in the OT! Latin translations of the Bible from as early as the 2nd century AD with small, individual manuscripts of particular books, and later in a translation by St. Jerome in the 4th century AD, soon became the standard "Bible" for many Christians. However, in biblical studies it is always best to regard the original languages.

The Text of the OLD TESTAMENT

The writings of the OT and NT differ in one very important respect. The writings of the NT were written in a very limited period of time, from 75 to 100 years. A short letter, such as **Philemon** or **3 John,** was most likely written in one "sitting." Even a long book such as Acts was probably written over a relatively short period of time. The majority of writings in the OT, however, were composed over much longer periods of time. In the case of the Pentateuch, this was a period of about 500 years!

In the case of the writings of the NT, because there was an original text, the goal of text criticism is quite well defined – to recover the original text. In the case of the writings of the OT, however, the goal of text criticism is necessarily different. Many of the writings of the OT were edited several times over a long period of time and, therefore, it is much less clear as to what was the original text. A similar problem holds true for Homer's *Iliad* and *Odyssey* which are believed to have gone through a literary history that is similar in nature to that of the OT. The goal of OT text criticism is, therefore, to shed light on the history of the text.

It is good to know that the Hebrew of the OT is now a difficult language to translate. Ancient Hebrew was written with no vowels, and it is written from right to left with absolutely no punctuation. For many, it is a difficult language to learn because the letters are very different in appearance from the English alphabet. However, it can be learned. Sesame Street has published videos that teach pre-school children to write and be able to read a few Hebrew words! So, don't be discouraged.

The most exciting discovery of ancient manuscripts in the case of the OT was at Qumran in Israel by the Dead Sea. These manuscripts have been dated to as early as the 1st century BC! One of the most spectacular finds was a complete manuscript of the entire book of Isaiah. The majority of the finds of manuscripts at Qumran consisted of small fragments. Modern technology has come to the aid of piecing these fragments together in TWO WAYS. First, as mentioned, by the use of DNA analysis all of the pieces written on animal skin can be can be related to the specific animal from which they came. Secondly, each fragment has been put on a computer and, therefore, the piecing together can be carried out by means of the computer.

The Masoretic Text

The text of the OT that is contained in most English Bible translations is called the Masoretic Text. This text is so named because it was prepared by the **Masoretes** who represented succeeding generations of scribes who lived during the period **500-1000 AD** and attended to the matter of transmitting the OT text with great accuracy. The continuous biblical text they arranged had its roots in ancient Israel, originating from manuscripts dating to the last two centuries before Christ. Scrolls and scroll fragments attesting to this were found at Qumran. The Masoretic text was written in a new kind of Hebrew writing where the vowels were indicated by small dots and teeny lines, above and below the letters – known as pointing.

If you look at the introduction to the OT in your Bible it will usually tell you what text it is using for the OT. For example, we are told in an introductory section to the *New Revised Standard Version* that the text behind the OT is the *Biblia Hebraica Stuttgartensia* (1977 edition.). This identifies a particular Masoretic manuscript of the OT.

The Greek Text of the OT

In the third century BC, Greek-speaking Jews living in the **Diaspora** (i.e. outside of Palestine) felt a need to have the text of the OT translated into Greek. Greek was the language of the eastern Roman Empire, and the language of the Jewish population in Egypt. The Greek translation was accomplished, in its first stage, during the third and second centuries BC by a number of different scribes. This text of the OT, known as the **Septuagint** (which means "seventy"), derives its name from a legend that it was translated by 70 scribes (actually 72; six from each of the twelve tribes) all of whom, working strictly independently translated it exactly the same, word for word … or so the legend goes.

The Greek translation of the OT served as the Bible for the Greek-speaking Jews through the 1st century AD. It served as the scriptures for the Christian churches outside of Palestine through the 1st century and for a long time afterward. It is the Greek OT that is found in the ***Codex Vaticanus.*** The Greek of the New Testament is primarily Koine Greek, a popular dialect of Greek. Many NT scholars think that Jesus quoted the Septuagint in his preaching, as is quoted in the NT. The actual wording of the quotations reveals that it was the Greek translation. The reason that Jesus would do this is because the language of the day was Greek. Overall, this may mean that Jesus read and spoke Greek for his preaching, that he spoke Aramaic – a dialect of Hebrew – in his home, and read and spoke ancient Hebrew in the synagogue and the Temple.

The biblical text upon which the Septuagint is based is for some of the books of the OT considerably different from the Masoretic text. For example, the Septuagint version of Jeremiah is one-eighth shorter than the Masoretic version. It is apparent from a comparison of the two texts that the Greek translation was made from an early form of the book of Jeremiah and that the Masoretic text represents a further development of Jeremiah. There is evidence for both of these two traditions in the manuscripts of Jeremiah found at Qumran.

The Christians of the 1st century AD, then, used two versions of the OT. Those living in Palestine used primarily the OT based upon the textual tradition that developed into the Masoretic text. The Christians living elsewhere, especially the Gentile Christians, used the Greek translation of the OT, the Septuagint. It is not a difficult matter to tell that they actually used both versions because when the authors of the NT writings quote from the OT more often than not they quote from the Septuagint but the other times they quote from the ancient Hebrew, Masoretic texts.

In general, throughout the centuries, **Masoretic scribes** were known for their precision in studying the scriptures. They counted every word used in the documents they were reading, often making lists of words and working to understand how words were related and pronounced. Sometimes they even counted letters. Most deeply religious Jewish scholars today know which word marks the very center of the Hebrew Scriptures. The Masoretic scribes invented a way of adding small points and little lines to the words because in ancient Hebrew there usually were no vowel letters and vowel sounds were just remembered. The system which these scribes invented was called **"pointing."**

Here is an interesting question to consider. Up to the time that the Greek translation was undertaken, the Jews had written all of their sacred texts in Hebrew. Thus, up to that time Hebrew was the language in which the religious thinking of Israel had been expressed. It is sometimes stated that God chose the people of Israel to be God's people because Hebrew was a language that could express adequately God's revelation of truths. How, then, could the writings of the OT be translated into Greek, a language that did not have the same religious vocabulary as that of the Hebrew? What were the consequences, therefore, of translating from Hebrew into Greek? What impact did this have on the early Christians who knew the Scriptures only through the Greek translation?

Here is another question to ponder. Should we, as Christian believers of the 21st century, be reading the Masoretic text, which is presented to us in most of our Bibles, or should we be reading the Septuagint text, which was the OT text read by the majority of Christians after the middle of the 1st century AD (which we must purchase as a separate book)? Perhaps, it makes sense to read and compare various versions to gain the best knowledge of the writings.

49

CHAPTER SEVEN

THE TRANSLATION OF THE SCRIPTURES

Introduction

We have determined that the Scriptures are truly writings that were composed in ancient times. This fact has a very important impact on our efforts to read them. The texts of the Scriptures were written in the language of the time and place in which the various writers lived. Thus, the Scriptures are written in ancient Hebrew, Aramaic and Greek with a few words of Babylonian and Egyptian appearing once in a while in the OT as well. They were not written in English because they predate the development of the English language.

We, the prospective readers, are left with a choice. We must either become fluent in the ancient languages ourselves or we must depend upon other people who are fluent in the ancient languages and at the same time are fluent in our modern language and will translate the Scriptures into words and expression that we can understand. Fortunately for those of us who are not able to take the former approach, the Scriptures have been translated into a multitude of languages spoken and read in the world today.

The Goal of Translation

Let us assume that we have before us one of the biblical texts in its original language and let us focus our attention on the matter of translating that text into English. It is the common practice among translators to refer to the original language as the **donor** language and to refer to the language into which the document is be translated as the **receptor** language.

The goal of translation may be stated in the following manner (this is not the only way it can be defined):

> It is my conviction that the primary purpose of translation is to make
> a message originally written in one language available in another
> language to people who have no knowledge of the first language.[30]

The first priority of the translator is, therefore, to make the message contained in the donor language as intelligible as possible to people who must rely on the translation to receive that message in the receptor language. There are two aspects involved in this that need to be stated explicitly. They are the following:

1. It is fundamentally impossible, in general, to completely attain this stated goal. This is most easily seen in regard to the translation of poetry (and the Scriptures are almost one third poetical). There is simply no way that a poetic passage can be accurately translated into a receptor language. Something of the full form and impact of a poem is always lost in the translation. The same is true in the regard to the translation of a narrative piece of

---

[30] Charles R. Taber, "Translation as Interpretation" in *Interpretation* 32 (1978): 132.

50

literature, although perhaps to a lesser extent. For a moment, imagine translating one of Shakespeare's sonnets into German or Spanish from the donor language English. What is lost? For example, the sound effect of the words will be different, the metrical flow of the words is different, images can be culturally very different, and the rhyme pattern is impossible to be retained.

2. Every person has a number of preconceptions of one sort or another, some of which the person is aware of and others of which he or she is unaware. Thus, it is very difficult for any person to translate a composition in a totally objective manner. For this reason translations by committee are usually to be preferred to translations carried out by a single individual.

Translating from One Cultural Context to Another Cultural Context

The texts that come to us in the Scriptures are not only in (ancient) foreign languages but they come from cultures far removed from ours in the 21st century. As a result, when undertaking to translate a biblical text, one is faced with the decision as to whether or not to translate the **cultural context**. To put it another way, many of the biblical texts are from an agrarian society and must be translated so as to be understood by people living in an industrialized urban society. How do you make passages about sheep and goats understandable to people who are familiar only with cars and subway trains? The arboretum in New York City had to put up a special exhibit so that the city children could learn where vegetables came from!

Here are quotes from a translation of the Gospel of Matthew, in the *Cotton Patch Bible,* in which the translator attempted to translate the biblical writing from the culture of Judah in the 1st century CE into the culture of the southern United States in the 20th century:

> When Jesus was born in Gainesville, Georgia, during the time that
> Herod was Governor, some scholars from the Orient came to Atlanta
> and inquired, "Where is the one who was born to be governor of Georgia?"[31]

> As Jesus was planning to go to Atlanta, he called the twelve aside and
> said to them along the way, "Look, we're headed for Atlanta, and the son
> of man will be handed over to officials and they will pass the death
> sentence on him. They'll hand him over to the mob to have fun poked
> at him, to be flogged, and to be lynched. And on the third day he will
> be made alive."[32]

It is not hard to see that this method of translation simply will not work. **Lynching** in Atlanta, Georgia, and **crucifixion** in 1st century Jerusalem are not exactly equivalent. The one cannot simply be substituted for the other without a considerable change in meaning. This type of translation is fundamentally flawed. Consequently, one is better off having to learn how sheep

---

[31] Clarence Jordan, *The Cotton Patch Version of Matthew and John* (Chicago: Follett Publishing Company, 1970), 16.]
[32] Jordan, 67 – 68.

and goats behaved and how shepherds and farmers lived in 1st century AD Palestine than to attempt to transpose the text completely into some other culture and historical period.

Methods of Translation

In general, there are four ways of translating a text: **word by word, formal equivalence, dynamic equivalence**, and **free translation.** Each of these methods has its own set of advantages and disadvantages. There is no one perfect way of doing translation. It is easier to grasp the situation if one first looks at the two extremes: word by word translation and free translation.

Word by word translation. In a word by word translation an equivalent word in the receptor language is substituted for each word in the donor language. Here is a word by word translation of the Hebrew text – using an **interlinear translation** -- of **Genesis 1:1-2** (which must be read from *right to left* as Hebrew is written)[33]:

the-earth and the-heavens God he-created in-beginning … (1:1)"   ←
surface -of over and-darkness and-empty formless she-was now-the-earth (1:2) ←

If we read the passage in the following way, would it make sense?

in beginning he created God the heavens and the earth
surface of over and darkness and empty formless she was not the earth

It is obvious that due to differences in word order, this form of translation is difficult to translate into English and read.

Here is a word by word translation of the Greek text of **Matthew 6:9-13**:

Therefore thus pray you:
Father of us the one in the heavens.
Let be revered the name of you.
Let come the kingdom of you.
Let be done the will of you
as in heaven also on earth.
The bread of us daily give to us today.
And forgive us the debts of us
As also we have forgiven the debtors of us.
And do not bring us into temptation
But rescue us from the evil one.[34]

---

[33]John R. Kohlenberger III, Editor, *The Interlinear NIV Hebrew-English Old Testament* (Grand Rapids, Michigan: Zondervan Publishing House, 1987), 1.

[34] J. D. Douglas, Editor, *The New Greek-English Interlinear New Testament* (Wheaton, Illinois: Tyndale House Publishers, Inc., 1990), 19.

Greek is read from left to right, as is English, and the word order of the Greek language is closer to English than Hebrew, so this reads more easily for us than a word-by-word translation of a Hebrew text. But there are still some differences in word order and phraseology, and in the ancient texts there are no paragraphs, no punctuation, and no versification. Therefore, this is also hard for us to read with understanding because it is so unfamiliar to us. In the ancient Hebrew there was no punctuation, and there were no vowels, and no sentence or paragraph construction.

Since a word by word translation cannot be read with ease and comfort, most modern translators of the Scriptures do not use this method.

Free Translation. The most common form of free translation is the **paraphrase**. The paraphrase differs from the word by word translation in that little or no attempt is made to preserve the word order and structure of the original. All of the effort goes into trying to convey, as clearly as possible, the general meaning of the original. This type of translation is usually much wordier than the original. Frequently entire sentences appear which are not part of the original text. Commonly, translations made by this method are written by a single author.

The Message (Eugene H. Peterson, NAVPRESS, 2002) is a good example of this method of translation. It is a translation of the entire New Testament with Psalms and Proverbs written in contemporary language. The author states that it is written so as to be readable and so you should read it first and go to the more academic study bibles afterward. It is suggested that you read a bit of a translation to get a sense of how it "feels." Is it easier to read or not?

The majority of modern translators have avoided the two more extreme methods of translation described above. They have chosen to use one or the other of the two less extreme methods: formal and dynamic equivalence. These two methods of translation may be described as follows:

Formal Equivalence. This method of translation is a **phrase for phrase or sentence for sentence translation**. It strives to preserve that literary and grammatical structure of the original as much as is consistent with making the translation easily read and understood. If there is ambivalence of meaning in the original, that ambivalence is retained in the translation. Modern translations based upon this method are *The Revised Standard Version* (RSV) and *The New American Bible* (NAB).

Dynamic Equivalence. This approach to translation is a **"meaning for meaning"** approach. It is a freer translation. Less effort is spent in trying to retain the literary and grammatical structure of the original and if there is ambiguity in the original this ambiguity is resolved. It is an attempt to reproduce the meaning of the original in the translation. Modern translations based upon this method are *The New English Bible* (NEB) and *Today's English Bible* (also called *The Good News Bible*), and *The Jerusalem Bible* (JB).

Revisions of Translations

It has been twenty years or more since the basic new contemporary translations of the Bible were published. Consequently, you will find that all of these translations are now available in a **"new" or "revised" translation.** If you go to a book store you will find a mixture of the old and the new. The following table sets forth the original translation and the new translation (along with its common abbreviation):

Translation	New Translation
Revised Standard Version (RSV)	*New Revised Standard Version* (NRSV)
New English Bible (NEB)	*Revised English Bible* (REB)
New International Version (NIV)	*New International Version*, Revised
New American Bible (NAB)	*New American Bible with Revised NT and OT* (NABRE)

Use of Inclusive Language

American society at the end of the 20th century and in the beginning of the 21st century became aware of the presence of gender bias in modern English. As a consequence of the women's liberation movement, many individuals felt strongly that the male gender bias in the English language was undesirable. There is, therefore, an increasing demand for the use of **"inclusive language."**

Many people today also feel that there is a broad male bias in the language of the biblical writings. Consequently, both the NRSV and the NAB with Revised NT have adopted a style which is not gender specific when referring to people and retaining the male gender-specific language for God only where necessary. In some other versions of the Bible a similar attempt has been made but to a lesser extent.[35]

There are pros and cons in considering the use of inclusive language in the Bible. An effort to change all male references in a Bible to include both male and female references sometimes results in an incorrect meaning. In the NRSV, a translation for Herod's murdering of all baby boys in and around Bethlehem in order to exterminate the baby Jesus now reads in the following way using inclusive language: "… he sent and killed all the children in and around Bethlehem who were two years old or under." (**Matthew 2: 16**) This is not only a poor translation, but an incorrect one. One wonders if editors of the NRSV simply changed all male gender-specific references by using a computer search without thinking about the effect of the changes in each case.

Use of "Church Language"

In the time when the original *King James Version* of the Bible was made it was the common practice to use words like "thee" and "thou." This way of speaking was incorporated

---

[35] Keith R. Crim, "Modern English Versions of the Bible" in *The New Interpreter's Bible*, V.1, 24 (Nashville, TN: Abingdon Press, 1994).

54

into the Bible and developed into a symbol of reverence for God. Remnants of this way of speaking persist often in the present day, e.g. in Christian church services or prayer groups when the "Our Father" is recited, everyone usually says "*Thy* kingdom come, *Thy* will be done."

Most modern translations have discarded this language on the grounds that it is an antiquated way of speaking. It is maintained, however, in one new Orthodox translation of the New Testament. In this version of the New Testament, Mark 11:1-2 reads as follows:

> And when they drew near to Jerusalem, to Bethpage and Bethany, towards the Mount of Olives, He sendeth forth two of His disciples, and saith to them, "Go ye into the village, the one opposite you; and straightway as ye enter into it, ye shall find a colt which hath been tied, on which no man hath sat. Loose it and bring it."[36]

Do you think that using this form of speech is a help in emphasizing the sacred character of the biblical text or does it function, today, as an obstacle to rapid reading and easy comprehension? You could ask yourself a similar question as follows: Does publishing the Bible with a leather cover and pages with gold edges aid in preserving the holiness of the Bible as opposed to publishing it as an ordinary paperback book?

A suggestion for further reading

For further reading about translation of the Scriptures, consider the following:

> *The Bible in Translation*
> Ancient and English Versions
> Bruce M. Metzger
> Grand Rapids, MI: Baker Academic 2001

This is a very comprehensive, thorough and accurate book by a renowned biblical scholar. It is only 200 pages and reads very easily. It covers the Jewish translation of the Hebrew into Greek that is the Septuagint and other early translations. It gives a fast moving history of English translations. It describes all of the modern translations and their subsequent revisions. Very valuable are the comparisons that Metzger makes between different translations. For anyone with an interest in translation of the Scriptures, this is one book that is a must buy.

Lessening Your Dependence on the Translator

If you do not know anything much about the ancient languages in which the biblical writings were originally written you can still help yourself avoid becoming totally dependent upon the translator.

---

[36] *The Orthodox New Testament, The Holy Gospels* V. 1 (Buena Vista, Colorado: Holy Apostles Convent, 1999), Mark 11: 1-2, 164.

The first and easiest step in doing this is to **read more than one translation**. If you are studying a passage, read it in several different translations. Read a formal equivalence and a dynamic equivalence translation - this will help to indicate if there are uncertainties in understanding the meaning of the text. Proceeding in this manner will also bring to light any text problems that might be present in the passage. Often, the footnotes in a good study bible will provide information on translation issues.

For independence from the translator to an even greater degree, one can consult an interlinear translation (word by word translation) of the passage. Doing this is of great help in determining the key words in the original language of the passage, even though you really don't know the language. Here are two such books:

John R. Kohlenberger III, *The Interlinear NIV Hebrew-English Old Testament*, Grand Rapids, Michigan, Zondervan Publishing House, 1987.

J. D. Douglas, Editor, *The New Greek-English Interlinear New Testament*, Wheaton, Illinois, Tyndale House Publishers, Inc., 1990

These books are readily available in libraries and in bookstores today. Also, the internet now has a choice of online interlinear bibles.

There is yet another step toward independence by consulting a **translator's handbook**. These handbooks are published by the United Bible Societies and there is one for each book of the NT and one for most of the books of the OT. These books contain a lot of helpful information about the meaning of the biblical text. They are readily available by contacting the United Bible Societies in New York. As a sample, here is the reference for the volume on the Book of Psalms:

Robert G. Bratcher and William D. Reyburn, *A Translator's Handbook on the Book of Psalms*, New York, United Bible Societies, 1991.

Part Two … The Texts of the Writings that are Holy Scripture
Regenerating the ancient texts
Translating the ancient texts
Interpreting an ancient text

CHAPTER SIX

THE TEXTS OF THE SCRIPTURES

Introduction

When you start to read the Scriptures, they read like any other writings except that these writings contain a large number of unfamiliar names, places and events. You will read names like Jehoshaphat (1 Kgs 22:41) and Athaliah (2 Kgs 11:1). In fact, the first eight chapters of 1 Chronicles consist of nothing but a long list of such names! The Scriptures also mention some names that may be more familiar: like Abraham (18th or 19th century BC/BCE) and David (10th century BC/BCE) and Paul (1st century AD). But these are all names of **very** ancient people. The Scriptures also mention places that existed a very long time ago like Sodom and Gomorrah. Some places that existed a long time ago still exist today like Jerusalem, Thessalonica and Ephesus. In addition, the Bible mentions events which took place a long time ago, like the **Exodus** in the 13th century BC/BCE (Ex chapters 12-15), the **Babylonian Exile** in the 6th century BC (2 Kgs 19), and the **crucifixion of Jesus** in 30/33 AD (Mk 15:22-41). The events also carry deeper meaning in their spiritual interrelationship across the centuries. For example: the Passover ritual represents the Exodus which gives meaning to the Last Supper of Jesus. The Babylonian Exile represents the fact that earthly nations and kings do not last forever and that people must put their trust in God. And the gift of absolute love for us by God is found in the crucifixion.

What is the significance of the fact that the Scriptures deal with people, places and events of so long ago? There are many contemporary historical novels which portray people and events of the historical past. Are the Scriptures really writings of this sort? Can it be that they are truly ancient works? How can we reliably determine which of these two possibilities is actually the case? Are the Scriptures authentic works of ancient times or just cleverly written modern works of fiction?

For one thing, there are a large number of manuscripts (handwritten copies) of the Scriptures. Also, there are a number of nearly complete copies of the Scriptures that have been dated to the fourth century AD. There are fragments of the writings of the Scriptures that have been dated to as early as the second century AD. In 1947, a complete scroll of Isaiah and parts of all of the other books of the Jewish Scriptures, except Esther, were discovered in caves at Qumran in Palestine, called the Dead Sea Scrolls. These manuscripts date to the first century BC! This is amazing … these scrolls are older than 2,000 years! Further evidence concerning the existence of the biblical writings in ancient times is supplied by the quotations which are found in the writings of non-biblical authors of the first and second centuries AD and also by the longer biblical quotations that are found in the early manuscripts of liturgical books. The writings of Scripture, therefore, are truly ancient writings.

The generation of texts in the 1st century AD

In ancient times a number of different surfaces were used for writing: among these were clay tablets, stone, leather, various metals, potsherds (*ostraca*), papyrus and parchment. In the case of the biblical writings dating to the 1st AD, the materials of papyrus and parchment are of greatest interest.

The following description of the making of papyrus and parchment manuscripts is from Bruce Metzger:

> The manufacture of **papyrus** was a flourishing business in Egypt, for the papyrus plant grew plentifully in the shallow waters of the Nile at the delta (cf. Job viii.11, 'Can papyrus grow where there is no marsh?'). About 12 or 15 feet in height, the stem of the plant, which was triangular in cross-section and as thick as a man's wrist, was cut into sections about a foot long. Each section was split open lengthwise and the pith cut into thin strips. A layer of these was placed on a flat surface, all the fibers running in the same direction, and on top another layer was laid, with the fibers running at right angles to the lower layer. The two layers were then pressed together until they formed one fabric - a fabric which, though now so brittle that it can sometimes be crumbled into powder, once had a strength nearly equal to that of good paper.
>
> **Parchment or vellum** (often used interchangeably; more precisely the word *vellum* is used to describe a finer, superior quality of parchment) was made from the skins of cattle, sheep, goats, and antelopes; especially from the young of those animals. After the animal's hair had been removed by scraping, the skins were washed, smoothed with pumice, and dressed with chalk.[37]

Manuscripts of literary works were written in a style of handwriting called **uncials.** This style of handwriting consisted of large, carefully executed individual letters (much like our capital letters). This style of handwriting was replaced in the 9th century AD by a style having smaller, connected letters called **minuscules.** Within each of these periods, there were also different styles of making the letters. Analysis of handwriting is one way that scholars can date manuscripts.

Ancient scrolls were made of papyrus, utilizing reeds that grew along wet river areas like along the Nile in Egypt and the Tigris and Euphrates rivers in Mesopotamia. The reeds were cut, split and then beaten together on a flat surface and dried to make a writing material. This created

---

[37]Bruce M. Metzger, *The Text of the New Testament*, 2nd Edition (New York, NY: Oxford University Press, 1968), 3-4.

a writing surface that had lines which were used for hanging the letters down from the line above, much like writing papers that are made for kindergarten students today (although they learn to build the letters up from a lower line.) It is common opinion that papyrus is not a durable material. But that is not the truth. Papyrus is quite durable under the right conditions. It does become brittle and is subject to disintegration when it undergoes repeated wet and dry periods. It will, however, survive very well if protected from moisture (being put in a clay jar for example) or being kept in a dry climate (like Egypt or the desert near Qumran). It does not survive for long periods in regions that have high humidity (like Greece) One reason that many scholars give for doubting the validity of the spurious *Gospel of Judas* is that it was written on papyrus and not found in Egypt.

Parchment scrolls, known also as vellum, were made from various animal skins, including sheep, oxen, and deer. The animal hides were cleaned, stretched on frames and dried, sometimes with pieces later sewn together. Just like the papyrus material, after a scroll was written it was wound on wooden poles. With the modern knowledge of DNA, scholars today are now able to piece together hundreds of fragments of manuscripts found by identifying the very animal from which the parchment was taken.

The literary works in the Greco-Roman world were usually put in the form of a scroll. This scroll was made by gluing together the individual sheets of papyrus or parchment and then winding the long strip onto a stick. The length of a normal scroll was usually not more than 35 feet in length as that length was about the longest that could be handled conveniently. The books of Luke and Acts in the NT would each have occupied a scroll some 30 feet in length.

In the 2nd century AD, Christians adopted the **codex;** it was a book form made by binding, on one side, a number of papyrus or parchment sheets, sewn together on one side to make something like a modern book. The codex form for saving treasured biblical writings developed quickly because they found it was much easier to use and to carry around.

Transmission of texts

We have considered how texts for the NT were generated in the 1st century AD. Now let us consider how manuscripts, once generated, were transmitted. There are two senses of the term "transmitted." There is the sense of transmission from the place of origin to the place of an individual or group to whom the document was written. There is also the sense of how a written communication gets to places other than to the place for which it was originally intended, or comeS down to other historical times at much later dates.

There is a manuscript of the Bible at the Vatican Library in Rome that dates to the 4th century AD. What is of interest to us here is understanding the way that a letter written by Paul in the middle of the 1st century AD came to be part of a manuscript that dates to the 4th century.

The Letter of Paul in the Vatican manuscript is not the original letter. It is a copy of the letter. To be more precise: it is a copy of a copy of a copy of a copy of the autograph, the original letter. Why is this so? First, constant use of a manuscript written on parchment or papyrus caused it to deteriorate and become unreadable. Such documents, therefore, had to be copied periodically in order to preserve their clarity. Secondly, as the number of Christians grew and their geographic distribution increased, a demand was generated for additional copies to satisfy the increased and more widespread readership.

By the fourth century AD, it was the common practice for copies of manuscripts to be produced in a **scriptorium.** However, there is a strong argument by archaeologists that the stone foundation discovered at Qumran near the Dead Sea, much older than the 4th century AD, was actually a scriptorium and there certainly an individual leading an ascetic life evidently copied and studied scrolls. They even have found ink wells! However, as the monastic tradition of Christianity developed – at first in the desert of Egypt and later through the Near East, monks took up the task of scroll work. In a typical scriptorium a number of scribes sat at writing tables or desks in a room. Each scribe was equipped with papyrus or parchment, pens and ink. A reader slowly read aloud the text that was to be reproduced and, as he read, the scribes would write down what they heard. The number of copies produced obviously depended on how many individual scribes were available to be working in the room. The copying of scriptural and liturgical manuscripts became one of the major works in monasteries beginning as early as the 3rd century AD when monasticism emerged in the desert of Egypt. Recall the story of St. Anthony who gave away all his possessions and went to live an ascetic life in a cave in the desert.

The production of copies was no easy task. We can learn about how hard this task may have been by noticing the colophons (notes) which the scribes frequently put at the end of their manuscripts. Here are three examples:

1. "He who does not know how to write supposes it to be no labor; but though only three fingers write, the whole body labors."[38]

2. "Writing bows one's back, thrusts the ribs into one's stomach, and fosters a general debility of the body."[39]

3. In an Armenian manuscript of the Gospels a colophon complains that a heavy snowstorm was raging outside and that the scribe's ink froze, his hand became numb, and the pen fell from his fingers.[40]

It goes without saying that the scribes must have believed that the task of copying the scriptures was of such importance that it was worth suffering extreme discomforts and enduring long hours of tedious writing. It is because of the efforts of these dedicated individuals that we have the scriptures to read today!

Manuscripts transmitted in this manner are subject to the introduction of certain types of unintentional errors and intentional changes of various sorts. Unintentional errors include: confusing Greek letters that resemble one another; omission of a line or passage; omitting a line or phrase not heard; confusing two words that sound the same; and incorporation of words or

---

[38] Metzger, 17.
[39] Metzger, 17-18.
[40] Metzger, 18.

notes written in the margin of a page into the text itself. Intentional changes include: changes resulting from a strong desire to harmonize discordant parallels; clearing up historical and geographical difficulties; conflation of passages; alterations made for doctrinal reasons; and addition of miscellaneous information and markings.

It is not important at this point that you understand the details of these types of unintentional errors and intentional changes. What is important is be aware that because of errors and changes, there are a large number of variant readings in the manuscripts that have survived to our time. It can be said, however, that these variant readings are only rarely of significant importance to the meaning or interpretation of the verse and, in fact, an intentional change can even result in a better understanding of the verse.

These unintentional errors and intentional changes are a mixed blessing. On the one hand, they are undesirable because they degrade the accuracy of the manuscripts in which they occur. On the other hand, however, they are highly useful in that they provide the means by which the manuscripts can be grouped into families and the history of the text tradition determined!

The Manuscript Evidence for the NT

During the years of transmission many copies of the manuscripts ended up being destroyed or succumbing to fire or natural causes. A few, however, ended up being put in libraries and private homes or stored in caves and then left there forgotten.

Now turn the clock ahead to the 18th, 19th, and 20th centuries. These centuries were a period of discovery! It was the period of finding many ancient manuscripts. A small number of those found were complete: for example, the Isaiah Scroll found in a cave at Qumran. The majority of manuscripts were only partially complete. The earliest consisted of only small fragments of once complete texts. The sum total of all of the manuscript evidence enables the text critics to reconstruct the ancient texts with a considerable degree of confidence.

Most often biblical manuscripts have been found in the course of excavations at various archaeological sites. Occasionally, however, important manuscripts were found in unusual circumstances. In 1844, Tischendorf was traveling through the Near East looking for manuscripts of the Holy Scriptures. While visiting the monastery of St. Catherine on Mount Sinai, he happened to notice some leaves of parchment in a waste basket full of papers that were about to be used to light the oven in the kitchen. When he examined them he found that they were part of a copy of the Septuagint version of the OT. This manuscript contained most of the OT, all of the NT and several additional writings. It is now known as the *Codex Sinaiticus*, dating to the 4th century AD.[41]

The manuscript evidence for the NT text which we now possess consists of over 5,000 Greek manuscripts (abbreviation: mss), some complete or nearly so and many only fragmentary. These manuscripts consist of the following four types:[42]

---

[41] Metzger, 42-44.
[42] Eldon Jay Epp, "Textual Criticism (NT) in "*The Anchor Bible Dictionary*, Vol. 6 (New York, NY: Doubleday, 1992), 419-430.

2. **Papyrus mss** – there are 94 of them dating from the 2nd century to the 8th century AD.

2. **Uncial mss** – these are continuous-text manuscripts written on parchment in uncial characters; there are some 270 of these. The most important of these are the following:

    f. **Codex Sinaiticus** – complete NT; dating to the 4th century

    g. **Codex Alexandrinus** – nearly complete; dating to 5th century

    h. **Codex Vaticanus** – all of NT except for an extensive portion of Heb through Rev, dating to 4th century

    i. **Codex Bezae Cantabrigiensis** – only 4 gospels (in the order of Mt, Jn, Lk and Mk), most of Acts and a small portion of 3 Jn, dating to late 4th to 5th century

    j. **Codex Washingtonianus** – the four gospels nearly complete (in the order of Mt, Jn, Lk, Mk), dating to early 5th century

3. **Minuscule mss** – there are several thousand of these; they all date to the 9th century or later.

4. **Lectionaries** – there are about 2,200 of these liturgical texts; they contain the readings for the Church liturgical year.

In addition to these four types of manuscripts, evidence for the early NT text is obtained from patristic quotations, passages of the NT quoted by early Christian writers, and from various versions -- translations of the Greek text into other languages, principally Syriac, Latin, Coptic, and Ethiopic.

The oldest manuscript fragment of the NT found to date is a 2 ½ inch by 3 ½ inch piece of papyrus containing a small portion of the Gospel of John. It dates to the 1st half of the second century AD. The most important manuscripts of the NT as a whole are the *Codex Sinaiticus* and *Codex Vaticanus,* both of which date to the fourth century as we have seen above.

What does a text of the Scriptures look like? You can explore one of the oldest (middle 4th century AD) and best texts of parts of the OT and the entire NT: it is called the Codex Sinaiticus. Just go to the following website entitled "codexsomaotocis.org."

The Science of Text Criticism

The term "text criticism" is the name given to the critical study of ancient manuscripts. **It is the basic assumption of those practicing this discipline of text criticism that the original texts of the NT writings are to be found within the manuscript evidence which is currently possessed.** The task of text criticism is to determine, on the basis of all of the manuscript evidence, the original text (called the "autograph") of each of the NT writings. This task requires an enormous amount of effort and a scholarly and detailed knowledge of the textual evidence.

A small group of highly skilled people have made the tremendous effort required to work through all of the manuscript evidence. Through their dedication and skill there is available, for our reading today, a text of the writings in the NT that is the closest to the original texts that has been available to Christian believers since the 1st century AD!

The Text Underlying Our Modern Translations of the New Testament

Look in the Preface to the NT in your Bible. Look for where it tells you what Greek text was used for the translation. For example, in *The Catholic Study Bible*, Second Edition with the Revised New Testament, it first reprints the Preface to the New Testament from the first edition which reads as follows:

> In general, Nestle-Aland's *Novem Testamentum Graece* (25th edition, 1963) was followed. Additional help was derived from *The Greek New Testament* (Aland, Black, Metzger, Wikgren) produced for the use of translators by the United Bible Societies in 1966.[43]

Then it prints the Preface to the Revised Edition of the New Testament which reads as follows:

> The Greek text followed in this translation is that of the third edition The Greek New Testament, edited by Kurt Aland, Matthew Black, Carlo Martini, Bruce Metzger and Allen Wikgren, and published by the United Bible Societies in 1975. The same text, with a different critical apparatus and variations in punctuation and topography, was published as the twenty-sixth edition of the Nestle-Aland *Novum Testamentum Graece* in 1979 by the Deutsche Bibelstiftung, Stuttgart.[44]

What does all this mean? This means, first of all, that Kurt Aland and the others have done a great deal of work to bring us what they believe to be the best reconstruction of the original text of the NT. We owe a large debt of gratitude to this group of scholars! Secondly, it means that the *New American Bible*, Revised New Testament is not a translation of the same text as the first edition New Testament of the *New American Bible*. Thirdly, it means that if you read the *New American Bible*, Revised New Testament you are benefiting from 12 additional years of work by Aland and his coworkers on the text of the New Testament.

For those of you who can read Greek or plan to learn to read it, the result of the work of Aland *et al* is readily available in many religious bookstores or from some book distributors (e.g. the Christian Book Distributors). Keep in mind that the original language of the NT was Greek.

---

[43] Donald Senior, Editor, *The Catholic Study Bible*, Preface To The New American Bible, First Edition Of The New Testament (New York: Oxford University Press, 1990), *iib.*
[44] Donald Senior, Editor, *The Catholic Study Bible*, Preface to The Revised Edition (New York: Oxford University Press, 1990), ivb.

At this point, it is important to remind ourselves also that the original language of the Old Testament was Hebrew with some Aramaic included (a dialect of Hebrew) and later translated into the Greek Septuagint; and that the New Testament was originally written in Greek. Some OT scholars even tell us that there are a few Babylonian and Egyptian words in the OT! Latin translations of the Bible from as early as the 2nd century AD with small, individual manuscripts of particular books, and later in a translation by St. Jerome in the 4th century AD, soon became the standard "Bible" for many Christians. However, in biblical studies it is always best to regard the original languages.

The Text of the OLD TESTAMENT

The writings of the OT and NT differ in one very important respect. The writings of the NT were written in a very limited period of time, from 75 to 100 years. A short letter, such as **Philemon** or **3 John,** was most likely written in one "sitting." Even a long book such as Acts was probably written over a relatively short period of time. The majority of writings in the OT, however, were composed over much longer periods of time. In the case of the Pentateuch, this was a period of about 500 years!

In the case of the writings of the NT, because there was an original text, the goal of text criticism is quite well defined – to recover the original text. In the case of the writings of the OT, however, the goal of text criticism is necessarily different. Many of the writings of the OT were edited several times over a long period of time and, therefore, it is much less clear as to what was the original text. A similar problem holds true for Homer's *Iliad* and *Odyssey* which are believed to have gone through a literary history that is similar in nature to that of the OT. The goal of OT text criticism is, therefore, to shed light on the history of the text.

It is good to know that the Hebrew of the OT is now a difficult language to translate. Ancient Hebrew was written with no vowels, and it is written from right to left with absolutely no punctuation. For many, it is a difficult language to learn because the letters are very different in appearance from the English alphabet. However, it can be learned. Sesame Street has published videos that teach pre-school children to write and be able to read a few Hebrew words! So, don't be discouraged.

The most exciting discovery of ancient manuscripts in the case of the OT was at Qumran in Israel by the Dead Sea. These manuscripts have been dated to as early as the 1st century BC! One of the most spectacular finds was a complete manuscript of the entire book of Isaiah. The majority of the finds of manuscripts at Qumran consisted of small fragments. Modern technology has come to the aid of piecing these fragments together in TWO WAYS. First, as mentioned, by the use of DNA analysis all of the pieces written on animal skin can be can be related to the specific animal from which they came. Secondly, each fragment has been put on a computer and, therefore, the piecing together can be carried out by means of the computer.

The Masoretic Text

The text of the OT that is contained in most English Bible translations is called the Masoretic Text. This text is so named because it was prepared by the **Masoretes** who represented succeeding generations of scribes who lived during the period **500-1000 AD** and attended to the matter of transmitting the OT text with great accuracy. The continuous biblical text they arranged had its roots in ancient Israel, originating from manuscripts dating to the last two centuries before Christ. Scrolls and scroll fragments attesting to this were found at Qumran. The Masoretic text was written in a new kind of Hebrew writing where the vowels were indicated by small dots and teeny lines, above and below the letters – known as pointing.

If you look at the introduction to the OT in your Bible it will usually tell you what text it is using for the OT. For example, we are told in an introductory section to the *New Revised Standard Version* that the text behind the OT is the *Biblia Hebraica Stuttgartensia* (1977 edition.). This identifies a particular Masoretic manuscript of the OT.

The Greek Text of the OT

In the third century BC, Greek-speaking Jews living in the **Diaspora** (i.e. outside of Palestine) felt a need to have the text of the OT translated into Greek. Greek was the language of the eastern Roman Empire, and the language of the Jewish population in Egypt. The Greek translation was accomplished, in its first stage, during the third and second centuries BC by a number of different scribes. This text of the OT, known as the **Septuagint** (which means "seventy"), derives its name from a legend that it was translated by 70 scribes (actually 72; six from each of the twelve tribes) all of whom, working strictly independently translated it exactly the same, word for word … or so the legend goes.

The Greek translation of the OT served as the Bible for the Greek-speaking Jews through the 1st century AD. It served as the scriptures for the Christian churches outside of Palestine through the 1st century and for a long time afterward. It is the Greek OT that is found in the **Codex Vaticanus.** The Greek of the New Testament is primarily Koine Greek, a popular dialect of Greek. Many NT scholars think that Jesus quoted the Septuagint in his preaching, as is quoted in the NT. The actual wording of the quotations reveals that it was the Greek translation. The reason that Jesus would do this is because the language of the day was Greek. Overall, this may mean that Jesus read and spoke Greek for his preaching, that he spoke Aramaic – a dialect of Hebrew – in his home, and read and spoke ancient Hebrew in the synagogue and the Temple.

The biblical text upon which the Septuagint is based is for some of the books of the OT considerably different from the Masoretic text. For example, the Septuagint version of Jeremiah is one-eighth shorter than the Masoretic version. It is apparent from a comparison of the two texts that the Greek translation was made from an early form of the book of Jeremiah and that the Masoretic text represents a further development of Jeremiah. There is evidence for both of these two traditions in the manuscripts of Jeremiah found at Qumran.

The Christians of the 1st century AD, then, used two versions of the OT. Those living in Palestine used primarily the OT based upon the textual tradition that developed into the Masoretic text. The Christians living elsewhere, especially the Gentile Christians, used the Greek translation of the OT, the Septuagint. It is not a difficult matter to tell that they actually used both versions because when the authors of the NT writings quote from the OT more often than not they quote from the Septuagint but the other times they quote from the ancient Hebrew, Masoretic texts.

In general, throughout the centuries, **Masoretic scribes** were known for their precision in studying the scriptures. They counted every word used in the documents they were reading, often making lists of words and working to understand how words were related and pronounced. Sometimes they even counted letters. Most deeply religious Jewish scholars today know which word marks the very center of the Hebrew Scriptures. The Masoretic scribes invented a way of adding small points and little lines to the words because in ancient Hebrew there usually were no vowel letters and vowel sounds were just remembered. The system which these scribes invented was called **"pointing."**

Here is an interesting question to consider. Up to the time that the Greek translation was undertaken, the Jews had written all of their sacred texts in Hebrew. Thus, up to that time Hebrew was the language in which the religious thinking of Israel had been expressed. It is sometimes stated that God chose the people of Israel to be God's people because Hebrew was a language that could express adequately God's revelation of truths. How, then, could the writings of the OT be translated into Greek, a language that did not have the same religious vocabulary as that of the Hebrew? What were the consequences, therefore, of translating from Hebrew into Greek? What impact did this have on the early Christians who knew the Scriptures only through the Greek translation?

Here is another question to ponder. Should we, as Christian believers of the 21st century, be reading the Masoretic text, which is presented to us in most of our Bibles, or should we be reading the Septuagint text, which was the OT text read by the majority of Christians after the middle of the 1st century AD (which we must purchase as a separate book)? Perhaps, it makes sense to read and compare various versions to gain the best knowledge of the writings.

CHAPTER EIGHT

INTERPRETING AN ANCIENT TEXT

Introduction

Reading the Scriptures is not like reading a textbook, or a story book, or a non-fiction piece on a topic of specialized interest. Reading the Scriptures and understanding them is unique and sometimes a challenge. As has been stated … the very first thing to remember, when beginning to read the Scriptures is that these ancient documents have been translated from the original languages in which they were written – Hebrew, Aramaic, and Greek. This means that the translators have the important job of **interpretation**. In translating the Scriptures, the need for interpretation occurs because the original languages do not have the same sentence structure, word order, or phraseology as found in the English language. In addition, knowledge of the ancient culture is needed, including an in-depth knowledge of how the ancient languages varied in different time periods in history.

Consider the fact that ancient Hebrew and Aramaic languages read from right to left and there are no punctuation marks or divisions such as paragraphs, or versification, line breaks, or rhyming in poetry. Modern translations, for instance, will print the Hebrew poetry as found in the Psalms, in the form of stanzas but this arrangement does not exist in the original texts. The English translators offer this printing help to aid us in recognizing the poetic literary form.

The original language of the New Testament Greek does read from left to right as most modern languages do, but often the word order and phraseology is quite different from English and like many languages there are words and expressions that are either idiomatic or somewhat non-translatable. The work, then, of the translator requires interpretation in order to place the original words in meaningful English expression.

An interesting experiment to do that easily demonstrates the need for interpretation in translation, without even having to know the ancient language, is to consult an interlinear translation[45] and see how each word is directly translated as it occurs in the text. You write down each English word (beneath the OT or NT words) in order as they appear (from right to left for the Hebrew of the OT, and left to right for the Greek of the NT). What do you have? As was described previously, you see an almost incomprehensible collection of English words, especially those taken from the Hebrew. Without consulting any translation, attempt yourself to

---

[45] Look for the hard copy editions of the interlinear bibles in your library. For the Old Testament, see: John R. Kohlenberger III, editor, *The Interlinear NIV Hebrew-English Old Testament* (Grand Rapids, Michigan: Zondervan Publishing House, 1987). For the New Testament see: J. D. Douglas, editor, *The New Greek-English Interlinear New Testament* (Wheaton, Illinois: Tyndale House Publishers, Inc.; 4th edition, 1993). In addition, you may find these interlinear bibles online. See: The interlinear bible online (a non-denominational site that offers a wealth of information on each original word); and **biblehub**. When you click on "Strong's numbers," you will see further information on the meaning of each word as it appears in the context of a particular passage.

put these words into readable English. You can stick as closely as you can to the original words (literal translation), or you can paraphrase it all, or you can think about the meaning and then construct the English words that express this central meaning, following the literal translation as faithfully as you can (dynamic translation). The most important thing you learn is that it is truly necessary to interpret the words. It is obvious that one needs to be a competent scholar, knowledgeable in biblical history, biblical languages, and biblical culture to conduct the best translation.

Understanding biblical interpretation is a topic of great importance. It is through interpretation that the meaning of the biblical text is brought to light for us today. Therefore, it is important to know the background of the translators of the Scriptures you read. There are differences that can occur in the theological understanding between translators. One can easily understand that a translator's own viewpoint can highly influence the translation. For a given passage of Scripture, it is sometimes observed that the Jewish, Catholic, Protestant, Orthodox and Jewish (in the case of the OT) translators will differ, sometimes quite dramatically. The work of good translation requires the work of those who can be loyal to the original texts and not be tempted to interpret along personal views and agendas. Many of the best translations are the work of translation committees, often with Jewish scholars working alongside Catholic, Orthodox, and Protestant scholars.

It cannot be emphasized too strongly that when the reader sits down to read the text of Scripture in English, in reality he or she is reading a text that has already been interpreted for the reader. **This makes it imperative that you be sure that you are reading a reliable translation of the text.** It is also wise to consult more than one translation in most situations of biblical study.

There is a significant difficulty in using a paraphrase of the biblical text, although it's tempting because such a translation reads easily and seems more readily understandable than a more literal translation. But the big danger is that the meaning which seems to read more easily is not the same as the meaning as the original biblical text.

Overall, interpretation can be understood as more technically being the work of what is called **exegesis,** a Greek word that means "to draw out." This is the serious work of examining a biblical passage in depth in order to find the "authentic sense of the sacred text or even its different senses."[46] In this way, the work of exegesis will communicate to every reader the original meaning. Therefore, "exegesis is the process of careful, analytical study of biblical passages undertaken in order to produce useful interpretations of those passages."[47] Well-known New Testament biblical scholar Daniel Harrington wrote the following in reference to NT exegesis:

> At the most obvious and fundamental level, the exegesis of a biblical text involves explaining a passage written in Greek most likely by a Jewish-Christian author under the sway of the Hellenistic culture of the Roman Empire to a twentieth-century audience of Americans (or whatever other

---

[46] Pontifical Biblical Commission, *The Interpretation of the Bible in the Church (Rome, April 15, 1993).*
[47] Douglas Stuart, "Exegesis," in *The Anchor Bible Dictionary, Vol. 2(New York, NY: Doubleday, 1992), 682.*

nationality group) who speak English and live in what is variously described as the post-enlightenment age or atomic age.[48]

There is interpretation of biblical texts in the scriptures themselves

Specific texts in the Bible often refer to other texts in the Bible, and in this way form a kind of interpretation. Since the Scriptures are inspired by God, it is helpful when a later writing in the Bible is quoting an earlier writing, because in this way we see how the original passage is being interpreted. A good example is when the gospel writers are quoting the words of a prophet of the OT. The prophet is being interpreted for people of the NT time. In the letters of St. Paul we often find him interpreting OT passages, for example, those that point to God's plan of salvation, beginning with Genesis. Consider the following examples:

a. The OT interprets the OT

There is interpretation of OT passages in the OT itself. For example, Jeremiah 31:29-30 is interpreted in Ezekiel 18. The Books of 1 and 2 Chronicles are largely a reinterpretation of the books of Samuel and Kings.

b. The OT is interpreted in the NT

The account in Gen 15:1-6 portrays Abraham as believing in God's promise that he would have an heir. In Rom 4:1-8 Paul interprets this passage as showing that Abraham was a person who was justified by his faith and not by his works. In a similar manner, James (Jas 2:18-23) interprets Gen 22:1-14 to support the position that Abraham was justified by his works! So, one can conclude that both faith and works are necessary.

In the Gospel of Matthew, the OT is interpreted in the sense of having been fulfilled by various events in the life of Jesus. In Mt 1:22-23 the birth of Jesus is said to have fulfilled a prophecy of Isaiah (Is 7:14). In Mt 2:5-6 a prophecy by the prophet Micah (Mic 5:2) is interpreted to have been fulfilled by Jesus' birth in Bethlehem. Similar cases are to be found in Mt 2:15, 2:17-18 and 2:23.

In numerous places in the NT, statements found in the OT are interpreted to be expressions of the life and person of Jesus Christ. One of the best examples of this is found in the first chapter of Hebrews (Heb 1:5-13). This passage contains, end to end, seven citations of passages of the OT all interpreted to apply to Jesus Christ – Ps 2:7; Deut 32:43; Ps l04:4; Ps 45:6-7; Ps 102:25-27; and Ps 110:1.

In his letter to the Romans, Paul interprets texts of the OT that apply to the relationship of the Jews to the Christians in his own time. For example, in Rom 10:18-20, Paul cites OT passages three times: (1) in Romans 10, v18 he quotes from Ps 19:4 to state that the Jews have heard the gospel, (2) in v19 he quotes from Deut 32:21 to state that God will make them (i.e. the

---

[48] Daniel J. Harrington, S.J., *Interpreting the New Testament*, Volume 1 of the New Testament Message Series (Delaware: Michael Glazier, Inc., 1979), 131.

Jews) jealous of the Gentiles, and (3) in v20 he quotes from Is 65:1-2 to restate the idea that the Gentiles have found God but the Jews have not.

The references in the NT pointing back to the OT establish the interpretation that Christ has always existed, indicating that he has always been present in the words which God inspired the authors of the OT texts to write. There is a theological reason for this. If Christ is truly man and God, then the divinity of Christ has always existed. An example can be found in the Prologue to the Gospel of John where Christ is called the Logos, the Word of God. "All things were made through him, and without him was not anything made that was made." (RSV John 1:3) Also, reading this passage in another translation, one can see the translators laboring to interpret the Greek words: "All things came to be through him, and without him nothing came to be. (NAB John 1:3) With both these translations, we understand that Christ was instrumental in the creation of the world. Christ has always been!

c. Types

There is another way in which the NT interprets the OT. That is in terms of **types** (also known as typology.) This method is frequently referred to as the "typical sense" of scripture. You can see this method of interpretation in Rom 5:14 where Paul refers to Adam as "a type of the one who was to come." The typical sense may be defined in the following manner: **The typical sense is that deeper meaning which persons, places and events have because they foreshadow other things yet to come**. The type and its object are never similar in every detail. The type is not meant to define the object but to represent its meaning in a symbolic way.

It should be kept in mind that the type and its subject necessarily exist at different time periods but are related by a deep meaning that connects them. It is only when the subject of the type later appears that the type is fully recognizable. The type of Adam was only fully understood when Christ came, as Paul is pointing out in his letter to the Romans (See Romans 5: 12-21.)

d. The NT is interpreted in the NT

Instances of one NT writing interpreting another NT writing are not hard to find. For example, Mt 10:10 is interpreted in 1 Tim 5:18. Another example is that of the parable of the sower. The parable is set forth in Mk 4:4-9; an interpretation is given in 4:14-20.

e. Misinterpretation of the NT by people reading the NT

It is stated in 2 Peter 3:14-17 that the letters of Paul are read by some people who misinterpret them, apparently because there are some things in them which are hard to understand. This statement gives testimony to the reality that the scriptures can be misinterpreted!

Senses of Scripture

Historically, in interpreting the Scriptures, it appears that there are various approaches to understanding the scriptural passages. In other words, there are different "senses" in which to interpret the words. These are known as the **senses of scripture.** It is not a question of using one sense or another sense, but one finds that often there is more than one sense to a given passage. For instance, a narrative can relate an event and all the stages of action that happened. And, yet, in another way the events can have a deeper more symbolic meaning. This can be seen in the biblical account of the Exodus of the Hebrew people from slavery. It was an historical reality, but at the same time the narrative tells of the care that God provided the faithful people with care and protection, revealing thereby who God is in reality. God is the life-giver.

St. Thomas Aquinas in the 13th century described four senses of Scripture. Primarily, he distinguished between the literal and the spiritual sense. In the account of the Exodus, the literal sense reveals the actual historical narrative events as they happened. The spiritual sense is what the event revealed about God and what God intended for the Hebrews, the people of God. The literal sense gave the meaning that is immediately drawn directly from the words written by the author. The extension to a spiritual sense is seen when the words are understood in a metaphorical or allegorical way, sometimes providing a moral content. Today, there are considered to be four senses to interpret Scripture, much like the thought of St. Thomas. These are: 1) **the literal sense,** 2) **the allegorical sense** – often called the typical sense, 3) the **tropological or moral sense,** and 4) the **anagogical or eschatological sense.** The **literal sense** is obvious as it is the direct meaning as imparted by reading the words. The **allegorical sense** provides the more spiritual aspect by using words and phrases, or even whole narrative accounts, that impart who God is and what God wills. The **tropological or moral sense** is the interpretation of a passage as it directs the reader to an ethical life. As an example, Moses receives the Ten Commandments on Mt. Sinai as the stipulations of the covenant between God and the people. They replicate the covenants between nations of ancient times which always included stipulations. At the same time, there is a moral sense because the reader learns how God wishes people to live. The **anagogical or eschatological sense** refers to a sense of what it all means in reference to the end times, or the whole purpose of how God proposes the destiny of mankind.

More on the Typical Sense

The existence of types is explicitly expressed in Rom 5:14 where Paul states that Adam is the type of Christ. This typology is also alluded to in 1 Cor 10:6-12. The typical sense may be defined in the following manner: the typical sense is the deeper meaning which persons, places and events inherently hold which then represent a type for foreshadowing other things yet to come.

Some examples of types that are to be found in Scripture are the following:
- Melchizedek is a type of Christ (Gen 14:17-20; Heb 7:1-3)
- Exodus is a type of baptism (Ex 14:22, 29-31; 1 Cor 10:1f)
- Jonah is a type of Christ (Mt 12:40)
- Raising of the bronze serpent is a type of Christ on the cross (Num 21:8; Jn 3:14f)

Types exist by virtue of the fact that there is one God and only one God active throughout the history of salvation and, consequently, salvation history is a continuously developing unity.

In some cases it is not the historical reality that makes something a type but rather its literary description. For example, Melchizedek undoubtedly had parents, but he is a type of Christ according to Heb 7:3 primarily because Christ can be regarded as "High Priest" like that of this former King of Righteousness.

The Allegorical Sense

There are specific passages in Scripture which demonstrate an allegorical sense. For example, the Parable of the Sower (Mk 4: 1-8) which is given an allegorical interpretation by Jesus (Mk 4:13-20). In Gal 5:22-31 Paul references the Abrahamic traditions of Genesis (Gen 16:5; 21:2, 9) and attributes an allegorical to them meaning applicable to Christian believers. These examples demonstrate that the authors are writing under divine inspiration. This is a case of the *sensus plenior* that reveal that a voice of God permeates the entire collection of biblical writings.

The *Sensus Plenior*

Accepting Scripture as having both a divine and a human author introduces the possibility that the Divine Author interacts with the human author resulting in a deeper meaning of which the human writer is not aware, a "fuller sense" or in French a ***sensus plenior.***"

God's plan of salvation has unfolded within history. The history of salvation is a progressing education of humanity, the OT being the record of the preparation for the messianic [coming of a messiah] fullness achieved in Christ Jesus. It seems only natural, therefore, to expect that God inspired words with meaning, brought to light only later with the more complete working out of the divine plan of salvation. It is interesting to observe that Hebrew is full of conceptual language with metaphors, images, and meanings that can expand into deeper and more profound meaning at a later time.

The Hebrew language is particularly suitable for carrying hidden meanings since the culture of the people of Palestine and later Israel was more conceptual than linear in thought processes. People in the ancient world were used to thinking in concepts that were represented by images and even events that related a deeper and profound meaning beyond the meaning on the surface. As the Scriptures were written by human authors and inspired by God, these meanings were only understood in the future. It is like a professor of elementary physics communicating an idea to students, knowing full well they will not understand it in its entirety until some future time. Pius Drijvers describes this in a more poetic form:

> The truths of the Old Testament obtain a new and clearer perspective
> through the fullness of the revelation in Christ, in the same way as the thin

sound of a twanged instrument is made fuller and deeper by the presence of a sounding board.[49]

The *sensus plenior* is defined by Raymond Brown in the following manner:

> The *sensus plenior* is the additional, deeper meaning intended by God but not clearly intended by the human author, which is seen to exist in the words of a scriptural text, or group of texts, when it is studied in the light of further revelation or development in the understanding of revelation.[50]

The *sensus plenior* is intended by the divine author and is, therefore, a true sense of Scripture. It is not a literal sense, however, since the meaning is not intended directly by the human author at the time of writing.

Good interpreters must know themselves

Why is it important to know yourself before you set out to read Holy Scripture? This is because when you read it, you read yourself into it. That is why you are reading the Scriptures in the first place – because you have questions about the meaning of life, who God is, and what God wants. You have to realize your own interpretive approach. Consider the case of a person who does not believe in the possibility of miraculous cures. When such a person encounters Jesus' cures in the Gospels, he or she may immediately attribute the healing merely to a psychological change which takes place in the one cured. The miraculous element is denied. However, if that person is an individual with faith, who believes that miraculous cures are possible, he or she will immediately believe the accounts of Jesus' healings are powerful signs testifying to the divinity of Jesus. Perhaps the reader feels very strongly that contemporary moral values are the norm and cannot accept the ideas on divorce that the Bible provides. Or, that person is open to learn the moral code given in the Bible, believing that it is, indeed, inspired by God and is meant to connect him or her with God's will.

Therefore, the reader of Scriptures should be on constant guard not to rely just on one's own opinions and attitudes but approach these ancient writings by being open to history, social issues of the ancient ages, language, and the spiritual aspect of God's work in inspiring the writings. Thereby, it helps to identify the *sensus plenior* and to see the inter-connectedness of texts. It is not sufficient just to state, "Well, this is what I believe." Such a statement is shallow and often useless without referring to solid scholarship and the biblical writings themselves.

Do the writings contained in the Holy Scriptures have meaning for us today?

The Scriptures are read as part of the liturgy in Christian churches in the hope that they will convey some meaning of spiritual value. And, the Scriptures are read by private individuals with the hope of finding some meaning applicable to their lives for particular life situations.

---

[49] Pius Drijvers, *The Psalms* (New York, NY: Herder and Herder, 1965), 10.
[50] Raymond Brown, *The Sensus Plenior*, 42.

Even though these writings were written for people who lived before the early 2nd century AD, Christians and Jews of the 21st century AD do believe they hold great value for life today.

This belief by 21st century Christians and Jews, and that of many people for centuries, is well founded. First, and foremost, it is because God who is the author of the Scriptures does not change. Hence, what God reveals remains valid through the centuries. Secondly, this is so because the fundamentals of human life do not change. Systematic and moral theologians still can relate modern studies of humankind to the anthropology of Aristotle and Plato. Along the same thought, people of the 21st century commit the same sins as the people who lived in the 1st century. In this sense there is nothing new under the sun.

Should a person let Holy Scripture dictate to them what to do?

Except that it is in written form rather than verbal, a book is not different from a conversation with another person. A book carries no greater authority than the author or authors who wrote it. One can grant a book no greater grounds for belief than the credibility of its author, or in the case of the Scriptures its authors – God and the human author.

What can we say in regard to interpreting the Bible as we read it? Recall that the Bible contains two types of material: material called "study stuff" and the sacred writings of Scripture. The material called "study stuff" is entirely the work of human authors and, therefore, the authority of this material depends solely on the academic and scholarly reputation of the authors. And, the translation and its inherent interpretation is also the work of humans. But, at the core is the holy text itself, the word of God.

The writings of the Holy Scriptures, were the result of both divine and human authorship. They are the product of an interaction of God with humanity over many centuries and to which we have given the name "inspiration." To these writings of the OT and NT, therefore, Christians have accorded the greatest authority. The things which these writings offer for people of ancient times to believe, we believe. The writings and their meaning have stood the test of time and have found unity even though they were written in a myriad of different social and cultural contexts. The type of person that these writings urge us to be, we will be inspired to be. The things that these writings tell us to do, we strive diligently to do. **We can only grant these writings this high degree of authority because they have God for their author.**

Through the course of history there have been those who sought to destroy the existing biblical texts. There have been those who purposely altered the meaning of the texts in order to satisfy their own idea as to what the texts should be saying. There were those who inadvertently allowed an erroneous text to continue to exist because of their own ignorance or poor scholarship. Overall, is it not possible to believe that a God who acted together with humans to produce a text would also interact with humans to ensure that a true text made its way down through the centuries? We must, however, make every effort to ensure that the text that we are working with is the best text that is available to us. There is evidence of this, some think, of a miracle by God's hand in preserving good texts when one considers the long Isaiah scroll discovered at the Dead Sea in Qumran. This scroll appears exactly written as we have it in a good translation of the OT in the 21st century, except for a few tiny and inconsequential differences.

Some important questions to ponder

1. Is it necessary to interpret the Scriptures?

The answer to this question is straightforward. In one word: YES. Unless you are fluent in ancient Hebrew, Greek and Aramaic you must rely on a translation. We have learned that any translation is also an interpretation. So when we read the Scriptures we are already involved with interpretation. Furthermore, any time you read something for meaning, you are inherently interpreting as you go. Interpretation is, therefore, a subject with which each individual must consider.

2. What is the significance of the reality that the Scriptures can be misinterpreted?

We read that the Holy Scriptures can be misinterpreted as clearly stated in the New Testament itself: 2 Peter 3:16-17. The fear of misinterpretation has had a great effect on Bible reading through the centuries. For example, consider the historical happening of the Protestant Reformation. The Protestants, at the time of the Reformation, set forth the idea that each person has the right to interpret the Scriptures. In reaction to this, and out of fear that individuals would interpret the Scriptures in a way that conflicted with the teaching of the Catholic Church, the magisterium of the Roman Catholic Church reserved to itself the official right to interpret the Scriptures. As a result, from the time of the Reformation reading the Bible on an individual basis was not often encouraged for Catholics. In reality, the Holy Spirit does help a reader to understand the holy texts and everyone should be encouraged to read them! Today, however, things have changed and Catholics are urged to read and study the Bible.

Other groups will intentionally change the texts to fit with their religious tenets. An example in the Jehovah Witness and Mormon bibles.

As one would expect, the existence of the possibility of misinterpretation has led to the generation of misinterpretations. Consequently, the person who reads the Bible and reads about the Bible must be on guard against accepting these misinterpretations. It is important to read and engage the biblical text for oneself. However, each individual must protect against misinterpreting the texts, and this is done by careful study with the aid of good scholarly materials and spiritual discernment. Certainly, God can help the reader to understand.

There is a tendency in adult Bible studies in parishes today to read a passage from the Bible and then to ask what each member thinks it means. This is the complete extent to which the "study" goes. There is great value in reading and sharing the Bible together in small groups but it is not sufficient to let the matter rest at that point. Here is what a scholarly professor had to say:

> As in understanding the human word, so too and much more in listening to
> the divine is there needed a great amount of labor, often arid and always

demanding, which has to be expended before we can say, "This is the word of the Lord!"[51]

To recognize that there is work involved in understanding the writings of the Bible, it is imperative to open our minds and our hearts to the nature of the biblical texts and to take into account that these writings were composed over a one thousand year period some two to three thousand years ago!

3. What is the impact of having professional interpreters?

The existence of professional interpreters is a mixed blessing for the believer. On the one hand, professional interpreters are absolutely essential for without them we would know little about the Bible and what the Holy Scriptures contain. On the other hand, there are a fairly large number of these professional interpreters and they are prolific writers. This can become overwhelming. But, most discouraging of all to the beginning student of the Bible – it is of the very nature of scholarship that these experts do not agree with one another.

Conclusion

At this point it is best to appeal to the Scriptures for a final word as to what course to follow on the issue of interpreting the Holy Scriptures:

> **Then, too, heed your own heart's counsel; for what have you that you can depend on more? (Sirach 37:13)**

> **Most important of all, pray to God to set your feet in the path of truth. (Sirach 37:15)**

---

[51] Stanley B. Marrow, S.J., *The Words of Jesus in Our Gospels* (New York, NY: Paulist Press, 1979), 3.

A brief history of the Jewish People and early Christian believers
The Scriptures related to geography
The Scriptures viewed as literary works
Additional human help for reading the Scriptures with understanding

CHAPTER NINE

A BRIEF HISTORY OF THE JEWISH PEOPLE AND THE EARLY CHRISTIAN B ELIEVERS

Introduction

The scope of the Bible in terms of "time" is remarkable – from an undefined time in the ancient past not recorded by any human through centuries when the people of God found themselves appealing to God for help, believing in God, and then periods of time when they forgot him or even rebelled against his word. Through it all, God is rejected by some because of the lack of faith and obedience. However, never does his compassion and patience fail. Before embarking on a reading and study of the Scriptures, it is so helpful to grasp the concept of the history of Israel and how it is so deeply connected to the arrival of God's Son into the world ... in human and incarnated time. Keep in mind: "… it is time to seek Adonai [God], til he comes and rains down righteousness upon you."[52] God created our world and put us in it to come into relationship with Him which will bring joy and peace (righteousness).

The timeline for the Bible and the way it presents the history of Israel - which includes all people of God – is nothing less than amazing. It is in a sense … timeless. We start with **primordial time** meaning that it begins in the beginning of time. The first book of the Bible is appropriately entitled "Genesis," meaning "Beginning." Next in Genesis, begins a history of God relating to his people beginning with the call of **Abraham** and then the **patriarchs.** Subsequently, we enter into the time of the people **enslaved in Egypt and their exodus** to freedom at the hand of God. The leadership of the people by Moses is highlighted by the most important event when he received God's promise of love and care in the **covenant on Mt. Sinai** surrounded by what we can the **Ten Commandments** which are really stipulations of the relationship. After forty years of wandering and wondering in the desert of the Sinai the people **settle in Canaan** – the promised land now known as Israel. The people rule themselves with **judges** and then desire a king. We see the development of the kingdom which later divides i **two kingdoms**. Throughout these historical periods we learn about God's reve¹ the continuing **covenant** given on Mt. Sinai, and **the account of Jo**

---

[52] *The Complete Jewish Study Bible, Insights for Jew & Christians* (Peabody, MA: Resources, Hendrickson Bibles, 2016), Hosea 10:12.

and the life and trials of Job and the remarkable story of Ruth. When the remaining kingdom becomes weak the Israelites are **conquered and exiled**. The prophets arrive on the scene and try and explain the errors and failures of the people in loving and obeying God. We read the remarkable **prophetic books** of Isaiah, Jeremiah and Ezekiel. In the Bible, the writings are the prophets are collected as "Major" and "minor" prophets – not meaning greater or lesser importance but referring to length and degree of content. When Cyprus the Persian king allows the people to **return from exile**, we have more prophets including Nehemiah, Malachi, and Ezra. The Book of Daniel, like the prophets, also tells of the preparation of the people, and God's promise to send a savior to reunite the people with God in a unique way through Christ. All of this s is a condensed summary and sampling the many writings of Scripture will enrich and fill out God's world of love and promise as it is revealed over centuries and centuries. They years and centuries build upon one another and prepare Jews for the fulfillment of God's promises … the arrival of his Son in the world to establish the everlasting kingdom. We eventually find the **Roman Empire** taking over Israel, Judea formally subject to Rome in 63 B. Herod the Great was appointed governor of Judea and although he was politically associated with the Jews, became an antagonist to Jesus. He built the Second Temple, standing in the time of Jesus – a magnificent huge fortress-like structure bounded by a palace for Herod. This is known as the "Second Temple Period," another way of structuring biblical time in terms of the Temple.

Primordial Time

This period of time is without date. It speaks of the beginning of the world and the heavens and the creation of living creatures. Some very fundamentalist bible readers understand these accounts to be factual and anchored in time. The interpret the text to say that God actually created the world in six days and then took a rest! This is a hard interpretation to support when one knows the ancient world of cosmological stories. There is mystery and deep symbolism in all the words of this time period. For example, "seven" is a sacred number understood in Hebrew anthropology as "complete" and "perfect." Instead of God taking a vacation on the seventh day he is entering the creation with his presence and embracing it. If we read chapters one and two of Genesis, we find two slightly differing stories. One begins with chaotic waters and darkness (Genesis 1). The other begins with arid land and introduces rivers and then vegetation and animal life (Genesis 2). One should not get upset with this. These are remarkable writings that point to a deeper and profound meaning of God as creator. In the actual Hebrew of Genesis, the word "Adam" means "earthling" and "adamah" means earth. Eve is the mother of the living and becomes the companion of Adam in a way that unifies the two as one. God is relational and loving and creates humans (Adam and Eve – the earthlings) in his image, two who complement one another, love one another, and care for each other. Knowing some of these actual Hebrew meanings of the words in the creation account help us to know what God inspired the writers to reveal. We also learn that God intends humanity to care for the earth and work together to build a people of God. The first word of Genesis means "beginning." It is the "beginning" of God building a people whom he can love and who love him. In chapter three of Genesis we learn about the fall of humanity from God. They want God's knowledge and power for themselves. They are not just a bad man and woman who break a rule and eat fruit! Each aspect of this account represents their desire to take God's gifts and power for themselves. God en takes them from the Garden of Eden but does not abandon them. It is like a parent who plines a child by taking away privileges until they realize their worth. Psalm 23 indicates that God always loves and provides for humans but wants their love. We will find a bridegroom image of God throughout the Scriptures which indicates he wants to become "one" with humanity in love. All of these aspects are so important to grasp in Genesis. God is not a punishing God with rules but like a father and mother who want love and respect from their child.

Abraham and the Patriarchs

Sometime around 2,000 BC, a man Abram who lived in Ur the area of the Fertile Crescent (bounded by the Tigris and Euphrates rivers), responded to a special call from God to travel eastward, leaving the land of his father Terah and going to settle in Canaan which was the land intended for God's people. God promises him and his descendants special care and identity as God's people. He took his wife and possessions and faithfully answered God's invitation. Eventually, we learn that God changed his name to "Abraham," with various theories on the meaning of this but most likely the insertion of "ha," a reference to God, in the middle of his name. Following Abraham are his son Isaac, and his son Jacob, and then his son Joseph who is known for being sold by his brothers to slave traders in Egypt. These men become known as the foundational pillars of Israel – the "patriarchs" of God's nation. We read about them and other members of the family including Abraham's wife who conceived a child only in her late age.

The Exodus – Moses and the Covenant,
and Arriving in Canaan where they ruled themselves with Judges

Due to famine that spread throughout the land of Canaan many of the Israelites went to Egypt where they eventually became slaves. After 400 years of this bondage in Egypt, about 1300 BC, God chose Moses to lead the people out o f Egypt and back to their land of Israel. They wandered in the desert of Sinai for 40 years, many of them despondent and questioning God. However, during this arduous time, they formed themselves into a nation. In a remarkable encounter between Moses and God, a covenant was promised and given by God. The Ten Commandments were stipulations of this bonding of God with the people. This time of escaping slavery and moving toward their "Promised Land" in Canaan is commemorated in the Passover and other Jewish festivals including Shavuot (Pentecost) and Succot (Feast of the Tabernacles.) It becomes the sign of God's care and the covenant of compassion he gave. When Christ celebrated Passover just before his crucifixion, he revealed "the new covenant," the fulfillment of God's loving promise of a bond with the faithful. Once arriving in Canaan, the Israelites began to conquer and take over most of the land. Their government during this period of relative peace was led by judges. We find all this told in the Book of Judges. However, as the strength of their political adversaries grew stronger, they longed for their own king. The Pentateuch, the first five writings of the Scriptures, the Book of Judges, Kings I and II, and Chronicles covers this period of time of the Exodus, and the Return to the Promised Land. Most important was the covenant and God's interaction with the people of Israel.

Settling in Canaan and the Monarchy

Israel had their first king, Saul (c. 1020 BC), which transition them from a tribal society to a monarchy under Saul's son, King David (c. 1004 to 966 BC). King David was able to defeat the greatest opponent to Israel, the Philistines, and established good relations with other nearby kingdoms. He is remembered for uniting the 12 Israelite tribes into one kingdom. He established a capital for the nation in Jerusalem and ceremoniously brought the ark of the covenant there. David is known to have written many of the Psalms and collected many of the others. He was succeeded by his son Solomon (965-930 BC) who strengthened the idea of a kingdom. He is best remembered for his establishment of the Temple in Jerusalem. During these early ages, staged at different times according to various scholars, the account of Jonah, Noah and the flood, and the life and trials of Job and the remarkable story of Ruth tell of God's covenant – a loving bond with humanity, the trials of life, and the marriage of God with humans to build a people of God.

The Prophets

Mystical and charismatic Israelites, known as the prophets, began to emerge pointing out to the people they had forgotten about God and trouble would come. They were given God-appointed gifts of preaching to reveal God's word. They gave advice to the kings – sometimes not happily received, and tried to teach the people about ethics and God's will. Their revelations were kept in the books of inspired poetry and prose that we still have today. Before, during, and after these prophets continue to preach and teach.

The Divided Monarchy

After the death of King Solomon (930 BC), the people became disgruntled and began to pull apart. This led to the division into two kingdoms, one in the south called Judah and one in the north called Israel. The capital of Israel was Samaria. This lasted about 200 years under 19 kings. Judah was ruled from Jerusalem for about 400 years with kings following the lineage of King David. Sadly, the growing strength and expansion of Assyria and Babylonia took over the northern kingdom of Israel and then crushed Judah in the south (722 BC). They destroyed the Temple in Jerusalem (586 BC) and took most of the Israelite inhabitants to exile in Mesopotamia. This period is known as "**the Exile**" (586-538BC), bringing a tragic end to what is now called "the First Temple Period." Solomon's Temple was totally destroyed and most of the Jews were taken away in exile to Mesopotamia.

Return from Exile

Prophecy continues when the Persian king allows the Israelites to return home to Canaan, after the kingdom of Babylonia falls to Persia. The prophets urging Jews to repent and return to reliance on God at this time include: including parts of Isaiah, Nehemiah, Jeremiah, and Daniel. Ezra begins the idea to rebuild the Temple.

The Roman Period

It is important to know that at the time of Jesus, it was the Roman Empire who ruled Judea and all of Israel. One thinks of the original languages of the Bible and it is telling that the "Old Testament" (which isn't so "old" in terms of God's revelations that are in it) was originally written mainly in Hebrew with some Aramaic, a dialect of Hebrew. Years before Christ –

beginning in the mid-3rd century BC and continued through the 2nd century BC, , this Hebrew version was translated by seventy rabbis into Greek because the language of the Roman Empire following the Empire of Alexander was Greek! This was called the Septuagint (the Seventy). Even at the time of Christ, the language of the world of Jesus was Greek. Of course, he spoke and read Hebrew in the Temple and synagogues, spoke Aramaic in his home, and perhaps even Greek when he preached. Scholars have found phrases of the Septuagint in his preaching.

When we read the New Testament we are in a new time period. Jesus was crucified in 30 to 33 AD. The Gospel writers began saving all the preaching and accounts about Jesus, perhaps with Mark as the first. In the 30 years following the death and resurrection most of the New Testament was written. We know that much of the material was saved in the minds and hearts of those who saw and believed Jesus. This is known as "oral tradition." And, it is important to note that the New Testament was written in Greek … not Latin as many might think.   The Latin translation came later probably beginning with the work of St. Jerome who died in 420 AD.

Jews vs. Christians

Many Christians today feel that there was always a divide between what we know as Judaism today and Christians. This is totally untrue. Jesus was a Jew! His family and apostles were Jews. And all the first who had faith in Jesus and followed him were Jewish. There were opponents as we learn in the Book of Mark and the Book of Acts. Eventually, the word went out to non-Jews known as Gentiles. Jesus even preached to the Gentiles! Today, things are very different. The Jews of Judaism exist in many sects and groups – much like Christians. There are the main groups: Orthodox, Conservative, and Reform. In getting to know their positions on Jesus, we find they are quite different. Then there are Messianic Jews who have realized who Jesus really was and is! For today, it takes patience and love for Christians to dialogue with Jews. But in this book. We will study the Jews of Jesus' day and their societal and anthropological views … which are so important to know. When did the Jews and Christians divide? And why?   These are difficult questions and long books have been written on this subject. However, for the study of the Bible we can see that the Israelites, later called Jews, were the people of God, God's people being built into a kingdom or nation for eternity.

CHAPTER TEN

THE SCRIPTURES RELATED TO GEOGRAPHY

Where do we choose to live? Oftentimes, it is decided by where we were born and grew up – the land of our parents and extended family. In modern time, however, people tend to have a bigger choice and will often follow a new job to an entirely new location than they place of origin. For the Israelites and Jews of Jesus' time, their home was with God and God established a location that would be their land. Abraham was called from Mesopotamia to Canaan to begin the story of the land of God's people.

Looking at maps and videos of the homeland God chose for Israel, the places where they wandered and settled due to famine which took the Israelites to Egypt, the conquering and exile back to Mesopotamia, the return to Canaan and the eventual coming of Jesus in Galilee, all have significant relationships to the land. One such example: after the Baptism of Jesus he goes to the desert for 40 days (reminiscent of the 40 years Israelites spent in the desert during the Exodus. The desert speaks of austerity and hardship – Jesus begins him ministry by experiencing the human plight of survival in a desert, and was tempted by the devil there.

Taking a very broad view, the events described in the Scriptures all take place in a rectangular shaped region on the earth. This area is bounded on the East by the Euphrates River in Mesopotamia and on the West by Italy and the city of Rome. This area is bounded on the North by the area that is now occupied by Greece and Turkey and on the South by Egypt. The part of this rectangle that is of greatest interest is that of the land of Canaan (Palestine) which borders the eastern end of the Mediterranean Sea.

When studying ancient civilization, we learn that populations developed near rivers, such as the Euphrates in the so-called "Fertile Crescent," the Nile in Egypt, and the Jordan in Israel. The obvious reason is they were a source of water, a place of fertile land for growing crops and raising livestock, and a means of transportation (eventually for trade.) Mesopotamia, the area of one of the world's oldest civilizations is a large area bounded by two rivers, the Tigris and Euphrates. Note the reference to rivers that appeared in the creation account in Genesis 2: 10-14. In Egypt, we find early civilization developing along the Nile River. And in Canaan, Palestine, we find the river Jordan flowing from the Sea of Galilee in the northern region to the Dead See (Salt Sea) to the south. Canaan is bounded on the West by the eastern reach of the Mediterranean (Great Sea) and by a ridge of hills and mountains to the East. Travelling to the South, one goes to Egypt and to the North to an area ruled by the Phoenicians in the time of Jesus, later to become Syria from there to the East.

When reading the Scriptures, it is so helpful to have maps, photos, and videos of these locales. Most study bibles include maps for this purpose. However, with today's computers, there are vivid bible maps available, even given in some cases with satellite views of the topography.

Knowing that Jesus grew up in Nazareth, in Galilee in the northern area of Palestine, we can come to understand the importance of fishing in the Sea of Galilee. We understand that Jesus calling the fishermen as his apostles probably was due to the fact that these men were stable and involved the main economy of the area. John the Baptist baptized in the Jordan, and the baptism of Jesus may be significant because he is entering a living, flowing river of life that indicated the purpose of his mission on earth. There were no fish in the Dead Sea – it was a place lacking in life and where we find the pillar of salt generated from the story of Lot's wife (Genesis chapter 19). When the Israelites finally enter the "Promised Land," there is great emphasis given to them crossing the Jordan into their land.

When we consider Egypt, we encounter a pharaoh whose civilization is strong and pyramids are being built to represent the strength of the land. Because many Israelites fled to Egypt due to famine, there were many communities established in the Nile area. They fell into slavery and their escape to the desert of the Sinai symbolizes once again a period of suffering and the opportunity to repent and return to God – trusting God's care. Mt. Sinai is found in the Sinai desert – itself a high mountain reaching upwards which to the ancient person was a way to communicate with the divine. In fact, think for a moment of the escape of the Israelites from Egypt under the leadership of Moses. They came to a water border that allowed them to enter the Sinai peninsula. The waters of the Red Sea (Reed Sea) parted giving them a chance to live. And the waters closed down on the evil soldiers of Pharaoh.

Abraham's homeland in the fertile crescent, the land of rivers and fertility, suggest what he was asked to leave and abandon when God called him and his family to Canaan. This area of Mesopotamia is also the area ruled by Babylonians who captured and exiled Israelites to their kingdom as workers in the field. From the lay of the land, we can understand that this was not a slavery but actually a nice life for many of them. Why did they yearn to go back to Canaan? For those still remembering God and his call, it was "their land."

When one visits the land of Palestine, visualizing it at the various times in biblical history, one discovers much deeper meaning. For instance, the area ruled by the Philistines bordered the Mediterranean giving them a strategic place to live. Their power and strength derived from the geography!

The basic elements in the geography of the Scriptures, are not incidental. Today, we have trouble visualizing conceptual, symbolic meaning. But seas, mountains, rivers, deserts, hills and caves take on vital meaning that helps us understand the scriptural texts. We think of mountains and we envision refreshing vacation lands for summer and fun skiing in the winter. Do we consider it a place to meet God? The Jordan River that originates in Israel in the north embraces the Sea of Galilee and then deposits in the South at the Dead Sea, one of the lowest points on earth. The topography to the west of the Jordan – which runs north to south, includes flat, lands, small hills, and small lakes. It is interesting to note that there are no natural harbors on the Mediterranean coast in Israel. At one point in history, under the reign of Herod the Great about 10 BC, came to be known as *Caesarea Palestinae*. Eventually, it was engulfed by the sea but maritime archaeologists today find much of the ruin under water. Also, running north to south in Israel, is an elevated desert area that is very mountainous. Sharp cliffs abound and it is here that the famous Qumran scrolls were discovered in a cave, known as the Dead Sea Scrolls.

In biblical studies, there is an important locale that provides an open storybook and wealth of information about biblical times and geography. It is the location called Qumran where the so-called "Dead Sea Scrolls" were discovered in the 1940s. Local Bedouin sheep-herders discovered these scrolls hidden in caves along the hills standing to the West and rising up above the area in elevation. The oldest scroll of Isaiah (which is complete) was found. Questions abound but why were these scrolls hidden there? Since the middle of the 20th century, more and more caves have been discovered going to the South. Many important early scrolls have been found, including non-biblical texts that describe spiritual ideas of various groups of Israelites who apparently had fled to these hills to live better lives. Corruption in the Temple in the first century, and especially at the time of Jesus was flagrant. Once again, the desert and the rugged hills became a place to regain good lives.

THREE MAJOR TERMS IN BIBLICAL GEOGRAPHY

We often hear these geographical areas referenced but let us stop and take special attention to their biblical meanings. The words are: Canaan, Israel, and Judah.

Canaan –

The area called Canaan existed in the eastern Mediterranean area from Stone Age prehistory (before 3500 BC). From 3500 BC to 2000 BC approximately, a culture began to solidify but with no written records yet discovered. From 2000 BC to 1550 BC city states developed. From 1550 BC to 586 BC, including what is known as the Late Bronze ages I and II, village societies began to form into kingdoms. Eventually various empires rose up ruling the area of what is now known as Israel – the Assyrian, Babylonian, Persian, Greek and Roman empires.

Israel and Judah

During the Iron age, the history of ancient Israel and Judah began. Israel was known as the "Northern Kingdom" and Judah as the "Southern Kingdom." As noted, eventually Judah fell and Israel remained the only kingdom. The life and mission of Jesus began in the Kingdom of Israel.

Conclusion

The maps included in study bibles and online on bible study pages are important for more than just mere maps locating cities and countries. They tell us much about what he sacred texts of the Scriptures are revealing in God's word. Many are divided into eras and we can see the threat of nearby kingdoms such as Babylonia, Assyria, and the Roman Empire. If we keep in mind the "time" frames of salvation history, we also come to see the relationship these "times" have to geography.

CHAPTER ELEVEN

THE SCRIPTURES VIEWED AS LITERARY WORKS

The Scriptures are literature

In a college catalog, it is quite common to find a course titled: "The Bible as Literature." Often, the Bible is presented in classes on World Literature. This makes a significant point: that the writings contained in the Bible are literature! Are the writings of the Scriptures really literature?

To answer this question it is necessary to first answer the question: "What is literature?" It first comes to mind that literature is anything that is written. But that characterization is too simple, as is easily demonstrated. Consider the following: "The dog is red. The house is very large. The airplane flew swiftly overhead." This is written, but most likely no one would consider this to be an example of what is commonly accepted as literature.

Literature is more than just something written. It is something that is written in an organized way and for some specific purpose. A poem is written to inspire, enlighten and be enjoyed by readers. A newspaper article is written to inform readers about news events and sometimes an editorial is written to persuade the reader to accept an editor's point of view.

In the sense of experiencing and communicating a viewpoint, an insight into life and its meaning, the writings of Holy Scripture are literature. At the heart of all books of Scripture is an experience of covenant, God's love for humanity and desire to be loved in a lasting relationship. The letters of Paul were written to persuade readers to correct their behavior, to inform them of his travel plans, and to express his wishes for their well-being. For the early Christians, the gospels were written to strengthen faith in Jesus Christ and convey a theological exposition reflecting on Christ and his life and teachings. In the particular case of the Gospel according to Luke, the author's intention was to inform a person named Theophilus about the Christian faith.

Now for a little twist. Does what we consider to be literature include the spoken word? Consider the following: a prophet orally proclaims a prophetic oracle – a message from God. Is that literature? If it is not literature when he speaks this oracle, does it become literature when, at some later time, a scribe writes it down? Think of a famous playwright. His or her plays are both written and read as literature, and yet also performed becoming a live event much like the use of the Bible in liturgy. It seems most reasonable to take the position that even though generated from oral tradition, later when the writings took written form, then it was literature.

The following remarks from the inaugural address of Donald G. Miller as Walter H. Robertson Professor of New Testament at Union Theological Seminary in New York, regarding the literary aspects of Holy Scripture are significant:

Another neglected emphasis in the critical process has been the cultivation of a true proficiency in literary appreciation. Although the Bible surpasses other writings in its source and significance, nevertheless it is literature. And its values are to be realized through approaching it according to the best canons of literary appreciation.[53]

… First, **appreciation is more than information**. We have too often confused knowledge with understanding; facts with interpretation; information with appreciation. …. To store the mind with technical facts and critical theories may lead to genuine appreciation; on the other hand, it may not.[54]

… But how is true appreciation to be acquired? It is to be done through a first-hand approach to the Scriptures themselves. The appreciation of any work of art is dependent upon a **personal acquaintance** with the object itself. True appreciation cannot be mediated.[55]

… **A recognition of the art form** in which the work is cast is indispensable. The force of a work is not to be found in mere words and phrases and sentences. These are but parts of a total literary structure, mere items in a compositional unity. The individual features themselves do not unlock the meaning of the work. The important thing is the function they perform in the composition of the entire work.[56]

… One further word should be said about proficiency in literary appreciation and that is that true literary appreciation is possible through a good translation. …. For the average man, whose best avenue of impression is his mother tongue, a deeper appreciation may be gained through an **excellent translation** than through the laborious struggle which wading through the original entails.[57]

The Scriptures are classic literature

In the previous section, we considered the Holy Scriptures as literature. Let's go one step further. The writings in the Scriptures are not just literature, they are **classic literature**. What is classic literature? According to Peter Cameron, it is writing that satisfies the following:

True classics are those that have stood the test of time by transcending cultural peculiarities and overly-specific interests. Their relevance reaches beyond the

---

[53] Donald G. Miller, "Neglected Emphases in Biblical Criticism" in Dikran Y. Hadidian, Editor, *From Faith To Faith* (Eugene, OR: Pickwick Publications, 1978), 10. [bolded phrases added by authors]
[54] Miller in Hadidian, 11.
[55] Miller in Hadidian, 12.
[56] Miller in Hadidian, 13.
[57] Miller in Hadidian, 16.

author's day and age so as to speak cogently to the questions and concerns of people of every era.[58]

Cameron points out that if a person is to derive full benefit from a classic writing, it is important to pursue the following three tasks:

First of all, in reading a Catholic classic we must remind ourselves why it was written. Invariably a book is authored with a specific purpose in mind. It intends to achieve some particular aim. Therefore, in taking up a classic, one of the first things we should do is to identify the author's objective. This is accomplished by examining the background and circumstances of the book.[59]

… Secondly, we must acknowledge for whom the book was written. Who was the author's audience? Why was the book important to them? What was going on in their lives? By trying to unite ourselves with the experiences of that target audience we can authentically appreciate both the strong points and the limitations of the text, for we are not the people the author had in mind. Sometimes we tend to forget that and grow frustrated when the author's writing fails to speak more directly to our current needs.[60]

… And thirdly, we must consider the cultural factors that color a given work. It is not uncommon to be put off by an older book because of its foreign sounding literary style. Nevertheless, in order to enter into the world of a classic we are asked to adopt a forgiving disposition that enables us to look beyond literary limitations, awkward expressions, and obsolete ideas.[61]

If we believe that the Holy Scriptures are classic literature, then we must read them in the same manner that we read all classic literature!

THE SCRIPTURES ARE AN ANTHOLOGY OF LITERARY WORKS

In a literary sense, God did not write a book! The Scriptures were not written to be read from front to back as you would read a lengthy modern novel. The Scriptures are not intended to be read in sequence as you would read a modern mystery by Ellery Queen, or a modern adventure tale by Jack London. Nor is the Bible to be read like a modern biography similar to those published about President Kennedy or a famous sports player.

The writings that make up the Scriptures are of a number of different literary types such as: psalms, historical narratives, gospels, letters, wisdom writings, prophetic oracles, and apocalyptic texts. Built on oral traditions of God's revelation, many different human authors and editors assisted in the writing which took place over a period of more than 1,000 years. It was even written in three different languages: Hebrew, Aramaic (a dialect of Hebrew), and Greek.

---

[58] Peter John Cameron, OP, *The Classics of Catholic Spirituality* (New York, NY: Alba House, 1996), xiv.
[59] Cameron, xv.
[60] Cameron, xvi.
[61] Cameron, xvi-xvii.

All the ancient sources of revelation which were written down are now collected in an anthology that we call the Bible, or more exactly the Holy Scriptures. It is common to find anthologies of English literature, usually huge volumes that are assigned by professors in college courses on English literature![62]

It is clear, therefore, that before one begins to read the Scriptures some consideration must be given to the problem of how to approach the Bible as an anthological volume. Is it best to start with the OT first while setting the NT apart? Or perhaps is it better to begin with the NT, reading the Gospels and Acts of the Apostles first, and then going to the OT to develop an appreciation for the Hebrew context of the NT. Or maybe it is best if one began chronologically by reading the letters of Paul first, the Gospels and Acts second and finally the rest of the NT third. There is only one **best** way to read the Scriptures: that is the way that **you**, **the reader**, chooses to read them!

In the particular case of the Holy Scriptures, however, there is an underlying unity which stems from the mystery of the one and only God being very much involved in their authorship and which is greater than the diversity of their human authorship. This reality must always be kept firmly in mind. Recall that this is what we learned is called the *sensus plenior* of the Scriptures.

Reading the Scriptures as Whole "books"

Is it important to read a biblical book in its entirety or is it sufficient to read it in small segments (e.g. as it is read in the liturgy on Sunday)? Putting this question in a different way, one can ask: "Can a person get the meaning from a biblical book by listening to it read in small segments at different times or is the full meaning only gained through reading the book in its entirety?"

In order to answer this question it is helpful to first consider the following question: "With what intention was this particular book of Scriptures originally written – to be read in small pieces or to be read as a whole entity?" The answer to this question is that it depends on the individual book! The Book of Psalms, consisting of 150 individual psalms, was intended to be used in a manner similar to a hymn book, and daily form of prayer, and not to be read as a whole. The Book of Ruth, however, was clearly written to be read as a complete composition. The Book of Jonah was likewise intended to be read as a complete work. The book of Sirach, being a handbook to be used in the instruction of young men, was certainly not intended to be read as a complete composition, all at one time.

---

[62] The Scriptures are like a textbook of World Literature. For instance, examples would be: *The Literature of Western Culture Through the Renaissance,* Volume I, Maynard Mack, General Editor which actually is a book that is part of the series, *The Norton Anthology of World Masterpieces*, published by W. W. Norton & Company in New York. And, Volume I of this series is a collection of writings by many different individuals and includes compositions of differing literary types dating to a period of over 2,000 years. It even includes a few of the writings contained in the Scriptures!

What about the Gospels? How were they intended to be read? It would certainly seem to be apparent that Luke intended his two-volume work, Luke-Acts, to be read as an inspiring history and hence as a complete work. Surely the Gospels of Matthew and John were intended to be read as complete works. The Gospel of Mark was likely written to be read as a complete work although a small number of scholars have proposed that it was intended to be read in an annual liturgical cycle. It's hard to imagine today, but in ancient Christian days it is thought that the entire Gospel of Mark was proclaimed in its whole in a liturgical service. Imagine attending church on a Sunday and listening to a whole gospel read? Actually, this brings to mind one minister today who visits many churches and in a special program recites the entire gospel of Mark by heart – and in a dramatic way.

Literary Forms

In treating the Bible as literature, we must first look into the types of literature of which the various writings are fashioned. What do we mean by the word "type?" We are inquiring here into the form of the writing which makes up the individual books. Is it **prose or poetry**? Is it a **historical narrative**, a **story**, a **letter** or a **collection of poems**?

Particular literary forms are an integral tool in communicating the meaning in a text. In poetry, for example, a great deal of meaning is generated by word order, word sound, relationship of words such as in repetition or in recurring instances, and in figures of speech – metaphors, similes, and allusions.

Certain subjects lend themselves naturally to a literary form. The material, for example, in 2 Samuel or the Acts of the Apostles is best presented in the form of historical narrative. Prophetic oracles and passages on wisdom are best expressed through poetry. Advice on Christian living and personal religious experience often takes the form of a personal letter to a group of Christians.

The writings of the Scriptures, considered as whole compositions, include the use of at least seven, major literary forms:

- Letters
- Narratives; including both historical narratives and folk literature (e.g. Ruth and Tobit)
- Gospels
- Collections of prophetic oracles
- Collections of Psalms
- Wisdom writings
- Apocalyptic writings

Within the writings of the Scriptures themselves, there are many, many more literary forms to be encountered. In the New Testament there are: parables, sayings, doxologies, farewell addresses, and miracle stories – to name only a few. In the Old Testament there are: taunt songs, funeral dirges, laments, proverbs, prayers, and many more. So when you are reading the Bible you must always be alert concerning the matter of what particular literary form you might be dealing with in your reading.

LITERARY ASPECTS OF THE WRITINGS OF SCRIPTURE

Introduction

Before you set out, in a serious manner, to read a written composition it is wise to inquire into certain literary aspects about the piece. For example, if you set out to read a poem, then you like to know: who is the poet; when was it written; what are the circumstances surrounding its composition; and what is the poet seeking to convey to the reader? When you set out to read the writings of Scripture the same is true.

Assume for the moment that you are about to read a particular one of the writings in the Scriptures. Here is a list of questions you might like to have answered **before** you start to read:

- Who was the author?
- Where was the author when he or she wrote it?
- Who were the intended readers?
- What was the historical context in which it was written?
- What was the author's purpose in writing it?

Indeed, if you look at one of the introductions to a book of the Scriptures you will find that these are among the subjects that are addressed.

There are specialized books, with titles like *Introduction to the New Testament,* which treat the subjects: contents, literary character, theological purpose, author, place and time of composition. Here the word "introduction" is used in a narrow technical sense. These specialized books discuss the subject of authorship, for example, by presenting arguments pro and con concerning the claimed author, and then finally reaching a conclusion. Books of this type can be very useful for gaining knowledge on these subjects.[63] A serious detailed study of a passage is called an exegesis.

Now we move two other topics: 1) authorship and 2) historical and social context.

Authorship

Here is an intriguing question about the NT: How many letters did Paul write? And here are the answers! Early on it was believed that Paul wrote 14 letters: Romans through Hebrews in your Bible. During this period Hebrews had the title: "The letter of Paul to the Hebrews." As early as the second century people questioned Paul's authorship of Hebrews. For example, some think it might have been Barnabus that wrote the letter to the Hebrews, or even a woman deaconess. Today, few people consider Paul to be the author of Hebrews and in many bibles the book bears the title: "The Letter to the Hebrews." ... And then there were 13! Today, many scholars accept the position that the Pastoral Epistles (1 and 2 Tim and Titus) were not written by Paul himself but by an individual or individuals who followed him. ... And then there were ten!

---

[63] A good example of such a book is: Werner George Kummel, *Introduction to the New Testament*, 17th Edition, translated by Howard Clark Kee (Nashville, TN: Abingdon Press, 1975).

In addition, today there are those who hold the position that 2 Thessalonians, Colossians and Ephesians are also not written by Paul himself. … And then there were seven! This last claim is a minor opinion.

There are two ways that one can obtain knowledge of the author of an ancient writing. First, there is **tradition.** In most cases the name of a person has become attached to a writing and passed along through the tradition. Thus, for example, Matthew, Mark, Luke and John, whom we call evangelists, are the traditional names for the authors of the four gospels. Take note that "tradition" is most important in theological and biblical studies. In reality, without tradition we might not have a bible at all.

The second way to determine the author is to **examine the internal literary characteristics** of the writing. The writing itself is examined for such aspects as: statements that may fix the date of its composition; characteristics of the grammar and vocabulary; and anything else that might provide a basis for identifying the author.

The problem that arises is that tradition and the internal analysis frequently seem not to agree! For example, tradition tells us that the apostle John wrote the Gospel of John. Many modern scholars, however, conclude from the internal evidence that the Gospel was most likely written by a person who was not an eyewitness to the events of Jesus' life, and therefore couldn't have been the apostle John. Similarly, tradition identifies the author of the Book of Revelation as the apostle John. By means of internal analysis, many modern scholars say that the "John" mentioned in Rev 1:1 could not be the apostle. These claims concerning John's authorship of the gospel and Revelation, however, may be proved incorrect by future studies and discoveries. There are other theories such as the possibility that the original writings and thoughts of John were later edited.

When tradition and internal analysis do not support each other, then the various arguments have to be weighed carefully. This weighing of the internal arguments against the tradition, however, is almost never carried out in a completely objective manner. The outcome depends greatly both on whether the scholar holds that tradition can be historically accurate or whether he or she relies only on the validity of the various aspects of internal analysis. For example, Orthodox and Roman Catholics generally are more likely to believe in the historical accuracy of tradition than are Protestants. Orthodox biblical scholars, however, are much more likely to believe in the historical accuracy of tradition in many details than are many Roman Catholic scholars today.

An important factor to remember is the nature of tradition. Many modern people have little concept of how ancient peoples could remember accounts very accurately and pass them along generation to generation. This is called "oral memory." Today only actors and actresses and musicians appear to develop oral memory. It is possible that a writing which is often considered by some scholars not to be written by an attributed author could be material that was carried in oral memory and written down at a later date, perhaps with some things added that make the writing appear to have later dating.

Historical and Social Context

It is quite apparent that the writings of the NT came into existence because particular people sought to communicate with groups (local "churches") at a particular moment in time under a particular set of historical and social circumstances. It is only through the historical reconstruction of the life and thought of the first century Christians and their cultural environment, therefore, that the writings of the NT can be fully understood. Each of the writings combines in its own way literary, historical, and theological perspectives. One must seek to understand each of the writings in its own particular literary, historical and theological context. This approach to the NT is set forth in Kee, Young and Froehlich.[64]

The attempt to study the writings of the NT in their context, as undertaken by Kee, Young and Froehlich, involves a degree of uncertainty. On the basis of the internal content of a particular writing it is usually not possible to determine, with precision and with certainty, the context of a given writing. For example, some scholars believe that Hebrews was written by Paul in the middle of the first century and others take the position that it was written late in the first century by an unknown Christian author. The historical and social factors applicable in the middle of the 1st century surely cannot be equally applicable at a date late in the 1st century due to the rapid advance of Christianity, the changing relationship between the Jews and the Christians, and political and social changes within the Roman Empire.

These considerations are applicable to the writings of the OT as well. The merging of the historical, the literary and the theological factors has been considered by Bernhard Anderson.[65] Anderson states in the Preface:

> In the case of the volume on the Old Testament the aim was to offer a fresh approach to the story of ancient Israel by interweaving the oft-separated elements of historical and archaeological research, literary criticism, and biblical theology.[66]

> … I remain firmly convinced that the only way to understand the faith of ancient Israel is to portray the historical drama reflected in the pages of the Old Testament.[67]

At the end of the 20th century and continuing into the 21st, an additional factor has come into prominence. This factor is the sociological background of the biblical writings. In this effort scholars are attempting to apply today's knowledge of the discipline of sociology to the ancient writings. So now many scholars are probing the sociological context of the writings of Scripture. All of this comes under the technical term, textural criticism, namely the examining of all the aspects of Scripture as literature.

---

[64]Howard Clark Kee, Franklin W.Young and Karlfried Froehlich. *Understanding the New Testament*, 2nd Edition (Englewood Cliffs, NJ: Prentice-Hall, Inc, 1965), vii-viii.

[65] Bernhard W. Anderson, *Understanding the Old Testament*, Third Edition (Englewood Cliffs, NJ: Prentice Hall, Inc., 1975). This book achieved great popularity and is now available in a 4th Edition and even subsequently updated by a second author.

[66] Anderson, xix.

[67] Anderson, xix-xx.

CHAPTER TWELVE

THE "STUDY STUFF" IN THE BIBLE

Every bible includes writings of two different kinds. First, there are the sacred writings that comprise the canon – the "books" of the Bible. Secondly, there are all of the various writings that make up the rest of the Bible. These are all just ordinary human compositions without any direct divine cooperation. There is no general term that designates all of these items. Soe will choose the title "study stuff" for this purpose.

If you look at a number of different editions of the Bible, and compare them, you will find that different editions have different kinds and quantities of "study stuff." If you happen to look at a study Bible, you may find that it contains as many as 600 pages of "study stuff"! The term we use as "study stuff" includes all kinds of information that may be provided such as footnotes, cross references, biblical dictionaries, maps, scholarly articles, and introductory material to every "book." In *The Catholic Youth Bible*[68] the "study stuff" is presented in such a way that it is so dominant that the sacred text is almost completely overshadowed! If, however, you look at a Reader's Edition you will find the barest minimum – perhaps a few sparse footnotes, a map or two and a glossary of terms - as in the Reader's Edition of *The New Jerusalem Bible.*

"Study stuff" is both a blessing and yet sometimes problematic. On the one hand, it can be very helpful by both providing information that is useful in understanding the biblical text and by making this information readily available so it is not necessary to seek it elsewhere. On the other hand, its presence can divert your attention from concentrating on the biblical text itself. In any case, it certainly makes the Bible a much larger and heavier book to carry around.

"Study stuff," however, is not a modern development. Many manuscripts of the New Testament contain "helps" for the reader. These "helps" assist the private reader, as well as the one who reads the text in public. They originated at various times and in various places; and, as you would expect, they grew in volume over the years. As an example, various early NT manuscripts contain one or more of the following "helps" for the reader:[69]

- ❑ **Chapter divisions** – the oldest system of chapter divisions is found in the *Codex Vaticanus* which dates to the 4th century.

- ❑ **Titles of chapters** – these titles were placed in the margins and provided a summary of the contents of the chapter.

- ❑ **Eusebian canons** – a system to aid one in locating parallel passages in the gospels which was devised by Eusebius of Caesarea (b. 260, d. 341 CE).

---

[68] *The Catholic Youth Bible* (Winona, Minnesota: St. Mary's Press, Christian Brothers Publications, 2000).
[69] Bruce M. Metzger, *The Text of the New Testament*, Second Edition (New York, NY: Oxford University Press, 1968), 21-31.

- **Hypotheses** – these were brief introductions to a book and provided the reader with information concerning the author, content and circumstances of composition.

- **Subscriptions** – brief statements placed at the end of a book to indicate that it had ended.

- **Glosses** – brief explanations of difficult words or phrases usually written in the margins.

- *Scholia* – interpretative marks of a teacher placed beside the text in order to instruct the reader.

- **Artistic adornment** – these consisted most frequently of ornamental headpieces at the beginning of a book and illuminated initials beginning the text of the book. In the Byzantine period, and in the Middle Ages, pictures and designs of various letters and words were inserted. These were all done with beautiful colored inks and consisted of very intricate designs, known as "illuminated manuscripts".

"Study stuff" which is external to the pages of scripture

Under this heading we will focus our attention on the "study stuff" that is found in the sections before and after the section containing the inspired writings. External to the body of the scriptural texts, there is "study stuff," which is intended to help the reader.

Examples of such things are: a **title page**; a page with **publishing information and the copyright,** which is to be used when citing the Bible in a footnote or bibliography. (Please do not make the mistake made by one student who cited *Nihil Obstat* as the author of the Bible. This is a Catholic notation that a particular edition of the Bible has been approved by a bishop! The Latin means: "nothing stands in the way.") Also, often there is a **Foreword**; the **Editors' Preface**; a **list of abbreviations** used; and an **explanation of the symbols** used throughout the biblical text. Usually at the beginning of each of the testaments of Christian bibles, and at the beginning of the Hebrew Bible, there is an introduction that gives **information concerning which ancient manuscripts were used in doing the translation and how the translation was carried out.** Knowledge of which manuscripts served as the basis of the translation and the method by which the translation was done is of great importance to the reader and was described in Chapter Six.

Maps! Maps are very helpful to the reader of the Bible. One hopes that the Bible contains at least a set of accurate and easily readable maps. A good set of maps should include: maps of the Ancient Near East – representing the various historical periods; a map of Palestine in the time of Jesus; and a map of the Mediterranean Sea and surrounding area in the 1st century showing Paul's journeys with a separate map for each of his three journeys. Some Bibles provide a map index, which is useful, if the number of maps is more than one or two. It is very helpful if the maps also show the topographical features. Today, more and more bible maps with study material are appearing online. One example is found at the website bibleatlas.

Many travelers have discovered that if they visit Israel, Syria, Lebanon, Egypt, Turkey, Greece, or Italy where many biblical events occurred that the Bible becomes much more real to them. It is important to study the maps provided quite carefully and to try and picture the context of the biblical texts. It aids remarkably to the reader in understanding the texts.

Tutorial articles. If you have a study bible, then your bible will also contain a number of articles addressing various topics of interest concerning the scriptures. These articles provide a lot of very useful information.

Here are a few examples of tutorial articles which can be found in several different study bibles:

> "Biblical History and Archaeology"
> "The Bible; God's Revelation to Man"
> "How to Read the Bible"
> "Geography of the Holy Land"
> "Languages of the Bible"
> "Historical and Geographical Background to the Bible"
> "Reading Biblical Poetry"

Be careful! These tutorial articles are written by knowledgeable scholars and they can capture your interest. One can become engrossed in reading these articles and be diverted from reading the biblical texts.

Glossary. Another very useful item to have in your bible is a **glossary**. This is a collection of words or terms that pertain to a limited area of knowledge. In the case of the Bible, the words and terms all apply to the texts in the Bible. This is very helpful to the reader because it saves the effort of going to an outside source for this information.

Concordance. One item that is very useful to have included in your Bible is a **concordance.** The type of concordance found in a bible lists the individual words found in the text in alphabetical order and identifies the place in the text where it is found. This type of concordance is useful because it helps you to locate a passage of which only one or two words can be recalled. Due to the limitation of available space, the concordance in a bible is quite limited. A complete concordance of the Bible, under the designation "Exhaustive Concordance," in book form or in electronic form, is available online and on library shelves.

A word of advice

It may happen that you come across a particular edition of the Bible that has one or two items of "study stuff" that you desire very much to have while most of the other "study stuff" is of no help to you. In this case, a good way to proceed is to go to a library and look for the Bible that contains the item or items that you desire and copy them. By doing this you build up a file of those things that help you most, saving them for further study without the need to buy more books. Copying things in the Bible has two big advantages: 1) when you copy, you can expand the text thus making the copy more readable than the original; and 2) when you copy you get the information on a more useable grade of paper on which it is much easier to write notes and comments and which a highlighter does not bleed through. For those individuals who prefer to write directly in their Bible, you may be amused to know that there actually is a bible containing an article titled: "What should I use to mark my Bible?" There are, indeed, special highlighters available just for the thin pages of bibles!

"Study Stuff" that is *within* the pages of scripture

In this section our attention is on the "study-stuff" that is found within the pages of the Scriptures themselves! At first thought, it may surprise you that one can speak of "study-stuff" within the pages of Scripture. But you will soon see that there is a considerable quantity of it to be found there. The danger of it being there is, of course, that human writing will mistakenly taken to be inspired writing. The study material is, in reality, written entirely by human scholars and has no divine revelation involved!

First, in our bibles we find that all of the writings have titles. The truth of the matter is that the writings have not always had the same titles that they now bear and at the time of their writing probably did not have titles at all. The names are traditional and you will observe small variations even today. For example, in *The New American Bible,* the Book of Romans is called: "The Letter to the Romans." Whereas in *The New Revised Standard Version,* it is called: "The Letter of Paul to the Romans." Including the name of a person who is traditionally held to be the author of the writing in the title can be a problem in those cases where the authorship of the traditional author is disputed. In the not too distant past, Catholic bibles used to announce: "The Letter of Paul to the Hebrews." Now today, since many scholars do not hold that Paul wrote the Book of Hebrews, the Catholic bibles name it "The Letter to the Hebrews." Unfortunately, the editors of the Catholic bibles, and the Protestant bibles as well, have not reacted to the now commonly accepted scholarly position that Hebrews is not a letter! Thus, the titles of the books must be classified as "study stuff." Obviously, titles are very helpful to the aspiring reader.

Secondly, in many Bibles you will find a short introduction at the beginning of each writing. This introduction provides useful information about the author, time of writing, purpose, and the historical context of it. This introduction, although very brief and usually not presenting the full range of scholarly opinion, can be helpful in providing some background so that the reader can begin reading the book with greater understanding.

Thirdly, frequently there is a set of footnotes at the bottom of the page. Sometimes these footnotes are collected together and placed at the end of the writing in which case they are more properly referred to as "end notes." Footnotes can be of three types: informational, interpretive, or a combination of the two. Informational footnotes are very helpful because they provide the reader with information about people, places and things which are encountered in the text. Interpretive footnotes can be helpful, but they can also impose upon the reader an understanding of the text which may only represent the personal opinion of the author of the footnote, who, in most cases, is unidentified. The interpretive footnote most often has the purpose of "preserving the reader from error." **There is the ever present grave danger, however, that the reader will attribute to the footnote the same inspired character that is attributed to the biblical text!**

This means that the information in the footnote is the stated opinion of a scholar or scholars and certainly is not divinely revealed.

Fourthly, some bibles give another set of **notes** as well. These notes pertain to other possible readings of a verse. Such notes are put in a special place somewhere on the page and are always in very, very small print. Oftentimes, the presence of such a note is indicated within the text by means of a superscript, lower case letter.

Fifthly, some Bibles give **references to other passages** in the Bible which are related to a passage in the text. These are called "cross references" and they may be placed in the margin of the text or gathered together on some other part of the page. In those places where a NT writer explicitly cites a passage from the OT, it is very helpful to have such cross references.

Sixthly, in our bibles we find every one of the writings divided into **chapters**. This system of chapter divisions was introduced by Stephen Langton, the Archbishop of Canterbury (d.1227). A word of caution is in order. **One should not depend upon the chapter divisions in determining the literary structure of a book**. There are a number of places where the chapter divisions are inappropriate. For example, the following: **Is 52:13-53:12** which is a single complete poem; **Acts 21:40; Acts 4:37 and 5:1**; and **1 Cor 12:31 and 13:1.**.[70]

Finally, there is the verse **numeration system**. This numbering system was introduced by Robert Stephanus in 1555. Stephanus was a printer in Paris. His system is now considered by most to be standard and is usually the same in all bibles. Nevertheless, there are some differences in details such as the following:

1. In the Psalms of *The New American Bible,* the brief introductions for the musicians, found at the beginning of many Psalms, are labeled "verse 1." In other bibles, this introductory comment is not included in the verse numbers.

2. In the writings of the prophets, some bibles may choose to follow the Hebrew verse numbering (specifically, the *New American Bible*). This introduces a difference in the verse numbers that can be confusing when comparing readings between two different Bibles.

The first complete bible to use both the chapter and verse divisions together was Robert Stephanus' edition of *The Latin Vulgate* (1555). The first English edition to incorporate both of these systems was *The Geneva Bible* (1560).[71]

WHY ARE THERE SO MANY BIBLES?

A Christian bookstore in Boston used to advertise that it sells 500 over different bibles. The 2017 Fall Catalog of the Christian book distributors puts 68 pages of bibles before the eyes

---

[70] Rev. Henry G. Graham, *Where We Got the Bible* (Illinois: Tan Books and Publishers, Inc., 1977 Seventeenth Printing), 58.

[71] N. Geisler and W. Nix, *A General Introduction to the Bible* (Chicago, IL: Moody Press, 1986), 338-341.

of the perspective customer! What factors can possibly account for this astounding number of different bibles?

Differences in the canons and translations certainly account for only a small part of this multiplicity. At this point in our study, it is easy to recognize two factors that could be responsible for it - external physical features and "study stuff." The external physical features are things like the size of the book - which range from very large family size bibles to small pocket size volumes; the type of paper it is printed on – thin paper that highlighter bleeds through to thicker paper; and the type of cover – leather, composite or paperback.

The "study stuff" accounts for the large number of variations. There are readers' editions that contain almost no "study stuff" and there are study bibles which can contain over 1,000 pages of helpful material. There are bibles that print the words of Jesus in red, instead of the usual black. There are bibles that contain maps; there are some that have a glossary; there are others that have helpful articles about history, culture and language. There are variations of every imaginable sort and a number that are not even imaginable.

Needless to say, as you begin to read and study the Bible, there are many possibilities for enriching and deepening your understanding of the writings because there is so much "study stuff" available. At the same time, and possibly more importantly, as you begin to read the words carefully, you will no doubt discover that they have a vitality and spiritual value that is undeniable. The most important principle in studying the Bible is to realize that actually reading the "inspired" text will connect the reader with the Author (God) who has composed it through the hands and minds of human beings.

In conclusion, now when we are asked, "Do you read the Bible?" … we have to carefully think of what that question means. Is the question inquiring about whether or not we are reading the Scriptures? Or is it more inclusive and mean: Are you reading the Scriptures **and** the "study stuff" as well? Life often seems to have tendencies that make our studies more complex as opposed to more simple.

III. EXPLORING THE CANONICAL WRITINGS BEFORE THE BIRTH OF JESUS

PART 1
THE ISRAELITE PERIOD

CHAPTER THIRTEEN
THE TORAH AND THE DOCUMENTARY HYPOTHESIS

For the ancient Hebrews and the Jews of today, the first five writings - Genesis, Exodus, Leviticus Numbers and Deuteronomy -   are called the "Torah." This is a Hebrew word that means "teaching" or "instruction." You will frequently find "the Torah" translated as "law" in Christian bibles but this is not the best translation of this word. The first five books contain a lot more than laws.

"Pentateuch" is also a name commonly given today to these first five books of the Bible. This name comes from " *penta*," the Greek prefix meaning five, and "*teuchos*," a Greek word meaning "jars" or "containers." The name has been borrowed by Christians from the Septuagint, the Greek translation of the Jewish Scriptures that dates to the third and second centuries BCE. At the time these manuscripts were made, scrolls were kept in large clay jars in Hebrew called a "*teuch*." As at Qumran near the Dead Sea, for example.

The contents of these five books fall naturally into eight parts as follows:

1. The primeval history (Gen 1:1-11:32).
2. The patriarchal history (Gen 12:1-50:26).
3. The enslavement of the Israelites in Egypt and their escape from Egypt (Ex 1:1-15:21).
4. The Journey to Mt. Sinai (Ex 15:22-18:27).
5. The covenant at Mt. Sinai – Ex 19:1 – Lev 27:34.
6. Preparations for the departure from Mt. Sinai (Num 1:1-10:10).
7. The wandering in the desert and the death of the Exodus generation (Num 10:11-36:13).
8. The final words of Moses and his death (Deut Chaps. 1-34).

Now let us proceed in the following way. Let's consider these eight parts in turn by first reading a sketch of the contents of the part and then reading a small number of sections of the actual biblical text itself. In this way, we will achieve some degree of familiarity with the biblical text of the Torah.

1. The Primeval History (Gen 1:1-11:32)

The primeval history begins with the creation of the world and concludes with the scattering of the post-flood population that happened after the account of the Tower of Babel. The Israelites, being inhabitants of the Ancient Near East had a desire to fit their beginnings as a people into the beginnings of the world as a whole as did their contemporaries. We see, then, that the sages of Israel formulated a narrative the begins with the primeval account of creation much like other Ancient Near Eastern (ANE) in Babylonian cultures (Gen chaps. 1-11).

Chapters 1-11 of Genesis, includes the following events:

God creates the world – God creates by his word; God creates humankind in his image and likeness, and he establishes the Sabbath (Gen 1:1-2:3).

The creation of all things including the man and his wife; the sin of the couple and their exclusion from the Garden of Eden (Gen 2:4b-3:24).

The offspring of Adam and Eve (4:1-26).

The marriage of heavenly beings to human women (Gen 6:1-4)

The flood as punishment of the sinfulness of humans and a new beginning; God makes a covenant with Noah (Gen 6:5-9:29)

The Tower of Babel prompts God to intervene, introducing a confusion of languages which then causes the people to scatter over the land. (Gen 11:1-9).

The reader of the primeval history faces a significant decision. Is the primeval history to be understood as being a true historical account of the beginnings or is it to be understood as being a mythological composition explaining how things came to be? The term "mythological" doesn't mean that the account does not contain truths, but that the details are mystical and spiritual in nature.

This choice can be stated in a little more detail as follows:

➤ Is Genesis chapters 1-11 a straightforward historical narrative describing the actual beginning of the universe and the earth involving real historical people and real human events? That is, were Adam and Eve actual people who lived in a real garden, and so forth?

➤ Is Genesis Chapters 1-11 a mythological narrative of the beginnings of the universe and of mankind? That is, is the account of the creation of the universe, the account of Adam and Eve and Noah, and the events of the flood and the tower of Babel history in the sense of being a myth?

The significance of this choice can be expressed on a very simple level: those who hold that Genesis 1-11 is an historical account should appreciate the hunt for Noah's ark; those who hold that Genesis 1-11 is a mythological composition, however, will be willing to learn about the symbolic meaning in the actual Hebrew words and search for the deeper spiritual meaning. There is always a deep reality – perhaps in a hidden manner – concerning the primeval history as it is told in an account revealing the mystery of God. It is not a matter of one view (strictly historical) or the other (mythical and mystical in nature) but the ability to see the more profound meaning in the primeval accounts. A scholarly statement of the mythological view of Genesis 1-11 is the following:

> In these myths we see more explicitly the multiple functions of traditional myth: to explore the transition from creation to the present world and to construct the categories and relationships that sustain a coherent world …. The transgression in these myths – disobedience (Adam and Eve), fratricide (Cain and Abel), illicit sexual union (Sons of God and Daughters of men), generalized evil (the flood), familial taboos (curse of Canaan), excessive ambition (Tower of Babel) – serve as narrative catalysts that impel the movement toward the emergence of the present world; they provide the necessary crises for the definition of the proper relationships in the Israelite ethical system. In response to these transgressions Yahweh introduces the qualities and limitations of the present world; from an initial human state of nakedness and innocence come the familiar traits of clothing, mortality, work, the division of labor, a limited lifespan, the multiplicity of societies and languages, etc. The proper ethical relationships are established in this process: between man and woman, brother and brother, father and son, nation and nation, and running all through all of these, human and God.[72]

Furthermore, they wove into this narrative a genealogical pattern from the first human being, Adam, to the patriarchs of early Israel: Abraham, Isaac and Jacob. This narrative is contained in Gen 1-11.

In the time when the compositions contained in Genesis Chapters 1-11 came into being, such mythic compositions were not meant to represent the passing of time, as we know it today. These chapters in Genesis, however, appear to contain a sense of time passing due to the fact that the narrative is broken up by five successive genealogies. These genealogies are introduced by the *toledot* formula: "these are the generations of" which appears five times: 2:4a, 5:1, 6:9, 10:1 and 11:10. [It occurs an additional five times in the second part, chapters 12-50: at 11:27; 25:12; 25:19; 36:1 and 37:2.][73]

---

[72] Romald S. Hendel, "Genesis, Book of" in *The Anchor Bible Dictionary*, V. 2, David Noel Freedman, Editor-In-Chief (New York, NY: Doubleday, 1992), 935-936.
[73] Richard J. Clifford, SJ and Roland E. Murphy, O. Carm., in *The New Jerome Biblical Commentary*, Edited by: Raymond E. Brown, S.S., Joseph A. Fitzmyer, S.J., and Roland E. Murphy, O. Carm. (Englewood Cliffs, NJ: Prentice Hall, 1990), 9.

Read the following sections of Genesis 1:1-11:32)
- 1:1-2:3 Creation of the universe and the first humans; the Fall.
- 2:4-3:24 Creation of the man and woman; their sin and punishment
- 6:5-9:17 Noah and the flood.

2. The patriarchal history (Gen Chaps. 12:1-50:26)

The patriarchal history is concerned with Abram (Abraham), his son Isaac, his grandson Jacob and his great grandson Joseph. The narrative is constructed from three groups of traditions: 1) Abraham and Sarah (Gen 11:27-25:18), 2) Jacob and his sons (Gen 25:19-36:43), and 3) Joseph and his brothers (Gen 37:50-626). These traditions were almost certainly transmitted orally for many, many years before being put into a written f

Read the following sections of Genesis 11:27-50:26:
- 12:1-3:1 The LORD calls Abram.
- 15:1-21 The LORD promises Abram an heir, and land, and makes a covenant with him.
- 17:1-27 God gives Abram and Sarai new names and institutes circum
- 37:1-50:26 The story of Joseph.

3. The Enslavement of the Israelites in Egypt and their escape from Egypt (Ex 1:1-15:21)

The Israelites, who came to Egypt in the days of Joseph, did well and multiplied. But eventually a pharaoh came to power who knew nothing of Joseph and he had concerns about having a large foreign population in his country. So he oppressed the Israelites and assigned them the task of making bricks. The Pharaoh treated them so harshly that they cried out to their god for help (Ex 2:23). God heard their cry and came to their rescue.

At the burning bush, God gave Moses the task of leading the Israelites against Pharaoh (2:23-4:31) and told Moses his name (3:13-14). Sometime later, God engaged the Pharaoh in a contest involving changing a staff into a serpent and ten plagues (Ex 7:8-13:10) God defeated the pharaoh. In connection with the 10th plague, the killing of the firstborn, God prescribed celebration of the Passover (12:1-18). That same night the pharaoh urged the Israelites to leave Egypt. The Jews departed, despoiling the Egyptians as they left (Ex 12:31-36).

The Israelites marched out toward the Reed Sea (popularly known as the Red Sea) and when they saw that they were being pursued by the Egyptians they cried out to their God as they had previously. God responded to their cry by creating a miraculous crossing of the water for the Israelites and resulting in death for the Egyptians. (Ex 14:10-15:21).

Read the following sections of Ex 1:1-15:21:
- 1:1-2:22 The enslavement of the Israelites and the early years of Moses.
- 2:23-4:17 The encounter of Moses with God.
- 7:8-13:16 The ten plagues (read the first nine very quickly).
- 13:17-15:21 The destruction of the Egyptian army and the rejoicing of the Israelites.

102

4. The Journey to Mt. Sinai (Ex 15:22-18:27)

After they had crossed the sea and the Egyptian army had met its end, the Israelites journeyed to Mt. Sinai in stages. During the journey, the Israelites constantly complained to Moses about not having water to drink or food to eat. At Mara, in the desert of Shur, they complained of not having water to drink; so the LORD gave them water to drink (15:22-25). In the desert of Sin (pronounced *sheen*) they charged Moses with having led them into the wilderness in order to kill them by starvation; so the LORD gave the people quail and manna to eat (16:1-3; 13-15). At Rephidim, the people again complained that there was no water to drink; so the LORD again gave them water again.

In the third month, on its first day, the Israelites arrived at the desert of Sinai and they pitched camp.

- Read the following portion of this journey: 15:22-17:1-7.

5. The Covenant at Sinai (Ex 19:1-Lev 27:34)

The Israelites came into the desert of Sinai and camped at the foot of Mt. Sinai. (19:1-2). The LORD then made a covenant with Moses and the people.

What is a covenant? In the OT, the Hebrew word "berit" is used to express the concept of a covenant and it refers to a binding agreement such as the covenant made between Jacob and Laban in Gen 31:44.

Boadt and other scholars contend that in the ancient Near East (ANE) there were two types of covenants, or treaties, between peoples: the parity treaty and the vassal treaty. The parity treaty was a treaty between kings of equal stature. The vassal treaty was between a king who was a major power and the king of a small nation that had been conquered by the great king, a people who were so weak that they had to cooperate with the great king. The Israelites, experiencing the power of Yahweh in the Exodus event, first expressed their relationship with God in terms of the vassal type of covenant similar to the Hittite treaties of the period 1400-1200 BCE.

The Hittite vassal treaties had a prticular form. The form of these treaties has been determined from an analysis of various kinds of treaties found in the ancient world. The following is a presentation of the six part form characteristic of a vassal-type treaty:

The Preamble in which the overlord, or great king, gives his name and title:

Historical Prologue in which the great king lists his past acts of kindness
        to the vassal as the reason for the vassal king's obligation to obey.

The Stipulations or Demands that the overlord binds the vassal to keep.

Deposit of the treaty in a temple and public readings at set times.

103

The list of witnesses is important to any contract (But for a solemn state
    covenant, the witnesses are the gods of the two lands.)

The Curses and Blessings end the treaty. The divine beings are called on
    to maintain the treaty in the divine courtroom by imposing rewards and

Chapter 19 of Exodus describes the events leading up to the giving of the covenant between Yahweh and the Israelites. The content of the treaty is contained in Ex 20:1-17.With these elements of a treaty in mind, we now can read through the passage. Observe that the first two elements of the vassal treaty, the preamble and the historical prologue, are here merged into one - the Exodus event serves both to describe the God who is entering into the treaty and provides the list of things which the great "king" has done for the vassal "king" – in this case the Israelites who are accepting a covenant with God. The stipulations are the Ten Commandments (or the Ten Words which is the way the Hebrew text reads.) Thus, the first three elements of the vassal treaty are present, although in modified form.

The fourth element, the deposit of the treaty in the temple and public readings at set times can also be seen to be present. Ex 25:1-22 gives detailed instructions for building an Ark of acacia wood to serve as the meeting place between God and Moses and the two stone tablets bearing the Ten Commandments are placed in this Ark. This later was replaced by placing an Ark with the copy of the covenant in the temple. The fifth element of the typical treaty, the witnesses, does not appear. But this is to be expected. Note that the usual witnesses in the Hittite treaty are other gods. In the case of the Israelites there is only one God, Yahweh, .instead one god of many gods. Hence, there are no other gods to serve as witnesses to the treaty.

The sixth and final element, the blessings and curses do not appear at all here in the Book of Exodus. They can, however, be found in the Book of Deuteronomy.

Under the covenant, the people were obligated to follow the Ten Commandments (Ex 20:1-21) and the regulations contained in the Covenant Code (sometimes called the Book of the Covenant) contained in 20:22-23:33 as these were stipulations under the covenant.

 After being accepted by all the people, the covenant was ratified by the sprinkling of blood (24:1-8).

Moses stayed up on the mountain for a period of forty days and nights (24:18). The people, thinking that Moses was never coming back down from the mountain, asked Aaron to make them a god who would be their leader (32:1). Aaron obliges the people and the covenant with the LORD is broken! Subsequently, the LORD forgives the people for what they had done and renews the covenant (32:30-34:35).

The concept of Covenant and the covenant that God made with the Israelites at Mt. Sinai, in particular, are of great importance in many of the writings contained in the Scriptures – b othin the Old and the New Testaments!

Read the following sections from Ex 19:1-Lev 34:

- 19:1-20:21 The making of the covenant and the Ten Commandments.
- 24:1-18 The ratification of the covenant.
- Chaps. 32-34 The matter of the Golden Calf and the renewal of the covenant.
- Lev 23:1-44 The liturgical year.

6. Preparations for the Departure from Sinai (Num 1:1-10:10)

This section of the Book of Numbers deals with the preparations that the Israelites undertook, at God's command (see 1:1; 2:1; 4:1 and so on), to prepare themselves for the journey from the desert of Sinai to the Promised Land. These preparations included: 1) a census of the Israelites, excluding the Levites (1:1-19); 2) assignment of the Levites to take charge of the tabernacle (1:48-54); 3) organization of the camp in accordance with the order of march (2:1-34); 4) the number, organization and duties of the Levites (3:1-4:49); 5) purification of the camp (5:1-4); 6) two examples of case law (5:5-31); 7) the Nazirite vow (6:1-21); 8) the priestly blessing (6:22-27); 9) the consecration of the tabernacle and the Levites (7:1-8:26); 10) celebration of the Passover (9:1-14); 11) statement of the divine guidance to be provided the Israelites on their march (9:15-23); and 12) the acquisition of two silver trumpets (10:1-10).

Read the following sections from Num 1:1-10:10:
- 6:22-27 The priestly blessing.
- 9:1-23 The celebration of the Passover at Mt. Sinai and the divine guidance to be given to the Israelites on their march.
- 10:1-10 The two silver trumpets.

7. The March in the Desert (Num 10:11-36:13)

The section 10:11-36:13 of the Book of Numbers falls naturally into two parts. The first part tells about the march from Sinai (10:11) to the plains of Moab across the Jordan from Jericho (22:1). The second part tells what transpired on the plains of Moab (22:2-36:13) and contains a number of cultic regulations introduced by the phrase: "The LORD spoke to Moses saying," as in 28:1 and 31:1.

The most important point of the book of Numbers is that the people who are present at the beginning of the book in 1:1 are not the same people who are present at the end of the book in 36:13. The people of the generation of Moses have all died! This circumstance is symbolized in the narrative by an account of a census of the people carried out at the beginning (in 1:1-54) and by a similar account of a second census taken at the end (in 26:1-62). None of the names of those of the first generation, with the exception of Joshua and Caleb, are the same in the both reports as is pointed out in 26:64-65.

What was the cause of this happening? The people had constantly complained about the lack of food and the dangers of the journey (e.g. 11:1-3; 11:4; 14:4) and God had tired of the people grumbling (14:20-35). The case of the Israelite men having sexual relations with Moabite women and participating in the worship of the Moabite gods (25:1-5) and the case of an Israelite man bringing a Midianite woman into his family (25:6-16) provided further motivation for this divine action. Even Moses was not allowed to go into the land that God was giving to the Israelites (27:12-14) because he had not been faithful to the LORD (20:2-13) in one instance. He was, however, rewarded in looking on the Promised Land from a high mountain point. At this time, leadership was transferred from Moses to Joshua (27:15-23).

Read the following sections from Num 10:11-36:13:
- 11:1-3; 11:4; 14:4; 14:20-35; 25:1-5; 25:6-16 and 26:64-65 – about the people and God.
- 20:2-13 and 27:12-14 about Moses and God.
- 27:15-23 The transfer of leadership to Joshua.
- 13:1-14:45 The account of the spies and the decision to attack.
- 22:2-24:25 Balaam and his prophecies.
- 28:1-29:40 Regulations governing various offerings (read quickly).

8. The Final Words of Moses and His Death (Deuteronomy Chaps. 1-34)

The Book of Deuteronomy is made up of three discourses by Moses and an account of his death and burial.

The first discourse (1:1-4:49) begins with a brief introduction (1:1-4). The body of the discourse divides into two principal parts: 1) an historical review of Israel's march through the desert (1:5-3:29) and 2) an exhortation to follow the teaching of Moses recalling what took place at Mt. Sinai (4:1-40). After identifying three cities of refuge (4:41-43), the discourse concludes with a short statement (4:44-49).

The second discourse is by far the longest of the three: 5:1 – 28:69! It falls naturally into two basic parts: First the making of a covenant with the people of Israel, consisting of 5:1-26:19, followed by instructions for what the people should do when they cross the Jordan River into the Promised Land and a list of blessings for obeying the covenant and curses for disobeying it (27:1-69). The first part of this lengthy discourse itself falls into three parts: 1) a reminder of the covenant made at Mt. Sinai and a re-statement of the Ten Commandments (Chap. 5), 2) a lengthy preamble to the law code that follows (6:1-11:32) and the law code itself (12:1-26:15).

The third discourse, 29:1-30:20, is the shortest of the three. As it stands, it has the form of a covenant ceremony. It begins with a statement of what God has done for the Israelites (29:2-9). This is followed, in turn, by recognition that the people are entering into a covenant with God (29:10-15), an exhortation warning the people what action God will take if they turn away from God to worship idols (29:16-29) and how God will respond if the people subsequently return to God (30:1-14). The discourse ends with a statement that the choice confronting the people is a choice between life and death (30:15-20).

Chapters 31-34 of the Book of Deuteronomy deal with the death of Moses. This section contains: the commissioning of Joshua to replace Moses as leader of all the people; a song,

106

attributed to Moses, which he is reported to have recited to all the people (31:30 – 32:44), and a blessing of all the tribes (Chap. 33). The death and burial of Moses are related in Chapter 34.

Read the following sections from the Book of Deuteronomy:
- 4:1-40 The heart of the first discourse.
- 5:1-27 The Ten Commandments.
- 6:4-9 These verses are very important to Jewish spirituality.
- 26:1-11 These verses contain a very ancient creedal statement (26:5-9).
- Chap 28 Blessings and curses of the covenant.
- Chap 34 The death and burial of Moses.

THE DOCUMENTARY HYPOTHESIS

If you look closely at the text of the five books of the Pentateuch a number of literary elements become apparent. Careful analysis of these elements by scholars, over a period of more than one hundred years, has led many of them to come to accept the position that these are not five independent writings but that they are actually a single continuous narrative! This belief in a single continuous narrative is known as the **documentary hypothesis**. It is "documentary" because it is held that the writing consists of several documents which have been joined together by one or more editors. It is a "hypothesis" because it is based entirely upon evaluation of elements observed in the text. No text of any of the original documents has yet been discovered. Thus, the literary history of these five writings is embodied in the **documentary hypothesis** and it is this that we will consider in this section.

The following sorts of elements can be observed in the text of the Torah (Pentateuch): [74]

Language Differences:

a. Different names of God: Yahweh (e.g. Gen 2:4b, 5, etc) [J Tradition]; Elohim [E Tradition](e.g. Gen 1:1,3, etc)

b. Different names for the same place: Sinai (Ex 19:18, 20)
   Horeb (e.g. Ex 17:6; 33:6)

Doublets:
a. Abraham says his wife is his sister: Gen 12:10-20 and Gen 20:1-18

b. The sale of Joseph into slavery: Gen 37:25-28a and Gen 37:21-24 and 28b-36

---

[74] Richard E. Friedman, "Torah" in *Anchor Bible Dictionary*, V.6 (New York: Doubleday, 1992), 605-622.

Contradictions:

    a. In the story of the great flood

        1. Different numbers of animals: One pair of each (Gen 6:19; 7:8-9, 15) and 7 pairs of each clean animal and 1 pair of each unclean animal (Gen 7:2-3)

        2. In 7:4 God promises rain; in 7:4 it rains, but in 7:11 speaks of the fountains of the great deep bursting and the windows of the heavens opening

    b. In the Decalogue

        1. Different reasons for the Sabbath: Ex 20:11 and Deut 5:15

        2. Different commandments: compare Ex 34:14-26 and both Ex 20:1-17 and Deut 5:1-21

These are only a couple of samples of the language differences, doublets and contradictions that can be found in the Pentateuch. For a complete listing of these phenomena, look up 'Torah' in the *Anchor Bible Dictionary.*

Scholars have found that all of the elements of this sort provide a basis for separating (they come to us interwoven!) the material of the Pentateuch into **four major narratives** as follows:

As collected and refined during the last two centuries of scholarship, these divisions of the text have come to be identified. There are four major divisions and some smaller passages joined to them. The four major texts are classified as follows: **J (Jahwistic),** a group of passages so named because they consistently identify the deity in narration (not in dialogue) as Yahweh (the siglum J following the German spelling); **E (Elohistic),** a group of passages that identify the deity only as God (elohim or el) until the time of Moses, at which time the name Yahweh is revealed (Ex 3:13-15) and is used in this group thereafter; **P(Priestly),** a group that also identifies the deity as El or Elohim until the name Yahweh is revealed (Ex 6:2-3, the siglum P reflecting its exceptional interest in priestly matters; **D (Deuteronomic)** comprising nearly all of the book of Deuteronomy, whose bank of terminology is blatantly different from the other three narratives J, E, and P.[75]

Each of the four divisions contains a number of elements that indicate the time and place of its composition. These elements are known as "historical referents." On the basis of these historical referents scholars have arrived at the following positions:

The **J and E** texts contain elements whose historical referents lie in the period of the divided kingdoms of Israel and Judah, ca. 922-722 B.C. The historical

---

[75] Friedman, 609-610.

referents of J indicate derivation from the S. kingdom, Judah. The historical referents of E reflect the conditions and interests of the N. kingdom, Israel."

Neither source shows any awareness of the fall of the kingdom of Israel nor of the dispersion of the N. tribes, which strongly suggests composition before the fall of Israel in 722 B.C. The very character of the two sources, each fitting one of the divided kingdoms, likewise points to composition in the period of the division. J's reference to Esau/Edom's breaking Israel's yoke from its shoulder (Gen 27:40) probably places its composition at least after Hadad's rebellion against Solomon or even after Edom's full independence from Judah in the reign of the Judean king Jehoram (849-842 B.C.). E offers few clues to narrow its composition further within the two-century period of division.

The P text contains elements whose historical referents lie in the period following the fall of the kingdom of Israel (722 B.C.) but prior to the fall of the kingdom of Judah (587 B.C.), with particularly significant elements indicative of the reign of the Judean king Hezekiah (715-687 B.C.).

The D text contains elements whose historical referents lie in the reign of Josiah, the great-grandson of Hezekiah.[76]

So, then, there are a J and an E narrative which date, in written form, to the time of the Divided Monarchy, a P narrative which dates to the time of King Hezekiah and a D narrative which was probably completed during or soon after the reign of Josiah.

The four narratives come to us combined into one continuous narrative. How did four independent narratives become combined into one? The best way to see how this was accomplished is to separate the four, one from another. So imagine in your mind that you have separated them and that they lie side-by-side on the table before you.

When J and E stand on their own, it is found that neither J nor E can be read as a continuous story. J and E taken together, however, do form a nearly continuous account. P, taken by itself, forms a nearly continuous account. These observations, combined with the dates of composition of the various narratives, lead to the following picture of the development of the Pentateuch:

1. **J and E, incorporating oral traditions, were written independently during the divided monarchy. They were later combined to form JE by an editor in the S. kingdom who cut out substantial portions of both narratives in fashioning the combined work.**

2. **P was later joined to JE, resulting in JEP, by an editor who went to great lengths to retain as much of his two source texts as possible without producing contradictions that were unacceptable.**

---

[76] Friedman, 612-615.

3. **The same editor who formed JEP, or a somewhat later editor, then added D to JEP by moving the accounts of the elevation of Joshua to leader and the death of Moses to the end of the Book of Deuteronomy. The result was JEDP, i.e. the Pentateuch as we have it.** [77]

This is the **documentary hypothesis** stated very briefly with little supporting evidence. Those who are intrigued by this should read the account by Friedman in the *Anchor Bible Dictionary* or, better yet, read his book: Richard E. Friedman, *Who Wrote the Bible*, HarperSanFrancisco, 1997.

Now, with this newly acquired knowledge of the literary history of the Pentateuch, go back to the beginning of this section and take another look at the various elements that we observed in the text of the Pentateuch. We see now that:

1. **Gen 2:4b** and following is the J account; **Gen 1:1-2:4a** is the P account

2. The doublet of Abraham and his wife: **Gen 12:10-20** is J and **20:1-18** is E

3. The doublet of the sale of Joseph: **Gen 37-25-28a** is J and the other is E

4. The flood story (**Genesis 7-8**): 7 pairs of clean and 1 pair of unclean is J and 1 pair of each is P (J held that a sacrifice was made to God after the flood so more clean animals were needed to avoid destroying a species. P held that sacrifice did not become part of Israel until long after the flood.)

5. God promises rain - in **7:12** it simply rains - this is J; **7:11** is P and refers back to **Gen 1:1-2:4** where the world is divided with waters beneath and waters above.

6. Different reasons for the Sabbath - **Ex 20:11** is P and **Deut 5:15** is D

7. Different commandments: **Ex 34:14-26** is J; **Ex 20:1-17** is P and **Deut 5:1-21** is D

So the documentary hypothesis does provide a reasonable explanation for the elements that are found in the text.

The most important thing that we have learned in this section is that the five books that make up the Pentateuch, as they come to us, constitute **one continuous narrative**. When we study the Bible we should read the first five books together as one work! Almost all of the commentaries that you will find on the shelves in the library or in the bookstores treat them, however, as five individual books and each book is presented and analyzed by a different commentator.

---

[77] Friedman, 618.

It is perhaps interesting to make one final point. You will have noticed that D comprises almost the entire book of Deuteronomy and that D does not appear at all in the first four books. Is this simply a matter of D being a fourth component of the Torah or is this a hint of something of significance that remains to be explained? We will find out in the next chapter that it is a hint that a great deal remains to be revealed about the Deuteronomy source, "D"!

CHAPTER FOURTEEN

THE DEUTERONOMISTIC HISTORY

Introduction

In 1943, Martin Noth (pronounced "Note") published his finding that the group of biblical books consisting of Deuteronomy, Joshua, Judges, 1 and 2 Samuel, and 1 and 2 Kings were not just seven independent works but in reality were a unified composition written by a single author. This conclusion by Noth still stands today.

It is now the common practice to designate this unified composition by the term: Deuteronomistic History and to abbreviate this term that is difficult to promounce by the symbol: DH. To designate those things pertaining solely to the Book of Deuteronomy it has been agreed to apply the term: Deuteronomic.

This is interesting to note: the Book of Ruth, which is found in the Bible after the Book of Judges is not a part of the DH. Ruth was actually written during the period of the Second Temple. It came to be associated with Judges because its narrative is set in that earlier time.

READING THE DEUTERONOMISTIC HISTORY
[The writings of Deuteronomy, Joshua, Judges, 1 and 2 Samuel, 1 and 2 Kings]

DEUTERONOMY

Begins: with the first speech of Moses (1:1-4:43).
Ends: with the death and burial of Moses and the succession of Joshua (34:1-12).

We have already encountered the Book of Deuteronomy as the fifth book of the Pentateuch. Here, we encounter it a second time, now as the first book of the DH. This Book of Deuteronomy deserves attention. On the one hand, it was then very important to the Israelites and is now of great importance to the faith and worship of the Jews of later times. Also, it is one of the OT books that is the most frequently quoted by the writers of the NT books.[78]

To understand the Book of Deuteronomy it is necessary to go back to the reign of King Josiah of Judah. Josiah commenced his efforts of religious reform in the year 629 BCE. According to the account in 2 Kings, chapter 22, some six to eight years later a document called "the Book of the Law" was uncovered by workers as they carried out some repairs to the Temple. And, at a later time, the Deuteronomist composed a comprehensive account of the history of Israel from the time of the Mosaic period to the fall of Israel and Judah, including the

---

[78] Bernhard W. Anderson, *Understanding the Old Testament*, 3rd Edition (Englewood Cliffs, NJ: Prentice-Hall, Inc., 1975), 352.

"Book of the Law" as chapters 12-26 and 28 of the part now known as the Book of Deuteronomy.[79]

Some scholars today have proposed that careful analysis of the text shows that it is probable that the first writer of the history ended his work with the fall of the Northern Kingdom, Israel. In their view, a second editor extended the work of the first one by adding to it the historical account of the fall of the Southern Kingdom, Judah, and by making some other additions. In the study of a religious tradition, as time passes historically the issues tend to become more complicated.

Now we can consider the following two things. First, let's look at Dt 5:5-22. These are clearly the familiar **Ten Commandments** given to Moses on Mt. Sinai (Horeb), although you are most likely more familiar with them as they are set forth in the Book of Exodus (Ex 20:1-17). But, notice that while they are referred to as commandments in Exodus, here they are called: "words" (5:5 and 5:22).

Secondly, we can continue and read Dt 6:4-8. This is a phenomenally important passage It is called the **Great Shema**, one of the most important Jewish prayers (6:4-5). However, it is known and treasured by Christian believers also because Jesus Christ, a Jew, called it the greatest commandment in the law (Mt 22:34-37). But, observe that in Dt 6:6 it is referred to as "words" and not as a "commandment." It may be interesting to know, also, that the Shema, is usually the prayer that is printed on a small – very small – scroll and placed inside a mezuzah, a small holder situated next to a door. The mezuzah is reverently touched when entering and exiting the door (in homes, in synagogues, in Jewish stores and places of gathering). This indicates reverence for the great Shema prayer that is, at least, more than 2500 years old!

You are probably wondering what difference it makes whether you call them "commandments" or "words." It makes a considerable difference! Let us let Richard Friedman tell us the difference:

> This is also a change in the presentation of the law in the Torah. Most of the commandments in the Torah have been given without reasons or explanations. From the law of the "red cow" (Numbers 19) to the Ten Commandments, one is not told why one must perform them, but only that God commands it (with a few notable exceptions). But the law code of Deuteronomy (12-28) is preceded by eleven chapters of history, explanation, and inspiration, and it is followed by two chapters of exquisite revelation of the relevance and value of the commandments. The Torah thus concludes with the message that the law is meant to be relevant, comprehensible, and meaningful in the people's lives. It is appropriate to seek out the meanings of the laws and, when interpreting the law, to understand that it is explicitly meant to enhance lives. One must not apply it in a way that causes injury or undermines its positive function in life.[80]

---

[79] Bernhard W. Anderson, 351.
[80] Richard Elliott Friedman, *Commentary on the Torah* (San Francisco: HarperSanFrancisco, 2001), 559.

We can see, then, why one must understand the Covenant as a revelation of "relationship" that God establishes with mankind, and the Ten Commandments are stipulations of that relationship. God is not revealed as a dictator that is barking out commands and subsequent punishment when they are not followed. In essence, the laws as our scholar, Dr. Friedman, states, "are meant to enhance lives." They are to reveal the life-giving of God and God's inestimable love for humankind and the creation.

There is one more passage in the Book of Deuteronomy that is worthy of attention: Dt 10:12-22. This passage has a lot to say about who God is. The meaning of the phrase "circumcise your hearts" will be encountered again in Paul's letter to the Romans 2:25-29, in the New Testament. It should always be remembered that the Hebrew people understood that God resides in the heart. In Hebrew anthropology, the heart is equated to the "soul" in New Testament usage.

One significant function of the Ten Commandments – or Ten Words – is the use of the Hebrew word *lo*, which means "no, not ever, never." This little word is biblically unique to the Ten Commandments. These "words" are guidelines for life. It is something like parents telling their teenager that he or she may NEVER drink and drive, or drive drunk because it means … death! They must NEVER do this. In the same sense, to worship other gods rather than God the Father is to reject the One who gives life, both physically and spiritually. It means "death." Therefore, the Hebrew word used in the list of the Ten Commandments is a short little word, *lo*. with a powerful meaning. This word *lo* – "no," "not ever," "never" means "not!" Most often the word of the other laws given in the Deuteronomistic History utilize another word which is a more "negotiable no," meaning one must not do it except in certain cases.

JOSHUA

Begins: with God's commission to Joshua following after the death of Moses (1:1-9).
Ends: with the death of Joshua (24:29-33).

The Book of Joshua divides naturally in three parts: 1) the conquest (Chs. 1-12); the division of the land (Chs. 13-21); and Joshua's farewell address and the renewal of the covenant ceremony (Chs. 22-24).

The portrayal of the Conquest provided by the Dtr is one of complete military triumph. (The Dtr indicates an editor or redactor who compiled this narrative.) It is presented as having taken place in three military campaigns: one to the east (Chs. 7-9); one to the south (Ch. 10) and one to the north (Ch. 11). This presentation of the Conquest probably represents a telescoping in time and a magnification of the completeness of the military victory compared to the historical fact.

The partition of the land is described by giving the boundaries of the areas allotted to each of the tribes receiving land. Following the partition, a number of cities of refuge were named and, finally, several towns along with their pasture lands were awarded to the Levites. All of this, however, points to the fact that God is helping them establish themselves as the people of God. Some readers flinch at the recounting of violent wars and the taking of land. They ask:

"does this condone aggressive war?" The answer by others is that the point is to understand that God is establishing a nation – a people – to be known as God's faithful. It is human writing through which shines a deep and profound spiritual truth of God as a life-giver.

Some significant passages in the Book of Joshua are the following:

- 2:1-24 In this passage, Joshua sends out two spies to view Jericho and its land. Rahab, a woman living in Jericho, protects the spies from the King of Jericho. Rahab's name appears again in connection with the genealogy of Jesus (Mt 1:5).
- 6:1-21 This passage is the account of the capture of Jericho in which the walls fall down.
- 23:1-16 This is Joshua's **farewell address**. The farewell address is an important literary form in the Scriptures.
- 24:1-28 (also 8:30-35) This is an excellent example of the covenant renewal ceremony. Bernhard Anderson refers to Chapter 24 as one of the most important in the Old Testament.[81]

JUDGES

Begins: with the time following the death of Joshua during which God raised up judges (see 2:16).
Ends: with the statement: "In those days there was no king in Israel; everyone did what he thought best" (21:25).

The Hebrew word, *shofet*, that is translated as "judge" is not limited to legal matters. The meaning of *shofet* is closer to the English word "ruler." The role of the judge in Israel was primarily that of a military leader and the authority of the judge extended beyond his or her tribe.[82] Many people are surprised there was a woman judge named Deborah.

Unlike a king, however, the judge did not receive authority on a hereditary basis. The judge was a charismatic leader who was raised up by God in a specific historical situation (2:16).

The accounts of the various judges all follow the same pattern. This pattern is set forth in general terms in 2:11-18. The pattern is as follows:

- The Israelites did what was evil in the sight of the LORD (v.11).
- The anger of the LORD was kindled against Israel (v. 14).
- The Israelites cry out to the LORD (this element of the pattern is missing in this passage – see example below).
- God answers their cry by raising up a judge (v. 16).
- The land rests until the death of the judge (v. 18).

A specific (brief) example of this cycle is contained in the account of Othniel (3:7-11). All but one of the parts of the cycle are clearly expressed here.

---

[81] Bernhard W. Anderson, 125. Reading all of pages 125-135 regarding the concept of covenant are most helpful.
[82] Anderson, 148-149.

Scholars have determined that the accounts of the judges are **not** organized in chronological order.

As examples, consider the following two notable judges:
- Deborah – Chapters 4 and 5 describe a judge raised by God who is a woman. Chapter 5 consists of the Song of Deborah; this song is an excellent example of early Hebrew poetry.
- Samson – Although Samson (Chs. 13-16) is well remembered it is often forgotten that he was a judge.

Note #1: Chapters 17-21 of the Book of Judges contains much valuable information about this historical period. Notice the repeated phrase: "In those days there was no king in Israel; all the people did what he thought best" (17:6 and 21:25 NAB). The subject of a king for Israel will come up again in 1 Samuel.

Note #2: In Catholic and Protestant Bibles the Book of Ruth follows immediately after the Book of Judges. The reason for this may be that the Book of Ruth begins with the phrase: "Once in the time of the judges….," leading some to think that this book belongs in the time of the Judges. Modern scholars, however, claim that the Book of Ruth was written down sometime during the 2nd Temple period for people living in that time. Of course, there is the question of "when" the Book of Ruth was written – was it composed in the 2nd Temple period or just written down then after centuries of oral tradition? Today's bible scholars usually feel the Book of Ruth is out of place in its location between the books of Judges and 1 Samuel. One thing that is more sure is that the Book of Ruth is not part of the DH.

1 SAMUEL

Begins: with the birth of Samuel.
Ends: with the death of Saul, his three sons, his armor bearer and all of his men.

One way that First Samuel can be divided into parts is the following:
- 1:1-4:1a – Birth of Samuel and his call
- 4:1b-7:17 – The Ark of the Covenant is captured by the Philistines and later returned.
- Ch. 8 – The people of Israel demand a king; their demand is granted by God.
- Chs. 9-11 – Saul is chosen to be king and is anointed by Samuel.
- Ch. 12 – Samuel's farewell address.
- Chs. 13-15 – Saul's kingship does not succeed; God regrets having made him King of Israel (15:35).
- Chs. 16-31 – The rise of David, after having to hide in order to escape death, is intertwined with the fall of Saul.

The birth of Samuel (1:1-2:11) is of considerable interest because Hannah was barren for many years and became pregnant with Samuel after praying to God for a male child. Hannah responds to the birth of her son with a song. This song bears many features that are similar to Mary's Magnificat (Lk 1:46-55). It is enlightening to read both of these songs together.

The call of Samuel to be a prophet (3:1-4:1a) is interesting because it makes it clear that it is God who calls the prophets and it makes it clear that it is God who speaks through a prophet.

Chapter 8 is a good read because it sets forth the idea that having a king is not necessarily a good thing. When the people persist in their demand, in spite of having been warned, God teaches them a lesson by granting their demand. You will see in the following books that God's warning had not been just idle words.

Reading Chapter 12 after having read Chapter 8 is helpful. Notice that in Verse 19 the people ask Samuel to pray to God on their behalf because they have added the evil of asking for a king to all their other sins! (Having a king would make them like their neighboring nations.)

2 SAMUEL

Begins: with David mourning the deaths of Saul and Jonathan.
Ends: with King David old and advanced in years, and the struggle for who would succeed him.

After mourning Saul and Jonathan, David is anointed King of the Judahites (2:1-4). Then, David reigned in Judah for some seven and a half years at which time the tribes of Israel came to him and anointed him king over all of Israel (5:1-5). Following this, David and his men captured Jerusalem and David established his family in that city (5:6-16).

After bringing the Ark to Jerusalem (ch. 6), David became concerned that the Ark resided in a tent while he resided in a house. At this time, God spoke to David through the prophet Nathan and promised David that his house and his kingdom would endure forever (7:1-17). In response, King David prayed to the LORD (7:18-29). This is a very important passage to read.

At some time later, David has an affair with Bathsheba, the wife of Uriah, and also arranges for Uriah, her husband, to be killed in battle (ch. 11). Chapter 12 moves forward rapidly: God is displeased with David's sin; God punishes David and the child they had conceived in this affair dies; David repents of his sin; and David and Bathsheba give birth to Solomon, the man who will succeed David as King of all Israel and Judah. Reading through this narrative can be as fascinating and as dramatic a depiction as seen on Discovery Channel or in the movies of the past.

Of special interest is the section in 2 Samuel, chapters 9-20 and 1 Kings 1-2. This narrative is known among scholars as the Court History of David and is held to be one of the best examples of prose in the OT. It is believed to have been written during the time that David was king and composed by a member of his court.[83]

Finally, also worthy of note are David's Song of Thanksgiving (22:2-51) and the last words of David (23:1-7).

---

[83] Anderson, 199.

1 KINGS

Begins: with the monarchy united; King David is old and advanced in years.
Ends: with the monarchy divided; Ahaziah reigns over Israel, the Northern Kingdom, and Jehoshaphat reigns over Judah, the Southern Kingdom.

It is clear from where the First Book of Kings begins and ends that it covers a very important period in the history of Israel. It is, therefore, an important book to read. This is a reading that one should plan to read someday, perhaps even suggesting it for a church bible study. The following are a number of important chapters for an interested person to eventually devote the time needed to read them.

Some of the important points in the First Book of Kings are the following:
- 1:25-2:12 The death of David and the accession of Solomon, David's son.
- Chapter 3 – Solomon asks God for wisdom; his request is granted. A demonstration of his wisdom is presented. The fame of Solomon's wisdom is summarized in 4:29-34.
- 4:20-28 A description of the magnificence of Solomon's reign is presented.
- Chapter 6 Solomon builds the Temple.
- Chapter 8 The dedication of the Temple and Solomon's prayer of dedication.
- 11:41-43 The death of Solomon.
- 12:1-24 The monarchy in Israel divides into a Northern Kingdom, Israel, and a Southern Kingdom, Judah.
- 1 Kgs 17:1-2 Kgs 2:1-12 The Elijah cycle. It is especially interesting to read the account of Elijah and the prophets of Baal (1 Kgs 18:20-46) and Elijah's meeting with God at Mt. Horeb (19:11-18). We will find in the Gospels of the New Testament that there were people who believed that John the Baptist was Elijah returned, and others who believed that Jesus was Elijah returned.
- 1 Kgs 19:19-21 The call of Elisha.

Let us pause for just a moment and consider a curious aspect to the descriptions of the reigns of the various kings of the divided monarchy and the way that they are presented. The beginning of the reign of a king in the southern kingdom (Judah) is described relative to the reigning kind in the north. See 2 Kings 15:1. The beginning of a king in the northern kingdom (Israel) is described relative to the reigning kind in the south. See 2 Kings 13:1. Overall, what do we learn from this curious situation? It appears there was inter-relationship between the northern and southern kingdoms.

2 KINGS

Begins: with an injury to King Ahaziah and his subsequent denouncement by Elijah.
Ends: with the fall of Judah and the release of Jehoiachin from prison.
Some significant passages in the book of 2 Kings are the following:
- 2:1-12 Elijah ascends to heaven.
- 2:13-18 Elisha succeeds Elijah.
- 2:19-25 and 4:1-6:7 Some miracles performed by Elisha.
- 13:14-21 Death of Elisha.

- **17:7-23 The Fall of Israel, the Northern Kingdom. Israel is taken captive into Assyria.**
- Chaps. 18-20 Reign of Hezekiah and his reform efforts.
- 21:1-18 The reign of Manasseh – He was a very bad king according to the biblical account (see vv. 10-15). However, there is an inspiring writing included in the Orthodox canon of the Bible (or in bible translations with the Apocrypha) that includes Manasseh's repentance before the Lord: The Prayer of Manasseh.
- 22:1- 23:30 The reign of Josiah. Hilkiah finds the book of the law in the Temple (22:3-20); Josiah responds by undertaking a reform movement (23:1-27).
- **Chaps. 24-25 The Fall of Judah with deportations to Babylon in 597 and 587 BCE.**

Conclusion

The Scriptures covered in this section are writings that oftentimes people ignore or with which they have never been familiar. They do, however, hold great significance for Christianity. To understand Christ's comment on the laws and how it is the "spirit of the law" that is important; to be aware of elements of worship; to realize how God does work in and among the people – are all examples of why these books are valuable. We read that scholars have identified passages in these writings as being particularly important passages of the OT. When one reads them over, it becomes obvious why scholars make these claims. In these Scriptures, the nature of God is revealed. Also, one learns what the real reasons are for why people should live according to what God plans. These writings demonstrate God's hope for humanity.

CHAPTER FIFTEEN

PROPHECY IN ISRAEL
& THE PROPHETS OF THE ISRAELITE PERIOD

Introduction

In popular thinking, the prophetic writings are divided into two groups: the major prophets and the minor prophets. The former group consists of **Isaiah, Jeremiah and Ezekiel** the latter group consists of the twelve prophets: **Hosea, Joel, Amos, Obadiah, Jonah, Micah, Nahum, Habakkuk, Zephaniah, Haggai, Zechariah and Malachi.** The terminology "major" and "minor" introduces a distinction that is based primarily upon length. Jeremiah, one of the major prophets, has 1,364 verses while Obadiah, one of the minor prophets, has only 21 verses.

We are going to study the prophets on the basis of the time in which they were called by God to deliver their prophecies. On this basis they divide into two groups: the pre-exilic and exilic prophets (8th -6th centuries BCE) and the post-Exilic prophets (after 538 BCE). Although the Bible groups the prophets from longest in length to shortest in length, it offers more meaning to read them in historical, chronological order.

PROPHETS ARRANGED HISTORICALLY
The prophets and their historical periods[84]

> 8th century BCE prophets: **Amos** (c.750), **Hosea** (c. 745), **First Isaiah** (c.742-700), and **Micah** (c. 722-701).

> Late 7th century BCE prophets: **Zephaniah** (c. 628-622), **Jeremiah** (c. 626-587), **Nahum** (c. 612), and **Habakkuk** (c. 605).

> 6th Century BCE prophets: **Ezekiel** (c. 593-573), and **Obadiah** (after 587).

The period of the restoration during and after the return from Exile in 538 BCE: **Second Isaiah** (c. 540), **Third Isaiah** (c. 540), **Haggai** (c. 520-515), **Zechariah** (c. 520-515), **Malachi** (c. 500-450) and **Joel** (c. 500-350).

A Word About Daniel

In the Orthodox Christian, Protestant and Catholic bibles, Daniel is placed between the major and minor prophets because some see it as a book of prophecy. In the *Tanakh,* Daniel is included among the writings. This disagreement most likely arises from a difference in opinion as to who Daniel was understood to have been. The Christians most likely understood Daniel to be a prophet in the distant past of Israel. The Jews most likely understood him to be the Daniel

---

[84] Anderson, 265.

introduced as a proverbial figure of wisdom in Ezek 28:3.[85] Locating the Book of Daniel with the writings is, perhaps, a more appropriate place since Daniel was probably written early in the second century BCE, long after the age of prophecy was believed to have ended. Furthermore, it is written in a form that is closer to that of the wisdom books than it is to the form of the prophetic writings. We will, consequently, study the Book of Daniel in association with the wisdom books of the Second Temple Period.

A Word About Jonah

In all of the major bibles Jonah is presented as one of the minor prophets. Jonah is not, however, anything like the other writings that are attributed to prophets. It is not a collection of prophetic oracles. In fact, it contains no oracles at all – only a report of Jonah's message to the citizens of Nineveh in verse 3:5. This composition is about a prophet, named Jonah, and his interaction with God and its purpose is to teach a lesson about God. The study of this writing will, therefore, be taken up in the chapter on folk literature.

The Nature of the Prophetic Writings

Who is a prophet? Our English word comes to us from the Greek word *prophetes*. In ancient Greece, a "prophet" was one who spoke for the gods. It adaptation into the language of the Bible means a prophet is one who speaks for God. The biblical sense of the Greek word *prohetes* accurately relates to the Hebrew word *nabi* which refers to one who communicates the divine will.[86]

The words of the prophets appear in the writings of Scripture as "oracles." These oracles are composed in short Hebrew poetic style. All the oracles have been collected together, then, in the books of the prophets.

Three very significant points follow from this definition:

- ❖ On the basis of this definition it is apparent that a prophet is a person through whom God speaks to the people. The prophet functioned as **God's spokesperson**. (See Jer 1:9).[87]

- ❖ The prophets saw themselves as messengers **sent** by God to communicate the word of Yahweh to the people.[88] The prophet Amos said : "The lion has roared; who will not fear? The Lord God has spoken; who can but prophesy?" (Am 3:8).
  A prophetic oracle frequently begins with the messenger formula "Thus says YHWH" and concludes with "the oracle of YHWH." (Amos 1:3-5; Jer 2:1-3; Is   45:11-13).

---

[85] Louis F. Hartman, C.SS.R and Alexander A. Di Lella, O.F.M., *The Book of Daniel*, Anchor Bible, V. 23 (Garden City, NY: Doubleday & Company, Inc., 1978), 7.
[86] Bernhard W. Anderson, *Understanding the Old Testament*, Third Edition (Englewood Cliffs, NJ: Prentice-Hall, Inc., 1975), 226.
[87] Anderson, 227.
[88] Anderson 229.

121

❖ The communication that the prophet delivered was **primarily directed to the people of his day**; however, there is also found an enduring message for all times. The task of the prophet was to communicate Yahweh's message for **now** [i.e. the "now" of the prophet!], and to seek the response of **the prophet's people today** [i.e. the "today" of the prophet's people].[89]

The belief that God spoke through the prophets was held by the Christians of the NT period. The author of the Letter to the Hebrews stated that: "In times past, God spoke in partial and various ways to our ancestors through the prophets" (Heb 1:1). The author of The Second Letter of Peter stated the same belief in an even fuller way:

> Know first of all, that there is no prophecy of Scripture that is a matter of personal interpretation, for no prophecy ever came through human will; but rather human beings moved by the Holy Spirit spoke under the influence of God. (2 Pt 1:20-21)

The Importance of the Historical Context

Each of the prophets was called by God at a specific period in the history of Israel. The prophetic message given to the prophet was related to the historic moment. This is one reason, for instance, why scholars will divide the long Book of Isaiah into three historical periods: Proto-Isaiah (First Isaiah), Deutero-Isaiah (Second Isaiah), and Tertio-Isaiah (Third Isaiah). The historical relevance, as an example, can be seen in First Isaiah (Is Chaps. 1-39 of Isaiah) which concludes with a lengthy historical "appendix" (Chaps. 36-39) that is adapted from 2 Kgs 18:13-20:19. In a similar manner Jeremiah concludes with an historical "appendix" (52:1-34) adapted from 2 Kgs 24:18-25:30.

It is apparent, therefore, that it is necessary in preparing to read one of the prophets to first learn something about the particular historical moment in which the prophet was active. Putting this another way, it is seen that the oracles of the prophets are read with greatest meaning if they are read together with the corresponding historical narratives contained in the books of history.

The Composition of the Prophetic Books

To speak of prophetic writings is perhaps somewhat misleading. In much of this material, the words appear to have first been spoken by the prophet, treasured by the people, and subsequently written down, presumably by a scribe. This leaves the question open as to whether the prophet delivered his message in fine poetical form or whether the message was subsequently put in poetical form by a scribe.

---

[89] Anderson 230.

Evidence supporting the view that scribes wrote down what the prophets said is perhaps provided by the following two passages from the book of Jeremiah:

This word of the LORD came to Jeremiah, after the king burned the scroll with the text Jeremiah had dictated to Baruch: Take another scroll, and write on it everything that the first scroll contained, which Jehoiakim, king of Judah, burned up. (Jer 36:27-28, NAB)

This is the message that the prophet Jeremiah gave to Baruch, son of Neriah, when he wrote in a book the prophecies that Jeremiah dictated in the fourth year of Jehoiakim, son of Josiah, king of Judah: …. (Jer 45:1, NAB)

One thing is clear. Christians of the first century CE truly believed that God spoke through the prophets, in many ways prophesying that a messiah was to come. That is to say, the prophet delivered a message that he had received directly from God. This was the belief of the early Christians, that God speaks to humanity, as supported by both **Heb 1:1** and **2 Pt 1:20-21**. This can definitely be seen happening even if written down by a scribe.

Some prominent literary forms in the books of the prophets

The Messenger Formula

A prophetic speech often begins with the phrase: "says the LORD" and frequently ends with the repetition of the same phrase. Examples of this are seen in: Is 45:11 and 13; Jer 4:1; 17:5; Amos 1:1; 1:5; 2:6 and 2:16.

The Call Narrative

First in the life of a prophet is the experience of receiving a **call** (or as it is also frequently called, the commission) from God to be a prophet. The written record of this experience is termed "the call narrative." Although the call comes first chronologically in the life of the prophet, it does not necessarily come first in the book because of the lack of a strict chronological order.

Amos tells us of his call to be a prophet in the following brief passage:

Then Amos answered Amaziah, ""I am no prophet, nor a prophet's son; but I am a herdsman, and a dresser of sycamore trees, and the LORD took me from following the flock, and the LORD said to me, 'Go, prophesy to my people Israel.' Now therefore hear the word of the LORD." (Am 7:14-16, NRSV)

Isaiah relates his call to be a prophet in a much more lengthy account than did Amos. The commission of Isaiah is received in conjunction with a vision of God sitting in the heavenly court (Is 6:1-13).For many people today, the words of Is 6:3 will most likely sound very familiar.

Here are some other examples of call narratives: **Jer 1:4-10; Ez 2:1-3:3.** There are call narratives for prophets outside of these fifteen books: Samuel **(1 Sm 3:1-18)** and Elisha **(1 Kgs 19:19-21).**

The Prophetic Oracle

It is well established that the prophets first delivered their messages from God orally. They were spoken. At some later time, they were written down – perhaps by the prophet himself or perhaps by one of his followers. These pronouncements are called "oracles." In general the word "**oracle**" is understood to represent words that are divine in nature, in a sense from the mouth of God through a human voice.

The **basic unit** in the books of prophecy is, therefore, the **prophetic oracle**. These oracles are quite brief in length and the prophet frequently delivered the message in the first person as if God was doing the speaking (e.g. Am 8:9-12). They are predominantly in the Hebrew form of poetry although sometimes they are in prose, Jer 8:4-7 being an example of the poetical form and Jer 8:1-3 an example of the prose form.

The oracles are frequently marked at the beginning, at the end, or less frequently both at the beginning and the end (e.g. Am 1:6-8) by an expression such as: "Thus says the Lord"(e.g. Am 1:3), "says the Lord" (e.g. Am 2:3), or "says the Lord your God"(e.g. Am 9:15). These expressions are used to indicate that the prophet is delivering a message from God. On the basis of these expressions and the content and form of the oracle itself, it is possible to identify the individual oracles which in the manuscripts are all "run together" (i.e. there are no breaks between them!). In most modern bible translations, the individual oracles are separated by "white spaces." If you compare bibles, you will experience the fact that in many places there are disagreements as to where the individual oracles begin and end (the "white spaces" being in different places). This indicates that it remains with the translators to judge where the oracle begins and ends.

Oracle of judgment

A common form of oracle is the **oracle of judgment**. An example of this type of oracle is **Am 2:6-8**. The following oracle is from Amos:

> Thus says the LORD:
> For three transgressions of Judah
> and for four, I will not revoke the
> punishment;
> because they have rejected the law of
> the LORD,
> and have not kept his statutes,
> but they have been led astray by the
> same lies
> after which their ancestors walked.
> So I will send fire on Judah,
> and it shall devour the strongholds
> of Jerusalem.
> (Am 2:4-5, NRSV)

124

Oracle of salvation

A less common form of oracle is the **oracle of salvation**. An example of this type is **Am 9:13-15**.

If you look closely at the oracle in Am 2:4-5, you will see that the first part of it states that God will impose a punishment and specifies that the offending party, in this case Judah, has done wrong in the eyes of God (v. 4). The last part of the oracle describes what the punishment will be (v. 5). This two part structure is common in this type of oracle, although the order of the two parts is sometimes reversed.

With the passing of time in later prophets, the short oracle was gradually supplanted by poems of greater length. This is evident in *Jeremiah and Ezekiel*. It can also be observed in *2nd Isaiah* (i.e. Is 40-55) which consists of a relatively small number of quite lengthy poems.

Editing of the Prophetic Books

The books of the prophets as they come "down" to us give evidence of having passed through a process consisting of three phases. These phases must have been something like the following:[90]

- ✓ The individual oracles were uttered by the prophet and at some later time written down by a scribe or one of his followers.

- ✓ The individual oracles were, at some point, fashioned into a coherent composition based upon organizational principles now only known by examining the text itself.

- ✓ At some still later point, other oracles, not directly related to those of the original prophet, were attached to the earlier oracles; the reason for the attachment of these later oracles being, perhaps, to interpret the earlier oracles for a later time.

The following quote from Lawrence Boadt is helpful in clarifying this matter:

> When trying to capture the spirit of the prophet's thought, readers often assume that every word comes from the prophet himself. Yet the titles of books under individual names such as Amos or Hosea do not imply that they contain just the words of Amos or Hosea, but also words **about, and in the tradition of**, the prophet. Nor are the oracles and sayings necessarily in the logical or chronological order that we would like. Ancient editors collected and arranged words spoken by these prophets in an order that seemed important to them but often escapes us. Editors frequently added words taken from disciples of the prophet, or even unknown prophetic words that are similar in theme and which add to the thought of the prophet in whose book they are included. Even more dramatically, later generations who cherished the words of an Amos or Micah

---

[90] John Barton, "Prophecy (Postexilic Hebrew)" in *The Anchor Bible Dictionary*, V. v, David Noel Freedman, Editor-in-Chief (New York, NY: Doubleday, 1992), 494-495.

occasionally added new applications and comments from their own centuries to the collected words of the long-dead prophet. [91]

A confirmation that this editing has occurred is provided by the manuscripts discovered at Qumran by the Dead Sea. The manuscripts of the Septuagint translation of the text of Jeremiah found at Qumran are 1/8th shorter and have a different arrangement of the contents than do the manuscripts of the Masoretic text (translated after the time of Christ) which are the basis for Jeremiah in most modern bibles. This difference can be explained if the modern version is compared to the Septuagint text from Qumran and it is noted that the additional length is due to a series of additions to the ends of the various units and to a rearrangement of the order of the contents. The Septuagint text is a translation of a version of Jeremiah earlier than that which appears in most English translations. In prior centuries, an earlier text which had been used by the translators of the Septuagint (Hebrew into Greek) was then both edited and rearranged before being translated for our English Bibles.

The Development of the Forms of Prophetic Literature

It is fairly evident that the early prophets borrowed forms from everyday life. For example, the "covenant lawsuit" was based on the proceedings of the law court. In the prophets, God is seen as bringing a lawsuit against the people to show that he has been offended. For example, in this presentation of a lawsuit against the nation of Israel in Hosea, chapter 4:

Hear the word of the LORD, you Israelites!
For the LORD has a covenant lawsuit against the people of Israel.
For there is neither faithfulness nor loyalty in the land,
nor do they acknowledge God.
2 There is only cursing, lying, murder, stealing, and adultery.
They resort to violence and bloodshed.
3 Therefore the land will mourn,
and all its inhabitants will perish.
The wild animals, the birds of the sky,
and even the fish in the sea will perish.
4Do not let anyone accuse or contend against anyone else:
for my case is against you priests!
5 You stumble day and night,
and the false prophets stumble with you;
You have destroyed your own people!
6 You have destroyed my people
by failing to acknowledge me!
Because you refuse to acknowledge me,
I will reject you as my priests.
Because you reject the law of your God,
I will reject your descendants.
7 The more the priests increased in numbers,
the more they rebelled against me.

---

[91] Lawrence Boadt, *Reading the Old Testament* (New York, NY: Paulist Press, 1984), 313.

126

They have turned their glorious calling
into a shameful disgrace!
8 They feed on the sin offerings of my people;
their appetites long for their iniquity!
9 I will deal with the people and priests together:
I will punish them both for their ways,
and I will repay them for their deeds.
10 They will eat, but not be satisfied;
they will engage in prostitution, but not increase in numbers;
because they have abandoned the LORD
by pursuing other gods.

However, it is also apparent that the postexilic prophets failed to follow in the footsteps of their predecessors. Instead of using images borrowed from their everyday experiences, these later prophets cast their writing into specialized forms which then became recognized as the "normal" prophetic style. The postexilic prophets did, however, imitate the earlier forms of prophetic speech. [92]

Certain forms that occur only sparingly in the pre-exilic prophetic writings, come into great use in the postexilic period. The allegory and the extended vision report are two such forms. A growing interest in eschatology (reference to end times) is characteristic of the later prophets. There is evidence to suggest that prophecy gradually changed from a largely oral communication into a written communication. Oral delivery, on the one hand, requires immediate impact and a form that can be easily remembered while written composition, on the other hand, remains on the page for a considerable length of time and then does not require such immediacy and ease of remembering since it is written on a keepsake scroll.[93]

On reading a book of prophecy

It is essential, when reading one of the prophetic books, to take into account that it is a collection of prophetic oracles. You cannot just read through such a book as if it were a secular story or some other type of systematic writing. It must be read in terms of the (small) units of which it is composed. It is essential to recognize this because the historical context (date) and even the audience can vary from one oracle to the next. Furthermore, it cannot be assumed that the order is chronological.

When reading the prophetic books it is essential to pay attention to the "white spaces," as mentioned. To see what the term "**white space**" means, go to Jeremiah 2 and take note of the separations between verses 3 and 4, 6 and 7, 13 and 14, 19 and 20, and so on. (You may find that in your Bible the white spaces come at different points in the text) These separations are the "white spaces." The function of these spaces is to inform the reader where one oracle ends and the next oracle begins.

---

[92] Barton, 494.
[93] Barton, 494.

If you compare several different translations of a prophetic book you will find that not all translations place the blank spaces at the same points in the text. In the manuscripts from which the various translations are made do not separate the oracles one from another; they are presented run together. The person doing the translation, therefore, must decide at what point each oracle begins and ends. It is not uncommon for the experts translating a text to disagree on this matter thereby giving rise to differences in the locations of the white spaces.

This is all the more important because, for the most part, the oracles do not appear in chronological order with the earliest first and the most recent last. For example, in the book of Isaiah, the call of the prophet comes in Chapter 6, not at the beginning of Chapter 1. Isaiah has been preaching for five chapters before he receives his call to be a prophet! It is not unusual in these books to find the most recent material at the beginning and the older material following it.

To study one of these books, therefore, you must first study the details of each of the small units - the oracles. Each must be appreciated fully on its own merit. Then you must study how they are grouped together - first into small groups and then into larger groups. Finally, you must step back and appreciate the book as a whole. The foundation of the book is certainly a collection of messages from God received by the prophet whose name is affixed to the book. But there may be an additional message from God brought to us through the work of an editor or editors, and one or more redactors who produced the final work.

Reading one of the prophetic books is something like doing a picture puzzle. You see these puzzles in the stores. Some have 500 pieces, some have 750 pieces and others have 1,000 pieces or more. When putting together a puzzle that is a beautiful picture – by fitting together, sometimes on the basis of matching the colors and other times on the basis of matching shapes, one piece at a time – it is obvious that the final effect of the picture and its meaning isn't seen until all pieces are placed. The prophetic book can be thought of as a puzzle to be fitted together one oracle at a time. Looking at it in this manner it is seen that Amos presents a relatively easy task – it only has some 27 pieces. Isaiah, on the other hand, promises to be much more of a challenge – it has a great number of pieces and they are quite intricately fit together.

Use a Good Commentary

Just from this very brief introduction to the prophetic literature it can be seen that you should not attempt to read a book of prophecy in depth without the aid of a good commentary! The information given in a study bible in introductions to the writing and in the footnotes (as well as attached maps, glossaries, etc.) is also invaluable. Each oracle must be understood in the context in which it was first delivered and in the context to which it may be been adapted later. The determination of its extent, the dating of it and the identification of its historical context requires a very great deal of careful scholarship. This task is best left to the scholars.

In comparing translations

The books of the prophets are among the most difficult books in the Scriptures to compare one translation with another. This is due to a number of factors: 1) The problem of the **white spaces** – determining where an oracle begins and ends, 2) the problem of whether to translate the passage as prose or poetry, 3) the problem of **verse numbering** – there is a Hebrew verse numbering and an English verse numbering, and 4) the problem of **translation** itself – these texts are intrinsically difficult to translate in themselves. This is a very real difficulty!

Looking ahead

This phenomenon of finding that the biblical text is constructed from small, independent units will come up again when we consider the gospels. At that time, we will find that, in a similar manner, they (except for John) have been constructed from small units.

Suggested Reading

Joseph Blenkinsopp, "Introduction to the Prophetic Books," in *Harper's Bible Commentary*, San Francisco, Harper & Row, 1988, 530-541.

THE MESSAGE OF THE PROPHETS

The major content of each of the prophets will be described below in the following short summaries:

AMOS

Amos says that he is not a professional prophet but a herdsman and dresser of sycamores and that God told him to go prophesy to the people of Israel, the Northern Kingdom (7:14-15). Among his oracles are the following:

- In 2:6-12, through Amos, God tells the Israelites some of the reasons why he is finding fault with them.
- Through Amos, God reviews some of the things he has done in order to encourage Israel to return to him (4:6-12).
- In 5:14-15, Amos states that God says he will show mercy if the people will hate evil and love good.

HOSEA

Hosea preached from his homeland – the Northern Kingdom. He founded the practice of treating the relationship between God and Israel in terms of marriage, a practice that was applied in the New Testament to the relationship between Christ and the Christian community. On the basis of this symbolism, the failure of Hosea's marriage to Gomer represents the failure of Israel to keep their covenant with God. The following is a sampling of the preaching of Hosea:

- 4:1-14, begins the series of oracles between 4:1-4 and 11:11, that ends with "oracle of the Lord." These oracles all express God's case against Israel except for verses 11:1-11, that expresses the thought that parental love is stronger than the misbehavior of the child.
- In 14:1, Samaria, the capital of the Northern Kingdom, is told that it will fall.

FIRST ISAIAH (Is Chs. 1-39)

First Isaiah is a very long writing and it is difficult to pick out a small sample to represent the whole composition. Hopefully the following will suffice.

- The call narrative which is very well known (6:1-13).
- In the 3rd edition of *The Catholic Study Bible* the following statement appears in a footnote:[94]

> **1:2-31** This chapter is widely considered to be a collection of oracles from various periods in Isaiah's ministry, chosen by the editor as a compendium of his most characteristic teachings.

On the basis of this statement let us accept the following seven oracles as representing Isaiah's teaching:
a. 1:2-3 God accuses Israel for not knowing God
b. 1:4-9 They have forsaken the LORD
c. 1:10-17 Things Israel should be doing
d. 1:18-20 The faithful must be willing and obey
e. 1:21-26 The LORD will restore Jerusalem
f. 1:27-28 The fates of the redeemed and the unrepentant
g. 1:29-31 Judgment on the sacred groves

MICAH

The superscription identifies Micah as a resident of Moresheth, a small village in the Judean hills, and that he was a contemporary of Isaiah. Micah's ministry was focused on Jerusalem and the Judean leadership. The following is a sample of his work as a prophet:

- The oracle 2:1-2 is one of the charges that the LORD has against Judah.
- In 4:1-5, the prophet Micah delivers that there will come a period of peace that is based on a just order where all are obedient to the divine will.
- In 6:8, Micah delivers a simple statement of what God seeks from every human being. This passage is well worth the time that it takes to read it!

ZEPHANIAH

The title of this composition tells us that the ministry of Zephaniah took place during the reign of King Josiah (640-609 BCE). Prominent among his prophecies are the following:

- Judgment on Judah (1:2-2:3)
- Judgment on Jerusalem (3:1-7)

NAHUM

Nahum prophesied in 612 BC against Nineveh at a time that was just a short time before its fall. Nineveh was the capital city of Assyria which had ruled for a very long time in a bloody and violent way over many nations. Assyria had devoured the Northern Kingdom in 722 BCE. The following is a sampling of the prophecy of Nahum:

---

[94] *The Catholic tudy Bible*, Third Edition, p. 990.

- In 1:2-8, the prophet Nahum presents a partial description of God.
- Nahum delivers a message that the end of Nineveh is inescapable (3:18-19)

HABAKKUK

The writing that is titled "Habakkuk" is very different from the writings of the other prophets. It does not contain a collection of prophetic oracles. Instead, it contains primarily a dialogue between the prophet, Habakkuk and his god Yahweh. Its primary content is as follows:

- The first complaint of Habakkuk (1:2-4) and God's first response (1:5-11).
- The second complaint of Habakkuk (1:12-2:1) and God's second response (2:2-4).

The most famous saying of this composition is without doubt verse 2:4 which reads as follows: "the just one who is righteous because of faith shall live." Remember that God is Life! Those who are "just" – those who are right with God and close to God – they will know God and be with God who is life itself!

CHAPTER SIXTEEN

THE BOOK OF PSALMS

Introduction

Since ancient times, psalms have been the core of Hebrew and Christian worship and prayer. Psalms are poetic hymns, many of which originated from the time of King David. Today, the most common encounter with psalms will be during a church service when often only a few lines of a psalm are sung or recited. A glance in most books of worship show that the verses being recited are a selection from the complete psalm. Seldom do the faithful experience a psalm either as a complete individual composition or as part of a collection. From a literary standpoint, however, it is important to encounter the psalms as complete compositions and as members of a collection as well.

It is also important to realize that in the Book of Psalms, one experiences mankind talking to God! The very fact that these compositions are part of the Bible means that it is a lovely form of prayer that is a conversation of the faithful with God. They are prayers that praise God, petition God for help, and reach toward an ever-deeper relationship with Him.

Looking at Two Psalms

The following are two psalms from the Book of Psalms:

Psalm 24
Of David. A Psalm.

The earth is the LORD's and all that is in it,
the world and those who live in it;
for he has founded it on the seas,
and established it on the rivers.

Who shall ascend the hill of the LORD?
And who shall stand in his holy place?
Those who have clean hands and pure hearts,
Who do not lift up their souls to what is false,
and do not swear deceitfully.
They will receive blessing from the LORD,
and vindication from the God of their salvation.
Such is the company of those who seek him,
who seek the face of the God of Jacob.

Lift up your heads, O gates!
and be lifted up, O ancient doors!
that the King of glory may come in.
Who is the King of glory?

The LORD, strong and mighty,
the LORD, mighty in battle.
Lift up your heads, O gates!
and be lifted up, O ancient doors!
that the King of glory may come in.
Who is the King of glory?
The LORD of hosts,
he is the King of glory.

Psalm 30
A Psalm. A Song at the dedication of the
Temple. Of David.

I will extol you, O LORD, for you
have drawn me up,
and did not let my foes rejoice over me.
O LORD my God, I cried to you for help,
and you have healed me.
O LORD, you brought up my soul from Sheol,
restored me to life from among
those gone down to the Pit.

Sing praises to the LORD, O you his faithful ones,
and give thanks to his holy name.
For his anger is but for a moment;
his favor is for a lifetime.
Weeping may linger for the night,
but joy comes with the morning.

As for me, I said in my prosperity,
"I shall never be moved."
By your favor, O LORD,
you had established me as a strong mountain;
you hid your face;
I was dismayed.

To you, O LORD, I cried,
and to the LORD I made supplication:
"What profit is there in my death,
if I go down to the pit?
Will the dust praise you?
Will it tell of your faithfulness?
Hear, O LORD, and be gracious to me!
O LORD, be my helper!"

You have turned my mourning into dancing;
you have taken off my sackcloth
and clothed me with joy,
so that my soul may praise you and
not be silent.
O LORD my God, I will give thanks
to you forever.

Looking at these two psalms, we observe the following:

- ❖ **The psalms are addressed to God** – This is apparent in the case of Psalm 30 (see 30:1). This is somewhat less obvious in the case of Psalm 24.

- ❖ **A psalm is written in the form of poetry** – A psalm is inherently poetical in nature. It should, therefore, be printed in the form of poetry, as it is in both the NAB and NRSV. This has not always been the case, however! The psalms in the older *Confraternity Version* are printed in prose. Because the psalms are poetry, the reader should always be on the lookout for the use of parallelism in the text.

- ❖ **Many psalms, like Ps 30, are expressed in the first person singular, "I"** – The fact that a psalm is expressed in the first person singular should not be taken to imply that the psalm is only to be utilized by an individual believer. In support of this, one needs look no further than the Creed which is recited during the weekly worship service. In many churches the congregation says "we believe" while in other churches the congregation booms out "I believe."

- ❖ **Every psalm has a type** – Psalm 24 is a liturgical psalm. It was intended to be used in conjunction with the liturgical action of entering the sanctuary. Psalm 30, on the other hand, is a thanksgiving psalm that was intended to be recited after recovery from a serious illness. As with all attempts to fit literary works into neat categories there will be exceptions: some psalms are of mixed types and a few psalms do not fit any of the types.

- ❖ **Every type of psalm also has a form** – All of the psalms of a given type are constructed on the basis of a number of "parts." These parts are common to all of the psalms of a given type. These "parts" are determined by comparing all of the psalms of a given type. This matter is complicated somewhat by the fact that not every psalm of a given type contains every one of the "parts" that characterize that type of psalm. It should also be pointed out that the order in which the "parts" occur differs from psalm to psalm.

- ❖ **Each psalm has a number** – This number is **not** part of the psalm; it only indicates the position of the psalm in the Book of Psalms. It serves to make it easy to locate the particular psalm in the book. For example, Psalm 23 of the

NAB and NRSV appears as Psalm 22 in the older *Catholic Confraternity Version*.

❖ **These two psalms have a heading** – The heading varies from psalm to psalm. For example, Psalm 33 does not have a heading; Psalm 18 has a very long heading; the heading of Psalm 35 only states that it is "Of David." **Note:** If you have a *New American Bible* (NAB) your verse numbers in the psalms may be one digit higher than the corresponding verse numbers in the NRSV version. This difference arises from the practice of the NAB to assign the number "1" to the heading rather than to the first verse, as does the NRSV version.

What is a Psalm?

What is a psalm? Very simply put, **a psalm is a Hebrew poetical composition**. What follows from this statement? Quite a great deal!

First of all, a psalm is a **composition**. This means that it a coherent literary piece purposely written to serve a specific function. Psalms serve one (sometimes more than one) of four general functions: prayer, praise, thanksgiving and instruction. The style and content of the psalm give evidence of its intended function.[95]

Secondly, a psalm is expressed by means of **Hebrew Poetry**. Mays puts it in the following way:

> Hebrew poetry is written in units that can be called lines and measures. Lines are usually composed of two or three measures (cola). In the printed text, lines begin at the left-hand margin and the following measure or measures are indented. In psalm 3 each verse is a line of two measures except for verse 7, which contains two lines. In Hebrew, the lines were composed so that they could be chanted or sung in a rhythm. Obviously, the rhythm cannot be reproduced in translations, but it is possible to turn psalms into metrical hymns and chants in English.[96]

Mays goes on to speak of **parallelism**, a very prominent formal feature of Hebrew poetry. Mays describes parallelism in the following manner:

> Parallelism is another formal feature of Hebrew poetry that can be observed in English, and it is far more important for the interpreter. The sense or content of the measures in a line is parallel. In one way of another, the sense of the second measure and the third, if there is one, corresponds to that of the first. Sometimes there is parallelism even between lines. The ways in which the parallels work cannot be reduced to a few categories. The parallels are as varied as the ingenuity of the psalmist allows. In verse 1[of Ps 3], the second measure repeats the first in

---

[95] James Luther Mays, *Psalms* (Louisville, KY: John Knox Press, 1994), 6.
[96] James Luther Mays,5.

other words. In verse 2, the first measure introduces a quotation and the second gives it. The first two lines are bound also. The first tells what the enemies do and the second, what they say. As one tracks the parallels through the rest of the psalm, one uncovers a typical variety of the relationships. Reading a psalm according to the parallels in measures and lines is important. The parallels make up one dimension of the artistic form and structure of thought in a psalm.[97]

Mays concludes by speaking about one other feature of the Hebrew poetry of the psalms: the **high density of rhetorical devices**. He says:

> Besides the formal features of lines, measures, rhythm, and parallelism, psalmic poetry is characterized by some semantic features. The psalms contain a high density of rhetorical devices. Similes, metaphors, idiomatic expressions, and hyperbole particularly are frequent. Psalm 3 illustrates several of the devices: metaphor, "God is a shield" (v.3); idiom, "strike the cheek and break the teeth" (v.7); hyperbole, the portrayal of the enemies as innumerable (vv. 1,2,6); and similes, all the "like" phrases in Ps 1. The density of these rhetorical devices in the psalms says something important to the interpreter. Psalms are not to be read in a literal way, as if the reference of their language were denotative on a flat level. As with poetry in general, their language is that of indirection and evocation. One has to read with a patient tentativeness and an awareness of the intentional, multivalent quality of the language.[98]

One very important aspect of the psalms remains to be emphasized. **The psalms are mankind speaking to God.** Humans are speaking from the depths of their being to the all-transcendent God. But at the same time, due to the nature of these writings being inspired texts, the Psalms represent God responding to human beings, revealing that it is proper and right that they address the transcendent Deity in this manner.

Types and Forms of the Psalms

Many people of the 21st century fail to realize that each psalm is a complete poetical composition having meaning and that the psalms come in different types with each type having its own particular form. There are **four prominent types** of psalms[99]:

1. **The prayer for help of an individual**
   These psalms have 6 elements:
   > a. They frequently begin with the **title "Lord"** and they are written in the first person as direct address to God.
   > b. The basic element is the **petition** in which the psalmist asks to be heard and/or helped.
   > c. There is a description of the **needs** of the psalmist (i.e. of the difficulty).
   > d. Supporting **reasons why** the petition should be heard.

---

[97] Mays 5-6.
[98] Mays, 6.
[99] James L. Mays, *Psalms* (Louisville, Kentucky: John Knox Press, 1994),19-29.

e. Confessions of **trust in God.**

f. Statement of a **promise** to praise God when the petition has been granted.

For a psalm that is a good example of this type see **Ps 13.** There is no standard order of the 6 elements; they can appear in any order.

2.   **Thanksgiving song of an individual**
     These psalms typically consist of 3 elements as follows:
     a.   Praise addressed to God that **rehearses** the cry for help and **reports** God's response of hearing and help.
     b.   A **summons** to a community of worship to join the praise and testimony to them.
     c.   A **presentation** of praise and/or sacrifice to keep promises made in the prayer for help.
     Typical psalms of this type are: **Ps 30** and **Ps 116.**

3.   **The corporate prayer for help**
     These psalms consist of 6 elements much like the psalms in category #1 above:
     a.   **Petitions** to hear and help (this is the principle element!).
     b.   A **description** of the trouble which includes: statement of God's absence or wrath, the community's humiliation and suffering, the power and arrogance of the enemies.
     c.   An **appeal** to the community's relation to God and of God's honor.
     d.   An assertion of **trust** in God.
     e.   **Rehearsal** of what God has done in the past for the community and perhaps even in the creation.
     f.   **Praise** is promised in gratitude for the help.
     Clear examples are: **Pss 44, 74, 79, 80 and 83.**

4.   **The hymn**
The hymn is the primary genre of praise. It is a song of praise of which God is the sole subject. Its language is that of joy. It states what God is like, has done and characteristically does! The cry "**Hallelujah**" is a hymn expressed in one Hebrew sentence. It consists of the plural imperative summons to praise (hallelu) and the short form of God's name Yahweh (*jah*).

5. There are **other literary types.** These include: psalms intended **to instruct** (e.g. **Pss 1, 19 and 119**); **procession and entrance psalms** (e.g. **Ps 118**); **songs of ascent** (e.g. **Pss 120-134**) and **royal psalms** (e.g. **Pss 2,101,110**).

The Origin of the Individual Psalms

The psalms were written over a long period of time: some of them may go back as far as the reign of King David (ca. 950 BCE); the most recent were composed in the postexilic period (after 538 BCE). Kselman states:

The times of composition of the psalms range across at least five centuries; the earliest psalm is probably Ps 29, which is adapted from early Canaanite worship, while several psalms contain contextual (e.g. Ps 126) linguistic or other evidence that they are from the postexilic period (Pss 51; 114; 137). While most psalms are Judean in origin, the language of internal references in several psalms suggest that they originated in the Northern Kingdom (e.g., Ps 80 and Ps 81, which contain references to Joseph); these most likely were brought to Judah after the destruction of the Northern Kingdom in 722 BCE. The majority of the psalms, however, originated in the preexilic, monarchic period, and are associated with the Jerusalem Temple.[100]

The psalm texts give evidence of the fact that they were composed initially by individuals of great poetic skill and firm belief. But the identity of these writers is entirely unknown because the psalm texts give little to no evidence of the specifics of the who, when and why of their composition.

Each psalm is a unique creation. Each psalm must have come into being at some specific moment in time and some specific historical moment. But as they come down to us they have been generalized, "smoothed" and now offer only a few clues as to their origin.

The Origin of the collection of Psalms

Mays describes the origin of the Book of Psalms in the following way:

> The composition, transmission, and collection of the psalms and the formation of the book were a very long process that stretched across eras of change. The preservation of the psalms was not a neutral archival process but involved the selection, reuse, revision and grouping of the psalms that went with their constant use in Israel's worship, the devotion of circles of the faithful, and the emergence of Scripture. The Book of Psalms is the deposit of that long process.[101]

Overall Organization of the Collection of Psalms in the Scriptures

It is not difficult to see that the collection of Psalms contained in the Scriptures has a particular overall organization. That organization is as follows:

- ❖ Psalms 1 and 2 function as an introduction to the entire collection.

- ❖ The book is divided into five parts, each part concluding with a doxology.
  - Book 1 – Psalms 3-41; doxology v. 41:13.
  - Book 2 – Psalms 42-72; doxology vv. 72:18-19.
  - Book 3 – Psalms 73-89; doxology v. 89:52
  - Book 4 – Psalms 90-106; doxology v. 106:48

---

[100] John S. Kselman, "Psalms" in *The New Oxford Annotated Bible*, Third Edition, Michael D. Coogan, Editor (New York, NY: Oxford University Press, 2001), 775.
[101] James Luther Mays, 19.

- Book 5 – Psalms 107-149; doxology Ps 150.

It should be noted that the concluding doxology of Book 5 has been elevated to the status of a psalm. Psalm 150, consequently, functions as both the concluding psalm of Book5 and the concluding doxology of the entire Book of Psalms.

Some scholars have suggested that this five-part structure is based upon the five part structure of the Pentateuch.

Psalm 151

Psalm 151 is considered to be canonical (inspired by God) by Orthodox Christians. It is not considered canonical by Jews, Catholics and Protestants.

The Greek text that we have of this psalm has been shown by the manuscript discoveries at Qumran to be a combination of two Hebrew poems. Verses 1-5, describing God's choice of David to be king, is the entirety of the first of these Hebrew poems and verses 6-7, telling of David's killing of Goliath, are the first two lines of the second Hebrew of the two poems.

The seven verses of Psalm 151 are written in the form of an autobiographical account as seen by the use of the first person singular, "I." It doesn't seem that it was not composed by King David, however, but many centuries later by an individual who is unknown to us today.

The first part of the psalm, verses 1-5, speak about God's choice of David as king and his anointing by Samuel. This is a condensation of 1 Sam 16:1-13. The second part, verses 6-7, tells about David beheading Goliath with his sword. These two verses make use of 1 Sam 17:51 but does not tell about David's killing Goliath with his "sling and stone" (1 Sam 17:48-50).

What is the theological meaning the lies behind the very brief Psalm 151. Daniel Harrington expresses this as follows:

> Psalm 151 reflects the main themes of 1 Samuel 16-17: God chose David to be the king of Israel despite his being a young shepherd, and used David and his slingshot to defeat the powerful Philistine warrior Goliath. The theological lesson is that the God of Israel can and does rescue his people from their sufferings in surprising ways. In danger of being conquered by the Philistines, Israel was delivered by a young shepherd with a laughably weak weapon. The mighty and faithful God can and does use such weak means as a way of showing that God (and not the armies of Israel) was responsible for the people's deliverance. This theological theme runs through both Testaments from start to finish.[102]

Conclusion

The psalms are a vibrant part of the OT and understanding that they are each a complete composition and that each one belongs to a certain collection of psalms helps the reader to delve

---

[102] Daniel J. Harrington, S.J., 171.

deeper into their meaning. The elements of Hebrew poetry, especially the parallelism, should be reflected upon carefully. The fact that the lines are the same in parallel meaning or exhibit opposite parallel meaning is an ancient way of expanding or detailing a concept, often something mystical and deep. It is not merely the teaching device that a kindergarten teacher uses to repeat and repeat. They are deliberately exploring a mystery about such concepts as creation, the Creator, and about the relationship of the sinner to a loving and sustaining God. To learn about the structure and literary devices of the psalms provides ever more meaning to the reader. Ancient patristic Christian writers and many Christians today see Christ at the center of the Psalms, not by name of course, but in his ever-existence. The Daily Hours of the Christian Church from ages past, connecting in origin with the daily prayer of the Hebrews at the time of Christ are built around the daily recitation and reflection on the Psalms. So, for all these reasons, the collection of Psalms forms a book of prayers that should be at the center of Christian study and life!

Part Two … The Exile and the Return
The destruction of Jerusalem followed by the Exile
The return from exile followed by the restoration

CHAPTER SEVENTEEN

THE DESTRUCTION OF JERUSALEM FOLLOWED BY THE EXILE

THE PROPHET JEREMIAH

Jeremiah was a priest who came from the village of Anathoth which was situated about three miles northeast of Jerusalem (Jer 1:1). His call to be a prophet came during the 13th year of the reign of king Josiah (627 BCE) and is life as a prophet that continued until the 11th year of king Zedekiah (587 BCE).

The call of Jeremiah

The call of Jeremiah is described in Jer 1:4-19. It can be divided into three parts by repetition of the phrase "The word of the LORD came to me" and by the phrase "But you:" verses 4-10, verses 11-19 and verses 17-19. In the first part, Jeremiah pleads that he is too young. God, however, responds by saying that "I am with you" (v.8) and "I place my words in your mouth" (v.9). In v.10, God assigns Jeremiah the task both "to destroy and to demolish" and "to build and to plant."

In the second part Jeremiah receives two visions. The first vision is of a branch from an almond tree. The almond tree is the first to bloom in the Spring and is called "the watcher" because its many blossoms resemble so many "eyes." This vision symbolized that God would be watching to see that his word was accomplished. The second vision was of a boiling pot with a spout that was pointed away from the north, symbolizing that God would bring the cities of the north against the cities of Judah.

In the third part, God tells Jeremiah to prepare himself for his mission and to stand up and tell the people everything that God had revealed to him. Jeremiah is told by God that "Judah's kings and princes, its priests and the people of the land" (v.18) will fight against him!

Jeremiah's early preaching

Jeremiah's early preaching, between the time of his call and the Deuteronomic Reformation of Josiah in 621 BCE (Josiah reigned 640-609 BCE), is found in the oracles contained in Jer 2:1-4:4.[103] During this time he delivered a message primarily of judgment and

---

[103] See: *Understanding The Old Testament*, Fifth Edition, Bernhard W. Anderson with Steven Bishop and Judith H. Newman, 2007, p.337.

much of it was expressed in the metaphor of marriage and sexuality similar to that of the prophet Hosea (see Jer 3:1-3, 6-10).

Example #1 Jer 2:9-13
In this oracle, God accuses the people of having "forsaken the fountain of living water," having forgotten about God in verse 13, and for having gone to foreign gods in verse 11.

Example #2 Jer 2:19
God again finds the people guilty of having forsaken him, the LORD. God also says: "the fear of me is not in you." The expression "the fear of God" is prominent in the Scriptures. It does not use the word "fear" in the sense of being "afraid" or terrified with a chilling fear like in a horror movie. It is used in the sense of reverence and awe. In this sense the expression appears prominently in Proverbs and Sirach in the OT, and in Acts and Romans in the NT. It is considered in the Scriptures to be an attitude that all faithful believers should possess!

Example #3 Jer 2:26-28
Jeremiah delivers an oracle here that says the whole house of Israel will be shamed by the way they have turned to idols.

Example #4 Jer 3:19-20
Jeremiah here once again delivers an oracle that accuses the people of having been unfaithful. It is interesting to note that in this oracle in verse 19 it expresses the fact that God wanted to be called "Father."

Jeremiah During the reign of Jehoiakim (609-598/7)

Jehoiakim was a tyrant. He was cruel and self-indulgent. As Solomon had done, he forced his people to build him great palaces (Jer 22:13). Those who opposed him courted death. He is the only known Judean king who dared to kill a recognized prophet of God (Jer 26:20-23)! He revived the paganism that his father, King Josiah, had tried to overcome with his great reform. Every member of Jehoiakim's family took part in making cakes for Ishtar, a pagan goddess considered Queen of Heaven (Jer 7:18). The rite of child sacrifice was practiced and idols were set up in the temple (Jer7:30-31, 19:5).

Example #1 Jer 7:1-5
In the first year of Jehoiakim's reign, Jeremiah received a word from the LORD that he was to deliver in the temple. This word is known as Jeremiah's Temple Sermon (7:1-15 and Chap. 26:1-11). The message of this sermon is that if the people will truly "amend your ways and your doings (v. 5)," then "I (God) will dwell with you in this place, in the land that I gave of old to your ancestors forever and ever "(v.7). But …! If the people will not do this then God will destroy the temple and Jerusalem as he did to Shilo (7:13-14)! Note that the impending doom is the result of the behavior of the people – they have brought it upon themselves.

Example #2 Jer 4:5-8
In this oracle, the people are advised to flee to the fortified cities because they have turned away from God which will bring "evil from the north" to make the land a waste and the cities to be in ruins and without inhabitants.

Example #3 Jer 5:1-9
In this oracle, verses 1-5 describe a search through Jerusalem to find just one person who acts justly, and seeks truth so that God can pardon the city. But no such person can be found and hence God must punish them (v.9).

Jeremiah during the reign of Zedekiah (597-587 BCE)

In the year 600 BCE, both Babylonia and Egypt were weakened. Jehoiakim tried to take advantage of this situation and made a bid for independence by withholding the tribute money that was owed to Babylon. The king of Babylon responded, in 598-597 BCE, by invading Judah. He removed all of the treasures in the temple and the king's house and he took all of the elite of the land into exile. Finally, he installed Josiah's youngest son, Mattaniah, as king changing his name to Zedekiah. All of this is described in 2 Kgs Chap. 24.

There is material concerning the prophetic utterances of Jeremiah under King Zedekiah scattered throughout Jeremiah 1-25 with a concentration of prophecies in Chapters 21-24. There is also a considerable amount of material of Jeremiah's prophecies under Zedekiah in the section devoted to Baruch's memoirs (Jer 26-45).

Example #1 Jer 21:8-10
In this part of the oracle Jeremiah delivers the startling message that those who remain in Jerusalem will die by the sword, famine and pestilence. Those who go into exile, however, shall live! The reason for this is that God has set his face against Jerusalem for its woe and not for its good (v.10).

Example #2 Jer 24:1-10
In this prophecy Jeremiah has a vision of two baskets of figs. The good figs represent the exiled people and God says that he will restore them to the land and "they shall be my people" (v.7). The figs that are so bad that they cannot be eaten represent the people who remained in Jerusalem which prophesied that they will be "destroyed from the land" (v.10).

The composition that is Jeremiah

The composition that we know as the Book of Jeremiah is sometimes a difficult one for the reader because, in part, it is one of the longest writings in the Bible – 52 chapters – and, in part, because of the way it is put together which can be confusing. In total, it is partly a collection of Jeremiah's oracles and partly a collection of writings about Jeremiah.

If someone surveys all 52 chapters, one finds that it consists of the following five parts:
1. Jer 1-25 consisting of oracles and accounts under three kings: Josiah, Jehoiakim and Zedekiah (as experienced above).

2. Jer 26-35 Prophecies of judgment and hope from the times of Jehoiakim and Zedekiah.
3. Jer 36-45 Biographical accounts of Jeremiah's work and personal suffering.
4. Jer 46-51 Oracles against foreign nations
5. Jer 52 An appendix describing the fall of Jerusalem in 587 taken from 2Kgs 25.

The genre (literary type) of the material contained in these 52 chapters has commonly become specified under three types:

Type A – Original oracles of Jeremiah's – almost always in poetry. These are most common in chapters 1 to 25 and 46 to 51.

Type B – Memoirs or biographical accounts about Jeremiah's work and personal suffering. These fall mostly in chapters 26-45 and are believed to be from Jeremiah's scribe Baruch.

Type C – Prose oracles that were edited, often extensively, by Deuteronomistic History. They are found in chapters 7, 16, 21, 32 and others.

All of this brings us to the realization that this composition is in reality a collection material about Jeremiah as much as it is a collection of his own sayings.

THE PROPHET EZEKIEL

Ezekiel, too, prophesied doom for Judah. In the case of Ezekiel, however, many of his prophecies came in the form of a symbolic action. A prophecy in this form comes as an action which the prophet carries out in front of the people. For example, in Ez 12:17-20, Ezekiel was instructed by God to eat his bread with trembling and to drink his water shaking with fear as a sign that the land will become a desolate place. Again, Ezekiel was instructed to pack a bag and travel to another place to symbolize the coming exile (Ez 12:1-3).

The Book of Ezekiel was composed with one of the highest degrees of order of any composition in the Scriptures. It is, therefore, easier to describe the content of this composition in some detail:

1:13:27	The call narrative.
4:1-5:17	Symbolic actions warning of pending divine punishment.
6:1-7:27	Oracles of judgment announcing Israel's total destruction.
8:1-11:25	A vision of the angels investigating Jerusalem for its idolatry and other sins; they find it guilty and God withdraws his presence from the temple.
12:1-14:23	A collection of oracles and symbolic actions stating the guilt and evil of King Zedekiah, the regular prophets, the priests and the people.
15:1-17:24	A collection of three parables or allegories that show the absence of faithfulness in Judah.
18:1-20:44	Three theological reflections on Israel's guilt.
21:1-24:14	Oracles warning about the coming attack of Babylon and explaining why the city must suffer destruction and exile because of its guilt.
24:15-27	The death of the prophet's wife, but he must not mourn her.

25:1-32:32   Oracles against the nations.
33:1-39:29   Oracles of restoration.
40:1-48:35   The new community[104]

This outline of content is offered because it may be of help when reading through the Book of Ezekiel.

FULFILLMENT OF PROPHECY IN HISTORY

The fulfillment of the prophecies of the destruction of Jerusalem and exile of the people is recorded in 2 Kings 24:10-25:30. This account describes a first attack against Jerusalem in 597 BCE which resulted in removal of all of the valuables from both the temple and the king's house along with a first deportation consisting of all the elite people (2 Kgs 24:10-16). It then describes a later two-year siege of the city (2 Kgs 25:1-3), horrors which are graphically portrayed in the five poems that make up the book of Lamentations. This siege was followed by a breaching of the walls of the city with the subsequent burning of the temple and all of the houses (2 Kgs 25:9) along with a second extensive deportation of people. This took place in the year 587 BCE. Finally it describes a group voluntarily exiling itself to Egypt (in 581 BCE; 2 Kgs 25:26). It is interesting to note that Ezekiel was taken with the first group to be exiled whereas Jeremiah went with the third group of deportees.

THE PLIGHT OF THE PEOPLE AFTER 587 BCE
A. In Judah and Jerusalem

At the time the exile began, some of the people of Judah and Jerusalem died in battle or as a result of starvation and disease (See Lam 2:11f, 19-21; 4:9f). The population was further depleted by three deportations in 597, 587 and 582 BCE that took away almost all of the educated and skilled people.

Most likely, the Babylonians left behind sufficient agricultural workers to ensure the production of products, such as grapes and olives, that could be exported. However, as a population, they were somewhat disorganized due to a lack of leaders.

The temple in Jerusalem had been burned to the ground as had many houses of the people. The foundation of the temple remained, however, so the place where the temple had actually stood continued to be a holy place where pilgrims came to offer sacrifice. Consequently, a religious culture continued to exist but it lacked a significant leader due to the several deportations. A consequence of this situation was the development of a number of unacceptable practices undertaken by the people (See Ezekiel 33:23-29; Is 57:3-13; 65:1-5).

The deportees who were taken to Babylon included all of the upper echelons of the population. When they reached Babylon they were not intermingled with the local people but were directed to live in their own settlements, located a few miles south of the city of Babylon. They were not completely free, but they were not treated as prisoners either. Life in captivity

---

[104] Lawrence Boadt: *Reading The Old* Testamen*t*, Second Edition (New York, Paulist Press, 2012) 342-343.

opened up for many of them, opportunities that would never have been available back in their former land. During the time of the exile many of them entered new trades and some of them became rich.[105]

Psalm 137 gives us a glimpse of the people in exile. In this psalm, the psalmist speaks about how their captors requested that the people sing songs of Zion to them.

A small number of people made their way to Egypt (582 BCE). Some of these people settled just inside of the border while others found their way into Lower Egypt. Still other Jews fled to other countries such as: Moab, Edom and Ammon.

The result of the deportation of the people of Judah and Jerusalem had a very significant long term effect which is nicely expressed by John Bright:

> Although there was as yet no Jewish Diaspora all over the earth, a trend had begun which would never permanently be reversed. Israel had begun to be scattered among the nations (cf. Deut 28:64). Never again would she be coterminous with any political entity or geographical area. Whatever the future might hold for her, there could be no full return to the pattern of the past.[106]

---

[105] John Bright, *A History of Israel*, Second Edition (Philadelphia, The Westminster Press, 1972) 346.
[106] John Bright, 347.

CHAPTER EIGHTEEN

THE RETURN FROM EXILE FOLLOWED BY THE RESTORATION

Prophecy

In the years when the prophets were prophesying destruction for Jerusalem and the temple and exile for the people, the messages of doom were not the only messages from God. Both Jeremiah and Ezekiel delivered messages of **hope – the promise of a restoration.**

If you look at Jeremiah, chapters 30 and 31, you will find a collection of oracles in which God promises to restore Judah, Jerusalem and the temple and to bring the people home from exile. Since God directs Jeremiah to write these oracles down in a book (Jer 30:2), these two chapters are sometimes called the "Book of Consolation." Surely all of these oracles were not uttered at the same time and in the same location but have been gathered together in order to make a more visible presentation. Jeremiah also delivered a prophecy that God would make a new covenant with the people of Judah (Jer 31:31-34).

A collection of prophecies of restoration is contained in Ezekiel as well (Ezek chaps. 33-48). The concept of restoration is expressed by Ezekiel in the imagery of a resurrection from the dead in his vision of the valley of the dry bones (37:1-14). Ezekiel also speaks of God in terms of the image of a good shepherd (34:1-24). He gives God's plan for a new Jerusalem and a new temple (chaps. 40-48). As Jeremiah had done, Ezekiel delivered a promise that God would give the people a new covenant (Ezek 36:22-28). Christian scholars find these prophecies relate to Christ, his triumph over death which will bring resurrection to all the faithful, and the fulfillment of the covenant with God.

Fulfillment of Prophecy

Toward the end of the Babylonian exile a prophet, known today only by the name Second Isaiah, prophesied that the end of the Exile was at hand (a section of Isaiah called Second Isaiah covering Isaiah chapters 40 to 55):

Comfort, give comfort to my people, says your God.
Speak to the heart of Jerusalem and proclaim to her
that her service has ended,
that her guilt is expiated,
That she has received from the hand of the Lord,
double for her sins.
(Is 40:1-2; NAB)

All of the words spoken by Jeremiah, Ezekiel and Obadiah became history when the Persians defeated the Babylonians in 587 and then, shortly afterward, Cyrus, the king of the Persians, proclaimed the following decree:

With regard to the house of God in Jerusalem: the house is to be rebuilt as a place for offering sacrifices and bringing burnt offerings. Its height is to be sixty cubits and its width sixty cubits. It shall have three courses of cut stone for each one of timber. The costs are to be borne by the royal house. Also, let the gold and silver vessels of the house of God which Nebuchadnezzar took from the temple of Jerusalem and brought to Babylon be sent back; let them be returned to their place in the temple of Jerusalem and deposited in the house of God. (Ezra 6: 3-5 NABRE)

Soon after the people who first returned to Jerusalem arriving from exile, they undertook to begin the task of rebuilding the temple. As described in Ezra 2:62-6:22, this project proved to be quite difficult and had to be carried out against considerable opposition from the people of the land (those people who remained in Jerusalem during the exile) and the Samaritans. The command of God through two prophets – Haggai and Zechariah; three official Persian decrees – two of them from Persian kings Cyrus and Darius; and years of work by the people of Jerusalem and Judah ... all contributed to the rebuilding process. The rebuilding of the temple was completed and it was rededicated in 515 BCE.

The restoration of the cult in Jerusalem continued slowly until the coming to Jerusalem of Ezra and Nehemiah near the end of the 5th century BCE.

The Prophet Second Isaiah

The prophet Isaiah lived in the 8th century BCE. The collection of oracles that is due to his work, known as "First Isaiah," comes to us in Isaiah chapters 1-39. The oracles mention the events surrounding kings Ahaz and Hezekiah of the Southern Kingdom, the threat of the Assyrians and further threats from the north.

However, the historical references in Isaiah chapters 40-66 mention the destruction of Jerusalem as a past event (Isa 40:1-2), refer to the present situation of the people as exiles in Babylon (Isa 43:14), and to Cyrus the Persian king as a deliverer of Israel (Isa 44:28). The setting for Isaiah chapters 40-66 is, therefore, the middle of the 6th century BCE, not the 8th century!

On similar grounds, it is evident that there also is a further division between chapters 40 to 66 into chapters 40-55 and 56-66. The second section, chapters 40 to 55, is known as "Second Isaiah." The third section in chapter 56 to 66, is known as "Third Isaiah." Since the names of these two prophets at the end of Isaiah are unknown they have been designated generally by "Second Isaiah" and "Third Isaiah."

Therefore, in the Book of Isaiah we have identified the following:
First Isaiah ... chapters 1- 39
Second Isaiah ... chapters 40 – 55
Third Isaiah ... chapters 56 - 66

Almost nothing is known about the person of Second Isaiah. His name is unknown, and it is not known how long he prophesied, and nothing is known about his background except what little can be deduced from his poetry. His call comes to us in Isa. 40:1-11. The prophet is told to speak to the heart of Jerusalem and to tell her that "her guilt is expiated" (Isa.40:2) and to go up on a high mountain and to be a "herald of good news" (Isa 40:9-11).

The work of Second Isaiah (Is 40-55) is many times referred to as "The Book of Consolation" because it does not speak of judgment or condemnation of Judah and Jerusalem. Its poetry is expressed in the language of rebuilding, restoring, renewing and even re-creating.

Scholarly analysis of the material of Second Isaiah has been made difficult by a lack of consensus concerning the length of the poems. The opinions as to the number of poems ranges from 15 to 70! For now, let us accept the division set forth by Richard Clifford in the *Catholic Study Bible*, 2nd edition. Clifford presents the following list of the poems in Second Isaiah along with a title for each expressing its content and meaning:

1. The Lord speaks good news to Israel (40:1-11)
2. Strength for an exhausted people (40:12-31)
3. Judgment in favor of Israel (41:1-42:9)
4. The divine warrior removes the obstacles to his peoples return (42:10-43:8)
5. Israel raised to be a witness to the Lord (43:9-44:5)
6. Witness to their maker (44:6-23)
7. The Lord appoints Cyrus king (44:24-45:13)
8. The Lord will not leave the holy city in ruins (45:14-25)
9. The Lord carries his people to his city (46)
10. The destruction of Dame Babylon (47)
11. Openness to the interpreting word (48)
12. The servant performs his task in the sight of the nations ((49)
13. The light that follows punishing darkness (50:1-51:8)
14. A prayer that the Lord destroy the foe and bring his people to Zion (51:9-52:12)
15. The many confess that the Lord upholds his servant (52:13-53:12)
16. Zion, the secure city of the Lord (54)
17. Come into the life-giving presence of the Lord! (55) [107]

In these poems, God continually speaks in the first person. For example: "I the LORD was there at the beginning" (Isa 41:6); "I am the LORD, LORD is my name" (Isa 42:8); "I alone am the LORD your God" (Isa 42:); "I, the LORD, am your God" (Isa 43:3).

In delivering the messages of salvation for Judah and Jerusalem, Second Isaiah makes use of oracles having special forms. One such form is called a "**proclamation of**

---

[107] Richard Clifford, "Reading Guide for Isaiah," *The Catholic Study Bible*, Second Edition (New York, Oxford University Press, 2011) RG288.

salvation." An example of this type of oracle is Isa 41:17-20. A second type is called the "**oracle of salvation**" and an example of this type is Isa 44:1-5. A third type of oracle is the "**idol parodie**" (Examples: 40:19-20; 41:6-7; 44:9-20; 46:6-7).

Second Isaiah frequently attaches titles to God such as: Savior, Holy One, Creator, The First and Last. Special attention should be paid to these titles because each one tells us something about God.

If you look closely, you will find that Second Isaiah has bracketed his collection of poems with two sayings about God's word. The first, Isa 40:6-8, states that the word of our God stands forever. The second, Isa 55:6-11, says that God's word will not return without accomplishing its purpose.

The word "servant" occurs 21 times in Second Isaiah. In 13 of these occurrences the word refers to Israel as a people. In four of the remaining occurrences scholars have maintained that the word refers to an individual: 42:1-4; 49:1-6; 50:4-11; 52:13-53:12. They have given a name to this individual: "Servant of the Lord." Also, these poetic sections are often called "the Suffering Servant Songs" because they appear to refer to Christ. The influence of these verses can be seen in the book of Daniel. With the coming of Jesus and his followers, however, these verses were applied to Jesus Christ.

The importance to the early Christian believers of the servant passages is attested to by the account of the encounter between Philip, the deacon, with the Ethiopian eunuch reported in Acts 8:26-40. The eunuch was reading Is 53:7-8 and asked Philip to tell him whether the prophet was saying this about himself or about someone else. The account tells us that Philip began with these two verses and then went on to proclaim Jesus. The reaction of the eunuch was his request to be baptized.

Psalm 126

This psalm seems to have its context in the return from exile. It consists of two parts: verses 1-4 and verses 5-6. This two part division is the result of an inclusion on the word "captive" in verses 1 and 4, and an entirely different subject in verses 5-6. The psalmist, in verses 1-4, apparently expresses the great joy experienced by the captives when they returned while in verse 4; and the psalmist seems to be asking God to bring home the captives who had not yet returned. Verses 5-6 appear to be an oracle from God promising that the effort to plant crops will be rewarded with a bountiful harvest.

The prophet Obadiah

The writing that bears the name Obadiah is the shortest of the prophetic books (21 verses). The writing contains no indication of a specific date, but based on its content it belongs to the period of the return from exile.

150

The content of Obadiah consists of the following:

1. 1b-4 A prophecy of Edom's destruction
2. 5-7 Edom at the hand of the nations
3. 8-9 Edom at the hand of God "on that day"
4. 10-14 Edom's offenses against Judah and Jerusalem
5. 15-18 Edom's fate will also be the fate of all hostile nations
6. 19-21 Reclamation and expansion of the territory of the exiles

As stated in verses 10-14, Edom had stood by and not come to the aide of Jerusalem at the time of its destruction. This incurred the hatred of the people forever after.

The prophet Haggai

The "Book" of Haggai is very short – two chapters totaling 38 verses. Nothing is known of the person of Haggai; neither the superscription nor the text itself reveals anything explicit about the prophet. All of Haggai's oracles were delivered in the year of his call – 520 BCE.

This composition is very straightforward. It is set down is a very tight chronological order covering the period from August 29 to December 18 of the year 520 BCE. The body of the book is divided into five episodes as follows:[108]

1. 1:1-11 Aug 29, 520 BCE – Haggai receives the word from God that it is time to build God's house (vv1:7-8).
2. 1:12-15a Sep 21 – The people obey God and start work on God's house.
3. 1:15b-2:9 Oct 17 – God tells the people not to be dismayed that this new Temple is not as large and glorious as the former Temple built by Solomon. He tells the people to "work" (2:4); that God will fill this new house with glory; and that the future glory of this house will be greater than that of the former Temple.
4. 2:10-19 Dec 18, 520 BCE – God says that from this day forward God will bless the people and the land (2:19).
5. 2:20-23 Dec 18 also – God tells Zerubbabel that he will be as a signet ring (2:23).

While many English translations present all of Haggai's oracles in prose form, as does the NRSV translation, it is probable that much of it is better expressed in the form of the original Hebrew poetry, as does the NABRE translation.

The prophet Zechariah

The book of Zechariah contains the work of two different prophets designated as 1 Zechariah(Chaps. 1-8), a contemporary of Haggai, and 2 Zechariah (Chaps. 9-14), a prophet dating to about a century later.

---

[108] W. Eugene March, "The Book of Haggai," in *The New Interpreter's Bible*, V. VII (Nashville, TN: Abingdon Press, 1996), 711.

151

The prophecies of 1 Zechariah can be divided into two sections: the first section, Zech 1:7-6:15, consists of eight vision reports and the second section, 7:1-8:23, includes a series of seven oracles dealing with the restoration of Judah (8:1-17).

The eight vision reports of Zech 1:7-6:15 describe the ways that God is working to help the newly formed community. They involve a new development in prophetic literature because the meaning of these visions is explained to the prophet by an angelic figure.

Six of the seven oracles of Zech 8:1-17 deal with how God will treat the people of Judah and Jerusalem. "I will dwell within Jerusalem," says God (Zech 8:3). God promises the old men and women will sit in the streets of Jerusalem again, and the city will be filled with boys and girls (8:4-5). God will bring back the exiles to dwell within Jerusalem and "they will be my people and I will be their God" (8:8).

The seventh oracle, Zech 8:14-17, contains a list of things the people must do: speak the truth to one another, judge with honesty and complete justice, do not plot evil against one another in their hearts, and do not love a false oath.

The prophet Malachi

Scholars are generally agreed that this composition was written sometime between the rebuilding of the temple and the time of Ezra and Nehemiah (the latter half of the 5th century BC/BCE). It is interesting to observe that the NRSV translation has the entire writing in the form of prose and the NABRE translation has the entire writing in the form of poetry. Malachi is structured in six literary units: 1:2-5; 1:6-2:9; 2:10-16; 2:17-3:5; 3:6-12; 3:13-4:3.

The content of the six literary units may be summarized as follows:

> 1:2-5 The LORD loves Israel but hates Edom.
>
> 1:6-2:9 The priests have despised the name of God by offering blind, lame and sick animals on the altar. Also they have caused many to stumble by their instruction.
>
> 2:10-16 The people have one father (God) but they have gone after other gods.
>
> 2:17-3:5 This unit speaks about those people who will not find favor with God – adulterers, those who oppress the hired workers in their wages, those who oppress the widow or the orphan, and those "who do not fear me (God),"
>
> 3:6-12 "Return to me, and I will return to you, says the LORD of hosts" (3:7b). It also says that the people are robbing God through their tithes and offerings (3:8-10).

3:13-4:3 The people have spoken against God. Those who
          LORD will be spared when God acts (3:16-18).

These six units have a distinctive literary form that is sometimes characte
In all of them two parties, God and some group, participate in a dialogue.

There are two additional verses at the end of Malachi. Verse 4:4
remember the teaching of Moses. In the last verse, 4:5, God promises to
the LORD. God is able to send Elijah because Elijah has never actually died (see 2 Kgs 2.11).
Christians have interpreted this promise to have been fulfilled with the coming of John the
Baptist in the time of Jesus.

Ruth

Ruth is found in the Roman Catholic canon of the Bible with the history writings. This is
misleading. The intention of this writing is not to expound history, but rather to tell a story with a
religious meaning. The account is told, however, against an historical background. The
background of this writing is the age of the Judges, which is why the book was placed
immediately following the book of Judges.

Although the historical setting of the writing is stated to be "in the days when the judges
ruled" (1:1, NRSV), thus about 1200 – 1025 BCE, many scholars believe this account was
written by a single author sometime in the late 6th century BCE. This position is based upon
recent linguistic analysis.[110] The identity of the author in this theory is unknown.

Ruth consists of four chapters with a total of 85 verses. A minority of scholars like to
describe this book merely as a short story with a lesson. It is important to know, however, that
most scholars will contend that it has far more worth than that. It is an important writing because
it helps to establish the pre-history of Jesus and contains some very important themes such as
kinship, friendship, and dedication to God. It is a writing that indicates that God's work is not
only for one national group of people. The story has three main characters:

- Naomi – The wife of Elimelech (1:3), a man of Bethlehem (1:1).
- Ruth – Daughter-in-law of Naomi, a Moabite woman (1:4).
- Boaz – A kinsman of Elimelech (2:1).

Scholars have proposed various ideas as to the intended purpose of the book of Ruth. Here are
two interesting possibilities:

- The reader should strive to be like the three main characters in the story. Thus:
  Whatever its date, however, Ruth is not a polemical
  book. The values it proclaims – loyalty, love of family,

---

[109] *The New Oxford Annotated Bible*, Fully Revised Fourth Edition (New York, Oxford University Press, 2010)
1351.
[110] *The Catholic Study Bible, Second Edition* (New York, Oxford University Press, 2011) RG165

and generosity toward strangers – are universal and timeless.[111]

- Consider the following inspiring interpretation provided by Kathleen A. Robertson Farmer:
    - The book of Ruth is about redemption – the word redeem" and its derivatives occurs 23 times in 85 verses.
    - In the story it is Naomi's life that is turned around. God accomplishes Naomi's redemption through the instrument of Ruth's faithfulness.
    - The author intended that the people of Israel identify themselves with Naomi. Thus the story of Ruth becomes a story of the redemption of Israel.
    - The people of Israel should believe that the redemptive efforts that God made on Naomi's behalf, God will also make on Israel's behalf. [112]

Ezra and Nehemiah

Both the *Catholic Study Bible* and the *Oxford Annotated Bible* place the writings of 1 and 2 Chronicles directly ahead of the compositions of Ezra and Nehemiah. The fact that the author of Chronicles quotes from Ezra, however, establishes that 1 and 2 Chronicles were written after Ezra-Nehemiah. This is likely the reason why Ezra and Nehemiah immediately precede 1 and 2 Chronicles in the Hebrew Bible. Despite the observation that 2 Chronicles 36:22-23 closely parallels Ezra 1:1-4, therefore, it will be best to treat Ezra and Nehemiah before taking up 1 and 2 Chronicles following the practice of the Hebrew Bible.

Although a few scholars still argue for treating Ezra and Nehemiah as separate works, recent scholarship has made a strong case for treating them as a single work by one author. In recognition of this unity the work, the term Ezra-Nehemiah is used.

Scholars agree on identifying the author as a person living in Palestine. With something less than unanimity, scholars fix the date of composition sometime early in the 4th century BCE.

The narrative of Ezra-Nehemiah is written in chronological order. It is recommended, therefore, that it be read, in order, from beginning to end. It is worthy of note that in the course of reading it, one encounters material from the memoirs of both Ezra and Nehemiah! Ezra chapters 7-10 and Nehemiah 7:73b-9:38 are from the memoirs of Ezra, and Nehemiah 1:1-7:73a is from the memoirs of Nehemiah. Along the way, the reader will encounter a considerable number of official documents concerning various aspects of the rebuilding process that occurred after the Exile. Through the narrative and the structure of it, the author of Ezra-Nehemiah focuses

---

[111] Tribble, 391.

[112] Kathleen A. Robertson Farmer, "The Book of Ruth" in *The New Interpreter's Bible*, V. II (Nashville, TN: Abingdon Press, 1998), 891-893.

154

attention on the role of the people themselves in the rebuilding of their temple, the city and their faith.

As a guide to reading the text of Ezra-Nehemiah the following outline will be of considerable help:

Ezra 1:1-11
> This section gives the edict of King Cyrus of Persia who gave permission to the Jews to return home from exile, while ordering a promise of assistance from their Babylonian neighbors (1:1-4). It also describes the reaction of the Jews and their neighbors to the official edict (1:5-11).

Ezra Chap. 2
> This chapter contains a list of the persons who returned to their homeland

Ezra Chaps. 3-6
> This section describes the restoration of the temple and its dedication in 515BCE.

Ezra Chaps. 7-10
> These four chapters describe the mission of Ezra and the restoration of the community according to the Torah. Ezra is described as "a scribe skilled in the law of Moses that the Lord the God of Israel had given; and the king granted him all that he asked, for the hand of the Lord his God was upon him" (Ezra 7:6).

Nehemiah 1:1-7:5
> These chapters come from Nehemiah's memoir. They describe how Nehemiah, the Persian King's cupbearer, becomes the governor of Judah and rebuilds the walls of Jerusalem.
>
> [Historical Note – In the ancient world, the "cupbearer" was a high ranking court official whose duty was to serve the wine at the king's table. This sounds like a job that would be much sought after. There is, however, a down side. Because of the constant possibility of plots and intrigues, it was the duty of the cup bearer to guard against poison in the king's cup. He was frequently required to demonstrate that the cup was poison free by drinking from the cup in front of the king and his friends! More than likely there was another position in the court with the title: assistant cup bearer.]

Nehemiah 7:6-73
> This section reproduces, with insignificant changes, the list of those who returned from exile given in Ezra 2:1-70.

Nehemiah chapters 8-13
> These chapters describe the celebration by the people of the completion of the return from exile, the restoration of the temple and the renewal of the worship cult. To accomplish these things had taken the people nearly 100 years! The public reading of the Torah described in chapter 8 is significant because it recalls the reception of God's teachings by the entire people at Mount Sinai.

1 Chronicles and 2 Chronicles

1 and 2 Chronicles are a continuous work, the break between the two coming between the death of King David at a natural dividing point. 1 Chronicles ends with the death of King David and the reign of King Solomon.

The content of 1 and 2 Chronicles consists of an alternative account of the historical narrative contained in 2 Samuel and 1 and 2 Kings. Chronicles is, however, a very selective retelling of the older narrative. If these two compositions are placed side by side and compared, the similarities and differences are easily seen. While in some passages the two are word for word the same, at other points there are considerable differences. For example: the episode with Bathsheba (2 Sam 11-12) and the psalms of David (2 Sam 22-23) are omitted from 1 Chronicles. The two writings of Chronicles constitute a rewriting of the historical traditions contained in 1 Samuel and 1 and 2 Kings.

What was at stake was the survival of Judah and Jerusalem. Before the Exile, life was carried out under a monarchy with national freedom and with the First Temple in Jerusalem. At the end of the Exile, the people faced a life without a monarchy, without a significant hope for national freedom and with a totally destroyed temple in Jerusalem – all which was the major purpose behind the writing of 1 and 2 Chronicles. One reason for rewriting the earlier traditions was to envision David as a second lawgiver nearly as great as Moses, and to make him a model for a community centered on the temple. A secondary motive for the rewriting was to remove the confusion between the roles of the priests and the Levites that existed in the earlier traditions.[113]

A second statement of the purpose of Chronicles is provided by John Collins:

> The aim of the Chronicler was to promote a view of Judaism that centered primarily on the temple cult and on active leadership of priests and Levites. The great contribution of David and Solomon was that they put the cultic system in place. Other kings are evaluated by the degree to which they maintained it. This temple-centered cultic view of Judaism, with its great emphasis on the leadership of priests and Levites, is characteristic of Second Temple Judaism. The Chronicler wanted to claim that this view of the cult of YHWH dated back to the time of David and Solomon, and was supported by consistent divine retribution in the history of Judah. The aim of the history was to legitimize and lend authority to this view of Judaism.[114]

A third view of the purpose Chronicles is a postexilic re-interpretation of the history of the Jewish people. Gary N. Knoppers expresses the purpose of this re-interpretation as follows:

> Both Kings and Chronicles end by describing the Babylonian invasion and exile in the sixth century BCE, but Chronicles also includes Cyrus's decree allowing the exiles to return to Judah (2 Chr 36.22-23), offering a clearer hope for the future than does the conclusion of Kings. In this way Chronicles contains and relativizes the tremendous tragedy of the Babylonian deportations soberly depicted in 2 Kings 24-25. Thus Chronicles, with its positive ending and emphasis on the power of repentance, may be seen as more optimistic than the history of Samuel-Kings, which it has rewritten. As the beginning of Chronicles introduces

---

[113] Lawrence Boadt, CSP, *Reading The Old Testament*, Second Edition (New York, Paulist Press, 2012) ,395.
[114] John J. Collins, *Introduction to the Hebrew Bible*, (Minneapolis, Fortress Press, 2004), 459-460.

the people of Israel and charts their emergence in the land, the ending of the book anticipates their return.[115]

Date

The date of the writing of Chronicles is stated by Allen as follows:

> The same impression of a dating late in the Persian period is given by the postexilic continuation of the Davidic genealogy in 1 Chronicles 3. .... In the light of this and the earlier evidence, the first half of the fourth century BCE seems to be the period when it was written. No Hellenistic features are present to warrant a later date.[116]

The author of Chronicles was writing to help his fellow believers. People reading the work today must keep in mind that Chronicles contains a **message for the author's contemporaries** in the early 4th century BCE! The reader's task is to read the books of Chronicles seeking the spiritual message that the author is giving to his contemporaries.

Chronicles is an epic work in its own right! It has, however, suffered in the Christian tradition because of its placement immediately after the books of Samuel and Kings. They have fared better in the Jewish tradition because they are placed at the end of the third division of the Hebrew Bible, the *Kethuvim* (the Writings). Its physical distance from the books of Samuel and Kings serves to emphasize that Chronicles originated in a different historical period than did 2 Samuel and Kings.

Content

The content of Chronicles can be divided into three sections as follows:
- o Genealogies beginning with Adam (1 Chr 1:1-9:34)
- o **The United Monarchy**
  - • David (1 Chr 9:35-29:30)
  - • Solomon (2 Chr 1:1-9:31)
- o The Kingdom of Judah (2 Chr 10:1-36:23) It is interesting to observe that the author does not include the independent history of the Northern Kingdom: Israel.

The Prayer of Manasseh

The prayer of Manasseh is considered to be canonical (inspired by God) by the Eastern Orthodox Christians. It is not considered to be canonical by Jews, Catholics and Protestants.

There are two different accounts of King Manasseh (698-642 BCE) in the Scriptures. The first account is found in 2 Kings 21:1-18. In this account Manasseh is stated to be entirely evil. The final sentence given to the description of his life says: "In addition to the sin which he caused Judah to commit, Manasseh did evil in the sight of the LORD, shedding so much innocent blood as to fill the length and breadth of Jerusalem" (21:16).

---

[115] Gary N. Knoppers, "1 Chronicles" in *The New Oxford Annotated Bible*, Fully Revised Fourth Edition, (New York, Oxford University Press, 2010), 576.
[116] Leslie C. Allen, 301.

157

The second account is contained in 2 Chronicles 33:1-20. This account is clearly based upon the account in 2 Kings since it is partly word for word the same. It is quite different, however in that it contains a description of Manasseh's conversion (33:11-17). This account says: "He humbled himself abjectly before the God of his fathers and prayed to him. The LORD let himself be won over: he heard his prayer and restored him to his kingdom in Jerusalem" (33:12b-13).

The Prayer of Manasseh is a penitential confession by a man living sometime in the period following the writing of Chronicles. Because this prayer pleased God even though Manasseh had been such a bad person, it was considered to be a model penitential prayer and it became very popular, and is included in the ancient Christian worship services.

The prayer is composed of three parts:
- An invocation of God (vv. 1-7)
- A Confession of sin (vv. 8-10)
- A request for forgiveness (vv. 11-15)

1 Esdras

The composition that is 1 Esdras is recognized as being one of the canonical writings only by the Eastern Orthodox Churches. It is not recognized as being in the canon by the Jewish, Catholic or the Protestant Churches.

1 Esdras is almost entirely parallel to sections of 2 Chronicles, Ezra and Nehemiah. It begins with King Josiah's celebration of the Passover festival in Jerusalem if 622BCE (2 Chron 35:1-36:21), follows with material that parallels almost all of Ezra, and concludes with material that is parallel to Nehemiah 7:6-8:12. The only portion that is unique to 1 Esdras is the section 3:1-4:63 which contains the fable of the three young body guards in the court of King Darius of Persia. Early Christian writers who cited 1 Esdras showed considerable interest in this story and King Darius' selection was the considered a very wise statement, "Great is truth, and strongest of all" (4:41 NRSV), which has become a popular saying. Tamara Cohn Eskenazi has this to say about 1 Esdras:

> Although the book largely overlaps other biblical books, its compositional pattern offers a distinct perspective on the history it recounts. It traces a trajectory between Josiah's Passover (1:1-24) and an unnamed holy day in the time of Ezra (9:49-55, parallel Neh 8:1-13). The destruction of Jerusalem, exile, and rebuilding that it narrates are framed by celebrations, which imply complete restoration and a return to the "good old days." It thereby depicts a more positive historical development than the longer report in Ezra-Nehemiah, which begins and concludes with challenges rather than festivities.[117]

The content of 1 Esdras, for the purpose of reading, may be outlined in the following manner:

---

[117] Tamara Cohn Eskenazi, "Introduction to 1 Esdras" in *The New Oxford Annotated Bible*, Fully Revised Fourth Edition, (New York, Oxford University Press, 2010), 1633.

158

Celebration of the Passover of Josiah 1:1-22
Death of King Josiah 1:23-33
Fall of Jerusalem, destruction of the temple and deportation of the people
(1:34-58)
First return from exile 2:1-15
Opposition of the local people 2:16-30
The contest of the three body guards 3:1-4:63
Second return of the Exiles 5:1-46
Rebuilding of the temple (5:47-7:15)
Ezra's mission 8:1-9:55
1. Ezra's commission 8:1-27
2. Ezra's journey to Jerusalem 8:28-67
3. Dissolution of mixed marriages 8:68-9:36
4. Public reading of the Torah 9:37-55

The principle focus of 1 Esdras is seen to be the rebuilding of the people of God by means of the restoration of the city of Jerusalem and its temple, renewal of the priesthood, reinstituting the traditional cycle of feasts, prohibition of marriages with non-Jewish women and the public reading of the Torah.

Conclusion

We can see in the writings that originate from the time of the Exile and return, and the resulting restoration of religious life for the Jews, that their religious traditions are now firmly re-established. The prophets have taught that God is involved with his people and their faithfulness leads to happiness and security. The prophecy found in 2 Isaiah, in the Suffering Servant Songs, appears to promise a redeemer. There is a lot of history throughout these writings but the important aspect in reading it all is to see the call of God and the response by the people, and his offer for a loving relationship and provision of life.

159

Part Three … The Writing of the Hellenistic Period
The writings of history
The prophets
The folk literature

Book of Joh
ch38-39 ❓
Proverbs ~11

CHAPTER NINETEEN

THE WRITINGS OF HISTORY

Introduction

The writings of 1 Maccabees and 2 Maccabees are two independent literary works. They are written by different authors, at somewhat different times and for different purposes. What these two literary pieces do have in common is that the historical periods they cover are overlapping. While 1 Maccabees covers the period 175-135 BCE, 2 Maccabees covers the period 180-161 BCE. It is seen on the basis of these considerations that the best approach is to study these two writings independently.

1 Maccabees

The identity of the author of 1 Maccabees is not known. Three factors combine to suggest that the author was an educated Jew living in Palestine: it was most likely originally written in Hebrew; much of its geographical data is accurate; and it was written in a style that is similar to other writings in the Hebrew Scriptures.

The narrative begins with the accession of Antiochus IV to the throne of Syria in 175 BCE and ends with the death of Simon Maccabeus in 135/134 BCE.[118] This work was probably written, therefore, near the end of the second century BCE. It is a straightforward historical narrative which states the date that each major action takes place.

Although it consists of only 16 chapters, 1 Maccabees is much longer than would be anticipated due to the fact that each of the chapters is very long - many times over 60 verses. In *The Catholic Study Bible*, Second Edition, the writing occupies 36 pages of small print, even though the quantity of footnotes is minimal. Reading this text can be quite tedious unless one has a more than average interest in reading about military actions that took place over 2,000 years ago.

First Maccabees starts out by telling of the actions of Antiochus IV, King of Syria, against the Jews and his desecration of the Temple in Jerusalem. It focuses on two generations of the Maccabees: Mattathias (2:1-70) the father, and three of his five sons: Judas (3:1-9:22), Jonathan (9:23-12:54) and Simon (13:1-16:24). Early in this period of time, the Temple was taken back, purified and re-dedicated (164 BCE). Later, the political independence of Judea was proclaimed (in 142/141 BCE). This period of political freedom lasted until the Roman invasion of 63 BCE.

---

[118] Robert Doran, "The First Book of Maccabees" in *The New Interpreter's Bible*, V.IV, Leander E. Keck et al, Editors (Nashville, TN: Abingdon Press, 1996), 3.

It is important to read about the attack on the temple by Antiochus IV (Chap. 1), the opposition to this attack made by Mattathias (Chap. 2), and the armed resistance to Antiochus IV mounted by Judas Maccabeus (3:1-4:35). Finally, read 4:36-61 which describes the purification of the temple and its rededication. Take note of the poems that have been included within this portion of the narrative [They appear at: 1:25-28,36-40; 2:7-13,51-64; 3:3-9, 45]. Also take note of how it is reported that Judas and his people realize that they are victorious only because God is on their side.

2 Maccabees

It is perhaps best to begin by repeating what was said above about the two books of Maccabees: they are two independent works. 2 Maccabees is not the second volume of a single work in two volumes.

The author of 2 Macc is unknown. Several features of the text, however, suggest a date for its composition of late second century BCE: the text was written in the typical Greek style of that period. The inclusion of a prologue evidences knowledge of Hellenistic historiographical conventions and the text itself shows knowledge of Greco-Roman literature of the late second century BCE. (Historiography is the study of history based on actual reliable sources from the time period and authentic details from those sources which can then be woven into a historical narrative.) Proposed dates for its composition range from 124 to 63 BCE.

This book covers events during the period 180-161 BCE, as stated in the introduction above.

Robert Doran summarizes the contents of 2 Maccabees in the following way:

> The narrative of 2 Maccabees is preceded by two letters addressed by the Jews in Judea to the Jews in Egypt, requesting that the Egyptian Jews celebrate the Feast of the Purification of the Temple – i.e. the Feast of Hanukkah. The first letter is dated to 124 BCE, while the second purports to be written in the time of Judas Maccabeus. The narrative portion of 2 Maccabees begins in the reign of Antiochus IV's predecessor, Seleucus IV. It provides more details about events leading up to the oppression of Judea in Jerusalem, highlights the martyrdom of Jewish resisters, and concentrates on the figure of Judas Maccabeus. The account ends, while Judas is still alive, after the defeat of the Seleucid commander Nicanor in 161 or 160 BCE.[119]

Introduction

The introduction to 2 Maccabees consists of two letters and a preface. The first letter is to the Jews living in Egypt and was intended to remind them to celebrate the Feast of Hanukkah

---

[119] Robert Doran, 3.

(called "Feast of Booths" in the text – probably due to confusion on the part of the author or to a mistake that entered the manuscript tradition during its transmission. Although the Feast of Booths is commemorated in the Fall, there is a connection to the Exodus in the memory of fragile "booths" – palm covered sheds – where those crossing the desert often had to live). The text of this letter states that it was written in 124 BCE.

The form of this letter is noteworthy because of its similarity to the form of the typical letter of Paul in the NT. The letter first identifies the sender and then the recipient. This is followed by a greeting. This is followed, in turn, by a prayer for God to help the recipients. The letter closes with a final request that they keep the festival. The letter is dated 124 BCE.

The second letter is directed to a man named Aristobulus and also to the Jews in Egypt. As did the first letter, this letter also urges the Jews to celebrate the feast of Hanukkah (2:18). The significant part of the letter is the account of the fire on the altar. In the time of Solomon, a fire came down from heaven and ignited the first burnt offering. This account relates that a similar event happened with respect to the altar in the Second Temple (1:18-22, 30-36). The letter also contains a prayer to God that is well worth reading (1:24-29).

The Preface (2:19-32), first provides the reader with a summary of the content of the composition in verses 19-22. It then goes on to describe what the author is trying to accomplish. The Preface (2:19-32), explains that the narrative of 2 Maccabees, 3:1-15:39, is a shortened version of a five-volume work by Jason of Cyrene. However, there is no known manuscript of Jason's composition in existence today. In *The Catholic Study Bible,* the work of the author is referred to as a "condensation" in 2:23, as a "digest" in 2:26 and as a "summary outline" in 2:28. One might ask as to whether this word choice is that of the author or whether it is that of the translator (compare it to the NRSV translation).

Contents

For the modern-day reader an outline of the contents of 2 Maccabees would be something like the following:

> 1. Introductory letters and preface (1:1-2:32).
> 2. Intrigues; profanation of the temple and abolution of Judaism (3:1-6:17).
> 3. Martyrdom of Eleazar (6:18-31).
> 4. Martyrdom of the seven sons and their mother (7:1-42).
> 5. Victories of Judas Maccabeus; purification and dedication of the temple (8:1-10:9).
> 6. Further struggles and victories of Judas (10:10-15:36).
> 7. Author's ending (15:37-39).

Whereas 1 Maccabees consists of a straightforward historical narrative, the narrative of 2 Maccabees contains numerous accounts of the miraculous. In the first eleven chapters of 2 Maccabees there are five such miraculous happenings: 3:24-28; 5:2-4; 10:29-31; 11:8-11.

The inclusion of letters in the narrative is notable. 2 Maccabees begins with two letters. There is a letter in 9:18-27 and four letters in a row in chapter 11:16-21, 22-26, 27-33, 34-38. It is interesting that letters appear to have become a common means of communication in the last two centuries BCE. It is, therefore, not surprising when one finds the letter popular in the first century CE and the New Testament.

Conclusion

The composition that is 2 Maccabees urges the recipients to celebrate Hanukkah. The text provides justification for this request by reminding them of the terrible circumstances in which the Jews had to exist and then of the heroic efforts of Judas Maccabeus to achieve freedom for the Jews and restoration and rededication for the temple. Notable features of this writing are the several heavenly interventions that are described, the account of the martyrdom of the seven brothers and their mother that has become so popular, and the description of the origin of the Feast of Hanukkah. It is also interesting to note that although Hanukah is mentioned in 2 Maccabees, the writing is not included in the Jewish canon. It is, however, considered to be a very writing by the Jews.

CHAPTER TWENTY

THE PROPHETS

Third Isaiah

A majority of scholars hold that chapters 56-66 of the "Book" of Isaiah were not written by Second Isaiah but by an associate of his. Chapters 56-66 presume that the people who have returned from exile along with those who originally remained in Judah and Jerusalem are working to rebuild the people of God.

Consider the poem in 58:1-14. This poem addresses the subject of fasting that is acceptable to God. In verses 6-14 God tells the people what is an acceptable fast. In vv. 6-7 an acceptable fast consists of releasing those bound unjustly, sharing bread with the hungry, sheltering the homeless and clothing the naked. In 9c-10a more things acceptable to God are set forth. Finally, in verse 13 it is stated that keeping the Sabbath is important to God. There is much food for thought in this passage.

In 60:1-3, the presence of God in Jerusalem and in the Temple is symbolized as light. Notice that in verse 2 the peoples of the nations are portrayed as being in darkness while the people of God are symbolized as being in the light.

The words in Is 61:1-2 may seem familiar to many. That is because they are said by Jesus at the beginning of his ministry (see Lk 4:18-19). Jesus was reading from Isaiah and interpreting it in a synagogue – pointing to himself as the prophet of God. "Today the scripture passage is fulfilled in your hearing."

"Arise, shine; for your light has come,
and the glory of the LORD has risen upon you.
for the darkness shall cover the earth,
and thick darkness the peoples;
but the LORD will arise upon you." (Isaiah 61:1-2 NRSV)

"The Spirit of the Lord is upon me;
because he has anointed me
to bring good news to the poor;
he has sent me to proclaim release to the captives
and recovery of sight to the blind,
to let the oppressed go free,
to proclaim the year of the Lord's favor." (Luke 4: 18-19 NRSV)

The section in Is 63:7-19 is a prayer for the return of God. The people have been in exile and have felt like God had abandoned them. Now they long for things to return to how they were before the fall of Israel and Judah and the ensuing exile in Babylonia. Notice that the people acknowledge that God is their father! Thinking of God as Father is not a totally new innovation in New Testament times, as some have thought.

Joel

All that is known about the person of Joel is his own name and the name of his father (1:1). Any attempt to place this composition in its place in the history of Israel must come from inside the book itself. On this basis, many scholars place the time of Joel's prophetic activity to be around 400 BCE.

Note: There is a frustration for anyone who tries to read both the NRSV and the NABRE translations. The NRSV has three chapters and the NABRE has four chapters! This difference arises because they are translating different texts. Comparison shows, however, that chapters 1 and 2 of both translations contain the same material. The difference comes after chapter 2.

The text of Joel divides into two parts. The first part, 1:2-27, tells of a crisis and its resolution. The second part, 2:28 - 3:21, contains cosmic symbolism and describes war with foreign nations.

The first part centers around the theme of the people having withdrawn from God, and then describes God trying to bring them back. It goes as follows:

1:1-12
In this section Joel describes the effects of a locust plague on various groups of people: the elders; drunkards; vine-dressers; priests; and the farmers.

1:13-20
This section is a plea for the people to cry out to the Lord. The priests should put on sackcloth and lament. The elders and all the people of the land should cry out to the LORD.
The writer says: "I cry, O LORD, and all of the wild animals cry to you."

2:1-11
These verses portray the locust swarm as approaching, referring to it as "God's army" (2:11).

2:12-17
In this section, the LORD says that "even now" (2:12) return to me with all your heart.

2:18-27
In this final section, the LORD takes pity on the people. God does not bring destruction but brings well-being instead.

Note: In 3:1-2 God says that the spirit of God will be poured out. These verses are cited by Peter in the NT in Acts of the Apostles 2:17-21(NRSV).
Jonah

The author is unknown. It is generally believed today that the 8th century prophet by the same name (see 2 Kgs 14:25) is perhaps not its author. The person who wrote Jonah probably wrote sometime during the 6th to the 4th centuries BCE.[120] The author made use of phrases and ideas from other writings of the OT. This literary technique supports a later date of composition rather than an earlier one.[121] We see then, that the Book of Jonah is collected with the prophets but also later as folk literature.

The genre of Jonah is debated. Some scholars consider it to be a fable because of the involvement of a large fish. Other scholars consider it to be a folk tale, while others consider that we may not fully understand what the experience may have been but it was that of a giant sea creature, according to Jonah.

Jonah is not at all like the other prophets. Most other prophets respond favorably to their call. In the first section, chapters 1 and 2, Jonah tries to flee from God's presence when he is called by God. God brings the prophet back by means of a large fish (The text does not say "whale"!) In the second section, chapters 3 and 4, Jonah is called a second time. This time he does as God asks but he gets angry when the Ninevites do not heed his message of warning, and God shows great mercy and does not destroy them. He is angry with God for not going through with his warning even though the people repented. God responds to Jonah's attitude by means of a giant plant.

The "story" of Jonah is told to bring a prophetic message to people of the writer's generation. At the time it was written, the people held the belief that if God warned of the destruction of a city or nation that the city or nation would surely be destroyed. This "story" illustrates the truth that God proclaims to be: "I who show favor to whom I will, I who grant mercy to whom I will" (Ex 33:19) and claims to be "The LORD, the LORD, a God gracious and merciful, slow to anger and abounding in love…." (Ex 34:6).

There is one more interesting aspect to Jonah. The very first Christians, as attested by frescoes in the catacombs – where early Christians were buried, used the image of Jonah in the fish, with Jonah emerging alive, as a sign of Christ's resurrection.

The cessation of charismatic prophecy

The age of charismatic prophecy began in about 750 BCE with the call of the prophet Amos, the herdsman from Tekoa, a village located a few miles south of Jerusalem, who was sent by God to prophesy in the Northern Kingdom of Israel. After Ezra's time, many believed that the age of charismatic prophecy had ended. They also believed that an age of prophecy would again accompany messianic times (Joel 2:28-29 NRSV; Joel 3:1-2 NABRE).[122]

The great charismatic prophets were called by God to deliver messages that interpreted the events of the time. They prophesied during the time of the monarchy and spoke of things like the destruction of Jerusalem, exile and the return from exile. After the time of Ezra the people

---

[120] Jonathan Magonet, "Book of Jonah" in *The Anchor Bible Dictionary*, Vol. III (New York: Doubleday, 1992), 941.
[121] Jonathan Magonet, 939.
[122] Anderson, Fifth Edition, 489

who were called prophets were the "cultic prophets" who took part in the worship services (see 1 Chronicles 25:1). (Note: this does not infer the new meaning of "cult" but meaning a "sect.")

In the Second Temple period, prophecy evolved into a new form of literature – apocalyptic. Although there are early evidences of apocalyptic writing in Ezekiel, Third Isaiah and Zechariah, it reached its full development in the Jewish writings of the last century BCE and the first century CE. A similar form of writing is found in the New Testament in the Book of Revelation.

CHAPTER TWENTY-ONE

THE FOLK LITERATURE

Introduction

Everyone is familiar with the story form. The love of the story –sometimes legend or myth, and sometimes literally true -- is not new. Stories have existed for thousands of years. It is not surprising, therefore, that we find different kinds of folk stories in the Holy Scriptures.

Several books of the Bible are written in story form. They are relatively brief narratives which clearly have a beginning, a middle, and an end. Words and actions reveal the characters.[123] These stories are believed to originate from ancient traditions which circulated for many years in oral form and were only later written down.

The writings we are now considering, literature that perhaps can be termed folktales or short stories, are essentially characterized by the following two observations:

- The setting of the book is considerably earlier than the time of its composition. For example, the historical setting of the book of Ruth is the time of the Judges (13th to 11th centuries BCE); its date of composition is sometime in the late 6th century BCE).

- The author makes use of historical people, places and times in order to bring a message to the readers of his own time.

Jonah

The genre of Jonah is debated. It is generally believed today that the 8th century prophet by the same name (see 2 Kgs 14:25) is not its author. On this basis, it is seen that Jonah satisfies the characteristics of folk literature.

The author is unknown. The person who wrote Jonah probably wrote sometime during the 6th to the 4th centuries BCE.[124]

The author made use of phrases and ideas from other writings of the OT. For example, there is a relationship between Jonah 4:2 and Exodus 34:6-7. This literary technique supports a later date of composition rather than an earlier one.[125]

The book of Jonah is divided into two sections: Chapters 1 and 2, and Chapters 3 and 4. In the first section Jonah is called by God but he tries to flee from God's presence. God responds the story of Jonah and the large fish. (The text does not say "whale"!) In the second section Jonah is called a second time. This time he does as God asks but the people repent and God

---

[123] Phyllis Trible, "Book of Ruth" in *The Anchor Bible Dictionary*, Vol. V (New York: Doubleday, 1992), 843.
[124] Jonathan Magonet, "Book of Jonah" in *The Anchor Bible Dictionary*, Vol. III (New York: Doubleday, 1992), 941.
[125] Jonathan Magonet, 939.

spares them. This angers Jonah because God has not carried through with what he prophesied and it makes him look bad. However, God's acceptance of the people's repentance is the central point of the narrative.

Tobit

This composition tells the story of Tobit, a descendent of the tribe of Naphtali, who along with his family is taken captive from Thisbe in upper Galilee during the reign of Shalmanesar (727-722 BCE), the king of Assyria. The story involves only seven principal characters – Tobit, his wife Anna and their son Tobias; Raguel, his wife Edna and their daughter Sarah; and Raphael the angel, who assumes the name of Azariah, in order to hide his identity.

Some modern-day scholars regard this composition as being a work of fiction, and set the date of its composition as sometime during the period 200-180 BCE. Most scholars, however, would not make such a radical claim about the writing. The highlights of this story are the prayers for death of Tobit (3:1-6) and Sarah (3:11-15), Tobit's and Sarah's prayer for life (8:4-7), and Tobit's song of praise (ch. 13). This book contains the very first form of a marriage ceremony.

Judith

Judith is a vivid narrative relating how, in a desperate situation, God delivered the Jewish people through the hand of a woman (Judith). It was originally written in Hebrew and although no Hebrew text has yet been found, the Greek texts that have survived testify to having been translated from the Hebrew.

The author was most likely a Jew living in Palestine. The unity of the text testifies to the fact that it was composed by a single author. It was written sometime in the 2nd century BCE.

Because the Book of Judith contains the names of Gentile persons who are otherwise unknown, the names of places that are otherwise unknown, historical inaccuracies of considerable significance and the heroine's names as the feminine form of Judah – the majority of scholars today regard this composition to be folk narrative. This text is noted for the many names for God that it contains.

Esther

The book of Esther comes down to us in two versions: a Hebrew version and a Greek version. The Hebrew text was written first, probably sometime during the period 165-140 BCE. The Greek version is the result of a translation along with editing of the text. The editing involved making both additions and deletions to the original Hebrew text along with the composition of lengthy additions to the Hebrew text (totaling 107 verses). This gives rise to the following complex situation:
- The Hebrew version is found in the Jewish Bible in the *Tanakh*.
- The Greek version is found with the books of the Apocrypha as in the *New Oxford Annotated Bible with the Apocrypha, Third Edition.*

169

- The *New American Bible* gives us the Hebrew version of the text along with the lengthy additions from the Greek text!

There is one further complication. The lengthy additions external to the original Hebrew text were not all added at the same time, were not all written in the same language, and were not all written by the same person! As if this were not enough, these additions appear in *The New American Bible* inside the text under the designations: A, B, C, D, E, and F while in the Septuagint (LXX) they are located at the end of the text as chapters 11 through 14!

The Book of Esther in the Hebrew version is directly connected to the Jewish Festival of Purim, a two day celebration (9:16-19, 20-22, 26-28, 31), and understood as its connection to Jewish history.

If you read the Hebrew version you will discover that there is no mention of God. If you read the lengthy additions that are part of the Greek version you will further discover that there is abundant mention of God and other aspects of religion. It is also interesting to note that this is the only book of the bible not found in the Dead Sea Scrolls at Qumran.

Baruch

The composition bearing the name of Baruch consists of three major parts: a prose prayer attributed to the exiles in Babylon (1:15-3:8); a poem about the elusiveness of wisdom and the identification of wisdom with the law (3:9-4:4); and a poem in which the theological significance of the Exile is explained and the hope of restoration is explored (4:5-5:9).

The author formed his composition out of three existing biblical passages: Dan 9; Job 28 and Is 40-55. He most likely did his work sometime during the period of restoration following the triumph of the Jews over Antiochus IV in 164 BCE.

Letter of Jeremiah

One Catholic scholar, Daniel Harrington, describes the composition as follows:

The Letter of Jeremiah purports to contain advice from Jeremiah to Jews exiled in Babylon on why they should avoid participating in non-Jewish worship. The structure of the book is set by nine refrains (vv. 16, 23, 29, 40, 44, 52, 56, 65, 69) in which the writer concludes that the pagan idols are not gods at all. After providing a historical setting in the exiled community in Babylon (vv. 1-6), the work gives ten reflections on the foolishness and uselessness of idol worship, concluding all but the last with the refrain. The reflections are repetitive and without any clear logical progression.[126]

This composition may be dated to sometime between 317 BCE and 100 BCE.

---

[126] Daniel J. Harrington, "Letter of Jeremiah," in *HarperCollins Bible Commentary*, Revised Edition, James L. Mays, General Editor (San Francisco, CA: HarperSanFrancisco, 2000), 787.

3 Maccabees

Note: The material contained in this section concerning 3 Maccabees is a condensation of the article by John J. Collins contained in *HarperCollins Bible Commentary*.[127]

This composition, 3 Maccabees, is found in some manuscripts of the Greek Bible but it is not included in two of the most important ones. It has not been accepted as canonical in the Protestant and Roman Catholic traditions. It is, however, recognized as being canonical in the Orthodox churches.

The book has nothing to do with the Maccabees. It consists of three episodes concerning Ptolemy IV Philopater, the King of Egypt (221-204 BCE). The first episode (1:1-5) is a brief account of how the king was saved from assassination at the battle of Raphia in 227 BCE. The second episode (1:6-2:24) is an account of the kings attempt to enter the Jerusalem Temple. The third episode (2:25-7:23) is an account of the king's persecution of the Jews living in Egypt and their deliverance.

The three accounts contained in 3 Maccabees are traditional stories and were most likely originally independent. It is a similar situation to the first six chapters in the Book of Daniel. In the view of John Collins, the reign of Caligula (37-41 CE) provides a plausible setting for the time when these three stories were joined together to form the book of 3 Maccabees.

One question addressed by the book is the matter of adherence to the letter of the law, including distinctive dietary laws (3:3-4), while at the same time showing loyalty to the king. The Jews who fail to follow their religion are shown contempt (2:33) and eventually receive vengeance (7:10-16).

---

[127] John J. Collins, "3 Maccabees," in *HarperCollins Bible Commentary*, Revised Edition, James L. Mays, General Editor (San Francisco, CA: HarperSanFrancisco, 2000), 837-839.

Part Four ... The Wisdom Writings
Job
Song of Songs, Proverbs and Ecclesiastes
The Wisdom of Ben Sira (Sirach)
Daniel and the Wisdom of Solomon

CHAPTER TWENTY-TWO

Wisdom Writings

Another literary category in the Bible contains what are called "wisdom books." In the ancient Near East, there was a culture of writings that were considered "wisdom," containing teaching by sages and wise men about the concept of a divinity and virtuous living. It often was derived from ancient oral stories but then eventually put in written form.

Biblical "wisdom writings" can also be called by the term "sapiential books." This term derives from the Latin word *sapientia*, meaning "wisdom." These writings include Job, Psalms, Proverbs, Ecclesiastes, the Book of Wisdom, the Song of Solomon (Song of Songs), and Sirach (Ecclesiasticus.) It should be noted that a very few Psalms are technically part of the "wisdom tradition." This is the reason that the Psalms are not included in this chapter under "wisdom writings."

We can now ask: "what is 'wisdom' as it is described in the Bible?" It means more than human knowledge, intelligent reasoning, or even the sense of being clever. It is on one level just plain good sense, judgment, and awareness of moral values (Proverbs 14:8). However, at a deeper level it is even far more profound. It is a sense that results from the relationship with God and the covenant in God's loving bond. It is a wisdom that provides meaning to life and is actually a divine gift provided by God to those who love him. It results from the experience of growing in closeness to God. Often, true wisdom is almost unspeakable and is known but can't be adequately described. It is gained in the unending quest to know more and more about God.

Job asks: Where is wisdom found?" The way to wisdom can only be enlightened by God – when a person is questing for God. The entire book of Job seems to pose man against God in this quest. Then finally Job turns humbly to God and gets God's response. "Man does not know the way to it. It is hidden from the eyes of all living things. God understands the way to it." (Job 28:12, 21, 23.) Here is the interlinear direct translation:

20

But whence does wisdom come? Where is the source of understanding?

21

וְנֶעֶלְמָה מֵעֵינֵי כָל־חָי וּמֵעוֹף הַשָּׁמַיִם נִסְתָּרָה׃

It is hidden from the eyes of all living, Concealed from the fowl of heaven.

22

אֲבַדּוֹן וָמָוֶת אָמְרוּ בְּאָזְנֵינוּ שָׁמַעְנוּ שִׁמְעָהּ׃

Abaddon and Death say, "We have only a report of it."

23

אֱלֹהִים הֵבִין דַּרְכָּהּ וְהוּא יָדַע אֶת־מְקוֹמָהּ׃

God understands the way to it; He knows its source

Use your understanding of biblical translation to draw out the meaning from the lines above, taken from an online bible interlinear.

JOB

Introduction

The Book of Job is greatly admired and loved by many. The "patience of Job" is proverbial. In James 5:11 it speaks of the patience of Job in reading a translation such as the old *Confraternity of Christian Doctrine* translation. However, modern translations of this same verse in the Book of James (in the NT) translate it as "endurance" rather than "patience." Job demonstrates his patience only in his response to disaster in the prologue (1:1 to 2:13) and his final resignation to the word of God in the epilogue (42:7-17). Besides the prologue and the epilogue, Job is anything but patient!

Who was Job? The main person of this book was not an Israelite. He was an Edomite sheik from the land of Uz, which was probably located in southeastern Palestine near Edom. Thus, the locale of the book was not Jerusalem but the edge of the desert.[128]

It is not possible to identify the author precisely with an associated date due to the lack of evidence upon on which to base a determination. It is not unreasonable to believe that the author was an Israelite sage who lived on the outskirts of Palestine. And it is perhaps not unreasonable to propose the Job was written sometime during the period of the 7th to the 5th centuries BCE.

---

[128] Anderson, 551.

This narrative is dealing with the human situation and matters of time and place are not of importance. He is concerned with matters of daily experience and with human life as it is lived from day to day.

The Text

Many people think that the Book of Job is just about suffering by a just person. seems to understand the problem treated in the Book of Job to be that of suffering by a just person. Bible scholar Anderson, however, proposes that the real problem presented in the writing is the following:

> But the problem of suffering – and its counterpart, the question of divine justice – provides the occasion for probing a much deeper question, namely, ***the character of man's relationship to God.***[129]

The Book of Job contains two primary literary forms. First, there is a prologue and an epilogue written in prose form. Secondly, there is a significant section in Hebrew poetry that presents the trial for Job and the eventual wisdom that is revealed to him by God. The Hebrew poetic sections appear to contain reflective, dramatic compositions added to a traditional story that may predate the composition of the book itself. It follows, then, that in order to understand the viewpoint of **the author of Job**, looks to the poetic part of the book perhaps independent from consideration of chapters 32-37 (see below). The composition of the traditional account in the prologue and the epilogue may have been woven together with other material from tradition in the middle.

The structure of the Book of Job may be summarized in the following manner:

- ❖ 1:1-2:13 Prose prologue
- ❖ 3:1-14:22 1st cycle of discussion
  - • Job's lament (Ch. 3)
  - • Eliphaz (Chs. 4-5) abd Job's reply (Chs. 6-7)
  - • Bildad (Ch. 8) and Job's reply (Chs. 9-10)
  - • Zophar (Ch. 11) and Job's reply (Chs. 12-14)

- ❖ 15:1-21:34 2nd cycle of discussion
  - • Eliphaz (Ch. 15) and Job's reply (Chs. 16-17)
  - • Bildad (Ch. 18) and Job's reply (Ch. 19)
  - • Zophar (Ch. 20) and Job's reply (Ch. 21)
- ❖ 22:1-27:23 3rd cycle of discussion[130]
  - • Eliphaz (Ch. 22) and Job's reply (23:1-24:17,25)
  - • Bildad (25:1-6; 26:5-14) and Job's reply (26:1-4; 27:1-12)
  - • Zophar (24:18-24? 27:13-23?)

---

[129] Anderson, 554.

[130] The third cycle of discussion has been thrown into disorder by later revisers. Given here is Anderson's reconstruction. It is clear, however, that the original form possessed a carefully developed literary scheme.

- Wisdom poem (Ch. 28) – Job's reply has been displaced by the later insertion of this wisdom poem.
- Job's reply and final defense (Chs. 29-31)

[Chapters 32-37: Who is Elihu? This is an intrusion into the literary scheme. It is generally thought that this material perhaps was added by a later Jewish writer who sought to uphold strict, orthodox Judaism even more vigorously than did the three friends in the account of their criticism of Job.]

❖ 38:1-42:6 Yahweh's answer from the whirlwind
- Yahweh's first speech (Chs. 38-39) and Job's submission   (40:1-5)
- Yahweh's second speech (40:6-41:34) and Job's repentance (42:1-6)
❖ 42:7-17 Prose epilogue

It might also be mentioned that some scholars believe that the book of Job portrays a courtroom-like scene where metaphorically humanity is holding God on trial. Another theory is that the intention was to present a theatrical-style drama. Of course, God has the final say and humanity learns a lesson!

At the very end of Job, we find an inspiring example of "wisdom writing." The resolution to Job's dilemma in testing and criticizing God is demonstrated in the paradoxical magnificence of God's own words, found in 38: 1-13. In this remarkable passage we see the following (at least):

God is Creator – not a human being
God is all knowledge – unlike man's limited understanding
God commands the forces of nature – like the sea before which man is powerless.

Job's response to God to help everyone understand is found in Job 42:1-6.

CHAPTER TWENTY-THREE

SONG OF SONGS, PROVERBS AND ECCLESIASTES

Song of Songs

In order to provide some introductory comments on this writing, we can observe a number of points from the introduction to the book in *The New Oxford Annotated Bible.*[131]

- ❖ Opinion is divided as to whether this book should be read as a single, unified poem or as a sequence of individual poems in a common style and idiom.

- ❖ The poem(s) features the voices of two lovers, one male and the other female, and their professions of love for one another. At times the two voices join in dialogue (e.g. 1:9-2:7; 4:1-5:1), but at other times they speak separately. The language is very sensuous.

- ❖ The superscription in 1:1 associates the poem(s) with Solomon, King of Israel (968-928 BCE). The nature of the Hebrew used along with its Aramaic expressions and possibly even Persian and Greek loan words, betray a postexilic date for its composition – perhaps sometime in the 4th or 3rd centuries BCE.

- ❖ Despite its late date, the poem(s) share many of its genres with Mesopotamian sacred marriage poems of the late 3rd and early 2nd millennium BCE. Also, many scholars see evidence that the writing has a form that resembles Egyptian love poetry has been interpreted symbolically as an account of the love between God and Israel.

- ❖ Christians interpreted the writing as an allegory of the soul's spiritual union with God. This allegorical interpretation was further developed over the centuries by Origen (3rd century CE), Bernard of Clairvaux in the 12th century CE and St, John of the Cross in the 16th century CE. Also, Christian tradition interprets the book in an allegorical fashion, reading it as an account of Christ's love for the Church.

Overall, the Song of Solomon presents sensuous and beautiful Hebrew poetry describing the profound passionate love that belongs to man and woman as images of God's love, and provides enlightenment on the depth of God's love.

Proverbs

The composition of Proverbs issues from the wisdom traditions of ancient Israel. It contains writings which have been collected over a long period of time and which consist of a number of different forms. The oldest material may date to the time of the early monarchy while

---

[131] F.W. Dobbs-Allsop, "Song of Solomon" in *The New Oxford Annotated Bible*, Third Edition, Michael D. Coogan, Editor (New York, NY: Oxford University Press, 2001), 959.

the final editing gives evidence of having been done during the post-exilic period (late 6th to early 5th century BCE).

Proverbs contains several different wisdom collections. Evidence of this is provided by the various headings that appear in the course of the text. Thus we find:

- Chaps. 1-9 "The proverbs of Solomon son of David, king of Israel" – a collection of wisdom poems and instructions.
- 10:1-22:16 "The proverbs of Solomon" – A collection of proverbs.
- 22:17-24:22 "The words of the wise" – A free adaptation of the Egyptian wisdom text: *The Instruction of Amenemope*.
- 24:23-34 "These also are sayings of the wise" – Another collection of sayings.
- Chaps 25-29 "These also are proverbs of Solomon. The men of Hezekiah, king of Judah, transmitted them."
- Chap 30 "The words of Agur, son of Jakeh the Massaite" – A collection containing a number of numerical proverbs.
- 31:1-9 "The words of Lemuel, king of Massa; the advice which his mother gave him" – A teaching from the queen mother to her son, the king.
- 31:10-31 No title – an alphabetic poem on the good housewife.

Consider the following description of the literary character of the book of Proverbs:

> In the Book of Proverbs we encounter a kind of literature that is quite different from the Torah, Prophets, or historical books. Conspicuously absent is any reference whatever to Israel and any interest in history at all. The book is in part a collection of proverbs or traditional sayings which almost by definition, have a timeless quality. In part it is instructional literature, presented as the teaching of a father to his son. This kind of literature is called "Wisdom literature" because of the frequency with which the words for wisdom and folly occur. While it appears only at the end of the Hebrew Bible, it was an ancient and widespread form of literature in the Near East, and it may well be more representative of popular thought in ancient Israel than the more cultic and distinctively Israelite literature.[132]

There is also a tradition that much of Proverbs was actually a manual for boys and young men teaching moral living – and that they were required to memorize it all!

Ecclesiastes

The Book of Ecclesiastes is a very good example of how people who encounter a book of the Bible in the liturgy fail to encounter the book as a whole literary work. We are all familiar with the passage 3:1-8: "For everything there is a season and a time for every matter under heaven: a time to be born and a time to die ... ." But how many individuals can give a brief statement of what the whole book of Ecclesiastes is about?

---

[132] John J. Collins, *Introduction to the Hebrew Bible* (Minneapolis, MN: Fortress Press, 2004), 487.

It is an interesting book to study, however. It is easy to read and relatively short, but at the same time the meaning of the book as a whole is puzzling. The scholars have offered a number of widely differing solutions to the problem of the book's meaning. It offers any person willing to make the effort a chance to do a little active and creative thinking!

The author identifies himself by the title in 1:1. But the meaning of the Hebrew word "Qoheleth" is not well understood. The ancient translators who translated the Hebrew Scriptures into Greek translated this title by the word (here transliterated) "Ekkleiastes" meaning, "one who leads a congregation." It is this title that comes down to us in the form of "Ecclesiastes." It has been translated as "preacher" in the past. Today it is more frequently translated as "teacher" (see NRSV translation; the NAB avoids the issue by leaving the word un-translated and simply using "Qoheleth"). All that is known about the "author" is the title that applies to him. But this does not tell us very much.

The author is identified as King David's son in 1:1. This, indeed, may be true. But some say that the linguistic evidence seems persuasive against this possibility. A number of internal points also argue against it. Most likely, therefore, it may be a case of attributing all wisdom to Solomon. Scholars will continue to mull over this question.

Regarding the questions: "Why read Ecclesiastes?" and "What wisdom do we encounter?" … consider that there is a focus to it all. Overall, the message concerns the vanity of attaching oneself too much to material things; to avoid the over-rated importance of humankind's power and control; and the forgetting of life's real meaning. God has a plan which ultimately gives human life a reality of happiness – happiness and joy to be found in and with God always.

CHAPTER TWENTY-FOUR

THE WISDOM OF BEN SIRA (SIRACH)

Sirach contains the same type of wisdom literature as Proverbs which we have discussed previously. It consists of numerous short pieces put together in some sort of loose structure. Many feel that it can be easily applied to our lives in the 21st century.

This book was written in Hebrew sometime during the period 200-180 BCE. This date is arrived at on the basis of the following observation. Chapter 50 is about the High Priest Simon II, who served as high priest during the period 219-196 BCE. From Ben Sira's description of Simeon it seems apparent that he was a contemporary, perhaps even a personal friend, of Simeon. From 1896 to the present day, only portions of the text of Sirach in Hebrew have been found. In all, about 85% of the Hebrew text has been recovered.

The author's grandson translated the book, into Greek, sometime after 132 BCE. This date is based upon the reference in the prologue to King Euergetes (probably Ptolemy VII Physcon Euergetes II) who reigned in the two periods: 170-164 and 146-117 BCE. The 38th year of his reign is, therefore, 132 BCE.[133]

Notice the statement by the grandson in his prologue that something has probably been lost in the translation. You should keep this in mind that you are, for the most part, reading the translation of a translation!

The author states his purpose in writing the book, in poetic form, in 50:27-29:

> Wise instruction,
> appropriate proverbs.
> I have written in this book,
> I, Jesus, son of Eleazar, son
> of Sirach,
> as they gushed forth from my
> heart's understanding.
> Happy the man who meditates
> upon these things,
> wise the man who takes them
> to heart!
> If he puts them into practice, he
> can cope with anything,
> for the fear of the LORD is
> his lamp.

---

[133] Patrick W. Skehan and Alexander A. Di Lella, O.F.M., *The Wisdom of Ben Sira*, The Anchor Bible, V. 39 (New York, NY: Doubleday, 1987), 8.

Note: *The "Jesus" here is not Jesus Christ but the son of Eleazar who has the name Jesus. In Hebrew, the name, Yeshua (Jesus), means "a savior."*

The grandson states his understanding of what his grandfather sought to accomplish in the first paragraph of the prologue as follows:

> Such a one was my grandfather, Jesus, who, having devoted himself for a long time to the diligent study of the law, the prophets, and the rest of the books of our ancestors, and having developed a thorough familiarity with them, was moved to write something himself in the nature of instruction and wisdom, in order that those who love wisdom might, by acquainting themselves with what he too had written, make even greater progress in living in conformity with the divine law.

This author, the grandfather Jesus ben Eleazar ben Sira, identifies his audience in 33:16-18:

> Now I am the last to keep vigil,
> like a gleaner after the vintage;
> Since by the LORD's blessing I
> have made progress
> till like a vintager I have filled
> my winepress,
> I would inform you that not for
> myself only have I toiled,
> but for every seeker
> after wisdom.

Again, like the Book of Proverbs, the Book of Sirach was intended for use in a school. It was, therefore, intended to be used by young men!

A Note about the Text and the Verse Numeration in Sirach

- ❑ The text exists today in both a shorter form contained in the manuscripts of the earliest date, and a longer form contained in manuscripts of a somewhat later date. In the case of Sirach, bibles today contain the short form based on the belief that the shorter form is the more original. (The long form can be found in the older Catholic bibles).
- ❑ A point of interest… the situation is reversed in the case of the Book of Tobit which also exists in a short and a long form. But in the case of Tobit it is the long form that is believed to be the more original. (The short form can be found in the First Edition of the *Revised Standard Version* of the Bible).
- ❑ A heads up! The verse numeration in the Book of Sirach has not been standardized. Therefore, the verse numbers in different bibles will vary. This is easily verified by comparing the text contained in the *New American Bible* with the text in the *New Revised Standard Version*.

From this brief consideration two things become apparent. First, since the contents of the majority of the book consist of individual, unorganized units, it is important to determine the beginning and end of each individual unit. In the course of doing this, the randomness and the repetition of the topics considered by the writer will become apparent.

Included here is a topical index, from Skehan and Di Lella[134], to show at a glance both the breadth of the topics contained in the book and how the same topic recurs over and over again.

I.   Wisdom and the Wise (1:1-43:33): "The beginning of wisdom is the fear of the Lord" (1:14) – 1:1-30; 4:11-19; 6:18-37; 16:24-17:23; 19:20-30; 24:1-31; 25:3-6, 10-11; 37:16-26.
  A. Praise of Wisdom's Author: 39:12-35; 42:15-43:33.
  B. Service of God and True Glory: 2:1-18; 7:29-31; 1o:19-11:6 17:24-18:14; 23:27; 32:14-33:15; 34:14-35:26.
  C. Prayer for God's people: 36:1-22.
  D. Autobiographical References: 24:30-34; 33:16-18; 34:12-13; most of 50:25-51:30.
  E. The Wise: 3:29; 14:20-15:10; 20:1-31; 21:11-24; 38:24-39:11.
    1. Wisdom applied to spiritual life
      a. humility – 3:17-24; 4:8; 7:16-17; 10:26-28.
      b. charity – 3:30-4:6, 8-10; 7:32-36; 12:1-7; 29:8-13.
      c. virtues and vices of the tongue – 5:9-6:1; 7:13; 195-17; 20:5-8, 13, 16-20, 24-31; 22:6, 27-23:4, 7-15; 27:4-7; 28:12-26.
      d. pride, folly, sin in general – 3:26-28; 10:6-18; 11:6; 16:5-23; 20:2-31; 21:1-22:2, 18; 25:2; 27:12-15, 28; 33:5; 35:22-24; 41:10.
      e. anger, malice, vengeance – 1:22-24; 27:22-28:11.
      f. evil desire – 6:2-4; 18:30-19:4; 23:5-6, 16-26.
      g. Other virtues and vices – 4:20-31; 5:1-8; 7:1-15; 8:1-19; 9:11-10:5, 29; 11:7-22; 15:11-20; 18:15-29; 25:1, 7-11; 27:8-21; 34:1-8.
    2. Wisdom applied to "practical" life
      a. parents – 3:1-16; 7:27-28; 23:14; 41:17.
      b. Children – 7:23-25; 16:1-4; 22:3-4; 25:7; 30:1-13; 41:5-10.
      c. women (including wife and daughters) – 7:19, 24-26; 9:1-9; 19:2-4; 22:3-5; 23:22-26; 25:1, 8, 13-26:18; 28:15; 33:20; 36:26-31; 40:19, 23; 42:6, 9-14.
      d. friends and associates – 6:5-17; 7:18; 9:10; 11:29-34; 12:8-13:23; 22:19-26; 27;16-21; 33:6; 36;23-25; 37:1-15.
      e. wealth – 10:30-31; 11:10-11, 14, 18-19, 23-28; 13:15-14:10; 25:2-3; 26:28-27:3; 31:1-11.
      f. poverty – 10:30-11:6, 14; 13:18-14:2; 25;2-3.
      g. enjoying life – 14;11-19
      h. loans – 29:1-7, 14-20.
      i. frugality – 29:21-28.
      j. health and doctors – 30:14-20; 38:1-15
      k. death – 38:16-23; 41;1-4.
      l. joy and pleasure – 30:21-27; 40:1-27.

---

[134] Skehan and Di Lella, 4-5.

m. manners and self-control at table – 31:12-32:13; 37:27-31.

n. household management – 7:20-22; 33:19-33.

o. travel – 34:9-12.

p. begging – 40:28-30.

q. good name – 41:11-13.

r. shame – 41:14-42:1d.

s. human respect – 42:1e-8.

Overall, this long list of topics offers a great deal of wisdom that is remarkably still relevant today. In this "wisdom" we discover the voice of God once again teaching us in his way to life and joy.

CHAPTER TWENTY-FIVE

DANIEL; THE WISDOM OF SOLOMON

DANIEL
The Traditional View

The book of Daniel is found in the Jewish Bible in the third grouping of books, the Writings. This location is undoubtedly due to the fact that Daniel was a righteous and wise man (see Ezekiel 14:14 and 28:3). In Christian Bibles, the book of Daniel is placed with the prophets; immediately after Ezekiel and just before Hosea. Placing the book of Daniel along with the prophets in the Scriptures surely arises from an opinion that Daniel was one of the prophets. Daniel is identified as a prophet in one manuscript found at Qumran, in Josephus's *Antiquities*, and in the Gospel of Matthew (24:115).

One can determine the historical setting of the book of Daniel by noting the kings who are mentioned in the text. Jehoiakim of Judah is mentioned in 1:1. The third year of Jehoiakim's reign was 606 BCE. The story of Daniel is said to have ended during the reign of Cyrus of Persia (10:1). The reign of Cyrus began in 539 BCE and, therefore, his third year was 536 BCE. Nebuchadnezzar of Babylon appears in 1:1, 2:1 and elsewhere. So then the setting of the narrative in the book of Daniel would seem to be during the years of the Exile in Babylon. This is well within the period of the prophets. It is interesting to observe that the account of Daniel, as determined from the text, spans exactly 70 years, a number of years that has considerable significance in the Bible as does the period of 40 years (the Exile of 40 years in the desert, and Jesus spending 40 days in the desert).

Thus, the traditional view of the book of Daniel is that the book deals with a historical person who was deported from Jerusalem to Babylon, and chronicles the experiences and visions he had in Babylon and thereabouts during the reigns of four kings: Nebuchadnezzar, Belshazzar, Darius the Mede and Cyrus (550-530 BCE).[135]

With this information in hand, one approaches the task of reading the book of Daniel as a writing similar to those of other prophets – a book consisting of a collection of prophetic oracles.

Outline of Contents
- Part I – Tales in the third person about Daniel and the famous account of his three friends – Shadrak, Mishak, and Abebnego who were thrown into a fiery furnace.
  - 1:1-21 The food test.
  - 2:1-49 The King's dream.
  - 3:1-100 (NAB) Daniel's three friends in the fiery furnace.
  - 4:1-34 Nebuchadnezzar's own account .
  - 5:1-30 Belshazzar's banquet and the writing on the wall.
  - 6:1-29 Daniel in the lion's den

---

[135] Louis F. Hartman and Alexander A. Di Lella, *The Book of Daniel*, V.23 (New York: Doubleday & Company, Inc., The Anchor Bible Series, 1978), 46.

- ❑ Part II – Daniel's Dreams and Visions Related by Himself (in the first person)
  - 7:1-28 The vision of the four bests and the man.
  - 8:1-27 The vision of the ram and the he-goat.
  - 9:1-27 The seventy weeks of years.
  - 10:1-12:13 The final revelation

- ❑ Part III – Three Additional Stories
  - Chapter 13 (NAB) Susanna.
  - Chapter 14 (NAB) Bel and the Dragon.
    - Bel (vv. 1-22)
    - The Dragon (vv. 23-42)

Note #1: It is immediately seen that the book of Daniel does not consist of a collection of prophetic oracles like those of the major and minor prophets. Clearly, it is not one of a kind with those books of the prophets!

Note #2: The NAB contains a number of additions to Daniel that are contained in the Apocrypha (and in a Protestant Bible that includes the Apocrypha under the title: "Additions to Daniel.") These additions to Daniel consist of: The Prayer of Azariah and the Hymn of the Three Jews (3: 24-90 NAB); Susanna, and Bel and the Dragon.

The Composition of Daniel

Any theory of the composition of Daniel must account for the following four factors:

- ❖ The stories in Chapters 1-6, on close examination, give evidence of having been written during the Persian period (539-333 BCE).
- ❖ The visions recorded in Chapters 7-12 give evidence of having been written in the early Maccabean period (2nd Century BCE)
- ❖ The book as it comes down to us is written in three languages – Aramaic, Hebrew and Greek. The section 2:4b-7:28 is written in Aramaic; the rest of chapters 1-12 are written in Hebrew; the additions to Daniel are written in Greek.

On the basis of careful analysis scholars Hartman and Di Lella propose the following theory for the composition of the book of Daniel:[136]

- ❑ The presence of historical inconsistencies in the text points to the conclusion that the writing was done at a later time when the time of the Exile was in the distant past.

- ❑ The six stories that comprise Chapters 1-6 may go back, in oral form, to the Persian period.
  - They contain many correct references to customs and terms used at the Persian court

---

[136] Louis E. Hartman and Alexander A. Di Lella, 13-14.

- The Greek names for the musical instruments in 3:5 probably do not antedate the time of Alexander the Great (336-323 BCE).
□ The vision of Chapter 7, without the later glosses [very small additions] in vss. 8, 11a, 20b-22, 24b-25, probably dates to shortly before 168 BCE. It seems to be a development of the ideas in Chapter 2.

□ The apocalypse in Chapter 8, without the later additions of vss. 13-14, 16, 18-19, 26a and 27b, was composed by another author (i.e. different from the author of Ch. 7) shortly after the desecration of the Temple in 167 BCE.

□ The revelation in 10:1-12:4 was written by a third author shortly before the summer of 165 BCE, when he expected a third campaign of Antiochus IV against Egypt (cf. Dan 11:40-44) – which did not take place.

□ Chapter 9, without the clearly interpolated prayer of vss. 4-20, was written by a fourth author after Antiochus' victory over Artaxias of Armenia in 165 BCE but before the religious persecution toward the end of 164 BCE.

□ The author of Chapter 9 is the final redactor of the complete book. He added his work to that of Chapters 7, 8, and 10-12 and, at the same time, revised each of these three other chapters by adding explanatory verses as follows:
  - To Chapter 7 he added vss. 8, 11a, 20b-22, 24b-25, all of which deal with the small horn which represents Antiochus IV.
  - To Chapter 8 he added vss. 13-14, 16, 26a and 27b which deal with the angel Gabriel and speculation on the length of time before the end of the persecution.
  - To chapters 10-12 he added 11:1 and 12:5-10, 13.

□ Two additional glosses were added sometime later, namely 12:11, 12:12 and the prayer 9:4-20, by one or more other persons.

□ Finally, a Hebrew translator put 1:1-2:4a and chapters 8-12 into Hebrew from the original Aramaic. His work was done around 140 BCE.

□ At some point, the additions to Chapter 3 and the stories of Susanna and Bel and the Dragon were added to the basic book, Chapters 1-12.

Conclusion

Hartman and Di Lella point out that:

....the book in its present form has an overall literary unity centering on the person of Daniel and a central theological purpose, viz. To inculcate courage and fidelity in the persecuted and disheartened Jews of Maccabean times ....[137]

---

[137] Louis F. Hartman and Alexander A. Di Lella, 16.

This is a remarkable conclusion as revealed by modern day scholarly analysis in considering the complex compositional history of the book.

Wisdom of Solomon

There is no consensus regarding the exact identity of the author other than that he was a Jew. He probably wrote in the Greek language in Alexandria, Egypt. He did his writing sometime during the period 30 BCE to 40 CE.

It is interesting to note that in the *Muratorian Canon*, which dates to 180-190 CE, the Book of Wisdom is listed among the New Testament Books![138]

Although the book was written in Greek, in the first part of the book (1:1-11:1), the Hebrew device of parallelism between the two colons of a line of poetry is used to great effect. (This may indicate poetic expression carried by oral tradition from an earlier period.) In the latter part of the book (11:2-19:22) a freer prosaic style of writing was used, revealing a familiarity and ease with Greek poetry and prose and, consequently, parallelism is much less in evidence.

Because of this change in style, a reader may encounter some difference in how the book is printed in comparing one bible with another. The *New American Bible* and the *New Revised Standard Version* both print it entirely in the form of poetry. In doing this, they both overlook the fact that the second part of the book would perhaps better be read and understood in a prose form. The *Good News Bible*, Catholic Study Edition, on the other hand, has seen fit to print the entire book in prose form (as it does for almost all of the Book of Sirach!)

The Book of Wisdom is divided into three major sections: 1) 1:1-6:21; 2) 6:22-11:1; and 11:2-19:22. Each of these major sections has its own internal structure. For our purposes here it will be sufficient to treat only the first of these sections.

Two major influences acted on the writer's thought: Hellenism and the Hebrew Scriptures. The author retains a Hebrew outlook while expressing his thoughts in a language that is understandable within Hellenism.

The prime influence and source for the thought for the person who composed the Book of Wisdom are the Jewish Scriptures.[139] The author makes use of them in every section of his writing. It is seen that:

✓ In the first of the three major sections, 1:1-6:21, the images from the creation and fall stories (Gen 1-3) are the basis for the argument on justice, death and immortality. There may also be influences from Is 52-58.

---

[138] Michael Kolarcik, S.J., "The Book of Wisdom" in *The New Interpreter's Bible*, V. V, Leander E. Keck et al, Editors (Nashville, TN: Abingdon Press, 1997), 438-39.
[139] Kolarcik, S.J., 441

✓ In the second section, 6:22-11:1, use is made of the personification of wisdom in Prv 8 and Sir 24. Chapter 9 is influenced by 1 Kgs 3:2 and Chr 1. And chapter 10 is a recalling of salvation history.

✓ In the third section of the book, 11:2-19:22, Exodus and Numbers provide the basis.

The author seeks to bolster the faith of his Jewish community that is under attack by powerful forces. Finally, the author advances consideration of the status of life after death that was prevalent in his time. The unambiguous declaration of everlasting life after death for the faithful was a late development in Hebrew thought (Dan 12:2-3; 2 Macc 7:9). Wisdom teaches about eternal life of the just after death by means of terms "immortal" (1:15; 3:4; 4:1; 8:17; 15:3) and "incorruptible" (2:23; 6:18-19).[140]

Finally, some scholars will evaluate the Book of Wisdom in the following way:

1. Book of Eschatology (having to do with end times)
   - exhortation to justice
   - speech of the impious, contrasts of the wicked and the just
   - exhortation to wisdom
2. Book of Wisdom
   - Solomon's speech concerning wisdom, wealth, power and prayer
3. Book of History
   - introduction, followed by diptychs of plagues (diptychs are small doubled references)
   - digression on God's power and mercy
   - digression on false worship and further plagues
   - recapitulation and concluding doxology.

Once again, we have a writing which is somewhat complex but with careful study can provide many interesting aspects that present over and over again the provision of God's care and love, and the difficulties that can follow from rejecting God.

---

[140] Kolarcik, S.J., 446-447.

CHAPTER TWENTY-SIX

THE HEART OF THE OLD TESTAMENT

Introduction

For the moment, let us focus our attention on that portion of salvation history that came before the birth of Jesus Christ. Let's inquire into the matter of whether or not any one of the historical events in salvation history before Christ holds greater precedence or core meaning than all of the other events which took place in this period. Putting this in a slightly different way, let us take as our objective the task of determining the answer to the following question: Does the OT have a heart and, if so, what is that heart?

Seeking the Heart of the OT

Make the following observation: take out your Bible and turn to the book of **Exodus**. Starting at the beginning skim along until you come to the place where the Israelites have escaped from Egypt. If you have done this you should be at **Ex 15:21** – just at the end of the song that occupies the first part of the chapter. Since Moses received his commission from God to lead the Israelites out of Egypt in **Exodus Chapter 3,** it takes some 12 chapters to accomplish the escape. We can observe that much space is devoted to the escape, leading one to think that this must be a very important event in the history of the Israelites. Let us follow up on this and see how this event plays out in the rest of the OT. For this purpose we include the following excerpt from the *Anchor Bible Dictionary* that demonstrates the multitude of references throughout the Old Testament that refer to the Exodus:

> **Later Biblical Allusions to the Exodus, and Their Significance.** Such allusions back to the Exodus-event are relatively numerous across the varied span of the OT writings. For the reader's convenience, they can be usefully grouped by function and in broad biblical sequences.
>
> a. The basic historical reason why Israel should **accept and obey** YHWH's covenant. In the introduction to the Ten Commandments, both at Sinai and in Moab (Ex 2:20; Deut 5:6), he is their deliverer from slavery in accord with ancient promise (cf. Gen 15:13-14; 48:21; 50:24-25, for what was envisaged). Reminders of Israel's covenant indebtedness to their deliverer from Egypt then recur in the settlement narratives (Josh 24:5-7,17, covenant renewal at Shechem; cf. Jgs 2:1-3, 12; 6:7-10, 13; 1 Sam 10:18-19), under Solomon (1 Kgs 8:51, 53; 9:9 = 2 Chron 7:22), then during the Divided Monarchy, Babylonian exile, and later (cf. Hos 12:9-10,13; 13:4; Amos 2:10-11; 3:1-2; 9:7, in terms of judgment: Mic 6:3-4; Jer 2:6-7; 7:22-26; 11:3-5,7; 32:20-23; 34:13). The editor of Kings (2 Kgs 17:7, 36), then others (Ezek 20:5-10; Dan 9:15; Neh 9:9-12) follow out this line. It also appears in the Psalms (78; 80:8; 81:6-7; 105:34-39; 106; 136:10-16).

b. A motivating reason for the Israelites' proper **treatment of each other** and of strangers, as pointed out by Sarna (1986:3-5), and at feasts. See Exod 22:21; 23:9; 23:15 (also 34:18); 29:44-46. Likewise, in Lev 11:1- 45; 18:3; 19:33-34, 36; 22:32-33 (cf. 25:54-55); 23:42-43; 25:36-38, 42:26:13, 45. Fleetingly, we have only Num 15:40-41 in that book. Contrast Deuteronomy - in the prologue (4:20, 34, 37), as a basis for gratitude (a., above); and motivation, 6:12, 21-23; 7:8; 11:3-4; 13:5, 10; 16:1 (feast), 12; 20:1; 24:18, 22; 26:6-10; 29:22-26. This theme thus extends across all aspects of the law.

c. Knowledge of the Exodus-event as showing the **sovereignty of the God** of Israel is credited by the Hebrew writers to people in Canaan in Joshua's time (Jos 2:10; 9:9), and to Transjordanians under the judges (Judg 11:13),. Cf. also the Balaam episode, Num 22:5, 11; 23:22; 24:8.

d. With the passing of time, the Exodus-event was used as an initial **dateline** (though not necessarily numerically) for the Israelites' history - much as the Egyptians would remark that something or other had never been seen "since the founding of the land" or "since the time of the god," in their case. Such "dateline" references occur during the settlement (Judges 19:30 - a deed, its like never seen since Israel left Egypt; the beginning of Eli's priestly line,1 Sam 2:27; the time span of Israel's disobedience, 1 Sam 8:8; and the starting point of Samuel's historical review, 1 Sam 12:6-8).This usage is found associated with the times of David (2 Sam 7:6, 23-24 = 1 Chr 17:5, 21-22). Solomon (1 Kgs 6:1, 480th year; 1 Kgs 8:16 = 2 Chr 6:5), and Manasseh (2 Kgs 21:15). Cf. Jer 16:14-15; 23:7-8; 32:20.

e. Allusions to the period of the Exodus occur as a basis for **comparison for later events,** such as under Saul (1 Sam 15:6; cf. usage in Isa 11:16 and Mic 7:15); and simply as a long past event, as with Solomon (1 Kgs 8:9 = 2 Chr 5:10; 1 Kgs 8:21 = 2 Chr 6:11), Hosea (2:15; 11:1), Haggai (2:5), and the Psalms (114; 135:8,9).[141]

All during early Hebrew history, therefore, from the settlement in Canaan (and probably even from Sinai), down through the history of the Israelites – to the Babylonian exile and beyond, there are many references to Exodus. They are expressed in different ways. This all forms an attitude of thanksgiving to God. God provides deliverance. It is the central reason for the people caring for others who have been oppressed like them. The Exodus creates a dateline for other events and as a comparison to everything else that happens. For the Israelites, it is history that is in the past but has a continuing vital importance.

The significance of the event of the Exodus is evidenced by looking at passages that appear to be **types of creeds**, found in Deuteronomy and Nehemiah. In Deuteronomy, we find an ancient liturgical statement which dates to a time prior to the United Monarchy, even perhaps to

---

[141] K.A. Kitchen, "The Exodus" in *The Anchor Bible Dictionary*, Vol 2 (New York: Doubleday, 1992), 701.

the time of Joshua who was the successor to Moses. This passage, **Deut 26:5b - 10**, goes as follows:

> A wandering Aramean was my ancestor; he went down into Egypt and lived there as an alien, few in number; and there he became a great nation, mighty and populous. When the Egyptians treated us harshly and afflicted us, by imposing hard labor on us, we cried to the Lord, the God of our ancestors; the Lord heard our voice and saw our affliction, our toil, and our oppression. The Lord brought us out of Egypt with a mighty hand and an outstretched arm, with a terrifying display of power, and with signs and wonders; and he brought us into this place and gave us this land, a land flowing with milk and honey. So now I bring the first of the fruit of the ground, that you, O Lord, have given me." (NRSV)

It is seen that this ancient liturgical prayer devotes the majority of its attention to the Exodus event, treating the Patriarchal Period and the Conquest in a compressed form. This ancient liturgical element is echoed in **Ezek 20:5-6**.

Now read **Neh 9:9-12** which also speaks of the Exodus event. Recalling that Nehemiah came to Jerusalem after the return from the Babylonian Exile (i.e. after 538 BCE), it is seen that the Exodus event retained its importance for the people of God for over 500 years. Of course, it retains that significance down to this present day for both Jews and Christians.

An important theme in **Second Isaiah (Is Chaps. 40-55)** is that of a new Exodus. Second Isaiah, writing just prior to the return from the Babylonian exile, describes Israel's return from exile in terms of imagery taken from the traditions of the Exodus.[142] The writer of Second Isaiah develops this theme in greater length in as described by Bernard W. Anderson and Walter Harrelson, eds., in *Israel's Prophetic Heritage*.[143]

The Exodus event came to be regarded as a revelation of who God is and how God acts. In **Ex 15:2** and **Hos 13:4** God is shown to be the savior. In **Ex 15:6, Josh 2:10; Is 43:14-17** and **Ps 66:5-6** God is shown to be powerful. And in **Ex 15:3, Ps 103:7-8** God is seen to be merciful.

Finally, the Exodus event came to be regarded as the event that made the Israelites realize that they were the people of God (see **Num 22:5,11; 1 Kgs 8:51; Dan 9:15; Hos 11:1; Amos 3:1-2 and Mic 6:3-4)**.

Today this significant event in the history of the Israelites is retold and relived in the liturgy of the **Jewish Passover feast**.

---

[142] Bernard W. Anderson, *Understanding the Old Testament*, 2nd Edition (Englewood Cliffs, N.J.: Prentice-Hall, 1966), 409-410.

[143] Bernard W. Anderson and Walter Harrelson, eds., *Israel's Prophetic Heritage*, Essays in honor of James Muilenburg, New York, Harper & Row, 1962.

Is the Exodus event the whole heart of the OT?

On the basis of all that has been said above it would seem obvious that we have, indeed, found the heart of the OT. However, this is not the whole matter. We have actually only found half of what we will call "the heart." We cannot be satisfied with half of a pie. We need to do a bit more work and find the other half as well. But it will not take us long to find the other half. We do not have to look far; it is right under our noses so to speak.

Look at the account of the Exodus in the OT and see how much space is given to the stay of the Israelites at Sinai. They arrive at the mountain in the desert of Sinai at the very beginning of **chapter 19** of Exodus. Now look to see when the departure from Sinai occurred. To find this you will have to go all the way to the **11th verse of the 10th chapter** of the Book of **Numbers!** The Israelites stay at Sinai from the 19th chapter of Exodus, all through the book of Leviticus, to the 10th chapter of Numbers - that is about **50 chapters of narrative**! If so much space is devoted to their stay at Sinai it must be because something of great importance happened there.

What happened at Sinai? Look at **Exodus 19:3-5.** Here Moses goes up the mountain to God and God tells Moses that "the One" will make a covenant with the Israelites. Is this covenant an important concept in the OT? If we look up the word **"covenant"** in a bible concordance –we will find that the word occurs over 300 times in the OT. Furthermore, if we look at which books it appears in, we will find that it appears in the majority of OT books. The **covenant** is the other half of the heart of the OT.

It is the Exodus event and the covenant, together, that comprise the whole heart of the OT. The brief passage in **Ex 3:9-12** serves to tie the two together:

> The cry of the Israelites has now come to me; I have also seen how the Egyptians oppress them. So come, I will send you to Pharaoh to bring my people, the Israelites, out of Egypt. But Moses said to God, "Who am I that I should go to Pharaoh, and bring the Israelites out of Egypt?" He said, "I will be with you; and this shall be the sign for you that it is I who sent you: when you have brought the people out of Egypt, you shall worship God on this mountain." (NRSV)

The covenant

The scholar Lawrence Boadt provides a truly in-depth study of the covenant that is important and fascinating. For future reference, the reader may someday want to look up "covenant" in Boadt's work. [144]

What is a covenant? The contemporary dictionary defines "covenant" as a formal, solemn and binding agreement. Today many Christian theologians refer to marriage as a covenant. In the OT, the Hebrew word **"berit"** is used to express the concept of a covenant and it refers to a binding agreement such as the covenant made between Jacob and Laban in **Gen 31:44**.[145]

---

[144] Lawrence Boadt, *Reading the Old Testament* (New York: Paulist Press 1984), 173-182.
[145] Boadt, 174.

191

Boadt and other scholars contend that in the ancient Near East (ANE) there were **two types of covenants,** or treaties, between peoples: **the parity treaty and the vassal treaty**. The parity treaty was a treaty between kings of equal stature. The vassal treaty was between a king who was a major power and the king of a small nation that had been conquered by the great king, a people who were so weak that they had to cooperate with the great king. The Israelites, experiencing the power of Yahweh in the Exodus event, first expressed their relationship with God in terms of the vassal type of covenant similar to the Hittite treaties of the period 1400-1200 BCE.[146]

The Hittite vassal treaties had a certain form. The form of these treaties has been determined from an analysis of various kinds of treaties found in the ancient world. No complete treaty has been completely preserved and none of the extant examples (those which survive to this day from the ancient world) hold all the characteristics that constitute the form. The form has to be determined from an analysis of all of the individual treaties found. It is apparent that the Israelites may have been using the concepts in these ancient civil treaties to express something new, their relationship to the God who was saving them. The following is a presentation of the six part form characteristic of a vassal-type treaty along with a sample taken from one of the treaties archaeologists discovered.

Constituent parts of the Vassal Treaty

1. **The Preamble** in which the overlord, or great king, gives his name and title:
   "These are the words of the sun Mursillis, the great king, the king of
   Hatti-land, the valiant, the favorite of the storm-god, the son of Suppululiumas
   the great king"(ANET 203) [Referring to an actual "Ancient Near East Treaty"
   - ANET as they were found by archaeologists.]

2. **The Historical Prologue** in which the great king lists his past acts of kindness
   to the vassal as the reason for the vassal king's obligation to obey:
   "Aziras, your grandfather, and Du-Teshub, your father remained
   loyal to me as their lord … Since your father had mentioned to me your
   name with great praise, I sought after you … and put you in the place of your
   father." (ANET 203-204)

3. **The Stipulations or Demands** that the overlord binds the vassal to keep:
   "If anyone utters a word unfriendly to the king or the Hatti-land
   before you, Duppi-Tessub, you shall not withhold his name from the king."
   (ANET 204)

4. **Deposit of the treaty in a temple and public readings at set times:**
   "A duplicate of this treaty has been deposited before the sun-goddess
   of Arinna …. In the Mitanni land, a duplicate has been deposited before
   Teshub …. At regular intervals they shall read it in the presence of the king
   of the Mitanni land and in the presence of the sons of the Hurri land." (ANET 205).

---

[146] Boadt, 176-177.

5.   **The list of witnesses** is important to any contract. But for a solemn state covenant, the witnesses are the gods of the two lands:
"We have called the gods to be present, to listen, to serve as witnesses:
the sun-goddess of Arinna … the sun god, the lord of heaven,, the storm-god,
the lord of the Hatti-land … the mountains, the rivers, the Tigris and Euphrates,
heaven and earth, the winds and clouds." (ANET 205-206)

6.   **The Curses and Blessings** end the treaty. The divine beings are called on to maintain the treaty in the divine courtroom by imposing rewards and penalties:
"Should Duppi-Teshub not honor these words of the treaty and oath,
may these gods of the oath destroy Dippi-Teshub together with his person,
his wife, his son, his grandson, his house, his land … But if he honors
these words … may these gods of the oath protect him with his person,
his wife, his son, his grandson, his house and his country." (ANET 205)[147]

Chapter 19 of Exodus describes the events leading up to the giving of the covenant between Yahweh and the Israelites. The content of the treaty is contained in **Ex 20:1-17.**With these elements of a treaty in mind, we now can read through the passage. Observe that the first two elements of the vassal treaty, the preamble and the historical prologue, are here merged into one - the Exodus event serves both to describe the God who is entering into the treaty and provides the list of things which the great "king" has done for the vassal "king" – in this case the Israelites who are accepting a covenant with God. The **stipulations are the Ten Commandments** (or the **Ten Words** which is the way the Hebrew text reads.) Thus, the first three elements of the vassal treaty are present, although in modified form.

The fourth element, the deposit of the treaty in the temple and public readings at set times can also be seen to be present. **Ex 25:1-22** gives detailed instructions for building an Ark of acacia wood to serve as the meeting place between God and Moses and the two stone tablets bearing the Ten Commandments are placed in this Ark. This later was replaced by placing an Ark with the copy of the covenant in the temple. The public reading of the covenant does not appear explicitly in the OT but **Joshua chapter 24** presents a covenant renewal ceremony which is similar to a public reading. Hence the fourth element of the typical treaty is essentially present. To this day, Orthodox Jews publicly read aloud the Exodus account on a yearly basis.

The fifth element of the typical treaty, the witnesses, does not appear. But this is to be expected. Note that the usual witnesses in the Hittite treaty are other gods. In the case of the Israelites there is **only one God, Yahweh,** instead one god of many gods. Hence, there are no other gods to serve as witnesses to the treaty.

The sixth and final element, the blessings and curses do not appear at all here in the Book of Exodus. They can be found in the Book of Deuteronomy. It is interesting to read through these

---

[147] Boadt, 177-178.

long lists of curses for those who reject God's covenant and the list of blessings for those who know God and become part of his covenant.

Take a moment and look at **chapter 24 of Joshua.** You will be able to identify many of the elements of the Hittite vassal treaty form in this passage. The setting is that of a convocation of the people at Shechem. The preamble is seen in verse 2a: "Thus says the Lord, the God of Israel ..." A rather substantial historical summary follows in verses 2b-13. The following two verses 14 and 15 contain the stipulations. The witnesses to the covenant are rather interesting. There are two witnesses: the people themselves (verse 22) and a great stone (verses 26 and 27). A sanction, which corresponds to a curse, is found in verse 20. The account states that Joshua wrote all of these things in a book but it does not say what he did with the book. Neither does it give any indication that there were periodic public readings of the book. So to a great degree, the covenant formulary is present in this account of the covenant renewal ceremony.

The covenant formulary is also to be found in the Book of Deuteronomy. But here we must keep in mind that Deuteronomy was written during the Exile in Babylon and perhaps edited after the Exile was over. Boadt points out that we have two sources of ancient vassal treaties, the Hittite treaties from the period 1400-1200 BCE and a number of Assyrian treaties from 700-600 BCE. So much time divides these two groups of treaties that it is not surprising that there are differences between them. Boadt says:

> The later Assyrian treaties show many of the same parts, although they sometimes lack the elaborate preamble and prologue of the Hittite types, while the list of curses and exotic punishments increases dramatically, perhaps to serve as a scare tactic to make the vassal keep the treaty.[148]

The covenant formulary is found in the book of Deuteronomy as follows:

Preamble **Dt 1:1**
Historical Prologue **Dt 1:2-4:40**
Stipulations **Dt 4:44-26:19**
Provision for periodic reading **Dt 27:8**
Witnesses None
Curses and blessings **Dt chaps 27 and 28**

Note the presence of an extended section of **blessings and curses** which is characteristic of the Assyrian type of treaty as mentioned above.[149]

There is one interesting facet of the Book of Deuteronomy that is worthy of note. In 622 BCE, the 18th year of the reign of King Josiah of Judah, workmen were making some repairs to the Temple in Jerusalem (2 Kgs 22:5). The high priest, Hilkiah, found "the book of the law in the house of the Lord" (22:8). When the king read the book which Hilkiah had found, he was motivated to make a covenant before the Lord (22:11-23:3). It is commonly believed by scholars

---

[148] Boadt, 178.
[149] Boadt, 351.

today that this book found in the temple constitutes what is contained in Deuteronomy chapters 12-26.

The significance of the covenant

Quoting from Boadt:

Berit is a term so rich it captures the heart of Israel's religious beliefs: (1) they are bound to an unbreakable covenant-union with their God; (2) he has made known his love and his mercy to them; (3) he has given them commandments to guide their daily life; (4) they owe him worship, fidelity and obedience; (5) they are marked by the sign of that covenant-bond. The covenant created the unity of the nation Israel, based not on blood relationship but on submission to the divine will and the confession that he alone is God. In turn, God pledges himself to be Israel's personal protector and helper, not only against foreign enemies, but against sickness, disease and chaos as well. Most of all, he will be present whether it is a time of prosperity or of failure, for he has laid claim to this people as his own. Yahweh is a personal God who demands personal loyalty. He gives no guarantee that his protective love and help always involves victory in battle, wealth in possessions, or increase of territory; it may at times include such gifts, but more often it describes the blessing that trust in the Lord will bring: freedom from fear in the promised land, the fruitfulness of children and crops, permanent peace and the joy of knowing God is near.[150]

The Heart of the Old Testament

We have arrived at the point where we can determine what is to be found at the heart of the Old Testament. It is the Exodus and the Covenant that God offered to the people during their trials in the desert. These are the two aspects of the very heart of the Hebrew Scriptures and it is on these elements that the messiah Christ comes to fulfill the Covenant in the New Testament. Remembering that the "Bible" of the time of Jesus was always considered to be the Hebrew Scriptures, this means that Jesus, his family, his disciples, his friends and those Gentiles, too, who joined "the Way" of Jesus, carried this treasure of the memory of the Exodus and the Covenant always in their hearts of faith.

---

[150] Boadt, 175.

IV. EXPLORING THE CANONICAL WRITINGS WRITTEN AFTER THE BIRTH OF JESUS

***Part One … Jesus and the Apostolic Period*:**
> The Gospel of Mark
> The Synoptic Problem
> The Synoptic Gospels of Matthew and Luke
> The Gospel of John
> Luke-Acts

INVITATION

One might expect that an investigation of the gospels will indeed begin by seeking to provide an answer to the question: What is a gospel? We will, however, not begin in this way. We prefer to defer answering that question until such time as you, the reader, has sufficient time to become familiar with each of the four gospels that are contained in the Scriptures. As we proceed in our investigations, you will become aware that three of the Gospels – Mark, Matthew and Luke - are quite similar to each other in both content and form. Because of the fundamental similarity these three Gospels have become lumped together under the group term: **Synoptic Gospels**. The fourth gospel, the Gospel of John differs considerably from the Synoptics in both content and form.

At the start, also, it may be helpful to consider the actual meaning of the word, "gospel" (*evangelium,* Latin form). From the online bible study site, Bible.org, we learn:

> The term *gospel* is found ninety-nine times in the NASB and ninety-two times in the NET Bible. In the Greek New Testament, *gospel* is the translation of the Greek noun *euangelion*(occurring 76 times) "good news," and the verb *euangelizo* (occurring 54 times), meaning "to bring or announce good news." Both words are derived from the noun *angelos*, "messenger." In classical Greek, an *euangelos* was one who brought a message of victory or other political or personal news that caused joy.
> In addition, *euangelizomai* (the middle voice form of the verb) meant "to speak as a messenger of gladness, to proclaim good news."[1] Further, the noun *euangelion* became a technical term for the message of victory, though it was also used for a political or private message that brought joy.[151]

The New Testament book, Acts of the Apostles, will also be considered in this part along with the Gospels. Our primary reason for including the Book of Acts along with the Gospel of Luke is that, in reality, they are a single writing in two volumes by the same author who is Luke. These two writings (Luke and Acts) are read with greatest benefit, therefore, if they are read one after the other. Although we treat the Gospel of Luke in Chapter 29 as one of the Synoptics, we have devoted Chapter 30 to the two-volume work Luke-Acts and consider Acts in some detail.

---

[151] "What is the Gospel?" Bible.org … "what is a gospel?" (Accessed October 23, 2017)

The scholars like to speak of the three stages of Gospel formation. They see these stages in terms of something like the following:

- First stage – The public activity of Jesus (the first third of the 1st century CE.
- Second stage – The apostolic preaching about Jesus (The 2nd third of the 1st century CE).
- Third stage – The gospels are put in final written form (Last third of the 1st Century CE).

History, however, does not move according to the neatly defined periods as determined by the scholars. In reality, the emergence of written gospels was the result of a more complicated and continuous historical process. The lifetime of Jesus, at least that part that constituted his public life, is well defined. His death is fixed at 30 or 33 CE and his public ministry took place in the one or two years prior to that. Following that, the period of apostolic preaching lasted until the death of the final apostle – Peter and Paul lived into the late sixties and the Apostle John of Zebedee until considerably later in the 1st century. The written gospels are then believed to begin with the writing of Mark in the period 65-70 CE, then continue with the writing of Matthew and Luke sometime in the decade of the 80s, and finally end with the writing of the Gospel of John sometime around 90 CE.

During the period of his life on earth, Jesus went about speaking with individuals and crowds of people. His presentation was entirely oral and the people received his teaching by ear and cherished them in their memory. His teaching was then passed from one individual to another orally. So very quickly the teaching of Jesus would reach the ear of people from other people who had not been eye witnesses of the teaching. Sometime later, the teaching of Jesus would reach the ear of the individuals who wrote the gospels. Most likely, the first one to undertake to write a gospel would have little but oral information with which to work. Thus, as we will come to see, the main reason for the gospels of Mark, Matthew and Luke to take on the form which they did is due to the fact that their authors were working with oral traditions (or perhaps some short-written forms of the oral tradition).

Let us begin our investigation of the gospels in the following way. We will take up first the study of the Gospel of Mark. We choose to begin with this Gospel because at the present time it is generally agreed by scholars this was the first, by some 20 years or so, the first complete gospel to be written. This position is referred to, in academic circles, as the "priority of Mark."

Many individuals have suggested that the best way to begin studying Mark is to sit down and read through it all at one sitting; "it will take only about an hour and a half," they say. We believe, however, that in the process of doing so an average reader will fail to notice many important features. We propose an alternative approach - taking on the Gospel one piece at a time. The wisdom of this approach will become apparent as we proceed.

In describing the Gospels, we could perhaps speak of the "atomic theory" of the synoptic gospels picking up on the knowledge that all matter is composed of atoms bound together by electrical forces. (The reader should guess which author of this book came up with this analogy!) Mark's gospel is constructed from small literary units joined together by means of changes in time or location.

At this point we would like to invite you to begin studying the Gospels by joining with us in an investigation of the Gospel of Mark.

CHAPTER TWENTY-seven

THE GOSPEL OF MARK

Introduction

We will begin our study of the gospels by treating the Gospel of Mark. in considerable detail. One reason for beginning in this manner is that Mark's Gospel is the shortest of the four gospels and, therefore, a good place to being. A fundamental reason for taking Mark first is that most modern scholars hold that Mark was the first gospel to be written. This is referred to, in the scholarly literature, as "the priority of Mark." Most scholars today also hold that Mark's Gospel was written sometime in the period 65 to 70 CE while Matthew, Luke and John were all written sometime after 80 CE. In modern scholarship, there is a minority opinion (in some places like Egypt, Syria, and Iran) that Matthew was earlier, written in Hebrew or Aramaic.

Reading Mark's Gospel

There is only one way to begin the study of the Gospel of Mark – in a thoughtful manner, you must read through the gospel from beginning to end. There is really no adequate substitute for doing this. In some ways, it appears to be like reading a story, but if read carefully you will discover that it consists of a fascinating collection of individual units (called pericopes) and that these must be read thoughtfully and carefully to get the full meaning of not only what is happening but what Jesus is doing and teaching.

Overall Structure

Having read through the gospel, you will most likely agree that on an overall basis it is arranged in a chronological order. Jesus is baptized in the beginning and then, after a period of public ministry, he goes to Jerusalem where he is arrested, mocked, crucified, buried and three days later rises from the dead.

In reading the Gospel of Matthew, we note the arious geographical locations that are mentioned. Jesus is baptized in the **Jordan River**. He is tempted in the **desert beyond the Jordan**. After this, he carries out his public ministry principally in **Galilee**. After a journey to **Jerusalem,** he enters the city and, after a short ministry there, he is arrested and is crucified. These geographical locations underlie the plan of the gospels of Mark and Matthew.

Detailed Structure

Let us now take a close look at the passages that make up the Gospel of Mark. It will very quickly come to light that the individual passages have certain particular literary forms. These include: miracle accounts, pronouncement passages, parables, sayings of Jesus, and accounts about Jesus. Our investigation will begin with the most readily identified form: the miracle accounts.

Miracle accounts

Consider the following passage:

> Just then there was in their synagogue a man with an unclean spirit, and he cried out, "What have you to do with us, Jesus of Nazareth? Have you come to destroy us? I know who you are, the holy one of God." But Jesus rebuked him, saying, "Be silent and come out of him!" And the unclean spirit, convulsing him and crying with a loud voice, came out of him. They were all amazed, and they kept asking one another, "What is this? A new teaching - with authority! He commands even the unclean spirits, and they obey him" (**MK 1:23-27** NRSV).[152]

This is called a **miracle story** in many commentaries. Observe that this story consists of three elements:

> 1) the circumstances are described,
> 2) the healing is recorded,
> 3) the reaction of the bystanders

These three elements are characteristic of the miracle account or story. Other examples of the miracle accounts are: the cure of Peter's mother-in law (**Mk 1:29-31**) and the cure of the leper (**Mk 1:40-42**). There are some 13 miracle accounts in all the gospels.

It is usual to distinguish **two types of miracles - healing miracles and nature miracles**. The cases presented above are healing miracles. There are six nature miracles: the stilling of the storm (**Mk 35-41**), the feeding of the five thousand (**Mk 6:34-44**), the walking on the water (**Mk 6:45-52**), the feeding of the four thousand (**Mk 8:1-10**), [Some scholars understand the feeding of the four thousand and the feeding of the five thousand to be two different versions of the same event, in which case there are only five nature miracles] and the cursing of the fig tree (**Mk 11:12-14, 20-22**).

Pronouncement passages

Let us consider next the sayings of Jesus that were transmitted along with an accompanying narrative. Vincent Taylor termed these units **"pronouncement stories."** Here is an excellent example of such a story - the question of paying taxes:

> Then they sent to him some Pharisees and some Herodians to trap him in what he said. And they came and said to him, "Teacher, we know that you are sincere, and show deference to no one; for you do not regard people with partiality, but teach the way of God in accordance with truth. Is it lawful to pay taxes to the emperor, or not? Should we pay them or should we not?" But knowing their hypocrisy, he said to them, "Why are you putting me to the test? Bring me a denarius and let me see it." And they brought one. Then he said to

---

[152] The word "unclean" in the context of Jesus' time does not mean "dirty" or "soiled." The term "unclean" in religious terms of the day means "not of God," "unholy," and in some cases "possessed by demonic forces."

them, "Whose head is this and whose title?" They answered, "The emperor's." **Jesus said to them, "Give to the emperor the things that are the emperor's, and to God the things that are God's."** And they were utterly amazed at him (Mk 12:13-17 NRSV).

This illustrates the chief characteristic of a pronouncement - they **culminate in a saying of Jesus.** It is the saying that is most important. Sometimes, the pronouncements are attached to other narratives. Two other examples are: **Mk 2: 15-17** and **Mk 2:23-26**.

Parables

Some people describe parables as metaphors or similes that use aspects of nature and everyday life to teach spiritual lessons.[153]   At the time of Jesus, it was a rabbinic custom to teach using parables. Consider a definition from the online site, Bible Study Tools:

> The range of meaning of the term "parable" (Gk. *parabole*) in the New Testament closely parallels that of the Hebrew *masal* in the Old Testament and related Hebrew literature. As well as referring to narrative parables, the term identifies similitudes (Matt 13:33 ; B. Pes. 49a), allegories (Ezek 17:2 ; 24:3 ; Matthew 13:18 Matthew 13:24 Matthew 13:36), proverbs (Proverbs 1:1 Proverbs 1:6 ; Mark 3:23), riddles (Psalm 78:2 ; Mark 7:17), and symbols or types (Heb 9:9 ; B. Sanh. 92b). "Parable" is a general term for a figurative saying.[154]

A genuine parable calls for deep reflection. The individual elements are carefully chosen by Jesus and represent everyday aspects for the people he is teaching. At this particular time, rabbis often told parables and it was recognized as a way to teach conceptual ideas, those aspects of faith which are deep and sometimes hard to comprehend. In many ways, the elements of the parable can be understood as signs that point to profound realities in the teaching of Jesus.

There are parables to be found in the Gospel of Mark. There is a small group of parables to be found in Chapter 4: the Parable of the Sower (3-8); the Parable of the Growing Seed (4:26-29); and the Parable of the Mustard Seed (4:30-32). An additional example is found in Mark 12:1-9, the Parable of the Wicked Tenants.

Two well-known examples include the Parable of the Good Samaritan in the Gospel of Luke (Lk 10:25-35; but read 10: 25-37 to see the whole context) and the parable form is found in Matthew 13:24-30, the Parable of the Weeds). These two parables have been chosen from Luke and Matthew because they best illustrate the parable form.

The parables of Jesus that come to us in the gospels are important for the following reason and summarized by Pageant as following:

---

[153] See: C. H. Dodd, "The Parables of the Kingdom," Revised Edition (New York: Charles Scribner's Sons, 1961) in Russell Pregeant, *Engaging the New Testament* (Minneapolis, Fortress Press, 1995),109.

[154] "Parable," Bible Study Tools (Accessed October 23, 2017)

Taken as a whole the parables set forth an authentic picture of 1st century Palestine. The use of parables in teaching was also common among the 1st century Jews. Many scholars believe, therefore, that it is through the parables that we come closest to the teaching of Jesus.[155]

Sayings of Jesus

According to the writing in the gospels, Jesus is never described as writing down his teachings. He apparently went about preaching and teaching orally to those who gathered around him. The sayings of Jesus expressed in the gospels, which include Mark, do share equally with the parables of Jesus in revealing his mission and teaching. People listened carefully and because of the strength of oral memory at the time, his teachings were transferred and carefully remembered and then passed down by what is called "oral tradition." So, it is not surprising to find that we have a record of his preaching and teaching preserved in the gospels. It should be remembered that these sayings are not all that Jesus preached and taught. At the very end of John's gospel, it is stated clearly: "But there are also many other things that Jesus did; if every one of them were written down, I suppose that the world itself could not contain the books that would be written" (John 21:25).

Here, there should be a word said about "oral tradition." In the ancient world, there were no books. Most people had no idea how to write and writing materials were extremely expensive even if they did. Humans had a capacity to remember which is being lost in modern times. It is called "oral memory." We can see this skill used by actors and actresses, those who hold technical jobs where it is necessary to access in the mind a number of codes or numerical values, and by musicians. Some musicians can go to hear new music and come home to play it, never using any music sheets. In ancient days, people passed along Hebrew poetic compositions, narratives, and oracles by oral memory. For instance, the Book of Proverbs, used to instruct young men, was most likely memorized by all the students. It is known that monks memorized the entire Book of Psalms. We now know Psalm 23 if we're lucky! Therefore, people who came to hear Jesus teaching would have remembered what he said, probably word for word. These were then deposited into what is called the "sayings source." Many scholars will claim that the oral tradition was more accurate in many ways than the written tradition (which is hard to imagine to us today.)

Individual sayings of Jesus come to us in the Gospels in two ways:[156]

1) Attached to something else, for example, **Mk 2:18-20 has verses 21 and 22 –** two originally independent sayings-- attached to it.

2) We find sayings in small collections of individual sayings, as in **Mk 4:21-25.**

Other examples of such collections are: **Mk 8:34-9:1 and Mk 9:41-50.** If you read these passages thoughtfully you will be able to see that they contain formerly independent sayings.

---

[155] Pregeant, 106.

[156] See Vincent Taylor, *The Formation of the Gospel Tradition* (New York: St. Martins Press, Inc., 1960), 89.

The sayings are now related to each other through the use of catchwords, i.e. a word in one saying is repeated in the next saying in the collection (this is easily seen in Mk 9:41-50).

Accounts about Jesus

The stories about Jesus have no common structural form. What they have in common is that they are all self-contained stories. Vincent Taylor[157] sees these accounts as vivid and colorful in character and as being units of the existing oral tradition incorporated directly into the Gospel by Mark. Examples of this type of story are the following:

Mk 7:24-30	The Syro-Phoenician Woman
Mk 10:17-22	The Rich Man's Question
Mk 11:1-11	The Entry Into Jerusalem

A word of explanation: literary forms always come with some variations. Hence, one example of a form will not always match, down to the least detail, another example of the same form. It is much like the rules of spelling and grammar in the English language where all have quite a number of exceptions (for example - "i" before "e" except after "c"). So, if you compare two miracle accounts one of them might be missing one of the three characteristic elements or one of them might have all three elements but in a different order.

The origin of the Individual Units

When you begin to read the Gospel of Mark, you will experience the feeling that Mark's gospel is composed from many small units held together by short statements concerning geography or vague statements about time. Detailed studies based on precisely this impression have brought scholars to the position that:

Generally speaking, at the beginning the traditions about Jesus circulated orally as independent units.[158]

The word "pericope," deriving from the Greek meaning "unit" is often used to refer to the individual units in the Gospels.

The most important event described in the New Testament is the death and resurrection of Christ, a significant portion of each gospel including John's gospel. Scholars notice that the details and description of the Passion of Jesus, his loving offer of his own death to conquer death and open up the relationship fully between the faithful and God, becomes a strong unit of writing in all the gospels, made up of pericopes.

---

[157] Vincent Taylor, *The Gospel According to St Mark* (London, The Macmillan Press LTD, 1966), 80.
[158] Howard Clark Kee, Franklin W.Young and Karlfried Froehlich, *Understanding the New Testament*, Second Edition (Englewood Cliffs, New Jersey: Prentice Hall, Inc., 1965), 83.

203

The writing of the Gospel of Mark

If you consider that Jesus was crucified in 30 AD/CE and the earliest gospel is the Gospel of Mark which appeared in the period 65-70 AD/CE, then the question immediately arises as to what happened to the traditions about Jesus in the intervening period of some 35 to 40 years. The answer is that the traditions about Jesus were passed on orally. It is hard for us today to recognize the importance of this fact because we depend on our newscasters on television, our iphones, ipads, and print media. The fact is that in all cultures oral transmission in earlier times was precise, for one reason due to its importance in keeping it accurate due to the lack that there were no permanent forms of writing to document the traditions.

In the first century AD/CE, the orally transmitted word was more highly respected by many people than was the written word. For instance, the Jews believed that the written sacred law had been handed down under the inspiration of God and at the same time they passed down orally the interpretation of this law from teacher to pupil for many centuries before it was finally written down, in 200 AD/CE. This written work, called the *Mishnah*, embodied the accumulated oral traditions. In a similar way, the Gospels embody many of the oral traditions about Jesus. But, in the case of the gospels, the period of oral transmission was only some 20 to 40 years. (Compare this to the probable transmission of oral tradition for the Pentateuch which spanned hundreds of years.)

Thesource materials that the author of Mark's gospel utilized were the units that made up the oral traditions concerning Jesus: the independent sayings; groups of sayings; parables; miracle accounts; pronouncement passages; and accounts about Jesus. Nothing is known about whether any of these individual units came to the author of Mark already joined together. Nothing is known either as to whether or not any of these units were written down before the author undertook the task of writing the gospel.

What Holds the Units Together?

We can find what holds the units (pericopes) together by looking at the opening words of each unit. If we do this, we find expressions like the following:

- "A leper came to him…" 1:40
- "Jesus went out again…" 2:13
- "One Sabbath…" 2:23
- "Again he entered the Synagogue: 3:1
- "Again he began to teach beside the sea." 4:1
- "In those days when there was again a great crowd…" 8:1

Notice how vague the references to time and location are. This has prompted scholars to believe that the units of the oral tradition circulated without reference to time and location and that Mark supplied the detailed chronological and geographical order himself for the purpose of giving coherence to his narrative. In some cases, the number of days or locations given may hold symbolic value. No person today truly knows the activity of Jesus on a day to day basis. There is even uncertainty as whether the ministry of Jesus lasted one year, as the Synoptic gospels indicate, or two to three years as the Gospel of John seems to indicate.

There is one additional method that the author of the Gospel used to move his narrative along – the summary statement. When you read 3:7-12 it is easily concluded that this passage is a summary of Jesus' activity provided by the author of the gospel in order to provide the narrative with a sense of the passage of time with ongoing activity all the while. The passage 6:53-56 is another example of the summary statement.

Evidence of the Author's Work

We have seen that the author's available material for composing the gospel consisted of independent units that circulated orally, most likely without any indication of time or location. It is natural to inquire, therefore, into whether there are any indications of conscious writing activity on the part of the author to be found in the gospel. We will quickly see that such evidence exists.

First Example

Read through Mk 1:21-39, paying special attention to verses 21, 29, 32, and 35. It is seen that all of these happenings took place in one location in a single 24 hour period. [When you come to read Mt and Lk, you will find that these same events are reported but that they are not attached together in a chronological sequence as they are here in Mk.]

Second Example

Read through Mk 2:15-3:6. This section contains a series of five pronouncement stories (2:15-17, 18-20, 23-28; 3:1-6). The conclusion of this series is that the Pharisees and the Herodians had begun to conspire to have Jesus put to death. Some scholars argue in favor of the position that these five units came to the author of the gospel already joined, but whether or not this was the case cannot be known with any certainty.

Third Example

A third example of the author at work is the fact that there is very little teaching of Jesus in the Gospel prior to Peter's confession in 8:29. There is, however, a substantial amount of his teaching in the Gospel after Peter's confession. This arrangement would seem to indicate that in the first part of the gospel the author of Mark was primarily interested in establishing that Jesus was the Messiah in order to provide this knowledge of who Jesus was as a basis for the authority of Jesus' teaching.

Fourth Example

Read through the section Mk 8:22-10:52. While you are reading note the following and watch for a pattern:

1. It begins with the healing of the blind man at Bethsaida (8:22-26) and ends with the healing of the blind Bartimaeus at Jericho (10:46-52).

2. Then there is the confession of Peter (8:27-30)

3. **Jesus then foretells his death and resurrection for the first time (8:31-33)**

4. This is followed by a teaching about following Jesus (8:31 - 9:1) which is followed, in turn, by some teaching of Jesus (9:2-29)

5. **Jesus then foretells his death and resurrection a second time (9:30-32)**

6. This is followed by a teaching pertaining to following Jesus (9:33-37) which is followed by more teachings by Jesus (9:38- 10:31)

7. **Jesus then foretells his death and resurrection for the third time (10:32-34)**

8. This is followed, as before, by a teaching about discipleship (10:35-45) which is not, in this case, followed by more teachings of Jesus.

This section is marked off by the two cures of blind men, and is a carefully structured section. Beginning and ending this section with cures of blind persons indicates that the eyes of the disciples and the eyes of the readers as well, will be opened in this section. The three-fold repetition of the foretelling of Jesus' death and resurrection provides great emphasis on the necessity for his death and repeating emphasis on the resurrection. Note that with each foretelling the amount of detail provided increases.

The Passion Narrative

One most important, final section of the Gospel of Mark remains to be discussed: the Passion Narrative. This section comprises all of Chapters 14 and 15. Each of the other three gospels has its own such narrative, also called "Passion Narratives" (Mt 26:1-27:66; Lk 22:1-23:56 and Jn 13:1-19:42). The narrative in John's Gospel is considerably longer that in the Synoptic Gospels due to the extended account of the Last Supper.

Was the author of Mark's Gospel the first person to formulate a Passion Narrative? One obvious conclusion seen in all four gospels in the New Testament is that the Passion Narrative is most important. Was Mark's the first such narrative? The answer to this question cannot be known with certainty. It is almost certain that many of the elements contained in the narrative originated within the oral tradition at an early time. Whether this came to be a connected account, perhaps even existing in written form, before becoming part of Mark's Gospel cannot be known.

Who was Mark?

All of this discussion on the literary units in the Gospel of Mark and how the author put together the gospel brings us to an obvious question: who was Mark? Scholars today have a wide disparity of opinion on this question.

It must be said, however, that there is also strong tradition concerning Mark from the early church supported by early writers who professed to know who Mark was. From these sources, we know that Mark was the companion of Paul mentioned in the Book of the Acts of the Apostles and was one of the Seventy Apostles – those mentioned in Luke 10: 1-16 as individuals sent out to preach and continue the work of Christ. Western scholars many times don't pay attention to the history of the Church that originated in Egypt in Alexandria, now known as the Coptic Church. Mark was a missionary there and is known as the first "pope" of the Coptic tradition, Christianity as it arose in Egypt. There is remarkable tradition that it was Mark's home where the disciples ate the Last Supper with Jesus at Passover and was the location of the Upper Room at Pentecost.

According to strong tradition, Mark's family history began in Cyrene, a city in North Africa. His father's name was Aristopolus and his mother's name was Mary. They were a Jewish family and yet he was educated in both the Hellenistic (Greek) and Hebrew cultures. Later, he became friends with the disciple Barnabus.

A note must be given here: even when reading very scholarly and trusted commentaries there can always be a difference of opinion. In some of the most modern biblical research, there appears sometimes to be a lack of interest in early tradition and writings.

CHAPTER TWENTY- eight

THE SYNOPTIC PROBLEM

Introduction

There are four gospels in the New Testament: Matthew, Mark, Luke and John. These first three gospels are grouped together under the title "Synoptic Gospels." The Gospel of John is separated from the other three because it has a different overall structure and a very different form of composition. We will take up John's gospel separately.

Remember that there are some scholars who support a theory that Matthew's gospel was the earliest writing of the gospels and was originally written in Aramaic. This is considered to be a minority opinion but one that is held especially when studying ancient Syriac and Coptic scriptures. The predominant opinion in the western world does favor, however, the "Two Source Theory" as a resolution of the Synoptic Problem which we will now describe.

Concerning the "Synoptic Problem, the term "*synoptic*" comes from Greek words meaning "seeing together."[159] This term is appropriately applied to the Gospels of Matthew, Mark and Luke because they are so remarkably similar in overall structure and in regard to their unitary form of composition. Because they share these similarities, they can be placed side-by-side and compared. We will soon see that this is a fruitful thing to do.

The Synoptic Problem

What is the Synoptic Problem? The Synoptic Problem is a term given to a particular aspect of studying these gospels. If you do a word by word comparison of the three gospels Matthew, Mark and Luke in their original language which is ancient Greek, you will discover that there is a great deal of similarity in both choice of words and word order. The degree of agreement is sufficiently impressive that many scholars have been prompted to set forth an hypothesis that there exists a literary relationship between them! The probable existence of this relationship has become known as the Synoptic Problem. One author of a recent book refers to it as the Synoptic Puzzle because the precise nature of it is something that must be determined.

A (small) number of solutions to this "problem" have been proposed but only one of them has achieved wide acceptance and has withstood the test of time: the Two-Source Hypothesis.

The two-source hypothesis

Picture in your mind some scholars in their offices, bent over their desks, colored pencils in hand, with the three Synoptic Gospels placed side by side. The scholars were painstakingly comparing the Greek texts word by word and underlining matching words with their colored

---

[159] Russell Pregeant, *Engaging the New Testament* (Minneapolis, Minnesota: Fortress Press, 1995), 100.

208

pencils. The two-source hypothesis is the result of all of this work by many scholars working independently.

The first step in this hypothesis is to establish that **Mark is prior.** What is meant by "prior" is that Mark was the first of the three Synoptic Gospels to have been written. Mark was written before either Matthew or Luke.

The second step consists of comparing Mark and Matthew very carefully. Many scholars concluded from this comparison that the relationship between these two gospels makes it a ppear that that Matthew borrowed from Mark! If you make the effort, you will find that almost 80% of Mark is included in the Gospel of Matthew. In a similar manner, it is determined that Luke borrowed from Mark and that about 60% of Mark's gospel is included in the Gospel of Luke. It is thought by scholars today that Luke and Matthew were using a written copy of Mark.

One more facet of this matter can be determined. Compare Matthew to Luke where each is borrowing material from Mark. In some places, Matthew and Luke do not follow Mark's order of events. However, they do not ever depart from Mark's order in the same place which means they worked independently of each other.

Up to this point we have established four specific conclusions:

1. **Mark is prior (written first).**
2. **Matthew used Mark as a source.**
3. **Luke used Mark as a source.**
4. **Matthew and Luke worked independently of each other.**

Mark is *one source* of the Two-Source Hypothesis. What is the second source?

Consider the following observation. Matthew and Luke share over thirty accounts of what Jesus said and did that are not contained in Mark. Here are a few examples: Healing of the centurion's servant (Lk 7:1-10; Mt 8:5-10,13); Beatitudes (Lk6:20-23; Mt 5:3-12); Woe to the Pharisees (Lk 11:37-52; Mt 23:4-7, 13-36); and parable of the leaven (Lk 13:20-21; Mt 13:33).

A word by word comparison of these passages in Matthew and Luke shows that they are so much alike that they must have come from a common source. This source, which was most likely a written wource, has come to be designated by the term "Q" which is known to refer to the German word "Quelle," meaning "source." The document Q is simply a hypothetical source. It quite likely consisted entirely of sayings of Jesus since we know of another such document: the Gospel of Thomas.

The hypothetical source Q is the *second source* of the Two-Source Hypothesis.

The term "Two-Source Hypothesis" is not an entirely complete description of the reality of the comparison of these three gospels. In the Gospel of Matthew there are a number of passages that are found only in Matthew. The designation "M" has been given to the source(s) which Matthew alone uses. The following are four examples of passages in Matthew that are attributed to "M":

1. Jesus speaks about anger (5:21-26)
2. Jesus speaks about comfort for the weary (11:28-30)
3. The interpretation of the Parable of the Weeds (13:36-43)
4. The Parable of the Net (13:47-50)

These additional sources could have been written or they could have been from an oral tradition … or some combination of both types. Nothing is more is known about them.

Similarly, the Gospel of Luke contains passages which are not found in the other three Gospels. The designation "L" has been given to the source(s) of these passages which are found only in Luke. These additional sources could have been written or they could have been from an oral tradition … or some combination of both types. Nothing is more known about them. The following are four examples of passages in Luke that are attributed to "L":

1. The Parable of the Good Samaritan (10:29-37)
2. The Parable of the Rich Fool (12:13-21)
3. The Slave's Wages (12:47-48)
4. The Parable of the Prodigal Son and His Brother (15:11-32)

So it is seen that what has come to be called the "Two-Source Hypothesis" in reality recognizes that there were additional sources that were uniqueto both Matthew and Luke. The term "two-source" is meant to refer to the two principal sources used by Matthew and Luke: **Mark and Q**.

Scholars have also determined that, in total, of Mark's 661 verses there are 528 verses (80%) that are shared with Matthew and there are 429 verses (65%) that are shared with Luke. Thus, of Matthew's 1,068 verses almost 50% are shared with Mark, and of Luke's 1,149 verses 37% are shared with Mark.[160]

THE TWO-SOURCE HYPOTHESIS IN DIAGRAM FORM

Two Source Hypothesis

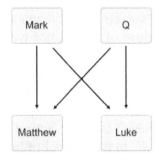

---

[160] Raymond E. Brown, *An Introduction to the New Testament* (New York: Doubleday, 1997), 111.

Therefore, in conclusion, we see that the components of the two-source theory, explaining the "Synoptic Problem," included the following sources:

> The Gospel of Mark
> The Q Source
> Material unique to Matthew
> Material unique to Luke

Remember that this is a "theory," albeit a good one that has been held by scholars for many years. Perhaps, the discovery of new scrolls might someday change the theory!

CHAPTER TWENTY-nine

THE GOSPELS OF MATTHEW AND LUKE

The Gospel of Matthew

Introduction to the significance of Matthew's gospel

The gospel of Matthew holds great significance in the history of the Christian churchy, perhaps this is the reason why it is the first gospel listed in most New Testaments, It has often been called "the Gospel of the Church." L. T. Johnson has the following to say about the Gospel of Matthew:

> Matthew is the Gospel of the church. Not only is it the only Gospel to use the term "church," ekklesia (16:18; 18:17), but both its contents and structure indicate an interest in providing clear and coherent guidance to a community of believers. In contrast to the Gospel of Mark's rather marginal early existence, Matthew has been from the beginning the Gospel most used by the church in its worship and in consequence, it has provided the text for most preaching and commentary. Already quoted directly by Ignatius of Antioch (ca. 115), it was given a full-scale commentary by Origen (ca. 185-254).[161]

A very important issue for the community that formed around Jesus and then continued to grow after his death and resurrection was the matter of continuity. This issue confronted the community in two ways. First, they faced the question: What is the relationship of the earthly life and ministry of Jesus in the 1st century to the life of Israel and activity of God on its behalf during the time before the birth of Jesus? Secondly, they faced a similar question: What is the relationship between the earthly life and ministry of Jesus and the life of the community as it continues to exist and grow in the time after his death, resurrection and ascension?

Achtemeier, Green and Thompson have the following to say about the Gospel of Matthew in relation to these questions:

> The first book in the NT does not circumvent these central questions, but begins to address them forthrightly, and immediately in its opening chapters. For this reason, the Gospel of Matthew, often called the First Gospel because of its location in the NT, functions as an effective bridge within the Christian canon of Scripture – from the OT to the NT. Readers of the Gospel of Matthew find here a portrayal of Jesus with deep roots in the OT together with branches that clearly embrace the church that grew out of Jesus' own ministry to restore Israel.
> This means, on the one hand, that Matthew has explored the vital relationship between Jesus' life and the history and hope of God's historic

---

[161] Luke Timothy Johnson, *The Writings of the New Testament*, Third Edition (Minneapolis, Fortress Press, 2010), 165.

engagement with Israel… the Evangelist has brought traditions about Jesus to bear on the needs of the still youthful Christian community struggling with important issues of power and authority, identity and witness, and, so of internal behavior and relations. Insisting on the church's genesis in the mission and message of Jesus and its continuity with historic Israel, Matthew works to aid his readers as they endeavor to find their way as a new religious movement in the Mediterranean world of the first century.[162]

The transition from traditional Judaism to Jesus and the church which – soon after the time of Paul, included both Jews and Christians, was not a historical development without confrontation. The Gospel of Matthew also contains considerable conflict between the Christians and the Jewish authorities and some of the Jewish people. Daniel Harrington has this to say about this conflict and Matthew's approach:

> After A.D. 70 Judaism was very much in transition. Several movements arose that claimed to provide the authentic means of continuing the Jewish tradition. Among such movements were the early rabbis ("scribes and Pharisees") and the early Christians (such as Matthew's community). The stakes were high (the survival of Judaism), the transition was at a very early stage (late first century A.D.), and tensions were severe (as Matthew 23 and other texts show). It is against this background that we need to understand Mathew's theological program, for it was intended as a way of preserving and continuing the Jewish tradition.[163]

The Gospel of Mark provided miracles, pronouncements, and sayings of Jesus, but we find much more teaching by Jesus in Matthew, particularly in the form of speeches. In Matthew, Jesus' teaching is found both spread throughout the Gospel and also highly concentrated into five separate speeches such as the well-known Sermon on the Mount 5:1-7:29. These speeches include the Sermon on the Mount, the Missionary Discourse, the Discourse with Parables, the Discourse on the Church, and the Discourse on End Times. Some scholars have identified these five speeches to be corollary to the first five books of the Bible, the Pentateuch, meaning that they were important teachings.

Introduction to its literary aspects

Author – Traditionally, the author of this gospel is understood to be Matthew, the tax collector (Mt 9:9) who became a disciple of Jesus (10:3). However, no verse in the text identifies the author, nor does any verse suggest that the author was an eye witness of the events he describes. Matthew is recognized as the author in the early church writings.

---

[162] Achtemeier, Green and Thompson, *Introducing the New Testament: Its Literature and Theology* (Grand Rapids, William B. Eerdmans Publishing Company, 2001) 89-90.

[163] Daniel J. Harrington, S.J., *The Gospel of Matthew*, Sacra Pagina Series, Daniel J. Harrington, Ed. Volume 1 (Collegeville, The Liturgical Press, 1991) 16.

Date – All that can be said about the date of its composition is that it was written sometime during the period between 70 CE, the date of the destruction of the Temple in Jerusalem, and 100 CE. Most scholars date it to sometime about 85 CE.

Original Language – Greek.

Place of composition – Syria or Palestine.

Literary structure

Like the Gospel of Mark, on the highest-level Matthew's gospel is ordered chronologically. On a secondary level, however, the ordering principle is geographic. Matthew appears to adopt Mark's geographic ordering in general and this can be immediately seen by setting the two gospels side-by-side.

	Mark	**Matthew**
The Infancy Narrative	------	Chaps. 1-2
John the Baptist, Baptism of Jesus, Temptation	1:1-13	3:1-4:11
Jesus' public ministry, largely in Galilee	1:14-9:29	4:12-18:35
Jesus journeys to Jerusalem	9:30-10:52	Chaps 19-20
Jesus' ministry in Jerusalem	Chaps 11-13	Chaps. 21-25
The Passion Narrative	Chaps 14-15	Chaps. 26-27
Resurrection appearances	16:1-8	Chap. 28
Shorter Ending	(16: 21)	
Longer Ending	(16:9-20)	
The Ascension	16:19-20	------

Matthew imposes two applications of the phrase "from that time" on the geographical ordering. In the first case, at 4:17, Matthew applies it to the beginning of Jesus' public ministry. In the second case, at 16:21, he applies it to the first time that Jesus speaks explicitly about his impending crucifixion. The use of this phrase on these two occasions neatly divides the Gospel into three parts. First, the initial use of the phrase in 4:17 divides what comes before it from what comes after it. This makes the case for taking 1:1-4:16 to be a literary unit with its own message. This initial use also marks the beginning of Jesus' public ministry, the termination of which is indicated by its second use in 16:21. The use of the phrase in 16:21 then divides the public ministry from what follows, which is Jesus' suffering, death and resurrection (16:21-28:20).

Matthew's Five Discoureses

The Sermon on the Mount (5:1-7:29)

This first discourse has become famous within Christian circles. It was originally directed to the disciples, Jesus' followers and to all of Israel that came to hear him (Mt 4:25). As it is cast in the second person, "you," it also becomes readily applicable to people of the present day as well!

Whole books have been written presenting explanations of what this speech says. In beginning to study the Gospel of Matthew, it is best to read through it slowly, and in a thoughtful frame of mind, and absorb from it whatever you can – using the bible's footnotes and study material if you can.

On Mission (10:1-11:1)

Having just informed the disciples that the harvest is abundant but the laborers are few (Mt 37-38), Jesus prepares the twelve disciples to go out to do missionary work among the people. Jesus gave the disciples authority over unclean spirits and to cure every disease. He instructs them how to carry out their assignment (Mt 10:5-15). He then tells them about persecution and how to understand it, in addition to words on one or two related matters.

The parable discourse (13:1-53)

Matthew has arranged his text so that at this point Jesus delivers a number of "parables." This third, of the five speeches, begins with the Parable of the Sower (Mt 13:1-9). The explanation of this parable is given to the reader of the Gospel in 13:18-23. Inserted between this parable and its explanation is a brief explanation of the purpose of speaking in parables (Mt 13:10-17).

Next Jesus sets forth the Parable of the Weeds. Once again, the explanation of the parable is separated from its presentation. This time the separation is provided by three items: 1) the Parable of the Weeds; 2) the Parable of the Mustard Seed; and 3) a short statement about Jesus' use of parables. The third speech concludes, after three more parables and a saying of Jesus that is applicable to the leaders of the community.

Advice to a divided community (Mt 18:1-35)

The fourth of the five speeches is composed of a small number of individual pieces. This speech opens with the teaching that unless we become like children we will not enter the kingdom of heaven. After a word about temptation to sin and the parable of the lost sheep, Matthew treats the matter of how to handle a brother/sister in the community who sins. The speech concludes with the Parable of the Unforgiving Servant.

The eschatological discourse (Mt 24:1-25:46)

In this the last of the five speeches, Jesus addresses the coming of the end of the age

The Gospel of Luke
Introduction

The writing that is known to us today as the Gospel of Luke is, in reality, only the first part of a two-part narrative. The first part describes the life of Jesus; the second part, Acts of the Apostles, extends the narrative to cover the early years of the growth of the early and growing Christian community.

Why was this narrative of Luke and Acts written in two parts? The most likely reason is a very practical one. Each of the two volumes is of such a length that it had to be written on its own individual scroll. They came to be separated, as we now encounter them, when the codex came into use. Luke was placed with the other three Gospels, and Acts came to be placed at the beginning of the period of first century evangelism.

Luke is popularly known for three aspects in its narrative. First, it is recognized on the basis of its birth narrative in chapters 1-2. It views the birth of Jesus from the perspective of the events surrounding Mary which makes it different from the birth narrative contained in Matthew which is centered on Joseph. Secondly, Luke is known to many people for the lengthy journey Jesus takes from Galilee to Jerusalem (9:51-19:48). This portion of the Gospel consists entirely of the teaching of Jesus and includes famous parables such as the Good Samaritan and many others. Thirdly, the entire Gospel of Luke stresses the need to provide assistance to the marginalized, dispossessed, and the poor.

The genre of Luke is thought by many scholars to be that of biography. Recently, attention has been focused on a type of biography contemporary to the time of this writing that has a form similar to that of Luke-Acts. It consists of two parts. The first part relates the life of the individual who is the focus of the biography and the second part presents what happens to the followers of the person in the biography. Other scholars have other opinions. One other view that has been put forward is "historiography." A dictionary definition of this term would be: the exposition of history based on the critical use of reliable sources, the selection of particulars from these materials, and the synthesis of a narrative that will stand the test of critical examination. Genealogical records (3:23-38), meals as scenes for instruction (5:27-39; 14:1-24; 22:14-38), travel narratives (9:51-19:48), speeches, and dramatic episodes such as Jesus' rejection at Nazareth (4:16-30) are all elements of historiography.[164]

What is the purpose that underlies this composition of Luke-Acts? This is perhaps best expressed by Achtemier, Green and Thompson in the following two quotations:

> … here we have a narrative whose aim is to present the timeline of the history of God's people so that it must pass through (and not bypass) Jesus and his disciples. Against this backdrop, the purpose of Luke-Acts would have been to strengthen

---

[164] Achtemeier, Green and Thompson, 152

the Christian movement in the face of opposition by ensuring them in their interpretation and experience of the redemptive purpose and faithfulness of God and by calling them to continued fidelity and witness in their service of the kingdom of God.[165]

As historiography, then Luke's narrative draws a continuous line from the Scriptures of Israel into the birth, life, death and resurrection of Jesus, and from Jesus into the fledgling community of Christian believers. By this means, Luke gives the Christian community continuity with Israel of old, identity with God's purpose, and validation as God's people. Luke thus teaches his audience who they are and how they are to live out the substance of their faith in discipleship.[166]

It is easily seen that the major aspects of the life of Jesus in the Gospel of Luke are the same as those in the gospels of Mark and Matthew. In the case of Luke, however, a prologue and a birth narrative are attached to the beginning. Thus, the outline for this gospel is as follows:

Prologue (1:1-4)
Birth narrative (1:5-2:52)
Preparation for the ministry of Jesus (3:1-4:13)
The ministry of Jesus in Galilee (4:14-9:50)
The journey to Jerusalem (9:51-19:28)
Jesus enters Jerusalem and teaches in the temple (19:29-21:38)
The suffering and death of Jesus (22:1-23:56)
Jesus' resurrection and ascension (24:1-52)

Luke's Narrative

1:1-4 The prologue
Luke provides a prologue, written in a high style of Greek that is the equal of other prologues found in contemporary Greco-Roman literature.

1:5-2:52
Luke's narrative begins by focusing on three individuals: Zechariah, a priest in the temple in Jerusalem; Mary, a virgin betrothed to a man named Joseph; and Simeon, a man who was righteous and devout. The events and interactions of these people are structured in a narrative by means of a movement from promise to fulfillment to songs of praise. In addition there is a parallelism between the narratives concerning John the Baptist and Jesus that clearly show that Jesus is the greater of the two. This birth narrative makes the identity of Jesus known – he is the Son of God.

3:1-4:13
Luke presents the "coming" of John the Baptist, which later terms John as "the Forerunner." Luke presents John as a prophet. After going to some length to specify the date of John's coming (3:1-2a), Luke follows with a description of John's ministry (3:2b-17). Jesus'

---

[165] Achtemeier, Green and Thompson, 149.
[166] Achtemeier, 153.

217

identity as the Son of God is confirmed by God during Jesus' baptism and this identification is further supported by a genealogy (3:23-38). Following the genealogy, Jesus' temptation in the desert is described.

4:14-9:50

This section describes Jesus' ministry in Galilee. Jesus' ministry begins with him teaching in the synagogues. Luke presents a sample of Jesus' preaching (4:14-30) that most likely is intended to serve as a summary for his entire ministry. In this section we are also provided with a number of examples of Jesus' healings.

Other highlights described in this portion of Luke's gospel include the following: the call of Peter; the members of the Twelve (the 12 apostles) are named (in 6:12-16); and Luke's version of a major sermon by Jesus is presented (6:17-49). This sermon, this time "on the plain" (in a field), is very similar to that of Matthew's sermon on a mountain slope. This similarity of Luke to Matthew is most likely due to Luke's use of the same source (namely Q). It is also possible that Jesus gave this sermon over and over, portrayed by Luke as given in a field, and in Matthew the same teaching given on a mountain.

Finally, this section ends with the issues of Jesus' and the nature of discipleship (9:1-50).

9:51-19:28

Jesus' journey to Jerusalem begins with the statement: "When the days drew near for him to be taken up, he set his face to go to Jerusalem" (9:51). Luke makes use of this journey to give the reader a major portion of the teaching and actions of Jesus. At the same time, the opposition of the Jewish authorities to Jesus intensifies.

Many biblical scholars are of the opinion that Luke has no underlying plan to this collection of teachings. Indeed, if you casually read through it, one notices it to be random and unorganized. Paul Borgman,[167] a professor of English at Gordon College, wrote his commentary on Luke's Gospel by working through a literary approach to the gospel proposing that this section has the form of a chiasm. A chiastic structure has the form: ABB'A' where A and A' are in a parallel relationship to each other, and similarly for B and B'. This is considered to be a ring structure because it ends up where it began – with A and A'. The most important point in the ring structure is the center, where the order reverses. Also significant are the first and last of the elements A and A'.

If the chiastic form is applied to the travel narrative in Luke's Gospel, two significant concepts are highlighted. First, the first and last elements of the structure speak of peace. Secondly, the important center elements speak of the kingdom of God. When applied to the travel narrative, the chiastic form is, of course, quite involved. Perhaps this is the reason why Borgman's hypothesis has never received the attention by biblical scholars that perhaps it deserves.

---

[167] Paul Borgman, *The Way According to Luke* (Grand Rapids, William B. Eerdmans Publishing Company, 2006), 78.

This section of the gospel contains a number of Jesus' well known parables. For example: The Parable of the Good Samaritan, 10:29-37; the Parable of the Rich Fool (12:13-21); the Parables of the Mustard Seed and the Yeast (13:18-21); The Parable of the Great Dinner (14:15-24); and the Parable of the Prodigal Son (14:11-32).

The section 17:11-19:27 of Jesus' journey has a special importance. The pace of the journey increases as Jesus moves from the region between Samaria and Galilee (17:11), passes through Jericho (19:1), and finally reaches Bethpage and Bethany which are near Jerusalem (19:29). In this section Jesus instructs his disciples about the significance of his arrival in Jerusalem.

19:29-21:38

This section includes four happenings. First, there is the Jesus' entry into Jerusalem. Verses 29-40 of Chapter 19 describe how Jesus arranged to be mounted on a colt (v.33; NRSV) and rode down from the Mount of Olives. Second, "as he came near and saw the city" (v.41), Jesus wept and then prophesied that the city would be destroyed. Third, he entered the temple and drove out those who were selling there. Finally, Jesus began teaching in the temple and continued doing so on a number of days (19:47-21:38).

22:1-23:56

This section is known as the passion narrative. It gives the reader a narrative that describes Jesus' arrest, trial, crucifixion, death and burial. It is interesting to compare Luke's narrative of these events to the other passion narratives provided in the other three gospels. In some ways it has small differences.

24:1-53

In this, the final chapter in his Gospel, Luke provides the reader with a short narrative describing the finding of the empty tomb (vv. 1-12). This is followed by the accounts of several appearances of the resurrected Jesus. Luke's Gospel concludes with a brief account of Jesus' ascension to the Father (vv. 50-53).

For Further Reading

If you have the time and the interest to read a very fine presentation of the Gospel of Luke, or if you are studying a passage from Luke, you might want to consult the following:

Paul J. Achtemeier, Joel B. Green and Marianne Meye Thompson. "The Gospel of Luke" in *Introducing The New Testament*. Grand Rapids, Michigan: William B Eerdmans Publishing Company, 2001.

CHAPTER Thirty

THE GOSPEL OF JOHN

Introduction

The Gospel of John is a highly mystical and spiritual reflection on the life of Jesus, presenting many theological ideas on the life and ministry of Jesus. . It is significantly different from the three Synoptic Gospels. There is a fundamental difference in the literary structure of this gospel and there are significant differences in vocabulary, chronology and theological concepts. The nature of these differences prompts one to treat this Gospel for its own merits. The beauty of having gospels that have different approaches to the life and mission of Christ is that they all reveal – in their own way – the remarkable revelation of God's salvation.

Author

Consider the following observations:
- A very strong tradition identifies the "beloved disciple" as the Apostle John, son of Zebedee and one of the Twelve, and as the author of the gospel.
- The gospel itself does not identify the author by name. It does make reference to a "beloved disciple," which can easily be understood to be the Apostle John.
- It can be deduced from the text that the author was a Jew who was fluent in Aramaic.
- Some scholars of the present day reject the traditional belief the Apostle John is the author and is to be identified with the "beloved disciple." Their reasons do appear weak and are strongly contradicted by tradition that is ages long.

Where does this leave the present-day reader who is not a biblical scholar? There are three possible positions from which to choose: 1) accept the traditional belief, 2) join in with the modern scholars, 3) suspend a decision until such time that more evidence comes to light.

Date
An ancient manuscript known as *p52* ["*p*" for papyrus] contains John 18:31-34, 37-38 and is dated to 110-125 AD/CE. This is the earliest papyrus manuscript of the NT.[168] The existence of this papyrus shows that the Gospel of John was in existence at the end of the first century. Its existence, therefore, establishes that the Gospel of John must have been written before 100-110 AD/CE. The earliest possible date is established on the basis of the belief that the gospel contains a reference to the destruction of the Temple in Jerusalem in 70 AD/CE (see John 2:13-22).

---

[168] Philip W. Comfort, *Early Manuscripts &Modern Translations of the New Testament* (Wheaton, IL: Tyndale House Publishers, 1990), 55-56.

Overall Structure

Most scholars see the Fourth Gospel as being divided into two major parts: The Book of Signs (1:19-12:50) and the Book of Glory (13:1-20:31).

The Book of Signs encompasses Jesus' public ministry and contains seven signs, interspersed with dialogues, discourses, and sayings. These signs show the divinity of Christ in deep and special ways. The seven signs are as follows:

- Changing water to wine at Cana (2:1-11)
- Healing of the official's son (4:46-54)
- Healing of the man ill for 38 years (5:1-18)
- Feeding the "large crowd" (6:2-14)
- Jesus walks on water (6:16-21)
- Healing of the man born blind (Chapter 9)
- Raising of Lazarus (11:1-44)

The Book of Glory encompasses Jesus suffering, death, and resurrection which opens a path to glory, overcoming human death by providing life eternal with God for the faithful… and showing Christ's return to the Father in Heaven. This Book of Glory includes: the Last Supper account (Chapters 13-17), the Passion Narrative (Chapters 18-19) and the resurrection narratives (Chapter 20). The Book of Glory concludes with the words of Jesus: "

"I ask not only on behalf of these, but also on behalf of those who will believe in me through their word, that they may all be one. As you, Father, are in me and I am in you, may they also be in us, so that the world may believe that you have sent me. The glory that you have given me I have given them, so that they may be one, as we are one, I in them and you in me, that they may become completely one, so that the world may know you have sent me and have loved them even as you have loved me. Father, I desire that those also, whom you have given me, may be with me where I am, to see my glory, which you have given me because you loved me before the foundation of the world. (John 17: 20-24 NRSV)"

As you can see, this passage requires quiet contemplation and reveals deep truths. In fact, when reading this from time to time, even more understanding can result in each reading!

Narrative and Discourse

The Gospel of John is characterized by the use of narrative and discourse in combination. Narrative is an account of an event and a discourse is a speech or conversation. Frequently a narrative is followed by a discourse which develops the meaning of the narrative. For example:
- 3:1-10 narrative; 3:11-21 discourse
- 5:2-18 narrative; 5:19-47 discourse
- 9:1-34 narrative; 9:35-10:18 discourse

As a consequence, one must read the Fourth Gospel differently than one reads a Synoptic Gospel which is put together out of small units (called "pericopes") as we have seen. In John's Gospel the words of Jesus appear fuller and more poetic.

Johannisms

What is a Johannism? A Johannism is a distinctive literary construction, word or concept which occurs frequently in the Fourth Gospel. Some of the words are, of course, seen in t he Synoptic Gospels but not in the same way as found in John's Gospel. There are a considerable number of these Johannisms but we will consider only a sample.

First, there is the **statement-misunderstanding-clarification** sequence. A good example of this structure is to be found in Jn 3:3-5. It goes like this:

- Jesus makes the following statement:

"Very truly I tell you, no one can see the kingdom of God without being born from above." (NRSV)

- Nicodemus replies but he misunderstands what Jesus is asking:

"How can anyone be born after having grown old? Can one enter a second time into the mother's womb and be born?"

- Jesus then responds by clarifying what he is asking. In this case by making it clear to Nicodemus that he is not speaking of a physical birth:

"Very truly, I tell you, no one can enter the kingdom of God without being born of water and Spirit."

Other examples are: 4:10-14 and 4:31-34.

Secondly, there is the frequent use of **dualism**. Note the occurrence of pairs of opposites in the following: light and darkness (1:5), spirit and flesh (3:6), life (eternal life) and death (3:36), heaven and earth (3:31) and above and below (8:23).

Thirdly, there is the special **vocabulary** of the Gospel of John. As you read the Gospel you will encounter the terms: believe, know, glory, truth, hour, life, world, come, witness, remain, and sent.

Fourthly, we find a number of times Jesus speaks using the phrase **"I am,"** (called appropriately the "I am statements." See the following:
- "I am the bread of life" (6:35,41,48)
- "I am the light of the world" (8:12; 9::5)
- "I am the door of the sheep" (10:7,9)
- "I am the good shepherd" (10:11,14)
- "I am the Son of God" (10:36)
- "I am the resurrection and the life" (11:25)
- "I am the way, and the truth, and the life (14:6)
- "I am the true vine (15:1) [169]

---

[169] Stanley B. Marrow, *The Words of Jesus In Our Gospels* (New York: Paulist Press, 1979), 130.

These "I am statements" can be Jesus' way of indicating who he truly is, as related and in reference to God's response to Moses in Genesis: God said to Moses, "I am who I am." (Ex 3:14)"

Fifthly, there is the portrayal of Jesus as **God's agent.** The Jewish institution of agency was based on three major principles:

- An agent is like the one who sent him. This is utilized in 5:23;12:44,45; 14:9; and 15:23.
- The sender is superior to the one who is sent. This is found in 13:16.
- The agent carries out his mission in obedience to the sender. This is utilized in 6:38; 8:28-29; 8:42; 12:49 and 14:24. [170]

Let us now consider some of the significant ways in which the Fourth Gospel differs from the three Synoptic Gospels. Here are a number of ways:

- In the Synoptic Gospels Jesus' public ministry occupies only one year; Jesus moves about Galilee and then at the end goes to Jerusalem to his death on the cross. In John, Jesus goes to Jerusalem on three different occasions.
- In the Synoptics, Jesus celebrates only one Passover; in John Jesus celebrates three.
- In the Synoptic Gospels, the cleansing of the Temple takes place at the end of Jesus' ministry; in John it takes place at the beginning of his ministry.
- The Fourth Gospel reports a meeting between Jesus and a Samaritan woman at a well; this incident does not appear in the Synoptics.
- The Fourth Gospels reports the miracle of the raising of Lazarus from the dead; this is not found in the Synoptics.
- In John, the account of the Last Supper occupies 155 verses (5 Chapters). In the Synoptics this account takes 25 verses in Luke, 15 verses in Matthew and only 10 verses in Mark.

Do these details cause any real difficulties for biblical scholars? The answer is "no." When looking more closely at all these details, reasons can be given to explain the apparent disparities.

Two significant passages in John's Gospel

The Prologue

The introduction to John's Gospel is a mystical hymn that speaks of Jesus as the Word, describing the Word as God the Creator. There is no birth narrative of Jesus as we find in Matthew and Luke. This gospel begins, in the beginning, describing creation, parallel in a mystical way to the first words of Genesis, "in the beginning." It indicates that Jesus, the Word, has always existed and is the "communication" of God the Father to humanity. It is a unique

---

[170] Peder Borgen, "God's Agent in the Fourth Gospel" in J. Neusner, Editor, *Religion in Antiquity: Essays in the Memory of Erwin Ramsdell Goodenough, Studies in the History of Religion* (Leiden, Netherlands: E.J. Brill, 1968), 138-141.

passage and holds great interest for many Christians in its deeply mystical aspects. In reflection, we see Matthew and Luke describing the incarnation of Jesus as the earthly Jesus and John giving us the eternal and ever-existent Jesus, especially in the Prologue. Mark's gospel begins with the baptism of Christ, to identify his mission on earth. When we put them all together, we come to understand a little better that Jesus is truly a human and totally God! The Prologue of John, however, presents us with a special view of the eternal aspect of Jesus who is God the Father's communication with humanity.

> If John has been described as the pearl of great price among the NT writings, then one may say that the Prologue is the pearl within the Gospel. In her comparison of Augustine's and Chrysostom's exegesis of the Prologue, M. A. Aucoin points out that both held that it is beyond the power of man to speak as John does in the Prologue. The choice of the eagle as the symbol of John the Evangelist was largely determined by the celestial flights of the opening lines of the Gospel. The sacred character of the prologue has been reflected in a long-standing custom of the Western Church to read it as a benediction over the sick and over newly baptized children.[171]

Notice how many of the typical Johannine terms appear in this Prologue. Life (v4), light and darkness (v5), sent (v6), know (v10), receive (v12, 16), believe (v12), truth (v14,17) and testify (v15).

Many have observed that there are parts of the prologue which have a parallelism that is like that of a hymn. Some say the parallelism takes on the character of ancient Hebrew poetry, due to its parallelism. This observation has prompted some to propose that the author of the Fourth Gospel has taken an existing hymn (possibly Hebrew or Aramaic because of its parallelism) and adapted it to serve as the beginning to the Gospel.

What is the purpose of the Prologue? Its major function is to relate the incarnate Jesus as God's Son, to the Father. God comes into creation from Heaven (the Incarnation) and returns after his resurrection to the right hand of God in Heaven. The Gospel itself can then be seen as relating the journey of Jesus from Heaven and then back to the Father.

More highlights in the Gospel of John

The Raising of Lazarus (11:1-53)

□ In the last days of Jesus on earth, and before his arrest and crucifixion, we witness a remarkable miracle that gives meaning to his death and resurrection. The account of the raising of Lazarus is structured as follows: Lazarus' illness and death (vv. 1-16), preparation for the raising (vv. 17-37), the raising of Lazarus (vv. 38-44), the reaction of the Jews (vv. 45-53). **1:19-51 John the Baptist comes and Jesus calls disciples 2:1-22 The sign at Cana and the cleansing of the temple**

---

[171] Raymond E. Brown, *The Gospel According to John*, The Anchor Bible Series, V. 29A (Garden City, New York: Doubleday & Company, Inc., 1966), 18.

Jesus turns water, in large pottery jars meant to hold "waters of purification," to wine (vv1-12). There are a lot of symbolisms in this account. The reference to the third day looks ahead to his resurrection. Jesus' reference to his hour looks ahead to his death. The occasion is a wedding feast which is traditionally has messianic overtones (see parables in Mt 22:1-14). The abundance of wine recalls Amos 9:13-14. In calling the water to wine miracle a "sign," we see that the meaning of this event points to something deeper – which is what signs always do. The cleansing of the temple episode is explained by Jesus by quoting from Ps 69:9 (Zeal for your house…) and concludes in the form of a misunderstanding as the Jews think Jesus is speaking about the temple but in reality he is speaking of his body.

2:23-3:36 Jesus instructs Nicodemus; John the Baptist instructs his disciples

Jesus' discussion with Nicodemus is in the form of a misunderstanding – Nicodemus and Jesus are speaking on different levels (vv. 3:1-9). This discussion then moves into a discourse by Jesus (3:11-21). This is the first of Jesus' discourses in the Gospel. And, once again John the Baptist contrasts his role with the of Jesus' role.

4:1-42 The woman at the well in Samaria

The success of Jesus' encounter with the Samaritans shows sharp contrast to Jesus' encounters with the Jews from Galilee and Judea with whom he met constant opposition.

4:43-54 Healing of the court official's son

The court official is with Jesus in Cana and the official's son is in Capernaum. Jesus says to the official to go home, that his son will live. And the son is healed (v. 50).

5:1-47 The healing of the man at the pool and Jesus' discourse

This is the third of the seven signs in the Gospel of John. Archeologists have uncovered a double pool with five colonnades (porticoes) in Jerusalem and the copper scroll from Qumran has authenticated the name of a pool in Jerusalem as Bethzatha.

6:1-21 Jesus feeds five thousand men and walks on water

The feeding of the five thousand is the fourth of the seven signs in the Gospel of John (see v.14). Because of this sign the people recognize Jesus as "the prophet who is to come into the world." However, the people most likely thought that God would send a prophet like Moses (Deut 18:15).

Jesus' walking on water is the fifth of the seven signs in the Gospel. This event shows Jesus' divinity because walking on water is attributed to God in Psalm 77:19(20). In addition, this is most likely the first instance in the Gospel where Jesus speaks of himself as "I am" since a literal translation at this point would be "I am." (v.20). "I am" is the name God (Yahweh) God speaks to Moses at the burning bush (Ex 3:14)!

6:22-71 Jesus' bread-of-life discourse and reactions to it

The bread-of-life discourse (vv.35-51a) is preceded by an introduction (verses 22-34) and is followed by the reactions of the Jews (vv. 51b-58) and Jesus' followers (vv.59-71). At the beginning of the discourse Jesus declares: "I am the bread of Life." This is the first clear use of the combination of "I am" with a predicate. In effect, Jesus is saying: "What you long for in the religious symbol of the bread of life is to be found in me."

7:1-7:52 Jesus dialogues with the Jews

Jesus goes to Jerusalem for the Jewish Feast of Tabernacles and in the middle of the celebration he goes to the temple to teach the people.

8:12-59 Jesus debates with the people

This section of the Gospel begins with an "I am" statement by Jesus: "I am the light of the world." The theme that dominates the whole chapter is that of fatherhood and sonship. In verse 18, Jesus reveals that God is his Father who was the one who "sent" him. Jesus as the one who is "sent" is a prominent feature through John's Gospel.

9:1-41 Jesus gives sight to a man born blind from birth

The healing of the man born blind is the sixth sign (of seven). At the time of Jesus, nobody knew of anyone born blind having received sight (v.32).

10:1-21 Jesus as the good shepherd

This section consists of two parts: 1) a brief lesson on sheep and sheepfolds (vv.1-5); and 2) a discourse by Jesus. And, this introduction furnishes Jesus with the opportunity of making two "I am" statements: "I am the gate" (v.7) and "I am the good shepherd" (v.11).

10:22-42 The Father and I are One

Jesus makes the amazing statement that he and the Father are one. The Jews think this this gives them grounds for charging him with blasphemy and justification for putting him to death.

11:1-44 Jesus raises Lazarus from the dead

Jesus raises Lazarus with a verbal command – thus revealing himself **to be** the resurrection and the life which he had said of himself back in verse 25a. The question Jesus asks in verses 25b-26 is a question that he could ask each one of us today!

11:45-54 Reaction of the Jews to the event

Many of the Jews who had come to the tomb with Mary believed in Jesus after what he did. Some of them, however, went to the Pharisees and told them what Jesus had done. The Chief Priests and Pharisees convene the Sanhedrin. The Sanhedrin decides that the best thing to do would be to put Jesus to death. But, Jesus goes to Ephraim, which was near the wilderness, because his hour had not yet come.

11:55-12:11 The anointing of Jesus

A woman anoints the feet of Jesus at the home of Lazarus in Bethany.

12:12-19 Jesus enters Jerusalem

All four of the Gospels reference Ps 118:26 (NAB).

12:20-36 The hour of Jesus arrives and Jesus interprets his death

Jesus announces that his hour has come in v.23. Verses 25 and 26 teach us about discipleship and they are directly applicable to us in the 21st century. Verses 27 through 28 contain a prayer of Jesus to glorify God's name. In the coming events, and this prayer is answered by a voice from heaven.

12:37-43 Unbelief and Belief among the Jews

First, the author explains the unbelief of the Jews, in spite of all of Jesus' signs, on the basis of two quotations from Isaiah: 53:1 (LXX) and 6:10. The latter verse appears in all four Gospels in relation to the unbelief of the Jews.

12:44-50 Jesus sums up his public ministry

The Farewell Meal   13:1-38

13:1-11 The foot washing

13:12-20 Discourse by Jesus on communal service

13:21-30 Jesus foretells his betrayal

13:31-38 The love commandment and foretelling of Peter's denial

Farewell Discourse 14:1-16:33

14:1-11 "I am the way, and the truth, and the life"

14:12-24 "If you love me, you will keep my commandments"

14:25-31 "Peace I leave with you,; my peace I give you"

"I am the true vine, and my Father is the vinegrower" (15:1-17)

"I have chosen you out of the world" (15:18-16:4a)

Jesus' Farewell Prayer 17:1-26

17:1-8 Jesus prays: Father, the hour has come; glorify your Son so that the Son may glorify you, since you have given him authority over all people, to give eternal life to all whom you have given him. And this is eternal life …" (John 17:1-3)"

17:9-23 Jesus prays for the faith of the community

17:24-26 Jesus concludes his prayer

The Passion Narrative of the Gospel of John   18:1-19:42
Introduction

A "passion narrative" is an account that demonstrates deep and abiding love. For Jesus, this love was demonstrated by his suffering and death followed by his resurrection. In Paul's letters the account of the death and burial of Jesus formed the heart of the Christian proclamation (1 Cor 11:23; 15:3-51). This reference to the passion of Jesus also took a prominent place in the proclamation of Peter's words in Acts (3:12-26; 10:34-43). Due to the important meaning of Christ's death and rising, it is not surprising to find the passion narratives as a core section of all four Gospels. The passion narrative in John's Gospel is a narrative that moved from its very beginning and moved throughout the entire writing to conclude in "Jesus' hour." The "hour" is the glory of offering his own life in order to bring humanity back to complete and eternal union with God. For John's gospel, the crucifixion is Christ's hour of exaltation (3:13-14; 8:1-8; 12:32) and glorification (12:23; 13:31-32; 17:1)!

18:1-12 The Arrest

18:13-27 The Interrogation by Annas

18:28-19:16a The trial before Pilate

19:16b-37 The crucifixion and death of Jesus

19:38-42 Jesus' burial

The Resurrection of Jesus 10: 1 - 31

20:1-18 The first appearance of the resurrected Jesus

20:19-23 Jesus' first appearance to the gathered disciples

20:24-29 Jesus' second appearance to the gathered disciples

20:30-31 The ending

21:1-14 The miraculous catch of fish

21:15-23 Jesus talks with Peter

21:24-25 The formal conclusion - The author declares himself to be the Beloved Disciple.

Conclusion

The Gospel of John is a gospel of signs pointing to the divinity of Jesus and his eventual path to glory. The keywords as explained are deep and profoundly mystical concepts that are woven together in a writing that reveals Jesus as the Son of God sent to bring humankind to a new life, a new future, and an eternal life of joy and being with God.

CHAPTER THIRTY-one

Luke-Acts

Narrative Unity

Most scholars of the 21st century agree that Luke and Acts comprise one work in two volumes. The major reason put forward for the work existing in two volumes is a very practical one. In the first century CE, the maximum length of a scroll was about 35 feet in length. Each of these volumes would entirely fill such a scroll. In recognition of the unity of these two volumes, the title "Luke-Acts" has been adopted for this writing.

Other reasons for holding the position that Luke and Acts are a single work by a single author are the following:

- The author speaks of the Gospel of Luke as being the first book. Then he states that the second volume, the Book of Acts, is directed to Theophilus, as was his Gospel.
- The beginning of Acts covers the same events in Christ's life that the last chapter of the Gospel did; compare Lk 24:44-52 and Acts 1:1-11.
- The focal point of the two volumes is seen to be the city of Jerusalem. The whole movement of the Gospel is toward Jerusalem and the whole movement of Acts is the growth of the Christian community out and away from Jerusalem.
- Events in the Gospel are parallel to events in Acts. For example: Mary, the mother of Christ, appears at the beginning of each volume; the apostles perform miracles which are indeed from God but look similar to the miracles performed by Jesus; Paul's final journey to Rome and his martyrdom is parallel to Jesus' journey to Jerusalem which ended in the crucifixion of Christ.
- The crucifixion of Jesus and the martyrdom of Stephen are presented with considerable similarities.
- Prophetic fulfillment plays a similar role in Gospel of Luke and in Acts (see Acts 3:24; 13:40; 15:15; 28:25-27).
- Happenings prophesied in the Gospel are fulfilled in Acts. For example, Jesus' foretelling of the tribulations of his chosen witnesses is fulfilled in Acts (4:3-5, 14; 5:17-42).

Luke and Acts became separated and treated as two separate works very early in Christian history. There is no known manuscript that joins the two volumes and all of the Patristic Fathers of the early centuries of the church refer to the two as individual works. This probably is due to their great difference in literary form, with the Gospel of Luke being so similar to the Gospels of Mark and Matthew as a literary form, and the fact that the gospels of Luke and Acts initially were written on two separate scrolls.

It is interesting to note that if Luke-Acts is considered as one writing in two parts then it comprises nearly 30% of the entire New Testament. Paul, then, is not the major contributor to the New Testament as is popularly believed!

Matters of Introduction

Author – We have just seen that the Gospel of Luke and the Book of Acts are written by the same author. Early Christian traditions identify this person as Luke, the companion of Paul mentioned in: Philemon 24; Col 4:14; and 2 Tim 4:11. We will, therefore, refer to the author of Luke-Acts as Luke.

Date – The most probable date is around 85 CE.

Audience – There are several considerations about the name "Theophilus," to whom the Gospel is directed. The question is: how one understands the name "Theophilus"? Consider the following points:

- "Theophilus" is a proper name that was commonly used from the 3rd century BCE onward. Consequently, there is no reason to hold that it does not apply to a real person. However, the name, Theophilus, also means "lover of God."
- The use of the title "your Excellency" before it indicates that this person was known to be highly placed, or well off, or both highly placed and well off in the society in which he resided. It does not, however, necessarily mean that he was a Roman official.
- In Luke's prologue (Lk 1:1-4), he states that he has written an orderly account so that Theophilus may realize the certainty of the teachings that he has received. It seems fair to conclude from this statement that if Theophilus is actually an individual to whom Luke is writing, he was either a believer or a catechumen (that is, a person being instructed on becoming Christian).
- It is, perhaps, still an open question as to whether or not Luke wrote for Theophilus alone or for a large number of Christians of whom Theophilus, in some sense, was the leader, or representative.

Genre – Many words have been put on paper in support of one or another of the possible genres that can be applied to the gospels. In this, the twenty-first century, it seems that some scholars have come to the conclusion that the gospels are in fact biographies of Jesus. They are certainly not to be considered biographies in the modern meaning of the word, but they look very much like biographies when held up against other such works dating to the first century CE. Scholars of the period contemporary to when Luke wrote his gospel have shown that some biographies have a two part form similar to that of Luke-Acts: the first part presents the deeds and teachings of the master while the second part presents the deeds and teachings of the master's followers.

Literary features – Luke fashioned his composition in Acts out of three major gospel literary forms: *narratives*, *summaries* and *speeches*.

Consider the following:

- Narratives of type A – In Luke's prologue to his gospel, he speaks of having written down a narrative account. Narratives of this type are just simple narratives. An example of such narratives is Acts 2:1-12 – the coming of the Holy Spirit at Pentecost.

- Narratives of type B – These narratives constitute a very select group. Narratives of this type are phrased in the first-person plural rather than in the third person (singular or plural). They are, consequently, known as the "we sections." There are four of these "we sections": 16:10-17; 20:5-15; 21:1-18; and 27:1-28:16.

- **Summaries** – The term "summary" has come to be the term used to represent short general descriptions of Jesus' activity. There are three summaries that are several verses in length: 2:42-47; 4:32-35; 5:12-16. In addition, there are a number of summaries consisting of only one or two verses in length. Examples of the shorter ones are: 6:7 and 9:31.

- **Speeches** – The speech is a common literary form in Acts. As much as 25% of the material is given over to this form which attests to the importance of this literary form in Acts. An example of this form is the following: Acts 2:14-36. This is Peter's address to the people following the event of Pentecost. There are some 25 to 30 speeches in Acts; seven by Peter and seven by Paul with the remainder attributed to a variety of individuals.

- **Structure** – The overall structure of Acts is based upon a combination of time and geography. The flow of time throughout Acts is linear – the work is laid out in chronological order. Geographically, Acts moves in accordance with Jesus' command to the disciples to be his witnesses in Jerusalem, throughout Judea and Samaria and to the ends of the earth (1:8). It is easily seen that Acts begins in Jerusalem (1:1-8:3). Then the narrative moves to Judea and Samaria (8:4-40). From there, Paul's journeys take him around the Mediterranean world until he is finally, as a prisoner, imprisoned and finally martyred in Rome.

- **The reception of Gentiles into the believing community** –
Jesus was a Jew born of a Jewish woman, and grew up as a Jew in a Jewish family and society. His chosen apostles were Jews and all of the members of the early believing community were Jews as well. When Gentiles sought to become members it was necessary to decide whether or not these individuals would have to be circumcised. The Apostolic Council made the decision that they would not have to undergo circumcision but that they must avoid the worship of idols, observe certain dietary restrictions and refrain from eating or drinking blood of animals sacrificed to idols.

A fascinating question is this: Is the Apostolic Council posed in the writing in a structural way to show its importance? The Council was important as shown in the narrative describing it by the appearance of the phrase "apostles and presbyters" five times and by the presence of very important people, namely Paul, Peter, and James, who was the brother of the Lord and bishop of Jerusalem.[172]

A Walk through Acts, Chapters 1-15

At this point taking a quick walk through the first half of Acts is illuminating. This will accomplish three objectives. First, it will acquaint you with this very important writing from the 1st century CE. Secondly, it will provide ample illustrations of what has been mentioned above. Finally, hopefully you, the reader, will find this composition a "good read."

In this quick walk through Acts Chapters 1-15, it is helpful to proceed in the following way. First read the passage specified in the bold type. Then read the descriptive paragraph that goes with that particular passage. It is important that **you** actually read the passage first and then only read the paragraph after doing so. This makes it possible for you to form your own understanding of it before being influenced by the short paragraph provided. The purpose of the descriptive paragraph is to point out one or two features of the text that you have just read. No attempt will be made to explain meanings which can be spiritually inspiring. Of course, it is always necessary to consider more study material that follows from these brief descriptions.

Now, let us begin our walk!

1:1-26 Acts begins by recounting Christ's appearance to the disciples after his resurrection and repeats the account of his Ascension which is also found at the end of Luke's gospel. In the process, it provides Luke the opportunity to bring before the readers at the outset Christ's promise to send the Spirit and his commissioning of the Apostles to be his witnesses (1:1-11). Following the Ascension, the apostles and a few others return to Jerusalem. It is there that they will experience the coming of the Holy Spirit, Pentecost. Upon their return, the first order of business is to   determine a replacement for Judas Iscariot (1:12-26) who had betrayed Christ and then killed himself.

2:1-41 Luke next reports the coming of the Holy Spirit at Pentecost. The happening of this event is first described (2:1-13) and then follows Peter's speech. (2:14-36). The reaction of the crowd is described along with an estimate that – on that day – about 3,000 people were baptized (2:14-41), an evidence of growth in numbers of this early community of faithful.

2:42-47 At this point, Luke inserts a rather lengthy summary statement of the status of the believing community.

---

[172] An additional indication of its great importance has been suggested, perhaps indicating another feature as a "structure" – namely its central position in this part of the writing. The narrative of the Council is located at the precise center of the composition. Joseph Fitzmyer, in his commentary *The Acts of The Apostles* (Doubleday 1998), points out that the center comes after 12,443 words and that chapters 1-14 contain 12,385 words and chapters 15-28 contain 12,502. The Council is, therefore, very close to being at the center! So what do you, the reader, think? Is this good evidence that the Council of Jerusalem is related as a structural element or not?

3:1-4:31 Luke next tells the reader about a man, over 40 years old, who had been crippled from birth and who was cured by Peter and John (3:1-10) in the name of Jesus. It is interesting to observe that this report has the form of a miracle story familiar to us from our reading of the Gospel of Mark. The cure is followed by a speech made by Peter (3:11-26) in the name of Jesus. While Peter was still speaking, some of the leaders of the Jews who were angered by Peter's speech reacted to it by taking Peter and the others into custody. The next day, after finding no way to punish them because of the aroused state of the believing people, they had to release them (4:1-22). Following their release, they went back to their community and they all proceeded to pray together to God (4:23-31).

4:32-33 At this point Luke inserts another summary statement.

4:34- 5:11 Perhaps picking up on v.32, Luke now presents the community rule concerning property or houses (4:34-35) and then proceeds to give us two examples. In the first example (vv.36-37), a man named Joseph (who is also called Barnabas) follows the rule precisely because he has sold land and donated the proceeds to the community. In the second example (vv.5:1-11), a man named Ananias and his wife Sapphira break the rule by withholding some of the proceeds and they both suddenly die, indicating the importance at this moment to support the nascent church.

5:12-42 In this section, the leaders of the Jews once again try to stop Jesus from teaching. Luke begins by first describing for the reader the success that Jesus' followers were having with their fellow Jews. The apostles were performing many signs and wonders, the people esteemed them, and large numbers were being added to the community of believers every day. A large number of people even came from the towns around Jerusalem (vv. 12-16). In response, the high priest of the Temple, and the Sadducees put the apostles in the public jail. An angel, however, lets them out of the jail and ultimately, after they are flogged, they are let go (vv. 17-42).

6:1-6 Due to the increase in the number of members, the leaders of the community recognize that it is necessary to appoint assistants to the apostles so that the apostles can continue to carry out their mission of the ministry of the word and prayer. At that time, a group of seven men are selected; and among them is a man named Stephen.

6:8-8:3 Luke now presents the martyrdom of Stephen. After detailing the charges against Stephen (6:8-15), Luke reports Stephen's speech (7:1-53) which includes a review of Jewish history from the time of Abraham until Solomon (which is a common thing at the time for rabbis to do, referring to the "salvation history"). Stephen's martyrdom is then described (7:54-8:1a). In the aftermath of this event a persecution breaks out and the believers, except for the apostles, are scattered. Saul (Paul's Hebrew name) was a Roman citizen and his Roman name was "Paul." He continued to persecute the believing community of Christ's faithful (8:1b-3).

8:4-40 Those who had been scattered went around preaching the word. Philip went to the city of Samaria and performed signs there and both Peter and John paid him a visit there (8:4-25). An angel of the Lord sent Philip to an encounter with an Ethiopian eunuch whom he instructed and then baptized.

9:1-9 In the midst of Saul's efforts to persecute the believers, he has a phenomenal encounter with Jesus (who has already died and ascended to Heaven after 40 days) which is presented here in three parts. This is the remarkable account of the conversion of Saul. First, the setting is given (vv.1-2). Secondly, Saul's encounter with Jesus is described (vv.4-6). He merely "falls to the ground" … no horse! Finally, the aftermath is described (vv. 7-9).The term "the Way," used here in v.2, is the name used by the community of believers for itself. It is used again in Acts at: 18:25; 19:9,23; 22:4; 24:14, 22.

This is a good moment to spring a surprise quiz. See if you can answer the following four questions to see if your careful reading matches the details many people describe:

- Did Saul see Jesus?
- Did Saul fall from a horse as he is shown doing in a number of famous paintings?
- Did Jesus tell Saul to go to the Gentiles?
- What did Jesus tell Saul to do?

The vision of Saul is presented two more times in Acts (22:4-16; 26:9-18) and is also described by Saul (Paul) himself in Gal 1:13-17. How do you answer these four questions in each of these cases?

9:10-19a The account of how Saul regained his sight is described in this passage. The passage seems to indicate that Saul did have a vision of Jesus since Ananias makes the statement in v.17 that: "Saul, my brother, the Lord has sent me, Jesus who **appeared** to you on the way by which you came, …"(NAB). In the passage here, the Lord states that Saul has been chosen to preach to the Gentiles, kings and Israelites.

9:19b-22 Saul proclaims Jesus in the synagogues of Damascus.

9:23-30 After a long while the Jews at Damascus plot to kill Saul but their plot becomes known and he escapes (vv.23-25). When he comes to Jerusalem, Saul at first has difficulty joining the community of believers because they feared him on account of his past. When the Hellenists (here meaning Jewish adherents) try to kill him, the brothers send him back to Tarsus.

9:31 This is a short summary statement.

9:32-43 This section relates two miracles performed by Peter in the name of Jesus. The first one takes place at Lydda and is the cure of a man who had been paralyzed and bedridden for eight years (vv. 32-35). The second takes place at Joppa. In this miracle Peter restores the life of a young girl who had become ill and died (vv. 36-43).

10:1-48 In this section, Peter has a vision of great import. Cornelius and his household receive the Holy Spirit and are baptized (they are Gentiles!). In the first episode, 10:1-8, Luke introduces us to Cornelius, a centurion of a Roman cohort called the Italica. Both he and the members of his family believe in God. One afternoon an angel appears to him and instructs him to send men to Joppa to bring back Peter. Cornelius follows this instruction as soon as the angel departs. In the second episode, 10:9-16, Peter has a vision. The day after Cornelius was visited by the angel,

Peter goes up on the roof to pray and he has a vision which is in symbolic form (vv.11-16). In the third episode, 10:17-33, the men who had been sent by Cornelius arrive. The following day, they take Peter back to Caesarea with them and introduce Peter to Cornelius, who then asks Peter to tell him all that God has commanded him to say. In the fourth episode, Peter gives a speech (vv. 34-43). This speech divides naturally into two parts. The first part, vv. 34-35, points out that God shows no partiality; anyone who fears God and does what is right is acceptable. [Note: The term "fear God" has a much deeper meaning than simple fear or just "religion" in general, as is popularly held by many individuals. It is a term that is encountered throughout both the OT and the NT, and refers to the "awe" held for our Transcendent God! Modern day authors may be treating this term too casually.] The second part, vv. 36-43, consists of a very good distillation of Luke's Gospel. While Peter was still speaking, the Holy Spirit comes upon all who were listening. Consequently, Peter baptizes Cornelius and his entire household (vv. 44-48).

11:1-18 In this section, the believers in Jerusalem confront Peter over the issue of admitting Gentiles to the believing community those who have accepted the word of God. Peter then relates to them all that has previously taken place in both Joppa and Caesarea. He tells them that the Jerusalem community accepts that God has given gifts of salvation to the whole world, "even to the Gentiles the repentance that leads to life" (11:18).

11:19-30 This brief section is concerned entirely with the believing community at Antioch. In the first part (11:19-26) we are told that Barnabas was sent to Antioch and that he brought Saul. Barnabas and Saul stay at Antioch for a whole year. It was there, at that the believing Christians in the community were first called "Christians" (v.26). [Note: The term "Christians" occurs elsewhere in the NT only at Acts 26:28 and 1 Peter 4:16.] The second part (11:27-30) of this section relates the event of a severe famine all over the world that was predicted by the prophet Agabus. The response of the community at Antioch was to send relief to the brothers who lived in Judea.

12:1-19 This passage tells us about King Herod's persecution of the Christians. Herod strikes at the believing community by having James, the brother of John of Zebedee, killed and he then puts Peter in prison under heavy guard. With the help of an angel, Peter escapes from the prison.

12:20-24 This passage tells us of the death of Herod. Herod's death is attributed to the action of an angel of the Lord.

12:25 This very brief verse is self-explanatory.

13:1-14:28 These two chapters tell us about the first of the three missionary journeys of Saul. At the request of the Holy Spirit, Saul and Barnabas are commissioned to go evangelize. This effort begins at Antioch (13:1-3) and ends in Antioch (14:26-28). Study material can provide many more details of this journey [Note: Bibles almost always have maps of Paul's three missionary journeys. It is helpful to consult one of these maps to see where Saul's first journey took him.] Luke begins to call Saul by his Roman name, Paul, in Acts 13:9.

15:1-35 This chapter is concerned with the meeting of the apostles in Jerusalem that has become known as the Apostolic Council. The purpose of the council was to settle a dispute between two groups of people. One group held the position that a man cannot be saved unless he is circumcised according to the law of Moses. The opposing group, which included Paul and Barnabas, strongly argued in opposition (vv.1-5). After much debate had ensued, Peter got up before the apostles and presbyters and addressed them saying that both Jew and Gentile are saved through the grace of the Lord Jesus (vv.6-12). Following this, James, the brother of the Lord, said it was his judgment that they should stop troubling the Gentiles and notify the Gentiles by letter that they only needed to avoid pollution from idols, unlawful marriage, the meat of strangled animals and blood (vv.13-21). A letter to that effect was prepared and delivered to Antioch by Paul and Barnabas (vv.22-35).

15:36-28:31 The rest of Acts informs us about Paul's second and third missionary journeys, his visit to Jerusalem which culminated in his arrest there and subsequently being taken to Rome in custody.

Conclusion

It is certainly true that Luke wrote both the gospel of Luke and the Book of the Acts of the Apostles. In terms of a biography of Luke's day, these writings look very much like a biography and a record of the outcome of the ministry of Jesus. The two writings, originally two scrolls, are linked by the repetition of events. There is a pattern in the gospel of Jesus taking his ministry toward Jerusalem and in the Book of Acts the apostles beginning the work of establishing a community, a ministry, and a way of life that is Jesus centered but expanding out into the world and including Gentiles (non-Jews). Many of the aspects of the early church community are described, the conversion of a man who was adamantly against Jesus and his teachings who became a significant "apostle" for Christ, and the inclusion of details about church office such as deacon, bishop, and presbyter (later to be called priests.)

PART 2

CHAPTER THIRTY- two

Paul and his letters

Invitation

When you read the Acts of the Apostles, and reach chapter 8, you encounter a man by the name of "Saul." He is actually also known as "Paul." It was the custom in the days of Luke's writing, around the area of the Mediterranean, for people often to have two names. Therefore, Saul and Paul are the same person. If you read a little further in Acts, you will find in Acts 13:9, that from this point only the name "Paul" is used in the writing.

When we first encounter Saul (Paul), he is in Jerusalem watching and then approving of the stoning of Stephen, the first Christian martyr. This immediately raises a question. What happened to Saul who had led the Jews in persecuting Christians to the point of brutal death? Why are his letters a major part of the New Testament? To understand, we need to see that Saul was a faithful Jew, born on the tribe of Benjamin, and educated by the well-known Rabbi Gamaliel. Let's hear what he says about himself, when in his life he had: "progressed in Judaism beyond many of my contemporaries among my race, since I was even more a zealot for my ancestral traditions. (Gal 1:14)" Later, Saul confessed in his writing that "I persecuted the church of God beyond measure and tried to destroy it. (Gal 1:13)"

Amazingly, God had a plan for Saul that he could never have expected. Paul states in his letter to the Galatians that God had special plans for him: "when [God], who from my mother's womb had set me apart and called me through his grace, was pleased to reveal his Son to me, so that I might proclaim him to the Gentiles. (Ga1: 15-16)" Paul calls himself, after a remarkable vision of Jesus, an "apostle." This is understood to mean that Jesus, after his death and resurrection and ascension to Heaven, came to him and directly called him to a special mission. When Paul experienced the vision of the resurrected Christ, he was baptized three days later. From Paul the zealous Jew came one of the most faithful and hard-working zealous Christians!

Why did Paul write letters? To understand why, we have to go back to the 1st century CE and understand that in that time travel from one place to another was arduous. There were no trains, planes, or cars. Most travel was by foot! And, in fact, we know that Paul walked more than 10,000 miles in his travels to tell his fellow Jews and Gentiles about the amazing Christ! Back at that time, communication between people was carried out most frequently by means of letters. So ... Paul used a letter to carry his advice and encouragements to communities and even particular people, when he could not talk to them in person.

How fortunate we are to have the opportunity to read a group of letters written by Paul 2,000 years ago! He was a man who preached the gospel of Jesus diligently even through horrible struggles and death threats. He was inspired because Jesus had revealed himself to him personally and he made the point that he had not been taught the gospel by another human being (Gal 1:11-12). He was able to convert both Jews and Gentiles (non-Jews), teach them the way to Christ and God's way of life, and then guide the communities which he had established. He was a man who endured remarkable hardships, such as beatings and imprisonments. At the conclusion of his life, Paul died a martyr in Rome, probably in the late 60s of the first century CE.

Paul describes his letters in the following way: "For we write you nothing but what you can read and understand, and I hope that you will understand completely … (2 Cor 1:13)." But, Paul writes about the mystery of God coming to us, Jesus who was totally a human and totally God. So perhaps it is not so easy "to understand." Consider the following remark about Paul's letters that is found in 2 Peter: "In them there are some things hard to understand …" (2 Peter 16).

Paul the Man

The year of Paul's birth is not known, but it is known that during his life he was persecuted by both Jews and Gentiles, and that he died a martyr's death in the middle 60s of the 1st century. Above all Paul was a Jew: born of Jewish parents of the tribe of Benjamin and, as reported in Acts, given the Hebrew name Saul. He was circumcised on the eighth day in observance of the law. Because he was a Pharisee with great zeal he was initially known as a persecutor of the Christian communities (Phil. 3:5-6; NABRE). He was, however, also born a Roman citizen (see Acts 22:28) and, therefore, he was also given a Roman name: Paul.

Paul tells us himself that he worked at a trade that required him to work with his hands (1 Cor 4:12; 1 Thess 2:9). Acts provides us the knowledge that this trade was tent making (Acts 18:3). Paul practiced this trade, from time to time, during the course of his missionary activity.

Paul's vision of Christ occurred near Damascus sometime during the period 32 CE to 36 CE. There are three accounts of Paul's vision reported in Acts: 9:1-9; 22:6-11; and 26:12-26. It is interesting to note that in none of these three accounts is Paul described as riding on a horse as has been so famously depicted in Western Art of the Middle Ages and the Renaissance. Further confirmation of this vision is provided by Paul himself in Galatians 1:15-16. Following his vision, Paul became the great Christian evangelizer who is so well remembered today.

During his missionary activity Paul traveled all over the lands of the Roman Empire around the Mediterranean – taking him from Israel all the way to Italy, his last journey taking him all the way to Rome. It has become the custom to divide his missionary activity into three journeys, each beginning and ending at Antioch. It was during the time of these journeys that he wrote his letters. It is apparent from the letters themselves that the purpose of this letter writing activity was to maintain communication with the communities that he had founded or visited at times when he was not able to visit them in person.

Letters in the First Century CE

A letter is a written communication between individual people or between groups of people. A letter is most commonly written over a short period of time like an hour, a day, or a week. More formal written documents, however, may be written over much longer periods of time. A letter was also something that had to be carried from the sender to the recipient(s) since there was no mechanized postal service in the days of the first century.

Papyri of several thousand letters have been unearthed in the arid regions of the Mediterranean world. These letters include many different types including the following: business, personal and bureaucratic. These letters appear to have had the function of making contact between sender and reader for the purpose of transmitting personal news, information or requests. Several ancient letters from the period 200 BCE to 100 CE are included in the Holy Scriptures, and are included in the Scriptures. Two letters are included in 2 Maccabees (1:1-10 and 1:11-29) and another two letters in The Acts of the Apostles (15:23-39 and 23:25-30). The Seven Letters to seven churches in Revelation (Chaps. 2-3) appear to replicate the custom of letter sending in the text of Revelation.

In the first century CE, letters were written by means of reed pens on sheets of papyrus or parchment. Because it was quite difficult to write legibly on rough surfaces, individuals lacking the necessary skill frequently made use of a skilled scribe. Thus, four ways of writing letters were in common use in the first century: 1) writing it oneself; 2) dictating it word for word; 3) dictating the sense while leaving the precise wording of the letter to an amamuensis (secretary or scribe); and 4) having another person write the letter without first specifying the details of the content. We encounter evidence of the practice of using a scribe in some of the letters of the NT, such as Romans (16:22) and 1 Peter (5:12), for example.

Letters are characterized by having a certain form. A personal letter has one form and a business letter a different form. The letter form common in the 1st century CE is displayed in the letter in **Acts 15:23-29**. It is seen from this example that the form of a personal letter in the 1st century CE consisted of three parts: a salutation, a body and a concluding farewell. The salutation included the name of the sender, the identity of the recipient and a greeting.

The method of delivery was by private courier or trusted traveler. In this regard it is interesting to consider the Book of Revelation which is addressed to seven churches. If you identify the seven churches on a map you will immediately see that if you move from one city to the next the order traces out a circular path which has its beginning and ending in Ephesus. It has been proposed that the manuscript of Revelation was originally delivered by being carried from one city to the next in just this order.

Paul the letter writer

Some fifteen years transpired between Paul's conversion and the writing of the earliest of his letters that has come down to us **(1 Thessalonians)**. When Paul wrote to particular congregations, it was a time occasioned by particular circumstances. All we know of these particular situations must be deduced from what Paul wrote as we have little or no independent information.

The fact that letters are "occasional" writings and not carefully written treatises means that Paul is not presenting his readers with systematic theological essays. This is a fact that in past was frequently not emphasized or sometimes completely overlooked. In recent years, however, this fact has gained considerable recognition:

> It has become commonplace to say that they should be studied not as theological treatises but as communications between two parties on specific occasions for specific reasons. Paul wrote not in order to work out the details of Christian teaching in an abstract way but to deal with concrete questions and problems. For

that reason, it is important to try to reconstruct the specific situations that occasioned the letters. [173]

The letters written by Paul were first encountered in an oral form by members of congregations. He would write to the community intending the letter to be read aloud in front of the assembled community (e.g. see **Col 4:16**). Robert Jewett points out that:

> Unlike our experience with these letters, in which very small sections are read aloud, the early church would have experienced even the longest letters in one sitting. [174]

Once you begin to read the letters written by Paul you will see that his letters have a form also. Paul's letter form is very close to the usual 1st century form but with two modifications. First, there is a thanksgiving added immediately after the salutation. Secondly, the body of the letter is divided into two sections: a doctrinal section, which is more theological, and a section of exhortations that focus on how the assembly members are to conduct themselves in the process of going about living their lives. Paul's letter form is as follows:

1. Salutation
    a. Identity of sender
    b. Identity of recipient
    c. Greeting
3. Body of letter
    a. Part A: Doctrinal section
    b. Part B: Exhortation
4. Closing greeting

A glance at the New Testament in the *New Oxford Annotated Bible*, Fourth Edition, we find the following in the Acts of the Apostles. There is a composition bearing the title: "The Letter of Paul to the Romans." A similar glance at the *New American Bible* shows that following Acts of the Apostles is a book with the title: "The Letter to the Romans." Underlying this simple observation is a fundamental reality: Paul's authorship of several of the letters has been challenged! At the present time, only seven of "Paul's letters" are accepted by all scholars as having been authored by Paul – Romans, 1 and 2 Corinthians, Galatians, Philippians, 1 Thessalonians and Philemon. The remaining letters have all been challenged and, more or less, scholars have come to accept that they are pseudonymous – that is to say that they are held to have been written by someone other than Paul. The authorship by Paul is a position backed by centuries of strong tradition. The position of pseudonymity is the outcome of various internal analyses of the writings but with no external evidence supporting that position. In the matter of authorship, it seems wiser to side with the strong ancient tradition and not to follow the results of modern analysis which have no external support and, hence, are not definitive.

---

[173] Russell Pregeant, *Engaging the New Testament* (Minneapolis, Mn: Fortress Press, 1995), 328.
[174] Robert Jewett, "Introduction to the Pauline Letters," in *Harper's Bible Commentary* (New York, NY: Harper & Row, 1988), 1126.

Reading the Letters of Paul

Reading the letters of Paul is not an easy task. Some of them are quite long; some are theologically involved; some are difficult to understand. We find support for this fact as attested in 2 Peter:

> And consider the patience of our Lord as salvation, as our beloved brother Paul, according to the wisdom given to him, also wrote to you, speaking of these things as he does in all his letters. In them there are some things hard to understand that the ignorant and the unstable distort to their own destruction, just as they do the other scriptures. (2 Peter 3:15-16 NAB, Revised Edition)

A letter written by Paul in the 1st century CE can be understood in three different ways. First it can be understood as a literary composition: a letter. Looked at in this way, it can be examined in terms of questions like: Who wrote it? When was it written? To whom was it written and what purpose did it serve? Secondly, it can be looked at in terms of being a historical document. Under this view, it can be examined in terms of questions such as: What was the historical moment in which it was written? Why was it written? And, what impact did it have on people in the historical moment?

Finally, although a letter is not specifically a theological document, it may contain theological statements. It can, therefore, be investigated in terms of the theological statements it contains. This is a complicated way of looking at it because there are a number of different areas of theology that it could include. One might set forth the following areas of theology to look for in one of Paul's letters:

1. Christology – the study of Jesus Christ, his person, life and mission; and consideration of all aspects of his divine and human natures.

2. Pneumatology – the area of theology that studies aspects of the Holy Spirit.

3. Soteriology – That area of theology that encompasses teaching about salvation. It includes human sinfulness, the relation between God and humans, the death of Christ, justification and sanctification. In recent times some scholars have included liberation theology and freedom from oppression under this heading.

4. Eschatology – The area of theology that deals with the "last things," the end of human life and the end of the world, and the eternal state.

5. Ecclesiology – The study of the community of the faithful (church).

6. Ethics – This is the area of theology that considers how to live a moral life on this earth.

Each of Paul's letters can be examined in terms of any one, several, or even all of these topics.

In order to make handling the large body of written material that constitutes the collection that is Paul's letters with more ease, let us adopt an imaginary three part scheme. Let us imagine each letter to be a large body of real estate, like a state for example. Furthermore, let us imagine that we are seeking to determine "the lay of the land" with the aid of satellites, drones and tour buses.

Let us undertake to examine each of the 13 letters in three steps. First, let us explore by satellite, from high altitude, each letter in order to determine its overall form. Secondly, let us explore each letter by means of a slow flight at low altitude by a drone in order to determine the contents of the body of the letter. This will provide us with a "map" (outline) of the contents of the material. Finally, let us investigate various individual sites (passages of the text) of the letter in order to examine them in greater detail because they are of particular interest.

Perhaps by engaging the letters in this imaginative way, reading these letters will be both more enjoyable and significantly more meaningful.

In what order will we study these 13 letters? The letters are presented in the Bible in accordance with two principles:

Principle #1 Letters to communities first; letters to individuals second

Principle #2 Letters presented in decreasing order according to length

In our study, the letters are taken up in a "loose" chronological order. A strict chronological order is not possible simply because there are too many uncertainties in the record pertaining to when and where the individual letters were written.

People, today, encounter the letters of Paul in nicely printed Bibles. Encountering them in this manner can obscure the fact that they were written almost 2000 years ago!

Utilizing Satellites, Drones and Tour Buses

The writings of Paul make up a major portion of the New Testament. What is needed is some way to deal with this large amount of material to make the study of it easier to carry out. For this reason, let us enlist the aid of satellites, drone and tour buses, as we mentioned.

Everyone is familiar today with how satellites can produce maps of large areas of the earth's surface. Let us, therefore, make use of satellite observations to discover the major form of a writing in the New Testament. This measurement will make evident to us whether the writing is indeed a letter or whether it is some other form of composition.

As a second step in our investigation of a composition of a letter by Paul, let us use a low flying drone to reveal a more detailed analysis of the structure of the composition (an outline). Experience shows that with an outline in hand it is much easier to understand a letter or other writing.

243

Finally, due to the large volume of material that has to be covered, it will be useful to use the concept of a tour bus to visit a limited number of passages in a given composition. This is just what one does on vacation in a foreign land. It is not possible to visit every interesting site in a city in a short period of time. One has to use a tour book and visit only a few locations of interest. Through the use of a tour bus it is possible to visit a few of the most significant passages of a given composition. Of course, there is always the possibility to return to the letters of Paul later and tour more interesting passages!

CHAPTER THIRTY-three

Paul's Earliest extant letters

Introducing 1 and 2 Thessalonians

It is thought, on the basis of the best determination of scholars, that these two letters were composed in 51/52 CE and within a few months of each other. 1 and 2 Thessalonians are the earliest written Christian compositions which have survived to the 21st century. They are, therefore, of very great significance. When these letters are encountered in one of our beautifully printed Bibles, it is easy to overlook their antiquity.

Thessalonica is located in Greece, at the head of the Thermaikos Gulf and at the foot of the Hortiates mountains. When you visit there, you experience the fact that it is situated on the side of a steep rise. The city was founded in 316 BCE and derives its name from a woman named Thessalonici who was a half-sister of Alexander the Great. In 167 BCE, Rome became the patron of the city and later, due to the loyalty of its inhabitants to the Roman emperor, the city was favored with the status of being a free city with an independent government.

When the Via Egnatia – a road connecting the East and West coasts of Greece extending west from Macedonia to the east – was constructed in 130 BCE, Thessalonica soon developed into a center for trade. Archaeological evidence suggests that the city also developed a rich cultural life. As Paul walked along this thoroughfare, he would have passed shrines of many pagan gods and talked with a variety of people having different religious beliefs. The Via Egnatia survives to this present day making it possible to walk in the actual footsteps of Paul and his companions.

The founding of the Christian community at Thessalonica is described in Acts 17:1-9. Paul and Silas came from Philippi to Thessalonica. On a number of Sabbath days, Paul went into the synagogue there and presented his gospel message about Jesus. "Some of them were persuaded and joined Paul and Silas, as did a great many of the devout Greeks and not a few of the leading women." (Acts 17:4). It was to these converts that Paul wrote these two letters.

There exists a very strong tradition which holds that Paul is the author of both 1 and 2 Thessalonians. Although everyone today accepts Paul's authorship of 1 Thessalonians, a certain number of scholars assert that a follower of Paul's, writing sometime after Paul's death, is responsible for composing 2 Thessalonians. (The technical term for such writing is: "pseudonymous"). The stronger argument, however, does side with the traditional identification of Paul as the author of 2 Thessalonians.

Why did Paul write these two letters to the Thessalonians? It seems that there may have been two reasons for writing 1 Thessalonians. First of all, Paul sent Timothy to Thessalonica to see how the Thessalonian community had progressed since his prior visit. Timothy had recently returned to Paul with very good news (1 Tim 3:6). Paul, consequently, wanted to write to tell them about his joy for their faithfulness and progress. A second reason may be that he wanted to give them some instruction concerning the issue of Christ's return. This is indicated by the inclusion in the letter of the teaching about the status of those people who have already died (1 Thess 4:13-18) and "the times and seasons" for the expected Second Coming of Christ (1 Thess 5:1-11). Paul's reason for writing his second letter is to assure the Thessalonians that the Second Coming had not yet happened as some people were wrongly teaching at that time (2 Thess 2:2).

When one is reading these two letters and the words "the gospel" are encountered, it must be kept in mind that Paul is referring to the life and message of Jesus that is contained in the oral tradition. These letters were written before any of the four Gospels were composed. The earliest of these, the Gospel of Mark is dated to the period 65-70 CE is which after Paul's death.

A word that is frequently encountered is "persecution" (as in 1:6; 3:3, 4, 7 and so on). In Paul's Thessalonian correspondence this word does not refer to a state persecution against a large number of people. The word seems to refer instead to the frequent everyday sufferings that the Thessalonians had to endure for trying to be good Christians while living in close association with non-believing Jews and Gentiles.

It is interesting to observe that the first major word that we encounter after the salutation, in the oldest extant Christian document of 1 Thessalonians, is "thanks." Paul gives thanks to God for all that the Thessalonians have accomplished because he knows that God has chosen them.

Paul's First Letter to the Thessalonians

Exploring 1 Thessalonians

As a first step in investigating 1 Thessalonians, let us employ some modern imagination and suppose that we are going to use some satellite surveillance and other observation equipment. So first we seek information from our observation satellite that will enable us to determine the overall form of the letter. The result obtained by making this analysis is the following:

    1:1 Salutation
    1:2-10 Thanksgiving
    2:1-5:24 Letter Body
            Part A Doctrinal Division (2:1-3:13)
            Part B Exhortation Division (4:1-5:24)
      5:23-28 Closing Greetings

Now that we have the form of the letter, let's continue our investigation by making a low overflight, utilizing now a drone flying at slow speed. Now we can see the letter body in order to see its contents. The result of doing this is as follows:

Body: Part A   Doctrinal Division (2:1-3:13)
        1. 2:1-12 The manner in which Paul conducted his ministry among the Thessalonians
        2. 2:13-16 The manner in which the Thessalonians received the word from Paul

3. 2:17-3:10 Paul recounts his sending of Timothy to Thessalonika
4. 3:11-13 Paul prays in concluding Part A

Body: Part B   Exhortation Division (4:1-5:24)
1. 4:1-2 Introduction to this division
2. 4:3-8 Holiness in sexual conduct
3. 4:9-12 Love one another; mind your own affairs; work with your own hands
4. 4:13-18 Concerning those who have already died
5. 5:1-11 Concerning times and seasons
6. 5:12-22 A number of counsels specifying proper behavior (Presented in the form of a list to facilitate recognition of them as individual modes of behavior and to make it easier to remember them):
   a. vv. 12-13a Respect those who labor among you (the leaders)
   b. v.13b Be at peace among yourselves
   c. v.14 Counsel the idlers, fainthearted, and weak
   d. v.15 Do not repay evil for evil; seek to do good to one another
   e. v.16 Rejoice always
   f. v.17 Pray without ceasing
   g. v.18 Give thanks in all circumstances
   h. v.19 Do not quench the Spirit
   i. vv. 20-21 Do not despise the words of prophets; test everything
   j. v.22 Abstain from every form of evil
7. 5:23-24 Paul prays in concluding Part B

This completes the part of an overall mapping in our investigation, utilizing the aid of a drone. In order to continue our investigation further, let us engage the services of a tour bus and proceed to look at the letter first as a literary piece, then as a historical document and finally as a writing including material that is theological in nature. To accomplish this, we will board the tour bus to carry us to a number of specific passages in the letter that are of special interest. Just as a ride on such a tour bus, we can't visit every single location!

1 Thessalonians viewed as a literary piece

As a literary piece, 1 Thessalonians is seen, from its form, to be a personal letter. Let us climb onto our tour bus and visit one or two passages where 1 Thessalonians shows itself as a letter.

Stop #1 1:1 The salutation

The salutation clearly states that the letter is from Paul, Silvanus and Timothy. The latter two individuals were co-workers with Paul and frequently traveled with him. Although three individuals are named as writers of the letter in the salutation, it is easily seen that only one of them, Paul, is the actual writer of the letters by the use of the first person singular "I" in verses: 2:18; 3:5; and 5:7.

The passage also clearly states that it is to the church of the Thessalonians. Paul intended it for the entire congregation. This is substantiated by Paul's command in 5:27 that it should be read to the entire congregation. It is interesting to note that the first "readers" were actually hearers.

Stop #2 1:2-10 The thanksgiving

A thanksgiving follows immediately after the salutation as it does in all of Paul's letters with the exception of Galatians. In Galatians, a rebuke and a curse occupy the position of the usual thanksgiving! In the thanksgiving, Paul gives his reasons for feeling thanks in regard to the recipients of his letter, in the present case it is the Thessalonians who had pursued the new faith with vigor.

1 Thessalonians viewed as a historical document

Stop #1 Salutation 1:1

There is a problem with the use of the word "church." This involves a question of translation. To the readers of today, the use of the word "church" brings to mind a building with a large number of individuals in attendance. In Paul's day, the Greek word in question meant "assembly" and was used in referring to small groups that met in a house. This was the home of a family – it was a house church. Translating the Greek word by the English word "church," therefore, does not seem to be the best choice. It can too easily lead the reader to make a misjudgment of the historical reality in thinking that at this time there was a large institutional church.

Stop #2 1:4-8 and 2:1-2

These passages present Paul's own account of how he and his co-workers conducted their ministry in Thessalonica. From this narrative it is apparent that Paul struggled hard to carry out his missions without impinging on the livelihood of the people he was seeking to evangelize. It is apparent that he handled his communication with the believers with great care.

Stop #3 2:14-16

Paul speaks out about the Jews who had opposed his ministry and later gave the Thessalonians difficulties. Remember that Paul, himself, was a Jew! It should not be concluded from this passage that Paul is anti-Jewish. Because he was himself a Jew, he is upset that his fellow Jews refuse to beliee in Christ. He will address the matter of the non-believing Jews in the future when he writes his letter to the Romans (see Chaps. 9-11).

Stop #4 2:17-3:10

This passage relates the reason Paul is writing this letter. He had tried to go and visit the Thessalonians but he was prevented from doing so. When he became very concerned over their welfare he sent Timothy to them to find out about their welfare. When Timothy returned with good news, Paul was motivated to write to them to tell them how he was happy he was for them.

1 Thessalonians viewed as a writing that contains theological material - Christology

Stop #1 1:1 Salutation

The salutation ends with the phrase "Grace to you and peace." These two words, "grace" and "peace," appear in the salutation of every one of Paul's letters! But see in 2 Thessalonians where Paul identifies the source of grace and peace: "Grace to you and peace from God our Father and the Lord Jesus Christ" (1:2).

Often in the Hellenistic world, people would greet one another with the Greek word *chairein*, a meaning equivalent to our modern day "greetings" or "hello, how are you?" Quite distinctly, Paul's letter always uses a different form of this word of greeting and he uses the form: *charis*. This word is usually translated ""grace" in bible translations due to the equivalent Latin word *gratia* that supplanted *charis* in Latin bibles. *"Gratia"* indicated a "gift" from God; however, the original word *charis* carries a much deeper meaning of "joy" or the blessing of "God be with you" which is true joy! Paul's use of the word *charis* reveals that Christians do experience joy in their lives in their relationship to the Lord. And, the second important word in Paul's greetings is "peace," derived from the Hebrew word *shalom*. In like manner, Jews then in the ancient days and even today greet one another with the word *shalom*, translated "peace," as a common daily greeting. But what kind of "peace" does *shalom* represent in its foundational meaning? When one considers the tragic rupture of mankind from God in the beginning of time, as recorded in Genesis, the word *shalom* connotes God's promise that one day there would be reconciliation – a loving and intimate rejoining of mankind and God, a true "peace" as then given in the word *shalom*, meaning "wholeness" and eternal union with God. All in all, then, Paul is consistently greeting the faithful communities to whom he writes with the hope that resides in all human hearts, indeed, the "joy" that comes from accepting Christ and having him abide in all their hearts, and the resulting "peace" that is the realization of once again being reconciled with God in the new beginning that Christ brought and offers to the world.

Stop #2 1:3

This verse contains the phrase "your work of faith and labor of love and steadfastness of hope." What is unusual about this phrase is the order of the three elements. Instead of the more familiar faith, hope and love, the order here in v.3 is the order that relates to salvation history: faith, love and hope. One has: "faith" in Jesus Christ; "love" while living on earth; "hope" in the coming of the day that Christ comes again.

Stop #3 1:9-10

This verse contains a brief statement of how the Thessalonians responded to the message of Paul: they turned from idols (they were initially Gentiles - non Jews) to serve a living and true God and to wait for his Son from heaven whom he raised from the dead. It is almost like some sort of creedal statement.

Stop #4 2:17-18

It seems clear from these verses that Paul was a firm believer in the existence of a supernatural being that opposed mankind, namely, the Devil. Is this statement, since it carries with it Paul's authority, convincing in the 21st Century?

Eschatology

Stop #1 4:13-18

In this passage Paul seeks to allay the concerns of those who think that those who have already died by the time Jesus returns will somehow be left behind. Paul assures these people that the dead in Christ will rise first (4:16). From this passage it is also apparent that Paul believes he will be among those still living (4:17)!

Stop #2 5:1-11

The matter here is when Christ will come. Christ will come like a thief in the night (5:2) and, consequently, Paul advises that everyone keep awake and be sober (5:6).

Ethics

Stop #1 3:12

In this verse, Paul prays for the Lord to make the people to increase in love for one another. This puts emphasis on how important this element of life is to the community. Paul addresses this issue again in 4:9-10.

Stop #2 4:1

It is interesting to see that in this verse Paul links "how you ought to live" with the concept of "pleasing God." How often do Christian believers base their decisions in life upon whether or not what they are about to do pleases God rather than themselves or other people?

Stop #3 4:3-8

Here, Paul directs our attention to a number of sexual relationships. In verse 8, Paul points out that the authority behind this teaching is God – the One who also gives the Holy Spirit to us. Apparently sexual matters are important to God and are gifts from God to be used for life not selfishness!

This is the last stop that we will make looking at the theological aspects of the letter. On the way back to our lab, let's make one more stop that seems worthy of special attention – 2:13. In this verse, Paul is speaking of "his Gospel" which he taught to the Thessalonians when he evangelized them. Paul will tell us in Galatians that he did not receive "his Gospel" from any human being but directly from God. Paul's teaching about "his Gospel," therefore, comes with great authority.

Paul's Second Letter to the Thessalonians

Exploring 2 Thessalonians

As we did in the case of 1 Thessalonians, let us go into our laboratory and examine our satellite data to determine the overall form of 2 Thessalonians:

> 1:1-2 Salutation
> 1:3-12 Thanksgiving
>> Explanatory note: In the original Greek, verses 3-10 comprise a single sentence and verses 11-12 are also one sentence.. In as much as verses 11-12 are a prayer and as can be seen from verses 2:16-17 and 3:16 that Paul likes to end a section with a prayer, one is prompted to understand 1:3-12 as a thanksgiving section.
> 2:1-3:16 Letter Body
>> 2:1-17 Part A Doctrinal Division
>> 3:1-16 Part B Exhortation Division
> 3:17 Paul's authentication of his letter by writing in his own hand
> 3:18 The closing greeting

Paul's second letter to the Thessalonians, therefore, clearly has the usual form of a 1st Century personal letter.

Let us continue our investigation of this brief letter by enlisting the aid of our drone to make a slow and low overflight of the body of the letter in order to obtain a map of the contents of the body of the letter. We obtain the following outline:

> Body: Part A Doctrinal Division (2:1-17)
>> 1. 2:1-12 Paul reassures the believers that Christ has not returned from heaven yet!
>> 2. 2:13-13-15 Paul tells them to stand firm and hold fast to what they have been taught
>> 3. 2:16-17 Paul's prayer ending the doctrinal division
> Body: Part B Exhortation Division (3:1-16)
>> 1. 3:1-5 Paul asks the Thessalonians to pray for him and his helpers
>> 2. 3:6-13 Paul speaks against idleness and to earn their own living
>> 3. 3:14-15 Paul speaks out against those who do not obey his teaching
>> 4. 3:16 Paul's prayer ending the Exhortation Division

2 Thessalonians viewed as a literary piece

First, let us look at 2 Thessalonians as a literary work – a letter. Once again, we will board a tour bus to continue our investigation.

Stop #1 Salutation

As was the case with 1 Thess, this letter is from Paul, Silvanus and Timothy, although in reality Paul is the one who is writing (see use of 1st person singular in 2:5 and 3:17). His intended readers are, as in the first letter, the Christians in the assembly at Thessalonica.

Stop #2 1:3-4

In this part of the thanksgiving, Paul expresses his thanks that the faith of his recipients is growing and that their love for one another is increasing. This puts emphasis on the importance of these two factors, growth of faith and increasing love for one another, in a church community.

Stop #3 3:17

This comment by Paul that he is writing "this greeting with my own hand" has been understood by many scholars to indicate that the letter was penned by an *amanuensis* (scribe or secretary). In the 1st Century an *amanuensis* could function in a number of different ways ranging from taking dictation to composing the letter for the "writer's" signature.

2 Thessalonians viewed as a historical document

Secondly, let us look at 2 Thessalonians as a historical document. To accomplish this we will return to our tour bus and visit a couple of specific passages.

Stop #1 1:3-4

The "persecutions and the afflictions" mentioned in 1:4 refer to the daily harassments of the Christians by both their Jewish and Gentile neighbors and not to persecution by the Roman state. As Paul points out in 1:5, this activity can be understood as testing to make the Christians worthy of the kingdom of God, because through this testing believers demonstrate their trust in God.

Stop #2 2:1-2

Paul tells the Thessalonians to disregard any claim they have received from others to the effect that the day of the Lord, Christ's Second Coming, has already arrived. Paul tells the Thessalonians that it will not come before the lawless one has been revealed.

Stop #3 2:15

The words "by our letter" is most likely a reference to Paul's first letter to the Thessalonians. That would establish that 1 Thess was written prior to 2 Thess.

Stop #4 3:6-13

Idleness was apparently a problem in the community at Thessalonica. This is evidenced by this lengthy passage which Paul devotes to the treatment of this topic. His concern is for the church having to pay to support the people who are not supporting themselves. This was an ever present problem in Paul's churches because this matter appears in a number of his other letters as well.

252

2 Thessalonians viewed as a writing that contains theological material

Finally, let us view Paul's letter as a writing that contains some material that is theological in nature. Returning to our tour bus for a third time, let us visit a number of passages of this type. In this letter the majority of this material is in the area of eschatology – so we will investigate this first.

Eschatology

Stop #1   2:1-12

The principal concern of this letter is that word is going around Thessalonica saying that the return of Jesus' return from heaven has already taken place! Paul is writing to assure the believers there that this is certainly not the case. Paul responds to this situation by telling the Thessalonians that Jesus' return cannot occur before the rebellion comes and the lawless one is revealed. This entire section is cast in apocalyptic style language similar to that encountered in Revelation.

Stop #2 1:5-10

Every human being has been given life. At first, this section seems like it is going to describe all the possible outcomes of that life but it turns out to be only two outcomes because Paul divides all humans into two groups: those who know God and those who do not know God. First, Paul considers those who do not know God and those who do not obey the Gospel of our Lord Jesus. The end for this group will be eternal destruction and separation from the presence of the Lord. One would expect a similar description of the end for those who did know God and who did obey the Gospel. But it does not seem to be there. This is probably because Paul's strong feeling against those who are giving out false teachings and his strong desire to keep the Thessalonian believers from following after them causes Paul to put all of his attention on the awful end of those who are wrongly teaching.

If anyone is interested in what is in store for the faithful believers, the answer is provided by Paul in his first letter to the Thessalonians. Go back and look at verses 4:17-18 and 5:9-10 and discover that eternal life with Jesus Christ is in store for the devoted believer.

Stop #3 1:11-12

This is the first of three prayers (2:16-17 and 3:16 are the others) that Paul includes in his letter, each coming at the end of a major section. These prayers teach us that prayer is basically talking to God. God makes use of our gift of speech to communicate with those who believe in God. Thus, everyone is able to pray. God asks that we do this constantly.

Secondly, these three prayers also teach us that when one truly prays then one is verbalizing what one believes. In prayer, an individual reveals what is in the inner self, in one's heart.

These prayers also show that it is effective to pray for other people (intercessory prayer). Prayer should not be self-centered.

These verses teach us that God is concerned with our hearts. The heart is the place where God is joined to the human being and abides. Paul prays for the Lord to direct the hearts of the Thessalonian believers to the love of God and to the steadfastness of Christ in 3:5.

Stop #4 3:3

In this verse, Paul again makes it evident that he believes in a real, personal entity, the Devil, who opposes humanity. Given that Paul received his Gospel from God, does this not make sense that we can believe this as a truth on the basis of Paul's authority?

At this point, let us conclude our investigation by observing that in 2 Thessalonians Paul does not devote much space to writing about subjects in the category of ethics. In 3:6-13, Paul addresses the matter of idleness which, therefore, must have been a problem of some consequence in Thessalonica. Paul describes how when he was evangelizing the people who lived in Thessalonica, he and his co-workers had made every effort to work hard and support themselves in order to set a good example.

CHAPTER THIRTY-four

Paul's letters to the Galatians and Philippians

Galatians and Philippians are considered together because these two letters were both written early in Paul's Christian ministry, perhaps sometime near the middle of the 1st Century. These two letters are also considered together because they differ greatly as to both content and tone and, therefore, furnish one with a good contrast. On the one hand, Galatians is a letter written to set matters straight in regard to some teachers who are telling the Galatians that circumcision is required for new converts (if they were not Jews) to become Christians. Paul is forcefully teaching that circumcision is not required and to give in to this is to cut themselves off from Jesus. Philippians, on the other hand, is a letter written while Paul was in prison. It expresses his joy for the people who have shared in his Gospel and that he anticipates their love will overflow more and more.

Introducing Galatians

This letter is addressed to "the churches of Galatia" (1:2) and, consequently, it is clearly intended to be read in a number of different churches. Galatia is the name applied to a region of Asia Minor. It lies in the middle of what is known today as Turkey.

Almost all scholars today accept that Paul is the person who wrote the letter. He made use of a secretary as is seen from 6:11 where Paul states the he is writing the ending of the letter in his own hand. The high emotional level on which it is written is evidenced by the omission of the usual thanksgiving and the mention of his wish that those who are seeking circumcision for all of the Gentile Christians would castrate themselves (5:12). This prompts many scholars to suggest that, in this case, Paul used the method of dictation and the scribe also wrote down his outbursts of feeling as when he referred to his readers as "O stupid Galatians" (3:1) and when he said of his opponents that he wished they "might also castrate themselves." Paul wrote this letter in the early 50s of the 1st century CE.

At the time Galatians was written, there was an ongoing dispute over whether Gentile converts should be admitted to the Christian assembly directly or whether they should be required to first be circumcised. This controversy led to what is known as the Council at Jerusalem. Paul reports his version of this council in Gal 2:1-10. Another understanding of the council is presented in Acts 15:1-29.

Introducing Philippians

The date of the writing of Philippians depends upon the location of where Paul is imprisoned. Unfortunately, there is no indication within the letter as to where this took place. Three locations are possible: Ephesus, Rome and Caesarea. The probable dates for the writing of the letter associated with these three locations are 56 CE, 61-63 CE and 58-60 CE respectively.

Let us ask: What is the immediate occasion of the letter? In the absence of outside information about this matter, we have to rely upon the contents of the letter for an answer.

Reading through the letter it appears that Paul is writing to the Philippians because he is about to send Epaphroditus back to them (2:25-30) and he wants to make sure that the Philippians will sincerely welcome his return.

There are no indications in the letter of any pressing problems within the Christian assembly in Philippi. The most explicit indication of a problem is Paul's urging of Euodia and Syntyche to be "of the same mind in the Lord" (4:2-3). There is a brief reference to "opponents" (2:28) but the nature of this opposition is not described, thus leading one to think that this was not a problem of great magnitude. This letter contains primarily expressions of Paul's good feelings toward the Philippians at Philippi.

Exploring Galatians

Let us go into our laboratory and look at the satellite data pertaining to Galatians and seek to outline its letter form. There results the following outline:
        1:1-5 Salutation
        1:6-10 Rebuke and curse (replacing the thanksgiving!)
        1:11-6:10 Letter Body
            Part A Doctrinal Division (1:11-5:12)
            Part B Exhortation Division (5:13-6:10)
        6:11-18 Closing Greetings

Having thus established that Galatians has the now familiar letter form, let us send out our drone and make a low and slow overflight to determine the details of the letter body. Doing this we obtain the following:

Body: Part A Doctrinal Division 1:11-5:12
    1. 1:11-2:10 Paul's Gospel is not of human origin
    2. 2:11-14 Paul's rebuke of Peter
    3. 2:15-21 People are justified by faith, not by works of the law
    4. 3:1-5 How the Galatians received the Spirit
    5. 3:6-29 God's promise to Abraham
    6. 4:1-11 We are children of God and, therefore, heirs
    7. 4:12-20 Paul seeks to heal strained relations between the Galatians and himself
    8. 4:21-5:1 Paul teaches by using the method of allegpory
           (allegory of Hagar and Sarah)
    9. 5:2-12 "If you let yourselves by circumcised, Christ will be of no benefit to you" (5:2)
Body: Part B Exhortation Division (5:13-6:10)
    1. 5:13-15 Love one another
    2. 5:16-18 Live by the Spirit
    3. 5:19-26 Works of the flesh and the fruits of the Spirit
    4. 6:1-10 A number of counsels pertaining to living one's life

We have now proceeded to that stage of our investigation of Galatians where we will climb on our tour bus and visit a number of passages to see what they have to say in a little more detail.

Galatians viewed as a literary piece

Stop #1 Salutation (1:1-5)

It has been seen from our satellite survey, that Galatians is a 1st Century personal letter. The letter is seen to be from Paul and the use of the 1st person singular in 1:6 proves that it is Paul who is doing the writing. In this case, however, the letter is said to be from Paul and all of the Christians who are with him.

Stop #2 Letter Body Part A (1:11)

In this letter, the two divisions of the body are greatly unbalanced. The doctrinal division (1:11- 5:12) is substantially greater in length than is the exhortation division (5:13-6:10). Paul is focused on his refutation of the claims of the pro-circumcision group, so much so that he is not interested in all of the other affairs of life in the assembly.

Stop #3 4:21-51

In this section of the letter, Paul makes use of an allegory, based on OT personalities, to prove his point. Do you think that Christians of the 21st Century find Paul's argument convincing?

Paul, in verse 27, cites scripture. He quotes from Is 54:1 from the Septuagint. The Septuagint was a Greek translation of the Old Testament that was made in the 3rd Century BCE. The Septuagint came to be the Bible of the Greek speaking Christians who did not know Hebrew.

Stop #4 Paul's comment about his writing (6:11)

On the basis of the highly aroused tone of Paul's writing in this letter one would certainly think that Paul would have personally written it. This remark, however, seems to indicate that he made use of an *amanuensis*. This same observation of the tone would argue in favor of Paul having used the method of dictation.

Galatians viewed as a historical document

Stop #1 1:6-10

This passage describes what is at the root of the situation that Paul is seeking to combat. There are some individuals that are seeking to confuse the Galatian faithful and to lead them away from the one true Gospel.

Stop #2 1:11-2:14

This is a lengthy autobiographical passage intended by Paul to establish the truth of the statement he makes in 1:11; the Gospel that he teaches is not of human origin. It consists of three parts. The first is a statement of what Paul will demonstrate. The second, is a long account of Paul's life from the time of his conversion experience through the council at Jerusalem. The third recounts a later incident at Antioch in which Paul rebuked Peter.

Galatians viewed as a writing that contains theological material - Christology

Stop #1 2:15-16

These verses tell us that we are justified through faith in Jesus Christ, not through works of the law. This is a basic truth of the Christian faith. It is encountered here in Galatians and will be engaged again when it is time to consider Romans.

In verse 16, Paul uses the expression "works of the law." What does Paul mean when he speaks of "works of the law?" This phrase refers to: circumcision; observing special days and months, and seasons, and years (see 4:10); and observing the purity rules. This phrase does not refer to the daily good deeds that a believer does or should do.

Stop #2:4-7

This passage has much to say about the reason God sent his Son to earth. This passage is worthy of considerable investigation.

Ethics

Stop #1 5:16-26

Paul urges the Galatians to "live by the Spirit." He follows this with the negative statement not to gratify the desires of the flesh. Because, he says, the desires of the flesh are opposed to the Spirit. Then he goes on to spell out what the desires of the flesh are (vv. 19-21) and what are the fruits of the Spirit (vv. 22-26).

Stop #2 6:1-10

In this section, Paul gives the Galatian faithful sever counsels that they should follow in the course of living their lives. Notable among these counsels is the one that states that a person will reap only what that person sows. The one who sows for the Spirit will reap eternal life from the Spirit.

This concludes our investigation of Paul's letter to the Galatians.

Philippians

Exploring Philippians

Once again let us go into our laboratory to examine the satellite overview of Philippians to determine its letter form. Doing so gives us the following outline of the letter:

> 1:1-2 Salutation
> 1:3-11 Thanksgiving
> Letter Body 1:12-4:9
> >   Part A Doctrinal Division (1:12-4:1)
> >   Part B Exhortation Division (4:2-9)
> 4:10-23 Letter closing

This establishes that Philippians does possess the now familiar letter form. It also reveals that this letter does not possess a fully developed exhortation division as do most of Paul's other letters. This letter focuses on joy (4 times) and rejoicing (6 times).

Now let us exercise our drone again and make a slow fly over at low altitude to determine the details of the letter content. Doing this results in the following outline:

> Part A Doctrinal Division (1:12-4:1)
> >   1:12-26 Paul speaks about his imprisonment
> >   1:27-30 Live your life in a manner worthy of the gospel
> >   2:1-11 On humility
> >   2:12-18 Work out your salvation with fear and trembling
> >   2:19-30 Paul's plans for Timothy and Epaphroditus
> >   3:1 A comment by Paul
> >   3:2-11 Righteousness comes through faith in Christ
> >   3:12-4:1 Righteousness is a goal to be persued
> Part B Exhortation Division
> >   4:2-3 Paul speaks about Euodia and Syntyche
> >   4:4-9 Counsels on living the Christian life

Now that we have put our drone back in its hangar, let's look at this letter in the usual three different perspectives.

Philippians viewed as a literary piece

Stop #1 1:1-2 Salutation

From this passage it is seen that this letter is from Paul and Timothy but, as before, it is really Paul who is writing (see 1:3). It is also seen that the letter is to all of the saints (believers) in Philippi.

One must be alert to the two titles of assembly positions that occur in 1:1, the "bishops" and "deacons" as translated by the NRSV. Because of the meaning which is attached to these two terms in today's world, they can lead one to read into the text a greater degree of institutional organization then actually existed in Paul's time. It is wiser to use "overseer" and "deacon" as does the NABRE translation which follows more closely the original Greek.

Stop #2 4:10

At this point in his letter, Paul writes a lengthy thank you for the financial assistance given to him by the Philippians during his ministry.

Philippians viewed as an historical document

Stop #1 1:7

In this verse, Paul states that he is writing from prison. Four of Paul's letters were written while he was imprisoned somewhere. The other three are: Ephesians, Colossians and Philemon.

Stop #2 1:12-14

Surprisingly, Paul cites two good effects that have resulted from his imprisonment; it has actually helped to spread the gospel and it has enabled his followers to speak the word with greater boldness and without fear.

Stop#3 1:21-24

In 3:21, Paul says that for him "living is Christ and dying is gain." In Paul's mind, dying is to be with Christ. One would be wise to come to view life and death as did Paul.

Stop #4 2:19-24

This passage presents the reader with a firsthand testimony of the worthiness of Paul's associate Timothy. We will discover more about Timothy when it is time to read the two letters that have come down to us written by Paul directly to Timothy.

Stop #5 2:25-30

This passage is concerned with the situation of Epaphroditus. Apparently he had come from the Philippians to help Paul during his imprisonment but had become ill and came close to death.   Probably one of the major reasons Paul had for writing this letter was to tell them that he, Paul, was going to send him back to his home.

Stop #6 2:1-6

This is a reference to those who are opposing Paul in Philippi. Apparently they are in favor of circumcision as were the opponents at Galatia. In this case, Paul does not seem to be nearly as angered as he was in Galatians. Perhaps this indicates that the issue at Philippi had not caused believers to abandon their faith. At this point in the letter, however, Paul does see fit to devote some space to summarizing his experience of circumcision (vv. 4-6).

Stop#7 4:2-3

In this section Paul focuses his attention on two women in the congregation who had a disagreement. He sought to smooth things over by urging the two of them to be of one mind. He backed this up by seeking help from one of his (Paul's) companions.

Stop #8 4:22

This verse is interesting because it tells one that there were Christian believers in the emperor's household at the time Paul was writing this letter.

Philippians viewed as a writing that contains theological material - Ethics and Eschatology

Stop #1 1:9-11 Ethics and Eschatology

Paul places this prayer at the end of the thanksgiving. It is interesting because Paul points out that one needs both knowledge and perception (or insight) to discern what is of value from what is not of value. For many people, it seems the need for knowledge, as the factor that enables one to develop discernment, receives too little attention. Also, take note of the mention of Christ's second coming in this passage.

Stop #2 1:27-30 Ethics

In the first part of this passage, verses 27-28a, Paul counsels the Philippians to live their life in a manner worthy of the Gospel which includes being a unified congregation. In the latter part of the passage, verses 28b-30 Paul states that God has granted them the privilege of believing in Christ and of suffering for him as well. This is an interesting way of looking at Christian life.

Stop #3 2:6-11 Christology

The section 2:6-11 is an ancient Christian hymn, or part of one, which was in service at the time that Paul was writing this letter. The text here is seen to be in two parts: verses 6-8 the pronoun "he" refers to Jesus and verses 9-11 relate how God (God the Father) honored Jesus. The reason for quoting this hymn here is to give an example of the humility that the Philippians should try to emulate.

Stop #4 2:14-16 Christology

It states in verse 15 that the Christian faithful "shine like lights in the world." In Paul's view, all Christian believers are chosen by God. Given this premise, it would seem that all Christians have an obligation to lead good Christian lives so as to function as examples for the other people in the world. Thus, one's calling to be a Christian comes with an obligation!

Stop #5 3:20-21 Eschatology

In this brief passage, Paul tells us that when Christ comes, Christ will change our earthly bodies to conform with his glorified body. Here Paul seems to be speaking about those people who are still living at the time when Jesus returns. Paul does not address the question of the type of body that the resurrected people will have.

Stop #6 4:4-7 Eschatology

When Paul wrote "the Lord is near" he could have meant that the return of Christ was not far off in a chronological sense. But it perhaps could have had a different meaning. If one understands "Lord" to represent God the Father then it could be an echo of Ps 119:151 where it states the God (LORD) is near. God is the almighty, the unfathomable other, and yet God is near! And people can talk to God through prayer! Along this same line of thought, read verses 6-7 as well.

Stop #7 4:9 A suggestion from Paul himself

In this passage, Paul gives the Philippians some advice. First, he gives them a short list of things that are good to think about. Secondly, he tells them to keep on doing everything that they have learned, received, and heard and seen in himself. If the Philippians follow this advice then, Paul states: "the God of peace will be with you."

Is there a teaching here for us living in the 21st Century? Certainly, there is. We can think about the things that Paul has listed in verse 8. We can also hear what he has to say by reading his letters and we can learn from his life by reading the autobiographical sections in his letters and by reading about his ministry in the Acts of the Apostles. Recall that he said that he received his Gospel directly from God and he backed this statement up by reviewing his life. Paul, therefore, speaks with authority and, consequently, the God of peace, will be with us as well if we do these things.

CHAPTER THIRTY-five

PAUL'S CORINTHIAN CORRESPONDENCE
INTRODUCING 1 CORINTHIANS AND 2 CORINTHIANS

Corinth

Corinth is located by an isthmus which separates the Aegean Sea from the Adriatic Sea in what is now Southern Greece. The seaport of Lechaeum was located two miles almost due north, providing access to the Adriatic Sea and the lands to the West. The port of Cenchreae lay eight miles to the southeast providing access to the lands to the East. Its most prominent physical feature is the Acrocorinth, a steep promontory by the city that rises some 1,800 feet in height. In Paul's day a temple of Aphrodite stood at the summit.

In the 1st Century, because of the frequent storms, mariners found it too dangerous to sail around Cape Malea, the southern-most point of land. Consequently, they went by way of the isthmus. For large vessels, the cargoes were unloaded and carried across the isthmus and then loaded on another ship. In the case of small vessels, both the ship and its cargo were dragged across the Isthmus and launched back into the water.

Due to its strategic location on a major trade route, therefore, Corinth became a wealthy commercial center. Politically, Corinth was the leading city of the Roman province of Achaia and it was accorded the status of a colony which gave it a special relationship with the Roman Empire.[175] It was known for its bronzes, and pottery.

The sailors and travelers who passed through Corinth brought with them their various religious beliefs giving the city a considerable degree of diversity. Poseidon was the chief god worshipped there. Altars to the gods Hermes, Artemis, Zeus and others have also been found. In addition to its religious diversity, the city had a great diversity of economic prosperity resulting in a substantial gap between rich and poor.

There was a proverb voiced by the Mediterranean seamen that stated: "Not for every man is the voyage to Corinth."[176]

Paul's founding of Christianity at Corinth

Paul founded the Christian mission at Corinth (1 Cor 3:6). His initial visit to the city is described in Acts 18:1-18a. According to this narrative, when he first tried to teach the Jews about Jesus, they "opposed him and reviled him" (18:6) and, consequently, he turned to the Gentiles. The Jews and Gentiles who did come to belief in Jesus were primarily not those wise

---

[175] J. Paul Sampley, "The First Letter to the Corinthians," in *The New Interpreter's Bible*, V. X (Nashville, TN: Abingdon Press, 2002), 774.

[176] Clarence T. Craig, "The First Epistle to the Corinthians," in *The Interpreter's Bible*, Vol. 10 (Nashviille, TN: Abindon Press, 1953), 4.

men in the society by human standards, powerful or of noble birth (1:26). Paul remained in Corinth for a year and a half, teaching in the house assemblies that he had established there.

It is not hard to see why Paul experienced difficulty with the Christian community that he had established at Corinth. On the one hand, the populace at Corinth possessed considerable diversity as to political belief, financial status, religious belief, occupation and undoubtedly philosophic belief. On the other hand, Paul was requiring the Christian assembly, consisting of people from the population at Corinth, to have oneness in regards to belief in God, interrelationships within the assembly, and a moral way of life. It was impossible for there not to have been problems!

Introducing 1 Corinthians

In Corinth in the 1st Century there were some Jews and many Gentiles – a total of about 600,000 in all. These people were some very wealthy and many quite poor. There were individuals professing belief in a variety of gods. There were people who were merchants, sea captains, sailors, farmers and transients of many types.

Paul worked to win converts from among the people who made up this diverse assembly of individuals. He was, to a degree, successful in his work. He won over some Jews and a greater number of Gentiles. He converted some from among the wealthy and significantly greater numbers from among the poor. He was successful in converting some of the sailors, some of the farmers, some of the merchants and some of the seafaring leadership.

The house churches he established had problems. This is not surprising given the high degree of diversity within the assemblies. These problems included: moral depravity; factionalism; difficulties in celebrating the liturgies; uncertainties about eating meat sacrificed to idols; resistance on the part of some individuals to accepting belief in a general resurrection; and different attitudes toward marriage because of a belief that the day of the Lord was near at hand.

After Paul had founded the Christian mission in Corinth and departed, he wrote them a letter which has not survived. Sometime later, he wrote a second letter which has come down to our time as our canonical 1 Corinthians. In this letter, Paul sought to correct some of these problems and to bolster the faith of the Corinthian Christians. This is the letter that we will be investigating in this chapter.

Introducing 2 Corinthians

Our canonical 2 Corinthians is, in fact, a very personal letter and one in which Paul has much to tell about himself and his ministry. Overall, it is a happy letter because he has been reassured by Titus, who just returned from a visit to Corinth, that the faith of the Christian community in Corinth was still strong and that the faithful there still revere the apostle Paul.

We appreciate that this letter contains a wealth of autobiographical material. The major part of the letter is devoted to Paul's discussion of his divinely appointed ministry and in defending that ministry against those who are attacking it. Paul's interest in the collection for the faithful in Jerusalem is also given significant treatment (Chaps. 8-9). In this letter, however, little attention is given to existing problems.

Canonical 2 Corinthians is in fact Paul's fourth letter to the Corinthian faithful. How this circumstance came about is the next subject that we will take up. Paul's third letter to the Corinthians is no longer extant.

What took place between the writing of 1 Corinthians and 2 Corinthians?

To answer this question, it is wise to first seek to determine the extent of Paul's contacts with the Corinthians. There were three ways in which Paul could have contacted the Corinthians: personally visiting them in Corinth; by letter, either to them or from them; and by a personal report from them. The only sources that are available to us for gathering this information are the two letters from Paul to the Corinthians: 1 Corinthians and 2 Corinthians.

Carrying out this task results in the following series of contacts:
1. A letter from Paul to the Corinthians prior to our canonical 1 Corinthians mentioned in 1 Cor 5:9, which is not extant.
2. A verbal report to Paul from Chloe's people (1 Cor 1:11) and a letter to Paul from Corinth 1 Cor 7:1).
3. A letter from Paul to the Corinthian Christians (1 Corinthians, canonical).
4. Paul makes a "painful" visit to the Corinthians (2 Cor 2:1).
5. Paul writes a "letter of tears" to the Corinthians (2 Cor 2:4 and 7:8).
6. Paul receives a verbal report from Titus (2 Cor 7:7)
7. Paul writes a letter to the Corinthian Christians (2 Corinthians, canonical).

It is seen from this list that Paul wrote a total of four letters to the Christians at Corinth, only two of which are extant – our 1 and 2 Corinthians.

What events transpired between the time Paul wrote 1 Corinthians and the time he wrote 2 Corinthians?

It is seen from the table above that between our canonical 1 Corinthians and 2 Corinthians that Paul made a visit and afterward wrote letter to the Corinthians. No description of the visit has survived and the letter is not extant. The only source of information is what we can find extract from canonical 2 Corinthians.

What was the cause of Paul's anguish? The cause is not directly described anywhere in 2 Corinthians. There is, however, a reference to a man who caused pain in v. 2:5. On the basis of the punishment described in 2:6-7, it can be surmised that this man was a member of the Corinthian assembly.

Paul's reaction to this man and the situation was very strong. In response, Paul first made a visit to Corinth (2:1). Then after he had returned to Ephesus, Paul wrote a letter, the letter of tears (2:4; 7:8,12).

There is a happy ending to this account. Titus met Paul in Macedonia with the news that the man causing the offense had been punished (2:6-8). He also informed Paul of the Corinthian's yearning, their lament and their zeal for Paul (7:7). Finally, Paul rejoiced because of the joy of Titus with regard to the Corinthians (7:13b-16).

Consequently, Paul wrote our canonical 2 Corinthians!

The Christian assemblies at Corinth after Paul's death

It is possible to get a view of how the Corinthians made out after the death of Paul. There is a letter, dating to about 97 CE, which very ancient tradition ascribes to Clement, the third Bishop of Rome. Today, it is commonly referred to as: Clement's First Letter.

The letter was written to the Corinthians at this time because there was a schism in the Corinthian church. The importance of the letter derives both from the view it provides information on matters in the congregation at Corinth and on the interrelationships of the Christian churches at the end of the 1st Century.

Clement's letter was widely read in the East and so, highly respected that it was included in the NT canons of Egypt and Syria. It was, however, unknown in the West until 1628 when the Codex Alexandrinus reached England.

Among the sources in which this letter is available, one can find it in the following:

Early Christian Fathers
Cyril C. Richardson, Translator and Editor
The Macmillan Company, New York, 1970

For those who may have developed an interest in learning history from letters written during the historical period of interest, you might be interested in taking a further step into Christian history and reading through the seven letters of Ignatius, bishop of Antioch. Ignatius wrote these letters as he was on his way to be martyred in the Coliseum sometime during Trajan's reign (98-117 CE). They are available in the book by Cyril Richardson referenced above. These writings are also available online: Early Christian Writers.

1 CORINTHIANS

Once again let's go into our satellite laboratory and analyze the satellite data pertaining to 1 Corinthians and see if we can determine an overall structure to the letter.

Having analyzed the satellite data, we arrive at the following overall outline of Paul's first letter to the Corinthians:
>   1:1-3 Salutation
>   1:4-9 Thanksgiving
>   1:10-15:58 Letter Body

      A. Matters reported by Chloe's people (1:10-6:20)
      B. Matters about which they had written (7:1-15:58)
  16:1-24 Concluding matters and greetings

It is seen that this is Paul's usual letter form with one deviation. The letter body is not divided into two parts on the basis of doctrinal and exhortation but rather on the basis of how Paul learned of the problems, whether from Chloe's people or from their letter to him. Because Paul is undertaking to answer questions about problems in the community at Corinth put to him by its members, the theological material and the exhortation are necessarily mixed together.

     It is time to take our mapping drone out of its hangar and to use it to do an overflight of the letter body at medium altitude. In this manner we can determine what, if any, structure there is to the body of the letter. This will be most helpful to have at hand when we undertake to visit specific passages by tour bus. As a result of carrying out this task there is obtained the following outline:

A. Matters reported to Paul by Chloe's people (1:10-6:20)
    1. The problem of factions within the community (1:10-4:21)
        a. The problem described (1:10-17)
        b. The wisdom of God and the wisdom of the world (1:18-2:5)
        c. Wisdom for the spiritually mature (2:6-16)
        d. Application to the situation of the Corinthians (3:1-20)
        e. Let no one boast about human leaders (3:21-23)
        f. Paul's authority (4:1-21)
    2. Moral standards of the Christian life (5:1-6:20)
        a. A case of sexual immorality - incest (5:1-5)
        b. Purge evil people from your midst (5:6-13)
        c. Lawsuits against other members (6:1-8)
        d. The unjust will not inherit the Kingdom of God (6:9-11)
        e. Avoid sexual immorality for your body is a temple of God (6:12-20)

B. Matters raised in the letter to Paul from the church in Corinth (7:1-15:58)
    1. Advice for men and women regarding various interrelationships and states of life (7:1-40)
    2. Regarding meat sacrificed to idols (8:1-13)
    3. Paul justifies not using his right to material support (9:1-18)
    4. "I have made myself a slave to all" (9:9-27)
    5. A lesson drawn from the days of the Exodus (10:1-13)
    6. Avoid idolatry (10:14-22)
    7. Seek the good of others (10:23-33)
    8. Paul tells them to imitate him and praises them (11:1-2)
    9. Christian worship (11:3-14:40)
        a. "Be imitators of me" and "I praise you" (11:1-2)
        b. On head coverings for men and women (11:4-16)
        c. The Lord's Supper (11:17-34)
        d. The use of spiritual gifts (12:1-14:40)

(1) Many gifts but one spirit; many parts but one body (12:1-31a)
(2) The way of love (12:31b-13)
(3) Prophecy is better than speaking in tongues (14:1-19)
(4) The function of these gifts (14:20-25)
(5) Rules of order (14:26-40)
10. The Resurrection (15:1-58)
    a. The Gospel teaching about Christ (15:1-11)
    b. How can you say there is no resurrection of the dead? (15:12-19)
    c. Christ is the first fruits of the dead and will be finally subjected to God (15:20-28)
    d. Two practical arguments against there being no resurrection (15:29-34)
    e. The type of body that one will have (15:35-49)
    f. The resurrection event (15:50-55)
    g. God gives us victory through Jesus Christ (15:56-58)

At this point, it is usually the time that the letter that is under investigation is viewed from three different aspects. In the case of 1 Corinthians, however, considerable effort has already been expended on looking at the letter in terms of its literary characteristics and its historical values. Consequently, let us restrict our considerations to viewing the letter from the perspective of a writing containing theological material.

1 Corinthians viewed as a writing that contains theological material

Stop #1 6:12-20

This is a short passage that speaks about sexual matters. But more importantly, it brings into play the concept of the "body of Christ." This is a concept of considerable importance that should be given more attention in sermons and homilies today.

Stop #2 11:17-34

In this passage, Paul considers the practice of celebrating the Eucharist. He focuses attention on three aspects of the celebration. First, Paul stresses the fact that the unity of the assembly is important to the celebration of the rite (vv.17-22). Secondly, Paul presents the words of the consecration that were traditional in his time (vv.23-26). This is the earliest statement of these words that has come down to the present day. Finally, in vv.27-32 Paul teaches that the person receiving communion must prepare carefully.

Stop #3 15:1-58

In this chapter , Paul teaches about the resurrection. While the whole chapter is significant, two points are of special interest. First, vv. 3-5 contain a tradition of the appearances of Jesus after his resurrection that is more ancient than Paul's writing of this letter. It is, therefore, of great value. Secondly, vv.42-44 teach us that when people "rise from the dead" on the last day, they will receive glorified bodies.

Stop #4 16:1-4

This brief passage is interesting because it is about giving money which proves that churches asking for donations is not a modern affair. It has been there from the beginning!

2 CORINTHIANS

Now it is time to begin our investigation of Paul's letter of 2 Corinthians. Already we have come to understand that the title 2 Corinthians relates to its status as the second of Paul's letters to the Corinthians in the Bible. In actual fact, it is Paul's fourth letter to the Corinthians because two of them are no longer extant.

Let us return to our satellite laboratory to examine the data pertaining to the overall form of this letter. Doing this, we find the following:

> 1:1-2 Salutation
> 1:3-11 Blessed (compassionate) God
> 1:12-13:10 Letter body
> 13:11-14 Final exhortation, greetings and benediction

This verifies that 2 Corinthians is in Paul's letter form, although the usual thanksgiving is here replaced by a passage (vv.3-11) that states God is compassionate. This passage divides into two parts. The first, vv.3-7, states God is blessed and the God is the Father of the Lord. God is the God of compassion and comfort (v.3). God comforts us in our troubles so we can comfort others as God comforts us (v.4). The second part, vv.8-11, cites a specific example of Paul's rescue, by God, from a deadly affliction.

Now it is time to obtain a more detailed map of the contents of the letter. In this case, we will investigate the letter body in two stages. The first stage will be at moderate altitude and moderate speed. This results in the following outline:

> A. 1:12-7:16 Paul's discussion of his recent relations with the Corinthians
>   1. 1:12-2:4 Paul on his travel planes and the need for changes
>   2. 2:5-13 Two matters: the man causing problems and Paul's visit to Troas
>   3. 2:14-6:10 Paul speaks about his ministry
>   4. 6:11-7:4 The bond between Paul and the church is renewed
>   5. 7:5-16 Paul speaks of Titus' return
> B. 8:1-9:15 The collection
> C. 10:1-13:10 Paul's defense of his ministry
> D. 13:11-14 Final exhortation and closing greetings

That completes the mapping of the letter body. It does, however, leave us with one point of curiosity. This letter is written by Paul and, consequently, in those sections where he is speaking about himself it is autobiographical material! This material is, therefore, of considerable value. It would be nice, therefore, to have the section 2:14-6:10 which speaks about his ministry in greater detail. This can be accomplished by making another flight using our drone but do this flight at an even lower altitude and at an even slower speed. Furthermore, let us dedicate this flight to Floyd V. Filson, since it is his outline that we will discover.

B. The great parenthesis: the apostolic ministry (2:14-6:10)
1. Thanks to God for using Paul in the ministry (2:14-17)
2. The Corinthians are Paul's letter of recommendation (3:1-3)
3. The superior ministry of the new Covenant (3:4-4:6)
a) God qualifies the ministers of this covenant (3:4-6)
b) The new covenant surpasses the old in splendor (3:7-11)
c) The boldness of the risen Lord's ministers (3:12-18)
d) The ministry of light against darkness (4:1-6)
4. God sustains his ministers in their wearing work (4:7-18)
a) The life of Jesus manifested in their bodies (4:7-12)
b) Faith in the resurrection sustains them (4:13-15)
c) Eternal glory will follow brief affliction (4:16-18)
5. The hope of an eternal home with the Lord (5:1-10)
a) Paul hopes to receive it before physical death (5:1-5)
b) He is content to die and be with the Lord (5:6-8)
c) The main thing: Be ready always for judgment (5:9-10)
6. The ministry of reconciliation (5:11-6:10)
a) Paul seeks to serve God and the Corinthians (5:11-13)
b) In Christ God reconciled men to himself (5:14-19)
c) Paul's urgent ministry of reconciliation (5:20-6:2)
d) His diligence and suffering in this ministry (6:3-10) [177]

Now we are in a position to move on to viewing 2 Corinthians from the three different perspectives – as a literary piece, as an historical document and as a writing containing theological material.

Viewing 2 Corinthians as a literary piece

It has clearly been established that 2 Corinthians is a letter from Paul to the church of God that is in Corinth. The addition of the phrase "with all the holy ones throughout Achaia" indicates that this letter was anticipated to be widely read outside of Corinth. Since this letter is to be read by such a widespread audience must be an indication that Paul thought it contained a good amount of material that would be of interest to them. One should look for material, therefore, that is fundamental in Christian living in its content.

Viewing 2   Corinthians as an historical document

This letter is the most personal of all of Paul's extant writings. It contains, therefore, a considerable amount of autobiographical material. The letter is as a consequence an excellent source for looking into the character of Paul. So let us ask the following question: What can we learn about Paul from 2 Corinthians? We cannot accomplish this by means of a small number of

---

[177] Floyd V. Filson, "The Second Epistle to the Corinthians" in *The Interpreter's Bible*, V. 10 (Nashville, TN: Abingdon Press, 1953), 268-269.

tour bus stops. We must turn for help from a scholar who has combed through the letter looking for information regarding Paul as an individual. Dr. J. Paul; Sampley has done just this and the results of his efforts are the following:

> Paul was a passionate man, given to a wide range of emotions. We observe his anger and distress in 2 Corinthians 10-13 not only as Corinthian opposition hardens against him, but also as some of his beloved drift away under outside influences. Also visible, though, is his heartfelt affection, his sense that he loves the more and is loved less (12:15). (20)

> As reflected in 2 Corinthians, Paul's experiences range from the most sublime to the most precarious. What can surpass his being caught up into the third heaven, into paradise (12:2-6)? It is also almost as difficult to imagine anyone having more hardships than Paul (4:8-12; 6:4-10; 11:23-27), including his thorn or stake in the flesh (12:7-9) and his Damascus escape (11:30-33). (20)

> Paul's self-descriptions are illuminating because they show a Paul not always victorious, not always triumphant, but often vexed, put upon, and, at times, almost overwhelmed. (20)

> Throughout 2 Corinthians, and indeed across all his correspondence, he has no real interest in theological notions for their own sake, but only as they engage life, as they bear on the way people comport themselves. His theologizing, therefore, is never abstract or abstruse; instead it is always engaged, always linked to life as real people – he and his hearers – are experiencing it. (21) [178]

2 Corinthians viewed as a writing containing theological material

Stop #1 5:6-10

One more aspect of Paul remains to be considered – his thought concerning "works." Much has been said about Paul's teaching about justification by faith. Many people hold that works do not matter. Here in 2 Corinthians, however, we find that Paul believes that works do matter. In 5:10 Paul states that we will all be judged according to what we did in the body.

Stop #2 2:14-6:10

This stop is a little different from the usual stops. Instead of a short passage this stop is for a rather large section – the section in the letter where Paul speaks about his own ministry. Making use of the outline we obtained from the extra low and slow drone flight, read through this section, to learn about his ministry from Paul himself.

Stop #3 13:13

This is a good place to conclude our investigation of 2 Corinthians. This verse contains one of the clearest statements of the Trinitarian nature of Christian faith.

---

[178] J. Paul Sampley, "The Second Letter to the Corinthians," in *The New Interpreter's Bible*, V. XI (Nashville, TN: Abingdon Press, 2000), 20-22.

CHAPTER THIRTY-six
PAUL'S LETTER TO THE ROMANS

Paul's letter to the Romans is longer than any other New Testament letter. It is deeply reflective on the issues of justification and the Law. This letter is one of the most studied letters of Paul because it contains both fundamental theological concepts and addresses poignant questions of Christian living. For early Patristic writers, especially including St. Augustine, this letter was highly important. Abelard in the Middle Ages delved deeply into the writing. During the Reformation, Luther and Calvin took up Paul's letter to the Romans as critical and most important. Finally, the theologian Barth demonstrated that the letter has played a major role in the development of theological thought through the ages. Lastly, some feel that disagreement over the meaning of theological concepts in Paul's letter to the Romans has perhaps caused some of the major tension between Christian denominations.

For many, it is not an easy writing to read and understand. It requires knowledge of Paul's Jewish background and anthropology, the Greek culture of the day, the relationship between Jews who followed Jesus and the Gentiles who were brought to faith in the Christian way. In many instances, Paul's rhetorical method of writing appears challenging. Noted contemporary biblical scholars Gordon Fee and Douglas Stuart have this to say about Romans:

> This letter is arguably the most influential book in Christian history, perhaps in the history of Western civilization. But that doesn't necessarily make it easy to read! While theologically minded people love it, others steer away from it (except for a few favorite passages), thinking it is too deep for them."[179]

Purpose

It is most likely that Paul had more than one purpose for writing this letter to the Romans. On the one hand, Paul may have been prompted to write because he had wanted to visit the Christians in Rome for a long time and now had the opportunity to do that on his way to Spain (15:22-24). On the other hand, Paul's motivation might have been prompted by the division between the Jewish and Gentile believers in the Roman assemblies. Scholar Douglas Moo has this to say:

> Accepting the majority view that this text reflects a division in the Roman community between Gentile and Jewish Christians, and that the division was over the continuing relevance of certain requirements related to the law of Moses, it is natural to think that Paul's main purpose in writing was to heal this division. This proposal would explain why Paul focuses so much of the letter on the relation of Jews and Gentiles, the role of the Law, and the status of Israel. These were the theological issues that lay at the root of the division in Rome; and Paul hopes that by changing their convictions about these theological matters he can achieve his goal of getting the two factions to "receive" each other (15:7).[180]

---

[179] Gordon D. Fee and Douglas Stuart, *How to Read the Bible Book by Book* (Grand Rapids, MI: Zondervan, 2002), 317-318.

[180] Douglas Moo, "Romans, Letter to the," in *The New Interpreter's Dictionary of the Bible*, Katharine Doob Sakenfeld, General Editor (Nashville, TN: Abingdon Press, 2009), 848.

A third reason for Paul writing this letter is suggested by Achtemeier, Green and Thompson who advocate that Paul sought to "remind" the Roman Christians of some central truths of their faith:

> An additional purpose for the letter is to present the Roman Christians with a "reminder," apparently of some central points Paul felt it was his mission to emphasize (15:15). It appears from the way he phrases this statement that he does not presume to instruct the Roman Christians in aspects of the faith of which they are ignorant, but rather that he intends to emphasize some points he thinks are central to their faith. That probably means that Paul has included traditions in his letter that he assumes are known to the Roman Christians since they were generally in circulation among other churches as well. Fragments of such traditions may be contained, for example, in 1:2-4; 3.25-26; or 4:25, as well as in other places. It may also mean that he includes some generalized instruction on problems that his experience has taught him are widespread among Christian churches, such as the problem of diet and the relationship between the weak and the strong (chs. 14-15).[181]

Uncharacteristically, Paul does not name any associate in the superscription (1:1). This supports the idea that Paul intended this letter to embody a clear exposition of his own thought.

Exploring Paul's letter to the Romans

To begin our exploration of this composition, let us go to our satellite laboratory and analyze the data from our satellite. Doing this gives us the following outline:

- 1:1-7 Superscription
- 1:8-10 Thanksgiving
- 1:11- 11:36 Letter Body A – Doctrinal part
- 12:1-15:13 Letter Body B - Doctrinal part
- 15:14-33 Paul's plans, the collection and request for prayers
- 16:1-23 Phoebe, greetings of individual believers in Rome, and other things
- 16: 25-27 Doxology

It is seen that overall, Paul's writing to the Romans has the form of a typical 1st century letter.

Usually at this point, we make use of our drone to make an outline of the contents of the letter. In this case, because of the complicated nature of Paul's letter to the Romans, we will take a different approach. We will drive by car to the college library and look for a commentary on Romans. A good commentary to select is the one by Joseph Fitzmyer, and we will make use of his outline of Romans.

---

[181] Paul J. Achtemeier, Joel B. Green and Marianne Meye Thompson, *Introducing the New Testament* (Grand Rapids, MI: William B. Eerdmans Publishing Company, 2001), 301.

Doctrinal Division (1:16-11:36)

Through the gospel the uprightness of God is revealed as justifying people of faith (1:16-4:25)
1. Theme announced: the gospel is the powerful source of salvation for all, Disclosing God's uprightness (1:16-17)
2. Theme negatively explained: without the gospel God's wrath is manifested against human beings (1:18-3:20)
3. Theme positively explained: God's uprightness is manifested to all sinners through Christ and apprehended by faith (3:21-31)
4. Theme illustrated in the law: Abraham was justified by faith, not by deeds (4:1-2

The love of God further assures salvation to those justified by faith (5:1-8:39)
1. Theme announced: justified Christians are reconciled to the God of love; they will be saved through hope of a share in the risen life of Christ (5:1-11)
2. Theme explained: new Christian life brings a threefold liberation and is empowered by the Spirit 5:12-8:13
3. Theme developed: Christian life, lived in freedom bestowed by the indwelling Spirit, has its destiny in glory (8:14-39)

This justification and salvation through faith do not contradict God's promises to Israel of old (9:1-11:36)
1. Paul's Lament about Israel's failure to accept Christ (9:1-5)
2. Israel's failure: it is not contrary to God's direction of history (9:6-29)
3. Israel's failure: it is derived from its own refusal (9:30-10:21)
4. Israel's failure: it is partial and temporary (11:1-36)

Exhortation Division (12:1-15:13)

Spirit-Guided Christian life must be worship paid to God (12:1-13:14)
1. Life in the world as worship of God (12:1-2)
2. Sober existence using God's gifts for all (12:3-8)
3. Counsels for Christian living in the community (12:9-21)
4. The relation of Christians to civil authorities (13:1-7)
5. The debt of love that fulfills the law (13:8-10)
6. Eschatological exhortation: Christian life as vigilant conduct (13:11-14)

The duty of love owed by the strong in the community to the weak (14:1-15:13)
1. Christian solidarity: its extent and its limits (14:1-12)
2. The marks of Christ's rule in the community (14:13-23)
3. Christ is our model in all conduct (15:1-6)
4. Welcome all who turn to Christ as Lord, Jew and Gentile (15:7-13) [182]

We now have an outline of the body and we should express our thanks to Professor Fitzmyer for having provided it to us. Let's now return to the bus depot and begin making tour bus stops at interesting passages.

---

[182] Joseph A. Fitzmyer, *Romans* The Anchor Bible Series, vol 33 (New York, Doubleday 1993), 98-101.

Romans viewed as a literary piece

Stop #1 1:1-7

The salutation identifies Paul as the one who is initiating the letter. Paul's authorship of this letter has never been questioned.

One has to read all the way down to v.7 to discover to whom his letter is written. Paul says it is "to all the beloved of God in Rome." Who were God's beloved in Rome? That is: were they Jews or Gentiles? Looking ahead to 16:3-16, the fact that there are Jewish names among the people he sent greetings to in Rome establishes that there were Jews in the Roman congregations. In his writing, Paul refers to Gentiles in the congregations, as in 1:5-6. So the congregation in Rome was a mixed assembly.

Stop #2 6:15-23

In the salutations of his letters, Paul most commonly refers to himself as a "slave of Jesus Christ." Today's translators most commonly translate the Greek word "*doulos*"(slave) by the English word "servant." This is not a good translation. Paul's meaning becomes clear in the section 6:15-23.

Stop #3 16:22

At this stop, one learns that it is Tertius who is actually writing the letter on parchment with an ink pen. The scholarly world is united in holding that Paul is the one who composed the letter and that the role of Tertius was to write down just what Paul said.

Helpful note of a literary sort – the diatribe

It will help considerably to recognize that the type of argumentation Paul is using is the "diatribe," which is a form of rhetorical speaking and writing of the day. Fee and Stuart describe this in the following way:

> Knowing two things may help you as you read. First, the argumentation Paul employs in this letter is patterned after a form of ancient rhetoric known as the **diatribe**, in which a teacher tried to persuade students of the truth of a given philosophy through imagined dialogue, usually in the form of questions and answers. Very often an imagined debate partner (interlocutor) would raise objections or false conclusions, which, after a vigorous "By no means!" the teacher would take pains to correct.
>
> You will notice as you read how thoroughgoing the diatribe pattern is. The imaginary interlocutor appears at several key places (2:1-5, 17-24; 8:2; 9:19-21; 11:17-24; 14:4, 10). Paul debates first with a Jew (2:1-5, 17-24), with whom he dialogues in most of the argument that follows, as he raises and answers questions and responds to anticipated objections (2:26; 3:1-9, 27-31; 4:1-3; 6:1-3, 15-16; 7:1,7,13; 8:31-35; 9:19; etc.). A Gentile interlocutor is finally introduced in 11:13-24. In both cases Paul begins by attacking ethnic pride (2:17-20; 11:18). Notice further how all of this is suspended when he comes to the exhortations that begin part 4 (12:1-13:14), only to be picked up again when the issue of Jew-Gentile relationships over food and days is brought to the fore (14:4, 10).

Sometimes this form of argumentation can be dizzying, especially when in the course of it Paul makes some sweeping statements that may look contradictory. But in the end, all individual statements have to be kept in the context of the whole argument.[183]

Romans viewed as a historical document

Stop #1 1:7

Paul states that this letter is "to all the beloved of God in Rome." Rome, in Paul's time, was the capital of the Roman Empire. The most important cities in the 1st Century CE world were: Rome in Italy, Alexandria in Egypt, Corinth in Greece, and Antioch in Syria.

The "beloved of God" for whom Paul was writing this letter were obviously Christians, but were they formerly Jews or Gentiles? From the time of its founding in the 8th Century BCE, it was a Gentile city which developed over the centuries largely because of its location. After Pompey's conquests of Palestine in 63 BCE, many Jews were brought to Rome as slaves and other Jews would have come because they were merchants and sought to do business there. Thus, by the time of Jesus, there was a mixed Jewish and Gentile population at Rome. Given the Gentile origin of the city and its position as capital of the Empire, it would seem most likely that the Gentiles would have greatly outnumbered the Jews.

How did the Christian community originate at Rome? Neither the letter to the Romans itself nor the Acts of the Apostles makes mention of any evangelization there by a particular evangelist. Rome, being the important city it was, suggests that it would certainly have been evangelized by a well-known missionary. Most likely, therefore, the Christian community at Rome got its start through the presence of Jewish Christians and their associated Gentile followers. Substantiation that the congregation(s) at Rome consisted of both former Jews and former Gentiles is provided by our next three stops.

Stop #2 2:10

This verse can be interpreted as indicating that the Christian community at Rome consists of both former Jews and former Gentiles.

Stop #3 16:3-15

This section of the letter provides a list of the names of people in the Christian community at Rome. It can be shown that: ten have Latin names; 18 have Greek names; and two have Hebrew names. This indicates that there is a mixture of both Jews and Gentiles in the community.

Stop #4 15:23

In this verse, Paul states that he had desired, for many years, to come to Rome to visit them. Since Rome was populated by a mixture of Jews and Gentiles, then given a

---

[183] Gordon D. Fee, Douglas Stuart, *How to Read the Bible book by Book* (Grand Rapids, Zondervan, 2002), 319.

long time to make converts the Christian community would certainly be a mixture of Jews and Gentiles.

Stop #5 4:7-8

Here, Paul makes a quotation from the Book of Psalms in the Old Testament. What is interesting is that in this quotation Paul is citing appears to be derived from the Septuagint text (LXX). The Septuagint is a Greek translation of the Hebrew Old Testament that was made around the 2nd and 3rd centuries BCE. It was originally made for the Jews living in the diaspora who did not know Hebrew. Apparently, therefore, the Septuagint translation was used by the Christians living in the Greek speaking areas. It is interesting to note that many Christians of the 21st Century use the Masoretic text and not the Septuagint. There are substantial differences between these two translations due to the fact that the Septuagint is a translation of an earlier version of the Hebrew text than is today's English translations of the Hebrew text.

Romans viewed as a writing that contains theological material - Christology

Stop #1 1:1-7

Note the unusual length of the superscription. The usual content of the superscription is contained in the 1st and 7th verses. In between, Paul has placed the following items:

- In v.1 Paul states that: he is "a slave of Christ;" that he "was called (by God) to be an apostle;" and that he was "set apart for the gospel of God."
- In v.2 Paul says that God promised the gospel through the prophets.
- In the following two verses, vv. 3-4, Paul says that the gospel is about God's Son. This statement is followed by a statement that God's Son is both human (descended from David) and divine (confirmed by his resurrection from the dead). These two verses are probably taken from an early confession of the faith predating the writing of the letter.
- In verses 5-6 Paul tells his readers that he was called through Jesus Christ to apostleship to bring the gospel to the Gentiles.

Stop #2 1:16-17

The principal theme of Paul's letter to the Romans is salvation through faith. This is clearly stated in Romans 1:16-17.

Now let's do something highly significant. Let us take as our goal to visit those passages that would provide us with all of the fundamentals of the Christian faith. Paul has not, to be sure, set all of these fundamentals down in one paragraph. We can, however find them distributed throughout the Chapters 1-8. To accomplish this will require us to make the following seven stops in our tour bus.

Stop #3 3:9-20

In this passage, Paul sets forth the fact that all people, Jews and Greeks alike, are under the power of sin.

Stop #4 3:21-31

      Having shown that all people are under the power of sin, Paul now states that all are justified through the redemption that is in Christ Jesus and apprehended by faith.[184] This section divides into two parts. The first part, 3:21-26, includes in vv. 24-26 a pre-Pauline formula about justification, redemption and expiation. The second part, vv. 27-31, considers some consequences of the first part and formulates the presentation in the style of diatribe.

Stop #5 5:1-11

      Paul first states that: "now that we are justified through faith, we are at peace with God…." Paul says, in v.8, that God demonstrates his love for us because while we were still sinners Christ died for us.

Stop #6 8:14-17

      The Spirit of God dwells in the person who has been justified. All who are led by the Spirit of God are children of God and if children of God then joint heirs with Christ!

Stop #7 8:31-39

      Paul asks: "If God is for us, who can be against us"? (v.31). Paul ends by saying that nothing will be able to separate the believer from the love of God manifested in Christ Jesus (vv. 38-39).

Stop #8 2:1-11

      One is saved by faith, BUT, at death, one will be judged by God according to his or her works during this earthly life. The Christian faith is bound to a "way of life!" This accounts for why Paul begins Chapter 12 with the word "however."

Stop #9 8:18-25

      In hope of future glory, one is saved.

This concludes our search for the fundamentals of the Christian faith.

      Now we come to a section of Paul's letter to the Romans which is significant but usually is not given the attention that it deserves: chapters 9-11. In these chapters, Paul takes up the subject of the future of Israel in the plan of God. One reason these chapters do not receive more attention may be that they require a knowledge of a number of Old Testament texts. We have, as a tour guide with us, a woman who can read both Greek and Hebrew and so will be able to explain these texts if that should become necessary.

Stop #10 9:1-5

      In these verses, Paul laments the fact that in spite all of the gifts that God has given to Israel (vv.4-5) the majority of the Jews have not accepted Jesus Christ.

Stop #11 11:30-36

      In verses 30-32, Paul is saying that the Jews were disobedient and did not accept Christ. One day, however, they will receive God's mercy and rejoin the people of God. There are two OT citations in this passage:

---

[184] Fitzmyer, 342.

1. 11:34 from the Greek text of Is 40:13. (NABRE footnote)
2. 11:35 from an old Greek version Jb 41:3a. (NABRE footnote)

Ethics

Stop #1 12:1-2

These two verses stand side-by-side as two separate statements. In 12:1, the word "therefore" indicates both that Paul is making the transition to the exhortation part of his letter and that what Paul is about to say next follows on the basis of what he has set forth prior to this in chapters one through eight. The word "therefore" in the very first sentence of Chapter 12 ties the matters pertaining to ethics inseparably to the Christological matters set forth in chapters 1-8.

In the first of these two sentences, Paul urges his readers to make their whole lives pleasing to God so that their very lives will be acceptable worship of God. In the second of these two sentences, Paul tells them not to be conformed to this world but to be transformed by the renewal of their minds in order that they will be able to come to know what is the will of God for them and also to be able to discern the good from the not good. In our lives today, which are so complex and fast paced, discernment is of great importance even more so.

Stop #2 12:3-8

In this passage, Paul treats the problem that some in the community may think too highly of themselves. He points out that people have different abilities (gifts) and that they should develop the abilities they have been given and to exercise proper humility.

Stop #3 12:9-13

In 12:9-13 Paul specifies a number of ways in which the individual members of the community should conduct themselves. This short paragraph contains an amazing number of "ways" which is better illuminated by presenting them in a list. This list follows:

- Let love be genuine
- Hate what is evil, hold fast to what is good
- Love one another with mutual affection
- Outdo one another showing mutual honor
- Do not lag in zeal
- Be ardent in spirit
- Serve the Lord
- Rejoice in hope
- Be patient in suffering
- Persevere in prayer
- Contribute to the needs of the saints
- Extend hospitality to strangers

This is quite a substantial list if you plan to follow Paul's teaching on the way to be Christian.

Stop #4 12:14-13:7

This section takes up relations of the Christian believers with the outside world. It divides into two parts: 12:14-21 and 13:1-7. The first part, 12:14-21, deals with everyday relations between believers and the ordinary populations. Paul has the following advice on this subject, expressing it in list form:

- Bless those who persecute you; bless and do not curse them.
- Rejoice with those who rejoice, weep with those who weep.
- Live in harmony with one another
- Do not be haughty, but associate with the lowly
- Do not claim to be wiser than you are
- Do not repay anyone evil for evil, but take thought for what is noble in the sight of all.
- If it is possible, so far as it depends on you, live peaceably with all.
- Never avenge yourselves, but leave room for the wrath of God; for it is written, "Vengeance is mine, I will repay, says the Lord."
- If your enemies are hungry, feed them; if they are thirsty, give them something to drink; for by doing this you will heap burning coals on their heads.
- Do not be overcome by evil, but overcome evil with good.

Paul follows this with 13:1-7 which takes up the matter of being subject to the governing authorities.

Stop #5 13:11-14

In this passage, Paul brings up a bit of eschatology in order to put pressure on his readers to act favorably on what he has told them in 12:1-13:10. Verse eleven is a reference to the coming "day of the Lord." Recall that in his earlier letters Paul had indicated that he believed Jesus could return even before he died.

That concludes our investigation of Paul's letter to the Romans. Let's return to the Depot and put our tour bus in the barn until we need it again.

CHAPTER THIRTY-seven

PAUL'S LETTERS TO THE COLOSSIANS, TO PHILEMON AND TO THE EPHESIANS

Introducing Colossians, Philemon and Ephesians

Why are Paul's letters to the Colossians, to Philemon and to the Ephesians considered together in the same chapter? This is because there is a relationship between Colossians and Philemon on the one hand and there is a relationship between Colossians and Ephesians on the other hand.

Colossians and Philemon are related by having been written by Paul from the same place and at about the same time and having been sent to the same place, Colossae. This is a deduction made from a careful comparison of the two letters. Consider the following observations:

1. Both letters state that they are from Paul and a co-sender identified as "Timothy our brother" (Col 1:1; Phlm 1) and each letter contains a similar phrase in its ending penned by Paul: "…writing this greeting in my own hand" (Col 4:18) and "writing this in my own hand" (Phlm 19).

2. Onesimus (pronounced: O-nes'i-mus), the principal figure of Philemon (pronounced: Phi-lee' mon), is also mentioned in Colossians (4:9). Paul says that Onesimus is a member of the community in Colossae and that he is sending Onesimus to Colossae with Tychicus. It seems likely that they would be bringing Paul's letter to Philemon along with them.

3. Both letters reference Epaphras, the founder of the community at Colossae, and at the time of writing was also a prisoner with Paul (Col 4:12; Phlm 23).

4. Archippus is mentioned in both letters (Col 4:17; Phlm 2).

5. Other names appearing in both letters are the following: Mark, Aristarchus, Demas and Luke (Col 4:10,14; Phlm 24).

These five observations lead one to the conclusion that Colossians and Philemon were written at the same time in the same place and to the same Christian community. They are, therefore, related by having been composed in the same historical moment and the same environment.

Among all the letters attributed to Paul, no two are so closely linked as are Colossians and Ephesians. This is important to note because of the apparent controversy among scholars today on the authorship of Ephesus, with some who hold a minor position that Ephesians was not written by Paul. Consider the following points:

1. There is one case of verbatim agreement of the wording between Colossians and Ephesians - the recommendation of Tychicus (Col 4:7-8 and Eph 6:21-22).

2. There are a number of striking parallels:
    Col 1:14/Eph 1:7
    Col 2:13/Eph 2:5
    Col 1:25/ Eph 3:2
    Col 126/Eph 3:9
    Col 2:19/Eph 4:16.

3.   There are also close similarities between the two letters regarding language, style and concepts. Margaret Macdonald observes:

In other words, Colossians and Ephesians disclose a similar world view, reflect some of the same community concerns, and generally represent a similar stage of development in Pauline Christianity....[185]

On the basis of these observations it is likely that there is a literary relationship between Colossians and Ephesians. The possible existence of a literary relationship between the two books makes it appropriate to treat them together. Taken together, these two letters demonstrate the close brotherhood and loyalty of the communities of Christians which Paul was establishing.

A word about authorship is in order. All three of these letters state in their salutations that they are "from Paul" and all scholars agree that the letter to Philemon is truly from Paul. There are, however, some scholars today who form a minority opinion that Colossians and Ephesians are, in fact, "pseudonymous." This means they doubt that Paul was the author and they were written by a person whose name we do not know. For those scholars who hold the major claim that all three letters are, indeed, truly letters of Paul, the reasons for their position are strong – especially the fact that all three have been attributed to Paul for centuries.

 In the case of Colossians, some scholars holding the minority opinion, maintain that it is pseudonymous, which is to say it appears to have been written by a follower of Paul some years after his death. They base their position on analysis of the theology behind the text and on computer analysis of the internal characteristics of the text, for example the vocabulary. They conclude from these analyses that the text differs from the seven letters that all accept as authentic Paul. Their reasoning can be contradicted when it is realized that Paul's theology could have developed over his lifetime plus the fact that people do accrue new words in their vocabulary.

In a similar manner, there are some scholars today who hold the minor position that Ephesians is also pseudonymous. These analyses, however, do not seem convincing enough to outweigh the strong tradition that supports Paul's authorship. The literary relationship that seems

---

[185] Margaret Y. MacDonald, "Introduction" in *Colossians and Ephesians, Sacra Pagina,* Vol 17 (Collegeville Minnesota: The Liturgical Press, A Michael Glazier Book, 2000), 5.

to exist between Colossians and Ephesians is easily accounted for if they were both written by the same author at about the same time.

COLOSSIANS

Investigating Colossians

Colossae is located about 110 miles almost due east of Ephesus in the upper Lycus River valley in what is now the modern country of Turkey (see: openbible.info/geo).

There is no sure way of dating the letter from its contents. A strong earthquake resulted in severe damage to the city of Colossae in 60 CE. Since there is no mention of this noteworthy event in the letter, one is prompted to think that it must have been written before 60 CE.

Satellite observation to determine the letter form

First let's utilize our satellite to determine the overall letter form:
    1:1-2 Superscription
    1:3-8 Thanksgiving
    1:9-46 Letter body
        1:9-2:23 Doctrinal division
        3:1-4:6 Exhortation Division
    4:7-18 Concluding greetings

Now, let's make a drone observation at low altitude to determine the details of the letter body (1:9-4:6). We obtain from this observation the following outline:

Body: Part A	Doctrinal division (1:9- 2:23)	
1. 1:9-14	A prayer on behalf of the Colossians	
2. 1:15-23	The Christ hymn and its application to the Colossian believers	
3. 1:24-2:7	Paul's authority in Colossae	
5. 2:8-2:15	On opposing arguments based upon human traditions	
6. 2:16-2:23	On matters concerning food, drink and festivals	

Body: Part B	Exhortation division (3:1-4:6)	
1. 3:1-4	Set your minds on the things that are above	
2. 3:5-17	Put to death all that is earthlyand clothe yourself with all that is of God	
3. 3:18-4:1	The household code	
4. 4:2-6	Some further counsels	

On the basis of these satellite and drone observations, let us move on to look at Colossians as both a historical document and a writing that contains theological material by taking our tour bus and visiting some passages of interest.

Colossians viewed as a historical document

Stop #1 1:6b-8
First of all, we learn from this passage that the gospel is bearing fruit and growing in the whole world (v.6b). Secondly, we learn of a missionary named Epaphras, who is a friend of Paul's.

Stop #2 2:1-5
In this passage one is given a glimpse into Paul's motivation and concerns. Paul also expresses his concern that the Colossians will be deceived by plausible arguments against the gospel. This is a problem in the present day as well, and one can imagine him saying today in a TWEET from heaven, what is in verses 2:4-5.

Stop #3 4:7-17
This section contains information about a number of people who were affiliated with Paul and shared in his ministry.

Colossians viewed as a writing that contains theological material

Stop #1 1:15-20
This section is part of an ancient hymn. It is printed as poetry in the NABRE translation, but the NRSV translation prints it as prose. It appears to be written like Hebrew parallelism, perhaps from an original hymn in Hebrew (although it appears in Greek in the New Testament). It is seen that it consists of two parts. The first part, verses 15-17, speaks of Christ's role in creation and the second part, speaks of Christ's role in salvation.

Stop #2 1:21-23
These verses constitute a single sentence in the original Greek text. In it, Paul addresses his readers directly, speaking first of their past life as Gentiles and then of their life in the present as Christians. Finally, he points out to them that they must "continue securely established and steadfast in the faith" (v.23). Paul thus emphasizes that the Christian must continue in the faith for the rest of their life on earth. Salvation is not some magical event that once it is experienced one can then go do whatever one wants.

Stop #3 2:8-15
Most notable in this section is the statement in v. 9 that in Christ "the whole fullness of deity dwells." This passage then goes on to speak about baptism

Stop #4 3:1-4
This part of the letter from 3:1-4:6 constitutes the part where Paul sets forth various counsels concerning how people should live their daily lives. This passage, 3:1-4, is a good overall statement of how one should live: "set your minds on things that are above!'

Stop #5 3:5-17
This passage provides a list of things that bad people do and also a list of things that good

people do. These good and bad aspects are representative of the elements of two different ways of life – one leading to Christ and the other leading away from Christ. The early Christians were in fact identified as "members of the way." It was only later that the term "Christian" came into use to designate them. It was known as "the way of life."

This concludes our investigation of Colossians.

PHILEMON

Investigating Philemon

Philemon is one of the shortest books of the bible. Its brevity accounts for the fact that it is not divided into chapters; it only consists of verses – only twenty-five of them! Because of its brevity we will dispense with satellites and drones and tour buses and instead simply walk around.

Philemon is a personal letter from Paul to a man named Philemon. In the salutation (1:1) it states that the letter is from Paul and Timothy but in the letter the use of the singular "I" shows that Paul is the person who is doing the writing. Also in the salutation (1:2) it states that the letter is to Philemon, Apphia, Archippus and "to the church at your house" (Philemon's?) but throughout the letter the pronoun "you" is in the singular indicating that Paul is writing to Philemon.

There is a historical situation underlying the writing of this letter. This situation is not known from any external source and, consequently, it must be deduced from the contents of the letter itself. One possible reconstruction from the contents is the following:

> This story consists of the events Paul refers to in the letter: Philemon incurs a debt to Paul (his conversion? v. 19b); Paul is imprisoned (v. 9; cf. vv. 1, 10, 13, 23); the slave Onesimus runs away from his master Philemon and incurs a debt to him (v. 15; cf. vv. 11-13, 18-19a); Onesimus is converted by an imprisoned Paul (v. 10; cf. v. 13); Paul hears a report of Philemon's love and faith (vv. 4-7); Paul sends Onesimus back to Philemon (v. 12), and he sends a letter to appeal to Philemon, guaranteeing repayment of Onesimus' debt but also calling in Philemon's debt to him (vv. 17-19); Onesimus and the letter arrive at Philemon's house (implied); Philemon responds to Paul's appeal (vv. 20-21); and Philemon and the church that meets at his house anticipate a visit by Paul (v. 22). [186]

Petersen has pointed out that few translations of Philemon have fully recognized the large number of contrasting expressions in verses 8-16. He says the following pairs of contrasts are to be found there: "command" and "love" (vv. 8-9a); "formerly useless" and "now useful" (v. 11); "whom I sent to you" and "whom I wanted to keep with me" (vv. 12-13); "not by necessity" and "but by free will" (v. 14); "parted from you for a while" and "that you might have him forever"

---

[186] Norman R. Peterson, "Philemon" in *Harper's Bible Commentary*, General Editor James L. Mays (SanFrancisco, CA: Harper & Row, Publishers, 1988), 1245.

(v. 13); "not as a slave" and "as a beloved brother" (v. 16a); "especially to me" and "but how much more to you" (v. 16b); both "in the flesh" and "in the Lord" (v. 16c).[187]

What is Paul trying to accomplish by means of this brief letter? Initially, Onesimus was a slave and Philemon was his master. Onesimus ran away and was later converted by Paul. Now in addition to the slave-master relationship, Onesimus and Philemon are both brothers in the Lord. Paul, in this letter, is dealing with the problem of how Philemon will deal with Onesimus upon his return. Will Philemon treat Onesimus as a slave or as a brother in the Lord, or both of these together?

EPHESIANS

Investigating Ephesians

Let us begin our investigation of Ephesians by going to our satellite laboratory and analyzing the data received from our satellite to determine the overall form of Ephesians. We arrive at the following outline:

1:1-2	Salutation
1:3-14	In praise of God, the Father, and Jesus Christ, his Son
1:15-23	Thanksgiving
2:1-6:20	Body
	2:1-3:21 Doctrinal Division
	4:1-6:20 Exhortation Division
6:21-24	Closing greetings

Having established that this composition has Paul's usual letter form, let's continue our investigation by making a low overflight, by drone, of the letter body (2:1-6:20). The result of doing this is the following:

2:1-3:21 Letter body: Doctrinal division
- 2:1-10   God made us alive with Christ
- 2:11-22   The unity of Jews and Gentiles made by Christ
- 3:1-13   Paul as the revealer of the plan of mystery hidden for ages
- 3:14-21   Intercessory prayer (vv. 14-21) and doxology (vv. 20-21)

4:1-6:20 Letter Body: Exhortation division
- 4:1   The basic exhortation
- 4:2-16   Unity in the body of Christ
- 4:17-5:20   A collection of points of exhortation
- 5:22-6:9   The household code
- 6:10-17   Stand firm in the spiritual battle
- 6:18-20   Final exhortations

This completes our mapping of the letter body, so let's put the drone away in its hangar and climb aboard our tour bus and visit some interesting passages.

---

[187] Norman R. Petersen, 1247.

Ephesians viewed as a literary piece

A first glance at this form reveals that it has the usual Pauline letter form with one modification. There is the addition of a passage, praising God and Christ, between the salutation and the thanksgiving.

Stop #1 1:1-2
The salutation (1:1-2) states that this letter is from Paul and in the early church this ascription of the letter to Paul was not questioned. In the 21st century, however, Paul's authorship has been challenged by some scholars who hold that this letter is pseudonymous. The reasons they give for taking this position are based on internal analyses of the content. There is no external evidence for their position and their analyses are not convincing.

The words "in Ephesus," in 1:1, are missing from some important manuscripts (hence these two words are enclosed in square brackets in some translations, e.g. NABRE). Consequently one cannot assume with absolute confidence that the letter was intended to be sent to the Ephesians alone. Indeed, the general tone of the letter, lacking the usual Pauline letter's addressing of particular and immediate issues and personalities, has prompted some scholars to propose that it was written as a circular letter intended for a group of Christian assemblies in Asia Minor.

A Note Concerning Ancient Greek Writing

It is important to realize that in the Greek original, the text of the letter contains a number of quite long sentences. It is the custom of the scholars who translate from Greek into English to render each of these long Greek sentences into a number of shorter English sentences. It helps, therefore, in understanding the meaning and structure of the text, to be aware of this truncation by today's translators. The long unbroken sentences with phrases taken together can deepen the meaning. Some of the longer Greek sentences, in their English translations, are the following: 1:3-14; 1:15-23; 2:1-7; 3:1-7; 4:11-16; and 6:14-20.

Ephesians viewed as a historical document

Stop #1 3:1-6
Paul tells the reader in the first verse of this section, 3:1, that he is in prison at the time of his writing. Four of Paul's letters were written while he was in a prison: Ephesians, Philemon, Colossians, and Philemon. Paul then goes on to speak of his conversion experience (vv.1-3) and mentions that he has written an earlier letter to the Ephesians (which is not extant). The remainder of this section Paul devotes to telling his readers that the Gentiles are co-heirs and co-partners in the same body (the Christian assembly). Paul also refers to himself as a prisoner in 4:1.

Stop #2 5:2
Behind this verse is a reference to Christ's death on the cross.

Stop #3 6:21-22
Paul sets the Roman assembly on notice that he is sending Tychicus to them to tell them what he (Paul) is doing and so that he (Tychicus) can encourage their hearts.

Ephesians viewed as a writing that contains theological material

Christology

Stop #1 1:3-14
In the original Greek, this passage consists of a single sentence! It is translated into English as a number of sentences because complicated sentences are to be avoided in today's English. This passage is divided into three parts based on the three members of the trinity: God the Father (vv. 3-6); Jesus Christ, the Son (vv. 7-12); and the Holy Spirit (vv. 13-14). These three divine beings are presented in relation to what they have each done for the Christian faithful.

Stop #2 1:15-23
Paul begins this section by telling the Ephesians that he constantly gives thanks, in his prayers, for their faith in Jesus Christ (vv. 15-16). Then Paul petitions God the Father for several things on behalf of the faithful (vv. 17-18). In the last part of the section, Paul focuses on what God has done through his great power and might. God has: raised Jesus from the dead; seated him at God's right hand; put all things beneath his feet; and gave him as head over all things in the church.

There is one interesting bit of anthropology in this section. In verse eighteen, one encounters the expression: "eyes of your hearts." In true biblical anthropology, the heart is understood to be the place of encounter with God and where faith and trust is held and treasured.

Stop #3 2:11-18
This section provides a strong statement to the effect that both Jew and Gentile are joined as one in the Christian church. Paul says in verse 17: "So he came and proclaimed peace to you who were far off (the Gentiles) and peace to those who were near (the Jews)."

Stop #4 3:14-21
This passage is one of Paul's prayers. It is a prayer to God the Father asking that God may grant that the Ephesians may be strengthened in their inner being with power through God's Spirit and that Christ may dwell in their hearts through faith. This is known in Orthodox theology as *theosis* and in Catholic theology as "indwelling." Paul also prays that the Ephesians may be able to comprehend the "love of Christ that surpasses all understanding." These concepts are well worth studying and meditating upon.

Stop #5 4:1-6
The focus of these six verses is on unity. After a brief introduction, Paul takes up the unity of the assembly for them to "love one another" (v.2). In v.3, Paul speaks of the

unity of Jew and Gentile by mentioning the "bond of peace." The phrase "one body" is a reference to the body of Christ and the reference to "the one hope of your call" is a reference to the return of Christ. The passage concludes with a reference to the one God and Father of all. It is sometimes pointed out that this last statement is like the Jewish Shema in Deuteronomy (Deut 6:4).

Ethics

Stop #1 4:7,11-16

Paul states that each of us has been given grace by Jesus Christ (v.7). We should, therefore, seek to live our lives so as realize and discern the grace that each of us has been given. The point is that "each of us" has been given grace, not just the people specified by Paul in v.11! Each of us must find the grace that is given to us and then try to live it out as best we can.

Stop #2 5:22-33

This passage clearly deals with the relationship between a husband and a wife, as they are to be "subject to one another." At first, it reads as if the wife should always be subject to her husband. But read on … the passage concludes with a call for the husband to love and be subject to his wife, as Christ loved the church and gave up his life for all of us. The relationship of mutual love and companionship is seen in a quotation that Paul brings up in v.31, deriving from Genesis 2:24. This implies a complete joining of husband and wife.

Stop #3 6:10-17

In this passage, Paul speaks of the Christian battling against the devil and the other demonic powers. Since he is picturing a battle in his mind, it is natural for Paul to outfit the Christian "soldier" as the Roman soldier was outfitted.

Stop #3 6:18-20

This is Paul's final prayer in this letter. In v.18 he tells the Ephesians to pray for each other at every opportunity. In vv. 19-20, he tells the Ephesians to pray on his behalf that God will inspire his speech so that he will be able to make known the mystery of the gospel with boldness.

CHAPTER THIRTY-eight

THE PASTORAL LETTERS

Introducing the Pastoral Letters

Since the 18th century, the three writings 1 and 2 Timothy and Titus have been called "the Pastoral Epistles." Today, in the 21st century, the word "epistles" has fallen out of common use in favor of the term "letters." Consequently, it is becoming the usual practice to refer to these three writings by means of the collective term "the Pastoral Letters." The modifying term "pastoral" is retained in the title because of its obvious applicability to the nature of these three writings. Timothy and Titus were now "pastoring" their churches as directed by Paul, and they were no longer on missionary trips.

Literary analysis shows that the three letters were written by the same individual. Since the earliest times this individual was understood to have been Paul. Ignatius, Polycarp, Tertullian and St. Clement of Alexandria all attest to Paul's authorship. All through the centuries these letters were understood to be composed by Paul. In the 19th and 20th centuries, however, a challenge arose to this common belief. Today, some scholars hold that the letters were not written by Paul himself but rather by a disciple of Paul, sometime after Paul's death. It is best to accept the traditional position of Paul's authorship over the new position of authorship by a disciple of Paul because this secondary and minor opinion totally ignores tradition and is based solely on the results that come from an analysis only on the internal features of the letters. Perhaps, someday more evidence will be found – such as lost and rediscovered scrolls – that will further clarify this question.

The place of the Pastoral Letters in the Scriptures testifies to the claim of Paul's authorship. They are included along with other writings by Paul whose authorship is not contested by anybody. Paul's writings are arranged in the order of letters to churches first, and letters to individuals second. Each of these groups is arranged in the order of length: longer to shorter. This explains why 1 and 2 Timothy and Titus are found before Philemon at the end of the writings of Paul.

The Pastoral Letters, being arranged in order of length, raises the question of their real order of composition historically. Careful literary analysis indicates that most likely they were written at the time Paul was in Rome where he suffered two imprisonments – the first around 60 or 62 CE and the second just before his death in about 65 CE (these dates are not known precisely). It is believed that 1 Timothy and Titus were written in the period between Paul's two imprisonments and that 2 Timothy was written during his second imprisonment as he was facing death. The three writings will, therefore, be treated in the following order: 1 Timothy, Titus, and 2 Timothy.

Timothy

Timothy was one of Paul's young fellow-workers (Rom 16:21) who was about 30 years of age. He was born of a Jewish-Christian mother and a Gentile father (Acts 16:1). He had a grandmother named Lois and his mother's name was Eunice (2 Tim 1:5). Paul required Timothy to be circumcised because Paul felt that the Jews in the area where Timothy lived would understand Timothy's decision to follow Christ with much more respect if he could claim a definite affiliation to being a circumcised Jew. He could then demonstrate that he realized Jesus was the prophesied messiah, as a full-fledged Jew. Timothy's Jewish identity was originally based on the fact that he was the son of Jewish mother (Acts 16:1-3).

Paul regarded Timothy as much more than a fellow-worker. He referred to Timothy as a "beloved and faithful child in the Lord" (1 Cor 4:17; Phil 2:22; and 1 Tim 1:2). The fact that Paul included Timothy as a co-sender of four of his letters is further testimony to their very close relationship: 1 Thessalonians; 2 Thessalonians; 2 Corinthians and Philippians. Timothy accompanied Paul on Paul's last trip to Jerusalem.

Titus

Titus is less well known than Timothy; his name does not appear in the Book of Acts at all. He is, however, mentioned in the letter to the Galatians where Paul refers to him as "my partner and co-worker" (Gal 8:23).

About 17 years after Paul received his call from God, he journeyed to Jerusalem taking Titus with him. Although Titus was of Greek descent, he was not required to be circumcised (Gal 2:1, 3), probably because he had no Jewish ethnic heritage at all.

Titus played the role of an envoy to the Christian community at Corinth. While there, he is known as having played a prominent part in healing disagreements in the relationship between Paul and some of the Corinthians (refer to 2 Cor 2:7; 7:6, 13; 8:6, 16-17, 23).

As Paul departed to do more missionary trips, he appointed Titus to stay in Crete to "put in order what remained to be done" and "to appoint elders in every town" (Titus1:5). Paul also invited Titus to join him in Nicopolis where Paul planned to spend the winter (Titus 3:12).

PAUL'S FIRST LETTER TO TIMOTHY

Exploring 1 Timothy

Let us return to the laboratory once again and examine our satellite data in pursuit of a letter form. In this way the following outline is obtained:

> **1:1-2** Salutation
> **1:3-6:19** Letter Body
> **6:20-21** Letter closing

This is not the familiar letter form that we have become accustomed to when reading the letters that Paul wrote to the several Christian communities, but it is the usual form of a 1st century personal letter. To learn more, now fire up the drone and let's use it to make a low overflight of the letter body:

1:3-11 Paul urges Timothy to stay in Ephesus to work against false teaching
   a. Paul's request (1:3-7)
   b. Paul teaches about the law (1:8-11)
1:12-17 Paul describes his experience of Christ and his conversion
1:18-20 Paul states why he is giving these instructions to Timothy
2:1-7 Paul asks for prayers and intercessions for all
2:8-3:15 Paul speaks of people in the assemble and those aspiring to office
3:14-16 Paul states why he is writing these instructions at this time
4:1-5 A warning against false asceticism
4:6-16 Various instructions for Timothy
5:1-6:2a Advice for Timothy concerning the groups of people in assemblies; especially widows, elders and slaves
6:2b-18 Concerning those whose teaching is not sound
6:9-19 On money and a call for Timothy to fight the good fight of the faith (a sandwich construction)
6:20-21 Letter closing: final advice for Timothy and benediction

Now let us move on to viewing 1 Timothy from the three different perspectives through the use of our tour bus.

1 Timothy viewed as a literary piece

Stop #1 Salutation
It is clearly seen that this letter is from Paul and to Timothy. There is no indication as to the geographical locations of either of these two individuals at the time of writing.

Stop #2 5:23
It can be seen from our low overflight of the letter body that there is an element of alternating of the various components in the content. For example, verse 5:23 seems to be completely unrelated to its surroundings. Another such happening would seem to be the middle of the sandwich construction in 6:9-19. The middle could be removed and the surrounding material would not betray its absence!

1 Timothy viewed as a historical document
   Stop #1 1:12-17
   At this stop we encounter another of Paul's autobiographical statements. In this case he speaks about his conversion to Christianity.

   Stop #2 1:18-20
   In this passage we learn that prophecies were made about Timothy in the past.

We also learn of two individuals, Hymenaeus and Alexander, who rejected their consciences and as a result lost their faith.

Stop #3 3:1-13

In this section one learns something about the type of people who served as leaders in the Christian assemblies. It is interesting to note that both bishops and deacons could be married. It is also interesting to note that both men and women could serve in the position of deacon.

Stop #4 6:1-2a

From this brief passage it is learned that some slaves had Christian masters and some did not. It is suggested that the slaves who had masters who were within the assembly should serve their master faithfully and all the more because of this relationship.

Stop #5 6:9-10

This passage treats those people in the congregation who **want** to be rich.
It is obvious that this desire could easily lead one away from the faith. But, what about the people in the congregation who **are** rich? They are discussed in 6:17-19. The section 6:9-19 is a sandwich construction – this type of construction is familiar to us from the Gospel of Mark.

1 Timothy viewed as a writing that contains theological material

Stop #1 1:1-2 Christology

Paul's terminology is interesting here. He says that he is an apostle by the command of God. This is probably a reference to his conversion experience. Then he refers to God as our savior and Jesus Christ as our hope. To refer to God (Almighty, the Father) as our savior is somewhat unusual, but to see Jesus as our hope is certainly a reference to Jesus' return at the end of time. The addition of the word "mercy" to "grace and peace" is somewhat different from Paul's more commonly expression of just "grace and peace."

Stop #2 1:3-5 Ecclesiology

Paul gives instruction that love comes from a pure heart, a good conscience and sincere faith. This is a truth that applies to the present day just as it did in Paul's time.

Stop #3 2:1-6 Christology

Paul first asks for supplications, prayers, intercessions and thanksgivings to be given for everyone, even kings, through Christ the mediator. It may seem like including kings and all who are in high positions is going too far but in reality worshipping God as a Christian requires the good will of the state officials. A prayer for the state officials is included in the liturgies of the 21st century as well.

Paul gives us a quotation from an early Christian creed or hymn that states four major aspects of the faith: First, that there is one God. Then, three things about Jesus Christ: he is the one mediator; he was himself human; and that he gave himself as a ransom. Since

Paul saw fit to quote it, it shows that Paul himself accepted it. That is very good testimony to its truthfulness. It should, therefore, be taken seriously.

Stop #4 3:14-16 Ecclesiology and Christology
In verse 15, Paul refers to the church as the "household of God." This description of the church is only natural because in Paul's time there were only house churches. The term "living God" originated in the days of the prophets when the Israelites were struggling against idolatry. That God was a "living God" formed a good contrast with the idols that had no life in them. Verse 16 is most likely a fragment from an early Christological hymn. Paul refers to the event that was Jesus as the "mystery of our religion."

Stop #5 5:1-6:2 Ecclesiology
This lengthy section deals with how Timothy is to relate to various members of the community. The bulk of the material has to do with the widows. Widows probably abounded in the community because of the early deaths of the male members through wars and sickness. The major concern was to encourage care of the widows and thus limit the number of women who qualified for financial support, which in turn avoided difficulties with church finances.

Stop #6 6:11-16
This section is a challenge! First of all, what is it? Is it Christology, or is it eschatology, or is it ecclesiology? The answer is: yes! The first verse, 6:11, is simple enough – in fact, it is good advice for all of us.

The questions begin in the next verse. Should it read "Fight the good fight" as in the NRSV translation or should it read: "Compete well" as in the NABRE translation? The difference here is whether to take the original Greek as indicating a military action (NRSV) or to take it to refer to an athletic contest (NABRE).

Moving on, also in 6:12, there is mention of a "good (NRSV; "noble" in NABRE) confession." What event in Timothy's life does the phrase "good confession" indicate? In verse 13, Paul begins by "charging" Timothy. What is the meaning of "I charge you" and why is it done "in the presence of" (NRSV and NABRE use "before") both God and Christ Jesus?

From verses 13 and 14, it seems that Paul has charged Timothy to "keep the commandment." What commandment is Paul asking Timothy to keep without stain or reproach until the appearance of our Lord Jesus Christ (NABRE)?
One final question remains to be resolved. Who is the "blessed and only ruler" whom Paul speaks about in verse 6:15, and is also the subject of the remaining verses of this passage?

At this point it is time to consult study material including footnotes and biblical commentaries. The inquisitive and industrious individual will seek out one or more commentaries and study sources to seek the answers to the questions. When individual words and phrases are in question, it will be necessary to go back to the original Greek language text. Another most useful tool is an interlinear text such as *The New Greek-English Interlinear New Testament* by Robert K. Brown and Philip W. Comfort or one found online (such as in biblegateway.com). An interlinear presents the text of the New Testament writings in the original Greek along with a word by word translation in English.

PAUL'S LETTER TO TITUS

Exploring Titus

Paul's letter to Titus is so short, only three chapters, that it is not necessary to engage the services of satellites, drones and tour buses. We will simply rent a car and conduct a drive around of the text. [At this point read quickly through the letter.]

Mapping of contents by rent-a-car drive around:
  1:1-4   Salutation

  1:5-9   Why Paul left Titus in Crete and the attributes needed to be an elder.

  1:10-16 Rebellious people and how to deal with them.

  2:1-15 What Titus is to teach the faithful
  1. What Titus should teach the different groups of people (2:1-10)
  2. The reason for teaching these things (2:11-14)
  3. Three counsels for Titus (2:15)

  3:3:1-11 Further things that the people of the community should do.
  1. 3:1-2 The things the people are to do.
  2. 3:3:3-8a The theological reason for doing these things
  3. 3:8b-11 The good people; handling the bad people
  3:12-13 Assignments for several of the workers
  3:14   Paul wants the people to be productive
  3:15   Final greeting

To further investigate Paul's letter to Titus, it seems appropriate to abandon our practice of viewing it from three different perspectives and then making use of a tour bus to look at specific passages. For this letter it seems more appropriate to make a walk through.

1:1-4
This salutation is unlike those in the other letters of Paul because of its content. The usual elements found in Paul's salutations are there but other material is included. The letter is from Paul, slave of God and Apostle of Jesus Christ (v.1), and is addressed to Titus (v.4). The usual conclusion bringing grace and peace to the recipients is there as well.

It is what is also included in verses 1 to 4 that is surprising. Two questions immediately come to mind. The first question is: what does Paul say overall in verses 1-4? At the end of verse 1, continuing through verse 2, he tells why he was made an apostle. In verse 3,

Paul states that at the proper time God entrusted his "word" directly to Paul. This "word" is what Paul referred to in his other letters as "his (Paul's) Gospel." Paul's use of the word "proclamation" indicates this meaning.

The second question is: Why did Paul include all this information in verses 1 to 4? Perhaps the answer is that Paul wanted to firmly establish his authority so that Titus would act on what was set forth in the letter. Paul's stress on authority in 2:15 provides support for this interpretation.

1:5-9

In this section, Paul tells Titus the reason why he (Titus) was left in Crete. Then, Paul goes on to say what qualifications are required for a good presbyter. It seems that in this instance the title "presbyter" and "bishop" are applied to the same person. It is to be noted that at the time this letter was written celibacy had not become the norm for church leaders. The Greek word "*presbyter*" later is termed "priest" (a different position than the ancient Jewish priests who offered sacrifices in the Temple in Jerusalem). And, the Greek word "*episcopos*" meant "presider."

1:10-16

In verse 9, Paul spoke about refuting those who contradict sound doctrine. He now takes up those individuals – whom he points out – who profess to know God, but they reject God by their actions.

2:1-15

In these verses, Paul directs Titus what to teach the various groups of people in the assembly about their conduct. He points out the following groups: older men (vv.1-2) and older women   (vv.3-5); younger men (vv.6-8); and slaves (9-10).

The section vv.11-14 is a christological statement giving the justification for what Paul said in verses 1-10. It is good to pause for just a moment here to reflect on how directly this section applies to Christians living today in the 21st century.

Here in v.15 Paul states both "to declare these things" and to "reprove with all authority." In this statement, it is seen how authority passes down from one generation to the next.

3:1-11

This section divides into three parts: 3:1-2; 3:3-8a; and 3:8b-11. In the first part (3:1-2) Paul specifies a number of things that Titus should remind the people to do.

In 3:3-8a, the second part, is a description of a Gentile's entry into the Christian community of the faithful. The "we ourselves" in verse 3:3 is understandable if one considers that Titus was himself a convert to the Christian faith and here Paul is using "we ourselves" to stand for Titus and himself. The one confusing factor in this interpretation is, of course, that Paul was formerly a Jew and not a Gentile! This second part ends with some wisdom about sacramental life.

In the third part, 3:8b-11, Paul first gives Titus his desires on how he should handle those people who are faithful to the teaching and then what he is to do with those people who do not follow and live the teaching.

3:12-13
Here we meet some of Paul's associates and learn a little about their assignments and travels. Paul and his associates were always on the move.

3:14
Paul expresses his desire that all the people should be ready to assist when urgent needs arise. This would seem to indicate that on Crete, where Titus was working, when emergencies arose and members required help that the people did not always come to their aide.

3:15
Missing in this benediction is the word "peace," as Paul usually gives in other letters. "Grace and peace" is Paul's more usual expression.
What is the significance of the word "all?" If Paul is writing to Titus why doesn't he simply say "to you?" Could the presence of the word "all" actually be an indication that Paul wanted the letter to be read to the whole congregation or that he knew it would be?

That completes our walk through of Paul's letter to Titus. Let us move on now to 2 Timothy.

PAUL'S SECOND LETTER TO TIMOTHY

Exploring 2 Timothy
This letter, 2 Timothy, is most likely the last letter that Paul wrote. This conclusion is supported by what Paul says of himself in 4:6-8. Our exploration of the writings of Paul is almost at an end.

As a first step in our exploration of 2 Timothy, let us analyze the satellite data we have collected to look for the letter form. We obtain the following outline:

1:1-2	Salutation
1:3-5	Thanksgiving
1:8-4:18	Letter Body
4:19-22	Closing Greetings

Having established that 2 Timothy has the usual letter form, let us move on and make a slow drone overflight to establish the details of the content of the body of the letter. The result of this observation and subsequent analysis is the following:

1:6-14 Paul challenges Timothy to be a courageous witness
1:15-18 Paul informs Timothy of the actions of some who turned away and one who did not turn away
2:1-13 Paul encourages Timothy to be strong and to accept rough treatment

1. Encouragement of Timothy
2. Bear everything patiently – Paul's example of himself

2:14-21 Timothy is advised to avoid false teaching
2:22-26 Paul advises Timothy on proper conduct
3:1-9 Paul counsels Timothy that many men will act badly in the last days
3:10-17 Paul tells Timothy to stand by the things he has learned
4:1-1-8 Paul adjures Timothy to proclaim the Gospel
4:9-13 Paul gives Timothy some instructions about people and things
4:14-15 A warning about Alexander the copper-smith
4:16-18 Paul speaks about Paul

It is time, once again, to look at a letter from three different viewpoints and then to board our tour bus and visit some interesting passages. In this case we will limit ourselves to only two viewpoints. We will view the letter as a historical document and its theological material. We will forgo viewing it as a literary writing because there is little more to be said by doing so.

Viewing 2 Timothy as an historical document

Stop #1 1:1
Paul was originally a well-trained Jew and then had an experience of Christ (Acts 9:1-9) and became a Christian (following "the Way") as a result. An event such as this has its historical side in an event: a light flashed, other people heard a voice, Paul was blinded. But, it also has its spiritual side. So, we will encounter it again under theological material. This event happened to Paul completely without any effort on his own part; consequently he interpreted the event to indicate the he was chosen by God.

Stop #2 1:5
From this verse we learn that Timothy's grandmother and mother were both Christian faithful.

Stop #3 1:6
Timothy had received the imposition of hands and, therefore, we know that he held some official ministerial position within the Christian assembly.

Stop #4 1:15-18
Here we learn that a lot of people deserted Paul in Asia, a province of the Roman Empire, and that Paul was helped by a person named Onesiphorus. Recall that Onesiphorus was the subject of Paul's letter to Philemon.

Stop #5 2:8-9a
Paul describes the resurrection of Jesus and that Jesus was a descendent of David. He notes that these are two important pieces of his (Paul's) gospel and that he (Paul) was suffering to the point of being imprisoned for going about teaching this gospel.

Stop #6 2:16-18

This section speaks of false teaching and furnishes us with the names of two individuals who should be avoided. We also learn that one of the major points of their false teaching was that the final resurrection due at the end of time had already taken place.

Stop #7 3:10-11

Here we learn a bit about Paul's life from Paul himself. It is a very nice summary of his experience.

Stop #8 4:6-8

This is another nice autobiographical statement by Paul pointing out that he is approaching the end of his life.

Stop #9 4:9-18

Here we find autobiographical material dealing with Paul's associates and Alexander the Coppersmith who Paul said did him a great deal of harm in resisting Paul's teaching.

Viewing 2 Timothy as a writing that contains theological material

Stop #1 1:1

In this verse, Paul makes reference to the vision he had while traveling on the road to Damascus because he refers to himself as an "apostle" (technically one directly called by Jesus). We encountered this verse under the category of historical passages. We visit it again here for its theological meaning. It clearly meant that God had chosen Paul for a special task. Through this event Paul came to know Jesus Christ and Paul was given the gospel (special "good news" to teach others and draw them into faith in Jesus).During his later life, Paul maintained that he had received this gospel directly from God.

Stop #2 1:14

From this verse we learn that the Holy Spirit dwells within us.

Stop #3 2:10-13

There is a large theological content in these verses. We see in these four verses that the Christian is chosen by God and has both salvation and eternal life through Jesus Christ (v.10). Then, if one is baptized one dies with Christ and then lives with Christ ... but if one denies Christ, God will deny the individual eternal life. If one is unfaithful, Christ always will be faithful. These are words, perhaps an ancient baptismal hymn, that show God is a relational God and wants the faithful to love and be faithful to this relationship – forever!

Stop #4 3:1-5

We have eschatology in these verses. They inform us as to what will happen in the last days. We Christians of today are living in the last days! Doesn't it seem like these verses are a good description of the days that we are living through?

Stop #5 3:14-17

This section is about the Scriptures. We learn that all of the Scriptures are inspired by God and we learn about some ways in which the Scriptures can be useful to us. This is a key passage to hold in mind in reading the Scriptures, and helps us to recall our conversation in the coffee shop about "inspiration of the Scriptures."

PART THREE – THE REMAINING WRITINGS OF THE NEW TESTAMENT

CHAPTER THIRTY-nine

HEBREWS

Introducing Hebrews

The Letter to the Hebrews is a remarkable writing that includes "exhortations." An exhortation means a call to emphatically encourage certain actions and way of life. Harold Attridge, one of the leading scholars on the Letter to the Hebrews, has made the following comment about its intended purpose:

> …Hebrews may be characterized as a masterpiece of early Christian rhetorical homiletics, or in its own terms a "word of exhortation"(13:22), addressed to believers in Christ who are in danger of becoming lax in their commitment. It attempts to revitalize that commitment by exhortations to faithful endurance that are grounded in a renewed understanding of traditions about the significance of Christ.[188]

The Book of Hebrews is a writing that requires careful reading, reflection, and study. This provides depth to this important book of the Bible. What is the best way to go about studying this composition? It is always best to begin by reading the entire work, from beginning to end, in a thoughtful manner without the use of outside assistance. Think for yourself first! Secondly, it is helpful to read a short introduction to the book like that presented in the *Anchor Bible Dictionary*. This provides an idea on what is important about the book as well as what is accepted by the majority of scholars and what is still a matter of scholarly debate. Then you will need to have a Bible at hand for the purpose of looking up some of the many citations of the OT that are contained in Hebrews – there are about forty or fifty of references to Hebrew scriptures. One interesting thing to remember here is that the author of Hebrews was using the Septuagint version of the Bible (the Hebrew translated into Greek many years before the time of Christ); so, this means that the wording may differ slightly in today's most popular bible translations that use the Masoretic text of the OT.

Finally, always take notes when doing these kinds of bible studies. You will undoubtedly be interrupted in your studies and will have to set them aside for a time, maybe even a long time, so you need to have something to come back to when you want to resume your work. Patience and persistence are necessary qualities to have when you are engaging in the study of the Bible.

Author, Place and Date

For many centuries, the title given to this composition was: The Letter of Paul to the Hebrews. However, in the twenty-first century the scholarly community is practically united behind the position that Paul was not the author. However, this position is not new. It was proposed as early as the 2nd century CE. Modern scholars base their position principally on stylistic features and theological grounds. They suggest that its original attribution to Paul may have resulted in part from Paul's reputation as a letter writer and in part from the reference to Timothy, a companion of Paul, in 13:22.

The author does not explicitly identify himself within the composition itself. He does, however provide one clue – he is a second-generation Christian believer (2:3). It is, therefore, a

---

[188] Harold W. Attridge, *The Epistle to the Hebrews*, in the Hermeneia Series (Philadelphia: Fortress Press, 1989), 1.

matter of conjecture as to who may have been the person who wrote it. A number of 1st century individuals have been proposed, but not one of them has gained the support of a majority of the scholars and, consequently, the author of this carefully crafted composition remains unknown.

In the present day, many Bibles – for instance *The New American Bible* and *The New Oxford Annotated Bible* – take this lack of knowledge concerning the author's identity into account and now give this composition the title: The Letter to the Hebrews. While recognizing this work of the scholars is commendable, the bible editors apparently do not feel a need to recognize the other two firm results of modern scholarship that the composition is neither a true letter nor is it to the Hebrews.

Where was Hebrews written? We can perhaps gain some insight into the answer to this question from the composition itself. Verse 13:24b states: "Those from Italy send you greetings" (NAB). This verse, however, does not make it clear whether the writer is in Italy with other Christians or whether the author is writing from some place outside of Italy and is with some Christians from Italy.

There is no way to give a precise date to the writing of this composition. A latest possible date can be assigned by observing that Hebrews is referenced in 1 Clement, an early Christian writing that is most commonly dated to around 96 CE. An earliest date of around 60 CE can be assigned on the basis of the author's statement that he is a second generation Christian and by combining the reference to Timothy in 13:23 and the assumption that this Timothy is the former companion of Paul. Beyond this range of 60 to 96 CE no further narrowing of the period is possible.[189]

There is one remaining fascinating theory that some scholars are considering today that Priscilla may be the author of this piece. She and her husband Aquila were close friends of Paul. She was the leader of a house church in Rome and ancient church tradition indicates she was a well-educated woman. Many authors from this early period of the church have been considered: Barnabus, Luke, Apollos (whom tradition says Priscilla taught the faith), and Priscilla herself. Here are some of the reasons for citing Priscilla as author of Hebrews by scholar Ruth Hoppin:

> A feminine voice is heard throughout the epistle. We find the parent-child relationship portrayed with tenderness and poignancy, interest in education, delineation of the compassion of Christ and keen compassion *for* Christ. A feminine voice is heard in the naming of women as models of faith, with direct and indirect allusions to many others. The inexplicable loss of the author's name so early in the letter's history bears more testimony to female authorship.[190]

No one knows for sure the author of the Letter to the Hebrews, but the theories are intriguing and worthy of more thought. If Priscilla is the author, this presents yet another level of depth to understanding the letter.

---

[189] Harold W. Attridge, "Hebrews, Epistle to the," in *The Anchor Bible Dictionary*, Vol. 3, Editor-In-Chief David Noel Freedman (New York: Doubleday), 97.

[190] Ruth Hoppin, "Priscilla, the Author of Hebrews" in *The IVP Women's Bible Commentary,* edited by Catherine Clark Kroeger (Downers Grove, Illinois: IVP Academic, 2002), 763

Addressees

Now, to whom was the letter written? Does the term "Hebrew" refer only to Jews who are now Christian, or to Gentile Christians who because of their new faith in Jesus are now called "Hebrews"?

The document itself does not present us with an explicit identification of the identity of the addressees. It does, however, give us one or two clues. Clearly, they are Christians (see 3:6,14; 4:14 and 10:23). They have been baptized (6:4-5; 10:22) and, consequently, have been fully instructed (6:1-2). The author makes abundant use of the OT but this does not require that his readers be only Jews since Paul makes considerable use of the OT in 1 Corinthians and the Corinthians were predominantly Gentile converts. We can assume, however, that his readers are very familiar with the Septuagint translation of the Scriptures because the biblical citations used by the author come from that version and he is able to both argue from nuances of the Greek translation and to make allusions to persons and events in Israel's history.[191]

It is apparent from the composition that the addressees are in the midst of some kind of crisis. The evidence as to the nature of this crisis that is provided for us in the document consists of the following:

- Some members of the community had been under extreme external pressure. They had been publicly exposed to abuse and persecution and also had associated themselves with people who were causing others to suffer. They had joined in the sufferings of those in prison and cheerfully accepted the plundering of their property (10:32-34). And this is going on at the time of writing (13:3).
- Some have become sluggish in hearing – not listening to the fullness of teachings of the faith (5:11; 6:12; NAB). What they are not hearing is the Word, the Scriptures.[192]
- Some members have apparently stopped coming to the assembly (10:25).
- The author's assurances of a coming judgment (2:2-3; 6:8; 10:25, 29-31; 12:18-24, 26-29) and assurances of a final revelation of Christ's lordship (2:8; 10:13) seem to indicate there is a weakening of faith in the fact these people were expecting Jesus to immediately return and because he hadn't come yet they were losing faith.

The conclusion that one is led to on the basis of this evidence is aptly stated by Harold W. Attridge as follows:

…. If such remarks reflect the actual situation of the addressees, a major element of their perceived problem would be the diminishing of the initial ardor of their Christian commitment. Such growing disaffection would be readily comprehensible in a community which had for some time accepted Jesus as the

---

[191]Fred B. Craddock, "The Letter to the Hebrews" in *The New Interpreter's Bible,* Vol. XII, edited by Leander E. Keck (Nashville: AbingdonPress, 1998), 8.
[192]Craddock, 68.

Christ, but was subject to external pressure and the disappointment of their first hopes.[193]

Purpose

The purpose of this composition has been understood in a number of different ways. Many possibilities have been based on a partial and selective reading of the text. Proceeding in this manner has led to a number of incorrect conclusions.

Based on an assessment of the text as a whole, Attridge arrived at the following conclusion:

> Whatever the precise causes of the problem confronted by the author and whatever his perception of that problem, he is engaged in Hebrews in an attempt to revitalize the faith of his addressees and put their commitment on a more solid footing.
>
> ….The author does not simply admonish his addressees and encourage them to a firmer commitment. He also attempts to secure that commitment through a deepened understanding of the person and work of the one who makes faith possible.[194]

Genre

The author is clearly writing this document at a time when he (or she) is separated, by some distance, from the intended readers. This can be seen from the following comment that is made: "I urge you all the more to do this, so that I may be restored to you very soon" (13:19 NRSV). Given this situation, it is natural to expect Hebrews to be a letter. This expectation appears to be fulfilled by the ending (13:22-25) which bears a strong resemblance to the typical ending of a first century letter. Hebrews, however, lacks any semblance of the typical letter in its beginning; and, in addition, it certainly does not read like a typical letter. In fact, it reads like and appears to be structured more like a formal composition.

In between its beginning and end, the text gives the appearance of alternating between exposition and exhortation prompting one scholar to comment:

> The rhetorical organization of the homily is masterful. Exposition and exhortation alternate throughout, building on each other with such force that the cumulative impact is persuasive and the conclusions undeniable.[195]

Fred Craddock sees the alternating exposition and exhortation as follows:

> Exposition 1:1-4
> Exhortation 2:1-4
> Exposition 2:5-3:6
> Exhortation 3:7-4:16
> Exposition 5:1-10
> Exhortation 5:11-6:20
> Exposition 7:1-10:18
> Exhortation 10:19-13:25 [196]

---

[193] Harold W. Attridge, 100.
[194] Attridge, 100.
[195] L.T. Johnson, 458.
[196] Craddock, 16.

The author plainly states, in 13:22, that he (or she) is writing "a word of exhortation." The same expression appears in Acts 13:15 where the leaders of the Synagogue ask Paul if he or one of his companions would like to speak. What follows, in Acts 13:16-47, is a lengthy speech by Paul which contains a number of OT quotations. A word of exhortation, therefore, refers to something that is like a homily or a sermon. While Hebrews, taken as a whole, is not composed as a single, carefully constructed sermon, it does include well defined segments which probably exemplify homiletic patterns and may be based upon independent sermons or homilies (e.g. Chaps. 3-4 and Chaps. 8-10). In addition, smaller well-defined units appear to replicate elements in this homiletic pattern (e.g. 2:5-18; 7:1-28 and 12:1-13).[197]

The homiletic pattern consists of four parts: 1) introduction announcing the major theme to be treated; 2) a text from Scripture is cited; 3) some expository comments leading to an exhortation and 4) a rhetorical flourish. An example of this pattern is provided by Chapters 3 and 4 as follows:

1) introduction (3:1-6);
2) text from Scripture, Psalm 95 (3:7-11);
3) expository comment (3:12-4:11) and 4) rhetorical flourish (4:12-13.

A similar example is provided by Chapters 8-10: introduction (8:1-6); Scripture citation of Jer 31:31-34 (8:7-13); expository comment (9:1-10:10) and rhetorical flourish (10:11-18).[198] Recognition of this homiletic pattern goes a long way in helping to understand the text. Attridge has the following to say about the composition as a whole:

In these concluding remarks the work is described as a "word of exhortation" (13:22). This designation aptly describes the bulk of the text and suggests that the most appropriate generic identification is a homily.[199]

Author's Use of the OT

Citations of the OT occur some 40 or 50 times in Hebrews. These citations come from 12 different books of the Bible. Twenty of the citations are from the Book of Psalms, seven are from Genesis and seven from Deuteronomy. The other books cited are: Exodus, Leviticus, Numbers, 2 Samuel, Proverbs, Isaiah, Jeremiah, Habakkuk and Haggai.

A Number of Theological Points

The beginning statements of Hebrews have similarities with Acts and Luke. These are the last days (Heb 1:2) and this division of time is also expressed in Acts 2:14-17 at the beginning of Peter's speech at Pentecost. In Hebrews 2:4 the testimony of God is supported by signs and wonders, acts of power and gifts of the Holy Spirit apparently similar to the signs and wonders that are reported in Acts 2:43 and 5:12, and the gifts of the Spirit that are mentioned in Acts 2:4.

The author reveals a belief in the fact that the Scriptures are inspired by the Holy Spirit both in the introduction to scriptural quotations (e.g. 3:7 and 10:15) and in explicit statements such as "God spoke through the prophets" (1:1) and "Now God speaks through a Son" (1:2).

---

[197] Attridge, 98.
[198] 98.
[199] 98.

The composition that is the Letter to the Hebrews is known for its presentation of the two natures of Christ: the divine and the human. Look at the following description of the reality of Christ (known as Christology) made up from statements extracted from Hebrews:

- Christ is the Son of God (1:2; 2:11; 5:8).
- He was appointed heir of all things (1:2).
- The worlds were created through Him (1:2).
- He is the exact imprint of God's very being and the reflection of God's glory (1:3).
- He sustains all things by his powerful word.
- Christ has passed through the heavens (4:14).
- Incarnation – God prepared a body for him (10:5-7); Jesus, for a little while made lower than the angels (2:9); a person of flesh and blood like all children of God (2:14-18).
- In the days of his flesh, Jesus offered up prayers and supplications (5:7).
- Although he was a Son, he learned obedience through what he suffered (5:8) and was made perfect through suffering (2:10).
- He has been tested as we have, yet without sin (4:15).
- He endured the cross, disregarding its shame (12:2).
- Jesus suffered outside the city gates (12:13).
- Jesus' death was sacrificial and atoning (1:3; 2:9; 6:6; 7:27;10:10; 12:12).
- He was resurrected (13:20).
- He passed through the heavens (4:14).
- He is seated at the right hand of God (1:3; 12:2).
- He will come again (9:28; 10:35-39)

In Chapter 11, the author first defines "faith "(11:1-3). Following this definition, the author presents a long list of people who have demonstrated a strong faith (11:4-40). Finally, the author exhorts those who are hearing or reading the words to "run with perseverance the race that is set before us" (12:1-2).

Concluding Benediction

The writing ends with a remarkably beautiful blessing prayer that reminds the faithful of God's purpose in sending his Son. There is hope stated in the God "of peace" who wants humankind to join with him and one another in the Lord, who raised Jesus the dead who was a shepherd of the flock, whose blood was a sign of the eternal loving bond with God, and who will bring the provision of life to all who do God's will.

> May the God of peace, who brought up from the dead the great shepherd of the sheep by the blood of the eternal covenant, Jesus our Lord, furnish you with all that is good, that you may do his will. May he carry out in you what is pleasing to him through Jesus Christ, to whom be glory forever [and ever]. Amen. (Heb 13:20-21. NAB Rev. NT)

CHAPTER forty

JAMES AND 1 PETER

Introducing James

Author and Date

In the greeting we meet "James" who was recognized in the early centuries as designating James, the brother of the Lord and leader of the Christian church in Jerusalem. This traditional position is also held by many scholars of the present day. Those who hold that James, the brother of the Lord, is the author must date it to some time prior to 62 CE, the probable date of his death.

It should be noted that an early writing called the *Proto-gospel of James,* describes Joseph as a widower and older man when he was chosen to betroth Mary. Joseph had children and these are known as the "brothers and sisters of the Lord" in the New Testament. There are, of course, other theories that James was only a cousin (the usual Catholic position today) or that Mary and Joseph had more children after Jesus was born (mostly by Protestants).

There are some scholars today, however, who hold the position that this composition is a pseudonymous work -- that is, it was written sometime after James' death by a member of a Christian congregation who most likely wrote under the name of James so that his writing would be recognized as having authority. This position is founded only on internal analysis of the text and is not convincing. Those who hold this position must date this writing to sometime after 62 CE and frequently assign a date late in the 1st Century.

Addressees

This composition is addressed to "the twelve tribes in the dispersion." The question is: "Who are the persons specified by this designation?" In the OT, the "twelve tribes" specified the people of Israel. On the surface, this text seems to be quite Jewish in nature so it seems appropriate to take this designation to specify all of the Jews living outside of Palestine.

A closer examination of the text, however, shows that even though Jesus is only explicitly mentioned two times (1:1; 2:1), there are references imbedded in the text to the sayings of Jesus and to other aspects of Christian belief. Consequently, it would be consistent with the custom of the early Christians viewing themselves as "the New Israel," to understand the phrase "the twelve tribes in the dispersion" as designating the Christian churches in a broad geographical area – in other words the Jews who accepted the prophecies and recognized Jesus as the messiah.

Investigating James

As has becomes our custom, let us go to our satellite laboratory to examine the satellite data. Doing this, we find that the satellite data shows that James has a salutation at the beginning but it does not have a formal ending – it simply ends. Furthermore, the satellite data reveals nothing about its content. This leaves us without any data – seen from a distance - with which to investigate this composition further.

In this situation, we must go to our drone and make a flight at moderate altitude and speed to see if we can determine something about James' content. But carrying out this operation results in a surprising finding. The drone flight yields no information at all about the content of James because there's no apparent overall structure!

Let us, therefore, take to the air ourselves. Let us rent a helicopter, like a Chinook, and fly around over James to see what we can find out. Perhaps flying at very low altitude and low speed we will discover things that were not observable by usual other methods. We seem to have happened upon a unique composition.

The result of our overflight in a Chinook helicopter is the following map of the content of James:

1. A collection of ten individual maxims – each one standing on its own
    a. 1:2-4 Trials test your faith
    b. 1:5-8 If you lack wisdom, ask God for it
    c. 1:9-11 On the poor and the rich
    d. 1:12 Blessed is the one who perseveres in temptation
    e. 1:13-15 God tempts no one
    f. 1:16-18 All good giving and every perfect gift is from above
    g. 1:19-21 Everyone should be quick to hear and slow to speak
    h. 1:22-25 Be doers of the word and not hearers only
    i. 1:26 If anyone thinks he is religious and does not bridle his tongue, his religion is in vain
    j. 1:27 Religion that is pure: care for orphans and widows
2. A group of four short "essays" on living life
    a. 2:1-13 Show no partiality as you adhere to the faith
    b. 2:14-26 Faith apart from good deeds is barren
    c. 3:1-12 The tongue is capable of both good and evil
    d. 3:13-18 On wisdom from above and wisdom that is earthly
3. A group of four short, stand-alone maxims
    a. 4:1-3 Where the wars and conflicts among you come from
    b. 4.4-6 To love the world means enmity with God
    c. 4:7-10 Submit yourselves to God; resist the devil
    d. 4:11-12 Do not speak evil of one another
4. A short group of two short "essays" on living life
    a. 4:13-17 You have no idea what your life will be like tomorrow
    b. 5:1-6   A warning to the rich
5. A group of four short, stand-alone maxims
    a. 5:7-8   Be patient until the coming of the Lord
    b. 5:9   Do not grumble against one another
    c. 5:10-11 Suffering and patience
    d. 5:12   Do not swear by an oath

6. A group of two: one short "essay" and one short, stand alone maxim
   a. 5:13-18 The prayer of faith (v.15)
   b. 5:19 Bringing back a sinner

Viewing James as a literary composition

This composition is frequently given the title: The Letter of James. It is often designated by this title in bibles and frequently in the biblical literature as well. It is easily seen, however, that although it does have the typical opening of a Greek letter (name of sender, identity of addressees, and greeting), its only ending is the period at the conclusion of its final sentence when it is translated in English. More significantly, its contents certainly are not that of a 1st century letter. On the basis of this brief consideration it seems wise to conclude that James is **not** a letter.

If James is not a letter then what is it? Its content consists predominantly of brief maxims of how to act and a small number of brief "essays." We have previously encountered two writings that also have this form in the collection of wisdom writings from the Second Temple Period: Proverbs and Sirach. James is, therefore, a composition that fits within the wisdom tradition!

Purpose

The purpose of the Book of James is clearly that of teaching. The author is seeking to instruct his readers, evidenced by the frequent use of direct address (see 1:2, 16, 19; 2:1, etc.). In addition, the verbs are predominately in the imperative mode. The aim of the writing is clearly lived practice and right acting.

Structure

James does not have any readily recognizable structure! The individual maxims and short "essays" do not display any readily recognizable order and they could be rearranged without any loss of meaning.

When one reads James, there must be careful attention to the units which make up the body of the composition. During one's reading, do not pay attention to the section headings provided by some translations as they impose a structure on the material which the material does not possess.

Viewing James as an historical Document

We have determined that James is a wisdom writing. In this particular case it is concerned entirely with what its readers and hearers should do and not do. There are no historical references on which to attach a date of composition. About all one can say is that it includes "wisdom" in doing more good and in not doing things that lead one away from God. In this kind of writing, there is no way to attach a specific time or place … it is timeless.

309

Viewing James as a writing that contains some theological material

James is almost all theological material, but let us hop onto our tour bus and visit a few passages that are of special interest.

Stop #1 The college library

We stop first at the college library to take advantage of a piece of work done by L. T. Johnson who has observed that the writer of James has a lot to tell us about God. Consider the following:

It would be difficult to find a New Testament writing with as rich a collection of statements concerning the nature and activity of God. James begins with the confession that God is one (2:19), but scarcely stops there. God is the living God, who makes "even the demons believe – and shudder" (2:19 NRSV) and is the "Lord of hosts" (5:4 NRSV). God is constant and without change (1:17) and has nothing to do with evil (1:13) or human anger (1:20). God is the creator of all (1:17), who, by a "word of truth," has "given birth" to humans as a first fruits of all creatures (1:18) and has created them in God's own likeness (3:9). God has revealed the "perfect law of liberty" (see 2:8-12) and will judge humans on the basis of that revelation (2:12; 4:12). God is fit to judge because God alone is able "to save and to destroy" (4:12 NRSV). God has implanted a word within humans that is able to save them (1:21) and has made a spirit to dwell in them (4:5). God directs human affairs (4:15) and declares righteous those who have faith (2:23). Above all, God is defined by the giving of gifts (1:5, 17; 4:6), especially those of mercy and compassion (5:11). God has promised the crown of life to those who love God (1:12; 2:5), has chosen the world's poor to be rich in faith and heirs of the kingdom (2:5), considers true religion to include the visiting of orphans and widows (1:27), hears the cries of the oppressed (5:4), raises up the sick (5:15), listens to the prayers made in faith (1:5-6; 5:17-18) rather than wickedly (4:3), and forgives the sins of those who confess them (5:15). This is a God who approaches those who approach (4:10) and enters into friendship with humans (2:23; 4:4), even while resisting the arrogance and pride of those who oppress others (4:6; 5:6).[200]

Stop #2 1:2-4

We all face trials of many different sorts and this is very good advice, therefore, for everyone.

Stop #3 1:12-15

This is also a piece of advice that is good for everyone. We all face temptations frequently. It is also good to realize that temptation does not come from God.

---

[200] Luke Timothy Johnson, "The Letter of James," in *The New Interpreter's Bible*, Vol. XII, Leander E. Keck, Convener and Senior New Testament Editor (Nashville, TN: Abingdon Press, 1998), 181.

Stop #4 1:22-25

The maxim to be doers of the word is very good advice. The reason why this is so will be explained in our next stop.

Stop #5 2:14-17 (Also read verses 18-26 for a fuller presentation)

To be doers of the words is not just a good practice – it is essential for the Christian! Faith and works cannot be separated. One cannot have faith without doing good works. This is a reality worth meditating about and our next stop also fits well with this.

Stop #6 4:4-5

The truth in these two verses is not limited to adulterers. This is a statement of a general truth – you cannot love both God and the world. Life is a daily struggle to deal with this reality.

Stop # 7 3:1-12

This brief "essay" on the tongue and how it is capable of being both a force for good and a force for evil brings into view another basic reality. The tongue, however, is an entity that is not capable of doing anything by itself. It has to be told what to do by another organ of the body – the brain. The problem, therefore, is with what is inside the individual.

Stop #8 4:13-16

A moment of experience on a commuter train in Washington, D.C. seems to sound a lot like this passage. Sitting on a train, waiting to depart for New York City, a man sitting three rows ahead and on the other side of the aisle breathed two heavy breaths and then died. This kind of experience is always remembered … evidencing a fact of our lives on earth.

Stop #9 5:13-18

This passage is theologically significant because of its application to the Sacrament of Holy Unction. It is also significant because of its statement in verse 16 that says that the prayer of the righteous is powerful and effective. This is a good thing to keep in mind in today's world which is so fast paced and impersonal.

This concludes our investigation of James.

INTRODUCING 1 PETER

Author

On the basis of the letter form, it is seen that the writer of 1 Peter is the apostle Peter (1:1). However, many scholars believe that Silvanus may have been the scribe or the one that delivered the letter. From the phrase, "I write you this briefly through Silvanus," (see 5:12), they identify Silvanus as the person who penned the letter and perhaps also as the one who carried it to those for whom it was intended. Tradition from early times, however, says that Peter is the author.

Some modern-day scholars hold that this composition is pseudonymous; that is, it was written by an individual other than Peter under Peter's name. Two major reasons usually presented in support of this position are first that the quality of the Greek and the evidence that the writer possessed some rhetorical training. This argues against its authorship by a Galilean fisherman, and secondly that the author consistently cites passages from the Septuagint (LXX) Greek translation of the OT Scriptures. These reasons, however, are not convincing.

Date

The date of this composition, if it is held that it was written by Peter, would have to be sometime prior to 64 or 65 CE – the date of Peter's death. If this composition is held to be pseudonymous. then its date would be sometime some time before the end of the 1st Century CE. because a pseudonymous composition would necessarily have to be written at some time after Peter's death. There is, of course, another possibility that the original letter could have been later edited.

Location of the writer

It appears that the letter writer was in Rome at the time it was composed, evidenced by the statement that "the chosen one at Babylon sends you greeting" in 5:13. This greeting demonstrates the location of its writer because "Babylon" was a code name used by the early Christians for Rome. See the use of this code name, "Babylon," in Revelation

Addressees

It is seen from 1:1 that the letter is addressed to a number of churches in Asia Minor. The Christians in this area would have been converts from a predominantly Gentile population. The repeated references to their lives before baptism supports this position that they were mostly formerly Gentiles.

Situation

The churches to which this letter was directed were clearly undergoing some kind of "suffering" at the time of its composition. This is evident from what is stated in: 1:6; 2:12, 19; and 3:16. The majority of scholars believe this suffering was not the result of a state persecution, but rather verbal abuse and social distress arising from differences existing between Christians and the local Gentile population.

Purpose

The writer of this letter expresses his purpose in 5:12 as follows: "I write you this briefly through Silvanus, whom I consider a faithful brother, exhorting you and testifying that this is the true grace of God. Remain firm in it" (NABRE).

Exploring 1 Peter

Now it is time to explore the composition that is 1 Peter by means of satellites and drones. First, let us go into our satellite laboratory and examine the data that our satellite has provided for us. Doing this we find the following:

> 1:1-2 Salutation
> 1:3-5:11 Letter body
> 5:12-14 Closing greetings

On the basis of this satellite observation it is apparent that 1 Peter is a 1st century letter.

To gather more information about the body of this letter, let us bring out our drone once again and make a slow, low altitude overflight of it. Doing this provides the following interesting map of the letter body:

> 1:3-12 A blessing of God for what God has done
>> a. vv. 3-5 God has given us a new birth to a living hope
>> b. vv. 6-9 The genuineness of your faith will be tested
>> c. vv. 10-12 The message of this salvation was given to the prophets
>
> 1:13-2:10 On Christian conduct – Part A
>> a. 1:13-16 "Be holy because I am holy"
>> b. 1:17-21 Conduct yourselves with reverence
>> c. 1:22-25 Love one another
>> d. 2:1-3 Long for spiritual milk
>> e. 2:4-10 You are a people of his own so that you can manifest God's glory in the outside world
>
> 2:11-3:12 On Christian conduct – Part B
>> a. 2:11-17 Christian conduct in the outside world
>> b. 2:18-25 Conduct of Christian slaves toward their masters
>> c. 3:1-7 Conduct of Christian wives and husbands
>> d. 3:8-12 Conduct of Christians toward one another
>
> 3:13-22 On suffering for righteousness – Part A
>> a. 3:13-17 Suffering because of righteousness
>> b. 3:18-22 The resurrection of Christ and baptism
>
> 4:1-11 On Christian conduct – Part C
>> a. 4:1-6 Spend what remains of your life on the will of God
>> b. 4:7-11 Let your love for one another be intense
>
> 4:12-19 On suffering for righteousness – Part B
>> Those who suffer should do so according to God's will
>
> 5:1-11 On Christian conduct – Part D
>> a. 5:1-4 Counsel for Presbyters
>> b. 5:5-11 Counsel for the younger members

Investigating 1 Peter

Having completed our satellite and drone observations of 1 Peter, let us now investigate the letter using our tour bus to visit specific passages that should interest us.

Viewing 1 Peter as a letter

Stop #1 1:1

The salutation tells us that this letter is from Paul and "to the chosen sojourners of the dispersion in Pontus, Galatia, Cappadocia, Asia and Bithynia (NABRE)." This points out two aspects of the recipients of the letter. First, they are a chosen group of individuals. This has roots in the Old Testament and the concept of the Jews being the chosen people of God. The second factor is that it refers to the Christians as being "sojourners." The Greek term translated here applies to a person who is living in a strange land. It is used here, however, in a metaphorical sense to refer to people living on earth whose real home is in heaven.

The five areas referred to here are all areas in Asia Minor, present-day Turkey, which lie north of the Taurus Mountains. This is a large area – over 130,000 square miles.

Stop #2 5:12-14

Verse 12 declares that Peter is writing this letter "through Silvanus." This expression understood as indicating that Silvanus did the actual writing, serving as Peter's amanuensis. Some scholars take it to be a reference to delivery of the letter by Silvanus. The phrase "the chosen one at Babylon" in verse 13 indicates that the letter was written in Rome. "Babylon" was used as a code name for Rome in the latter part of the 1st century as is also seen in Revelation 14:8; 17:5; and 18:2.

Viewing 1 Peter as a historical document

Stop #1 4:3-4

People from Cappadocia, Pontus and Asia are reported in Acts 2:9 as having been present in Jerusalem at Pentecost. After having heard Peter's speech and after having talked to the people they met there. these individuals most likely returned home bearing the message of the Gospel. This initial association with the Gospel was probably later supplemented by Christian missionary activity. The passage 4:3-4 suggests that the people to whom this letter is written are recent converts from the Gentile community.

Stop #2 4:12-19

The suffering being spoken about in this passage is clearly that of the daily types of sufferings that are experienced by the Christian faithful in daily life. This is clearly stated in verse 4:14. Nowhere in this letter is there a reference to a widespread persecution of the Christian faithful. This view is confirmed by 5:8-11.

Stop #3 5:1-4

The mention of "presbyters" (presiders later called priests) in this section gives evidence that there was some structure in the Christian communities at the time this letter was written.

Stop #4 5:6-11

This passage clearly states that God cares for **you.** So when life becomes difficult you always have this to fall back on for support. As stated above in **Stop #2** the suffering spoken of is just the individual daily sort of things and not a state persecution.

1 Peter viewed as a writing that contains some theological material

Stop #1 1:3-5

Here we learn that God, the Father, has given us a new birth into a living hope through his Son, Jesus. Furthermore, God has given us an inheritance that is imperishable – that is kept in heaven for us. In addition, we are being protected by the power of God through faith.

Stop #2 1:13-16

This passage tells us that the reason we should strive to be holy is because the One who called us (God) is holy. Verse 16 is a quotation from Leviticus (11:44 and 19:2).

Stop #3 2:11-17

This passage is significant for us in 20th century United States. The question of obeying a government that dominates the people is currently of some interest. It encourages allegiance to a government that is good and God-fearing. People living in countries like Syria certainly have experienced the opposite at this time. It should be noted that Christians living in the 1st century had little hope of overthrowing the Roman domination.

Stop #4 3:18-22

This passage is theologically rich. It has something to say about Jesus and about the Christian believer. There is mention of baptism.

Stop #4 5:5-11

This passage contains advice to the younger members of the assembly.

This completes our investigation of 1 Peter.

CHAPTER FORTY-one

THE THREE LETTERS OF JOHN

Introducing 1, 2 and 3 John

Authorship by the apostle John

Let us start off with a question: "Why would anyone consider treating 1, 2, and 3 John along with Revelation?" Both 2 and 3 John are real letters. 1 John is not a letter at all. As to what type of composition it is, however, the scholars cannot agree. The writing known as Revelation begins with seven letters and ends with an apocalyptic writing which describes the last days of this world and the coming of a new world. They are grouped together on the basis of the traditional belief that all four of these writings were written by the same author – the apostle John.

Many scholars of the present day challenge the traditional belief of a common authorship by the apostle John. It is very unlikely, they say, that an apostle would ever take the position of an elder in a church. On the other hand, many other scholars claim that it would have been natural for an apostle to be an elder in the community. The word "apostle" means one who is sent out on a mission to spread the faith. The literary piece known as 1 John was most likely, they say, written after the completion of the Gospel of John either by the elder or by an individual belonging to the "Johannine" (in the tradition of John) circle of house churches. Even though the author of Revelation identifies himself as "John," some scholars argue that he is not John the apostle but some other John. These arguments can get rather ridiculous, in lieu of centuries of tradition with John the Beloved Disciple, author of John's gospel, as the real author!

So we see that these four writings are treated together because they are related to the apostle John. This comes about in the following manner. The three "letters" of John are compositions that are written in the same basic terminology and theological concepts that are found in the Gospel of John. They may not have the apostle John for their author, perhaps, but they are well within the Johannine school of thought. In regard to Revelation, the traditional belief in John's authorship still seems to have stronger support than any arguments to the contrary.

The interrelationship of 1, 2 and 3 John

Please take a moment to make the following three observations. First, observe that 1 John does not have any of the features of a 1st century letter. Neither the writer nor the addressees are identified at the beginning and it lacks any semblance of a usual ending. Even more significantly, it does not read like a typical letter. Secondly, 2 John and 3 John are typical letters written by the same individual – the elder (presbyter). The one, 2 John, is written to a house church, to the "elect lady" (woman in charge) and her children. 3 John, is written to an individual named Gaius. Finally, the three writings are arranged in the Scriptures by the same two principles as were the letters of Paul: longer before shorter and letters to house churches before letters to individuals.

A case can be made for taking the position that 1, 2 and 3 John were all written by the elder. First, the letters 2 and 3 John are clearly said to be from the elder. In 2 John, the elder uses the imagery of the church being a lady and the members being her children. In verse 1, the image is used to represent the church to which he is writing and it is used again in v.13 with reference to the elder's own church. The position that the elder is the author of 1 John is supported by two bits of evidence. First, the elder does state in 3 John that he has written "something to the church" which means that he was the one who wrote 1 John. Secondly, the four-fold reference to "children" in 1 John (2:1, 18; 3:18 and 5:21) can be understood as a use of this same imagery of a lady and her children as used in 2 John.

An interesting hypothesis has been put forward by a few scholars. First, 1 John is a formal (note the introduction vv.1-4) theological composition written either by the elder himself or by another individual in the Johannine sphere of influence. Secondly, 2 John was written to serve as a cover letter written by the elder to go along with the formal composition. Both these compositions were intended to be read together before the community. Finally, the elder wrote 3 John as a letter of recommendation for Demetrius, the individual who would carry the three writings to the church assembly.[201]

Now we come to an interesting point. The one who reads the three writings in the biblical order would most likely be reading them in the chronological order of their composition. The one, however, who approaches them in a reverse order – that is 3 John, 2 John, and 1 John – would most likely be reading these three compositions in the order in which the recipients first experienced them, if the hypothesis suggested above should turn out to be correct. This is the order that we follow now.

One further argument in support of following the reverse biblical order is that it allows 2 John and 3 John to come out from under the shadow of 1 John. By this, one is allowed to engage both 1 and 2 John as individual writings. It is interesting to view them as such.

3 JOHN

Investigating 3 John

The letter of 3 John is the shortest book in the New Testament. It does not have chapters; it only has verses – 15 of them. We sent out our mapping helicopter and it has just returned with the following outline:

v.1	Salutation
v.2	Prayer for good health for Gaius
vv.3-4	Visit of the brothers
vv.5-8	The manner in which Gaius should treat the brothers
vv. 9-10	Diotrophes spreads evil about the elder and obstructs the brothers
v.11	Imitate what is good – Observe the chiastic structure here (abb'a')
v.12	recommendation of Demetrios

---

[201] Luke Timothy Johnson, *The Writings of the New Testament*, Third Edition (Minneapolis, MN: Fortress Press, 2010), 497-498.

vv. 13-14   The elder expresses his wish to visit them
v.15   Final greetings

3 John viewed as a literary piece

The composition that is 3 John is the shortest written document in the New Testament. The Greek text includes only 219 words or 251 words in the NABRE English translation. Its length is about equal to that of a typical 1st century letter and it is short enough to fit on a single sheet of papyrus.

Observe that verses 1-2 are characteristic of salutations and verses 13-15 are elements characteristic of letter closings. Since the remainder, vv.3-12 reads like the body of a letter it is natural to recognize 3 John as a real letter.

3 John viewed as an historical document

In approaching 3 John as an historical document it is helpful to first identify the people who are featured in the letter. These are the following individuals:

The elder (presbyter) – The Greek word translated as "elder" can indicate one who has some authority in a community or someone who is simply of an advanced age

Gaius – The individual to whom this letter was sent. Gaius was a very common name in the 1st century and nothing is known about this particular individual.

Diotrophes – A member of the same house church assembly as Gaius. He opposed the elder in two ways. First, he apparently did not accept the authority of the elder (9). Secondly, he actively opposed people in the assembly who tried to give hospitality to the brothers (here missionaries) and even tried to have them expelled from the assembly.

Demetrius –The individual who is being recommended by the elder. Many scholars hold that it was he who brought these three writings to Gaius and his house church.

The "brothers" – This term was frequently used by Paul to refer to the members of a house church. In this letter, however, the term is applied to a group of traveling missionaries who are working to spread the gospel (3, 5-8, 10).

The "friends" – This term is used in verse 15 to indicate people who are in a particularly close relationship with each other, even bordering on true brotherly love.

318

3. John viewed as a writing that contains some theological material

What is the purpose of verse 11? This verse appears to be a wisdom saying. Observe the form of this saying; it has a chiastic structure in the pattern ABB'A'. It could have been placed between Diotrophes and Demetrius to emphasize that one of these individuals is evil and the other one is good. It might have been more effective if the translators had placed it in a paragraph of its own between verses 9-10 and verse 12.

This completes our investigation of 3 John.

2 JOHN

Investigating 2 John

As we did with 3 John, let us call upon our mapping helicopter to make a fly-over of the composition. So, this results in the following outline:

1-3	Salutation
4-6	The commandment: love one another
7-11	Those who deny that Jesus came in the flesh
12	Writers desire to come in person
13	Final greetings

Because this letter is so short, let as move right away to viewing it from three different viewpoints.

2 John viewed as a literary composition

It is evident right away that 2 John is a typical 1st century letter. Verses 1-3 are the salutation, verses 12 and 13 constitute the final greetings leaving verses 4-11 to make up the body.

Equally evident is the fact that this is a short letter, only 245 words in the original Greek text and thus only missing out on the "title for shortest letter" by 27 words. Its length is, however, 291 words in the NABRE English translation which is 40 words longer than the NABRE English text of 3 John. Thus, we find once again that modern English is much more wordy than ancient Greek.

It is seen that 2 John is from the elder (presbyter), most likely the same individual who wrote 3 John. In this case it is addressed to "the chosen lady and to her children" which is clearly a metaphor for a house church and its members. The elder uses the same metaphor when speaking of his church in verse 13 as "your chosen sister and her children."

2 John viewed as a historical document
and as a writing that contains some theological material

In this brief letter, the historical and theological materials are intermingled. It is not possible to separate the one from the other. Because of this happenstance, we will treat them both together.

It is easily seen that the body of the letter is divided into three parts. The first part, vv. 4-6, presents the good teaching. It is good that some of the children (members of the community) are walking in the truth, but all of the children need to love one another more. The second part, v.7, calls to the reader's attention that many deceivers have gone out into the world and are teaching that Christ did not come in the flesh – an early form of a heresy called Docetism. The third part, vv.8-11, counsels the "children" that if one of these deceivers should come to their house not to receive him into the house or even to greet him. The elder is concerned that the "children" will lose what they have worked for and will not receive a full recompense. Notice that at this point the Elder has put a bit of eschatology into his presentation.

This concludes our investigation of 2 John.

1 John

Investigating 1 John

Let us go into our satellite lab and to analyze the satellite data that relates to 1 John. So, this results in disappointment. The data obtained by satellite does not reveal an overall form such as a letter. This result seems to confirm the efforts of the scholars who have been unable to agree on a specific form for 1 John as well as the elder's own assessment that: "I have written something" (3 John v.9).

So let's fire up our drone and see if a closer look will reveal anything about the structure of 1 John. Analysis of the data gathered in our drone flight results in the following outline of the content of 1 John:

1:1-4	Prologue – the Word of life
1:5-2:2	Walking in the light
2:3-11	Keeping his commands
2:12-17	The new status of believers and their relation to the world
2:18-27	A warning against anti-Christs
2:28-33 3:4-10	The sinless-ness of God's children
3:11-18	Brotherly love as the mark of the Christian
3:19-24	Assurance and our confidence in God
4:1-6	The spirits of truth and falsehood
4:7-12	God's love and our love
4:13-5:4	Assurance and Christian love
5:5-12	The true faith confirmed
5:13-21	Christian certainties[202]

---

[202] I. Howard Marshall, *The Epistles of John* (Grand Rapids, MI: William B. Eerdmans Publishing Company, 1978), 26.

Please keep in mind that this is not the only possible outline. Just as the scholars do not agree on what literary form 1 John has, they also disagree over outlining its contents.

Viewing 1 John as a literary composition

Stop #1 1:4

Notice the use of the construction "We are writing ….So that."

Stop #2 1:12

Notice the construction "I am writing to you …. Because."

Stop #3 5:13

Notice the construction "I write these things to…."

Explanation: This composition provides information to us with the use of a frequently used formula. As one reads through it, one quite often encounters a formula that begins with "I am writing" and ends with the phrases: "so that," and "because" and "to." The use of this formula provides the reader with useful information. We learn that the writer is aiming his efforts at the Christian members of the community, the ones who did not leave – see 5:13. He is writing so that his joy may be complete (1:4) and so that his readers may not sin (2:1). He is writing to children, fathers and young people because he knows something good about them (2:12-14). And he is writing because he knows that they know the truth and that no lie comes from the truth (2:21). Finally, he is writing to them because he is concerned that those who infiltrate into to their community will possibly deceive them and will seek to teach something other than the truth (2:26).

Viewing 1 John as a historical document

Stop #1 2:26

A clue to the major problem confronting the church, which the elder is targeting, is provided in 2:26 where it is stated that the elder's concern is with those who would deceive the members of the congregation. We have to go back to verse 2:18 to see what took place.

Stop #2 2:18-19

It is evident from these verses that a group of members had broken away and gone out on their own. The people who left most likely had friends who remained in the church. They would, therefore, still maintain some relationship with their former group and thus would have some opportunity for continuing to influence their friends. Thus, there was a danger for the members who remained, and were subjected to this continuing influence to gradually lose their faith and to leave themselves, at some later time. The elder is writing to prevent this from happening. That is the historical moment in which this composition was written.

Viewing 1 John as a writing that contains some theological material

Stop #1 1:1-4

This prologue is similar to the prologue of the Gospel of John. This prologue, however, features the apostle's experience of the life of Jesus. In the original Greek these four verses are a single sentence.

Stop #2 1:5-7

This passage tells us that God is light and in God there is no darkness. If we are to have fellowship with God we also must walk in the light.

Stop #3 2:15-17

Here we are instructed not to love the world or the things of the world. The reason for this is that anyone who does so does not have the love of the Father in him.

Stop #4 2:24-25

In these two verses the elder reminds his readers that Jesus Christ has promised his followers eternal life.

Stop #5 3:1-3

This passage has much to say about God's love for the people who believe in him. But take note of the fact that there is an obligation involved.

Stop #6 4:7-12

God has shown God's love for us by sending us the Son of God - Jesus Christ.
But it also tells us that if God so loved us then we must love one another.

Stop #7 4:16b-18

God is love.

Stop #8 5:1-5

This passage tells us that the one who is victor over the world is the one who believes that Jesus is the Son of God.

Stop #9 5:13-15

These verses present to us the welcome news that God will answer our prayers!

This completes our investigation of 1 John.

CHAPTER FORTY-two

REVELATION

Introduction

No book in the Bible is as full of imagery to engage the senses of the readers as is the book of Revelation. It speaks of: "four living creatures, each of them with six wings, are full of eyes all around and inside" (4:8, NRSV); white, bright red, black and pale green horses (6:1-8); a beast that comes up from the bottom of a pit (11:7); a "great red dragon, with seven heads and ten horns, and seven diadems on his heads" (12:3, NRSV); myriads and myriads of angels (5:11; a Lamb (7:10) and a woman clothed with the sun (12:1); earthquakes (8:5), stars falling from heaven (8:10) and a great mountain that was burning with fire (8:8).

At the same time, no book of the Bible has presented so many difficulties to its understanding. The many different theories as to its literary structure testify to the difficulty of understanding the book of Revelation. So varied are these theories, G.K.Chesterton once remarked:

> Though St. John the Evangelist saw many strange monsters in his vision, he saw no creature so wild as one of his own commentators.[203]

Definition of Terms

There is considerable confusion between the terms: apocalypse, apocalyptic, and apocalypticism. It is useful, therefore, to begin by defining terms.

A good definition of the term "apocalypse" is the following:

> A group headed by J. J. Collins expanded on earlier studies of the genre apocalypse by analyzing all of the texts classifiable as apocalypses from the period 250 B.C.E. to 250 C.E. and concluded with this definition: " 'Apocalypse' is a genre of revelatory literature with a narrative framework, in which a revelation is mediated by an other-worldly being to a human recipient, disclosing a transcendent reality which is both temporal, insofar as it envisages eschatological salvation, and spatial, insofar as it involves another, supernatural world"[204]

Chapters 7-12 of the book of Daniel and the book of Revelation are examples of this genre in the Bible. Chapters 1-6 of Zechariah and the book of Ezekiel also display many of the characteristics of an apocalypse.

---

[203] Quoted in Paul J, Achtemeier, Joel B. Green, Marianne Meye Thompson, *Introducing the New Testament*, (Grand Rapids: William B. Eerdmans Publishing Company 2001), 555-556.
[204] Paul D. Hanson: "Apocalypses and Apocalypticism" in *The Anchor Bible Dictionary*, V.1 (New York: Doubleday, 1992), 279.

Eschatology is the term used for the study of the events of the end-time, the final days of the world. Apocalyptic eschatology is a view of the end-time which sees the judgment of the wicked and the vindication of the just but holds that this can only come about through the destruction of this world and the resurrection of the faithful to a happy existence in heaven.[205]

Finally, the term "apocalypticism" is a term that describes a movement. It is a movement that is based upon the world view of apocalyptic eschatology as its ideology.[206]

Historical Context

Apocalypses are most often addressed to those living in times of suffering and persecution – so desperate that they are seen as the embodiment of supreme evil. If history is laid out in a pattern of divinely determined periods (enumerated in various ways), the author is living in the last of them. Hope of a historical solution has disappeared in favor of a direct divine intervention that will bring all to an end. Very often in a strongly dualistic approach, the apocalyptist envisions what is happening on earth as part of a titanic struggle in the other world between God or God's angels and Satan and his angels. In some apocalypses pseudonymity is a factor. The writer takes the name of a famous figure from antiquity, e.g., Daniel, a legendary wise man; Enoch, who was taken up to heaven; or Ezra, the great lawgiver[207]..

Purpose

Apocalyptic eschatology is a way of viewing divine plans in relation to mundane realities; God's final salvific acts are conceived of a deliverance out of the present order (see for example Is 65:17). The key to understanding the purpose of apocalyptic literature lies in understanding the origin of this eschatology.

Apocalyptic eschatology developed from prophetic eschatology. In prophetic eschatology the divine plan and acts were seen as being effected primarily through mundane events and human persons. As historical events and sociological conditions made it increasingly difficult to make this identification, and as the vision of ancient myth began to offer world-weary individuals a means of resolving the tension between brilliant hopes and bleak realities people tended more and more to favor the viewpoint of apocalyptic eschatology over that of prophetic eschatology. As this tendency progressed, apocalyptic movements arose which developed symbolic universes and apocalyptic eschatologies in protest against the symbolic universes adhered to by the societies within which the movements arose. An apocalyptic movement is, therefore, by nature a minority phenomenon.

---

[205] Hanson, 280-281.
[206] Hanson, 281.
[207] Raymond E. Brown, *An Introduction To The New Testament* (New York: Doubleday, 1997), 776.

It is in this context that we encounter the specific purpose of the apocalyptic literature. The apocalyptic movements were not concerned with systematic consistency. They were concerned with the immediate crisis which was most often one of considerable severity. The primary and immediate concern was to establish the identity of the members of the movement within the hostile environment and to both create and sustain hope for deliverance. The essential point here is that the apocalyptic literature was intended to bring latent hope to full flower (Hope is a theological virtue and as such exists in every Christian although it is frequently not well developed.)

Let us examine this point in more detail. Look for a moment at some of the situations in which apocalyptic movements have arisen. There is, of course, the case of the community within which the book of Daniel originated. This community existed at a time when Judaism was divided into two groups, the Hasidim and the Hellenizers, by the attempts of the Greeks to impose Greek culture on the Jews (early 2nd century BCE). Then, there is the case of the Christian community within which the book of Revelation originated. This was a community facing the threat of persecution. Again, in the Middle Ages when the Jews were expelled from Spain, a very traumatic experience that was considered by the Jews of that time as an Exodus. An apocalyptic community arose at that time a flourished for a time.

If one takes the position that the apocalyptic literature of these communities arose out of a need to **sustain** hope, then we must picture a community of people under great stress going about filled with the "glow" hope and we must picture the apocalyptic writings as issuing spontaneously from this. This picture does not ring true.

It rather seems more likely that a somewhat different situation prevailed. Consider a community under great stress within which there is great fear and trembling about one's survival from day to day, or a group of persons beset by worries about what the future holds in store for them. Within that community there is an individual who has confidence in the future and who possesses abundant genuine hope and who wants to share it with the other persons in the community. It is from this individual, with the intention of raising up in other people a firm hope similar to his or her own, that the apocalyptic writing arises. If this person is successful, **hope is brought to full flower in persons where it only existed in seed before.**

Genre

What is the genre of the book of revelation? Consider the following observations:

- Overall it appears to have the form of a letter: the author identifies himself and his recipients in 1:4-4-5 and there is a letter like closing in 22:21.
- The author refers to his writing as prophecy (1:3).
- It starts out with seven letters to seven churches (Chapters 2 and 3).
- The author states that he has received a teaching from God through both Jesus Christ and an angel sent to him by Christ (1:1).
- The author has a vision (1:10-11) and some of the things he saw are explained to him by an angel (1:20-21).

325

It would appear, therefore, that basically the book of Revelation is a letter. This conclusion is supported by the observation that if you mark, in order, the seven cities named in Chapters 2 and 3 you will find that they make a circle which suggests that this was a circular letter. Within the letter form, however, some of the contents are written in the genre of apocalypse.

Author

The author refers to himself as John. Tradition has identified the John here with John, the son of Zebedee, the apostle. Modern scholars reject this identification and propose that the author is some other, unknown, John.

It is interesting to note that many modern scholars accept "John" as the name of the author and then argue that the book lacks the basic characteristic of an apocalypse – namely, pseudonymity. This problem would seem to disappear if one were to take the position that the book was written by an anonymous believer in the name of John the Apostle.

Date

On the basis of the following evidence:
- The most reliable external evidence is a statement by Irenaeus that the book was seen at the end of the reign of the emperor Domitian (81-96 CE).
- The clearest internal evidence suggests a date after the destruction of the Temple in 70 CE.

It would, therefore, seem that the book is most reasonably dated to 95-96 CE.[208]

Unity

The majority of modern-day scholars take the position that the book of Revelation is a unity. This position is based upon the uniformity of style and vocabulary. It is also based on the closely-knit character of the book.[209] This is one reason why many scholars attribute the authorship to evangelist John.

Outline of Contents

To get some idea of the overall content of the book let it suffice to follow Raymond Brown in his *An Introduction to The New Testament*[210]:

---

[208] Adela Yarbro Collins, "Book of Revelation" in The *Anchor Bible Dictionary*, Vol. V (New York: Doubleday, 1992), 701.

[209] E.F. Siegman and J. Winkler: "Book of Revelation" in *The New Catholic Encyclopedia*, 2nd Edition, V. 12 (Detroit, Michigan: Thomson/Gale Group, 2003), 185.

[210] Raymond E. Brown, *An Introduction To The New Testament* (New York: Doubleday, 1997), 774.

- Prologue: 1:1-3

- Letters to the Seven Churches: 1:4-3:22
  - Opening Formula with attached praise, promise, and divine response (1:4-8)
  - Inaugural Vision (1:9-20)
  - Seven Letters (2:1-3:22)

- Part I of the Revelatory Experience: 4:1-11:19
  - Visions of the Heavenly Court: The One Enthroned and the Lamb (4:1-5:14)
  - Seven Seals (6:1-8:1)
  - Seven Trumpets (8:2-11:19)

- Part II of the Revelatory Experience: 12:1-22:5
  - Visions of the Dragon, the Beasts, and the Lamb ((12:1-14:20)
  - Seven Plagues and Seven Bowls (15:1-16:21)
  - Judgment of Babylon, the Great Harlot (17:1-19:10)
  - Victory of Christ and the End of History (19:11-22:5)

- Epilogue (with Concluding Blessing): 22:6-21.

Structure of the Book

The structure of the book of Revelation is much debated. There are two basic approaches: 1) a linear approach in which the visions are taken to be consecutive, and 2) an approach which takes the later visions to in some way recapitulate the earlier visions. Because of the many ways the details of the structure have been worked out by various scholars, a careful treatment of this aspect of the book is, therefore, not possible within the time limits imposed upon a one semester course.

The following is a brief listing of some of the ways the structure of Revelation has been understood[211]:

- The patchwork theory – The book is understood to be a compilation of different sources which have not been welded into a consistent whole.
- The poetic theory – The book is understood to be the work of a visionary prophet and poet. The author is not concerned with casting his work in a logically worked out plan.
- The symbolism theory – The author's design is exposed in terms of the symbolism of the book.

---

[211] Donald Guthrie, *New Testament Introduction*, Fourth Edition (Revised) (Downers Grove, IL: Intervarsity Press, 1990), 970-977.

- The drama theory – The book consists of a prologue, a seven act play and an epilogue.
- The sevenfold design theory – The number seven is the key to the structure of the book.
- Transposition theories – The two most prominent attempts to understand the visions on a consecutive basis both achieve their ends by making rearrangements of the text.
- The liturgical pattern theory – This theory holds that underlying the book is a primitive form of the Paschal Vigil.
- The concentric theory – This theory seeks to find in the book a concentric structure. Thus 1:1-8 is seen as corresponding to 22:10-21; 1:9-3:22 is seen to correspond to 19:11-22:9 and so on.
- The historical-prophetic theory – This approach regards the whole book as pointing ahead to the first advent of Christ.

Guthrie observes that there is probably an element of truth in most of these theories but it is impossible to determine if the entire book can be explained in terms of any one of them.

Use of Biblical Images

One prominent feature of the book of Revelation is the use of imagery available in the OT. It has been estimated that in the 404 verses of Revelation there are some 518 citations of and allusions to the OT. Eighty-eight of them are from Daniel. Others are from Isaiah, Jeremiah, Ezekiel, Zechariah, Psalms and Exodus.[212]

Overall, when reading Revelation, one notices different literary forms: seven letters and a true apocalyptic writing. In the beginning, the reader learns about what will happen soon (1:1-3). Next, there follows a somewhat longer introduction to the seven letters (1: 4 – 20). The churches are: Ephesus, Smyrna, Pergamum, Thyatira, Sardis, Philadelphia, and Laodicea – all churches in Asia Minor (now modern-day Turkey). These letters speak to the churches about what they have done well and where they have not done so well. The letters to the churches are then followed first by a vision of heavenly worship (chapter 4) which is followed by a vision of the scroll and the Lamb (Christ). Then, the narrative moves into full apocalyptic mode (chapters 6 – 20) after which the writing speaks of a new heaven and a new earth including a new Jerusalem. The writing then concludes with a brief epilogue (22:6 – 21). Notice the "river of life-giving water" and the "tree of life" that is now given to the faithful (22:11 – 2). It is also noteworthy that the Lamb is now the Bridegroom at a wedding meaning the faithful are now his spouse. (Rev 19: 6-9) All that occurred in the Old Testament and was prophesied, and all that Christ taught and did on earth and in his death and resurrection are now come to completion!

Selected Readings from the Apocalyptic Literature in the Bible.

Dan 12 This chapter speaks about the end of time. Note that it includes a resurrection of **some** of the dead.

---

[212] E.F. Siegman and J. Winkler, 186.

Rev 4   This chapter tells us about God: God is eternal (v9), God is creator (v11) and God is all powerful (v11). A good lesson to learn: The primary literary source of the NT is the OT! Observe that verse 8 of this chapter seems to be based upon Is 6:3. To fully understand the meaning of the NT it is absolutely essential to have a thorough knowledge of the OT.

Suggested Reading

Paul D. Hanson, A. Kirk Grayson, John J. Collins, Adela Yarbro Collins, "Apocalypses and Apocalypticism" in *Anchor Bible Dictionary*, V 1 (New York, Doubleday, 1992), 279-292. These five articles, on five aspects of apocalyptic literature, presented under this heading are written by experts in the field and are very informative. They are well worth the time it takes to read them.

CHAPTER FORTY-three

JUDE AND 2 PETER

Our approach to the study of Jude and 2 Peter will be based upon one important result of modern scholarly analysis of the two texts. Most modern scholars agree on holding the position that there is a literary relationship between the two writings. It is held that the author of 2 Peter borrowed from Jude. Our approach to these two writings is based upon acceptance of this scholarly position.

Our analysis will, therefore, take place in three steps. First, Jude will be investigated as a writing that stands on its own. Secondly, a case will be made to establish that the writer of 2 Peter did indeed make use of the text of Jude in formulating his composition. Finally, 2 Peter will be investigated.

Introducing Jude

It is easily seen that Jude is a short composition. Indeed, it is so short that it has not been divided into chapters. It consists of only 25 verses. It is also seen that it is a letter since it begins with a salutation (v.1) which is followed with an expression of a wish for mercy, peace and love for the recipients and its ends with a benediction (vv.24-25).

The salutation informs us that the writer of this letter is Jude and identifies him as the brother of James. If this "James" is understood to be "the brother of the Lord" who became important in the Jerusalem church, then Jude would be the Jude who also was a brother of the Lord.

This brings us to a difficult point. Scholarly studies of the content of this letter seem to show that the letter fits more comfortably into the period at the end of the 1st century than it does into a time that is close to the lifetime of Jesus. If this assessment is accepted, then someone living late in the 1st century has written it under the name of Jude, the Lord's brother. That is … the letter is pseudonymous. This is the position that is accepted by a majority of modern scholars. There is also a minor opinion, that the content of the letter was passed along in oral tradition and then later written down.

The date that is assigned to the letter clearly depends upon one's position as to its authorship. If the writer was Jude, the Lord's brother, then it would most likely have been written before 70 CE. If, however, it was written by someone under Jude's name then it would have been written sometime in the period 80-100 CE.

There are numerous references to Jewish literature – both canonical and non-canonical. There are references to Jewish biblical writings in: v.5 to Num 14:29-37; v.6 to Gen 6:1-4; v.7 to Gen 19; v.9 to Deut 34:5-6; V.11 to Gen 4, Num 22-25 and num 16. Verses 8 and 9 seem to reference a non-canonical writing known as the *Assumption of Moses* and vv.14-15 seem to be based on 1 Enoch, a non-canonical sacred writing.

Investigating Jude

Our drone is all fueled up, so let's send it out on a low and slow flight to obtain information about the body of this letter. Doing this we obtain the following outline (but remember there are no chapters; only verses!):

> Verses 3-4 Occasion of the letter
> Verses 5-16 The intruders
> > a. 5-7 God always punishes sinners
> > b. 8-10 The intruders are described
> > c. 11-13 Author denounces the intruders
> Verses 14-16 Author tells the readers of a prophecy
> Verses 17-19 Author reminds the readers of the Apostolic predictions
> Verses 20-23 Author tells the readers how to react to the intruders

Jude viewed as a letter

Stop #1 Verse 1a

This first verse states that the writer of the letter is Jude a brother of James. It has already been said that if James is taken to be James the brother of the Lord, then the Jude who wrote this letter is the Jude who is also a brother of Jesus.

Stop #2 Verse 1b

This statement announces to whom this letter is written. It is such a non-specific statement, however, that any less general identification of the recipients is a matter of speculation.

Jude viewed as a historical document

Stop #1 Verses 3-4

In these verses the writer informs the reader that he has altered his original plan to write to them about the salvation that they share and instead he is going to write about some intruders who have "stolen in among you." Jude tells the readers that these intruders deny Jesus Christ and pervert the grace of God into licentiousness.

Stop #2 Verses 8 and 10

In these verses we learn a little bit more about the activity of the intruders, who are now identified as dreamers. We are told that they: defile the flesh; reject authority; slander the faithful ones; and they slander whatever they do not understand.

Stop #3 Verse 12

On the basis of this verse it seems that the intruders are fellow Christians because they are admitted to the community meals.

Stop #4 Verses 17-19

Behind this verse is the belief of the faithful that Jesus' return would not be long in coming. Jude recalls a teaching of the apostles that in the last time there would be scoffers and that it is these persons who are causing divisions within the community of believers.

Jude viewed as a writing containing theological material

Stop #1 Verses 20-23

In these verses Jude gives his readers a number of counsels as to how to deal with their situation. These counsels are easily seen to be good for the Christians of the present day.

Stop #2 Verses 24 and 25

The benediction is interesting for the concepts and imagery that it employs. There is something to be gained to consult a bible commentary and bible dictionary with regard to this passage because it appears to be a doxology – a lovely prayer that may have been a part of an early prayer service.

This completes our investigation of the Letter of Jude.

Introducing 2 peter

The New Testament includes two letters attributed to Peter in its canon. They differ, however, as to length, literary form and in quality of Greek grammar. For these reasons, most biblical scholars agree in holding the position that these two compositions were not written by the same author.

The very first verse in the composition that is titled 2 Peter states that it is written by Peter, the apostle of Jesus Christ. Acceptance of 2 Peter into the canon, however, met with considerable resistance in the early Christian assemblies. As late as the 5th Century some of the local churches still refused to grant it acceptance as a holy and inspired writing. The major cause of this delay seems to be that there was some doubt as to its being an authentic writing of St. Peter. Today, many scholars hold the position that 2 Peter is a pseudonymous writing. Let us not make a decision on this matter here. Let us pursue it in the course of our investigations of this composition.

Investigation of 2 Peter

Let us once gain go into our satellite data laboratory and analyze the data. If we do this we find that 2 Peter appears to our satellite to be a short letter:

        1:1-2 Salutation
        1:3-3:18a letter body
        3:18b Doxology

It is easily seen that the salutation is unusually lengthy and that the closing is unusually brief!

An overflight by drone at slow speed and low altitude results in the following outline of what appears to be the letter body:

1: 3-11 A brief presentation of the Christian life
    1. 1:3-4 The acts of God in salvation history
    2. 1:5-9 Support your faith with seven virtues
    3. 1:10-11 Make your calling and election sure
1:12-15 Peter's testament
1:16-19a Author says he was an eye witness of the transfiguration
1:19b-21 True prophecy comes from God
2:1-22 False teachers bring destruction
    1. 2:1-3 They are doctrinally unsound and morally corrupt
    2. 2:4-10a History foreshadows the false teachers
    3. 2:10b-16 Lust and irreverence determine their behavior
    4. 2:17-22 Their promise of freedom is actually slavery to sin
3:1-13 A explanation for why Christ has not returned as he promised
    1. 3:1-2 Introduction
    2. 3:3-4 Scoffers will ask: "Why hasn't Christ returned?"
    3. 3:5-7 The present earth has been reserved for fire
    4. 3:8-10 The Lord is not slow; the Lord is patient!
    5. 3:11-13 We wait for new heavens and a new earth – what sort of people should we be while we wait?
3:14-18a What to do while waiting for Christ to return

Let us move on and look at 2 Peter first as a letter, then as an historical document and finally as writing that contains some theological content.

2 Peter viewed as a letter

Stop #1 1:1-2

This salutation informs the reader that this letter is from Symeon Peter and is to a very general audience. Symeon is a less typical Greek transliteration of the Hebrew name "Simon." The lack of a specific designation of addressees could be an indication that this letter was intended for a wide audience.

Stop #2 3:1

In this verse the writer states that this is the second letter that he has written to them. Could the writer be aware of 1 Peter and, consequently, be referring to this as his second letter? If that is the case then the recipients could well be the same ones designated in 1 Peter, that is: the believers living in Pontus, Galatia, Cappadocia, Asia and Bithynia.

2 Peter viewed as a historical document

Stop #1 1:12-15

333

In verse 14 the writer of the letter states that Jesus has revealed to him that his death is soon to come. That statement makes it clear to the reader that the body of the letter is written as a testament (or as sometimes called: a farewell address). The literary genre of the testament is found a number of times in the Old Testament. For example: Jacob in Genesis 49; Moses in Deuteronomy 33:1-29; Joshua in Joshua Chapter 24. This genre is also found in the New Testament: Jesus in Luke 22:14-36 and in John chapters 13-17; and Paul in Acts 20:17-35. This letter is written in the form of Peter's testament.

Formal analyses of the testaments that appear in the Scriptures have identified a number of common features in them. Knowledge of these common elements is helpful in seeing that 2 Peter has this literary form. These elements are the following:

1. Prediction of death or departure
2. Predictions of future crises for followers
3. Virtues urged; ideal behavior prescribed
4. Commission
5. Legacy[213]

Can these elements be identified in 2 Peter? The answer is: Yes. The author identifies his approaching death in 1:14. He predicts future attacks on the group by false teachers and false prophets in 2:1-3 and 3:1-7. He urges the virtue of faithfulness in 1-4, 16-18 and in 3:1-2. There is an implied commission in that some individual will read this letter to the members of the assembly. Finally, he leaves a legacy, namely, the truth about God's just judgment (2:4-10 and 3:8-10) and by calling for the correct reading of Paul's letters (3:15-16).[214]

Does the apparent fact that this letter was written in the form of Peter's testament prove that it was written by Peter himself? A careful reading of the body of the letter will reveal that the answer is no.

Stop #2 1:16-18

These verses clearly state that the writer of the letter declares himself to have been present at the Transfiguration of Jesus. Does the writing of this letter in the form of Peter's testament and the statement that the author was present at the Transfiguration of Jesus establish conclusively that it was written by Peter himself? Withhold your decision until you have visited the next two stops.

Stop #3 3:3-4a

The fact that the writer is stating here that a delay in the return of Jesus was predicted indicates that such a delay has actually occurred at the time of his writing.

Stop #4 3: 8-9

Here the writer presents an explanation for the delay in the return of Jesus that is taking place at the time of his writing. Recall that in 1 Thessalonians 4:15 and 4:17 Paul stated

---

[213] Jerome H. Neyrey, *2 Peter, Jude* (New York, NY: Doubleday, 1993),164.
[214] Neyrey, 164

that he expected to be alive at the time when Jesus returned. Talk of a delay in Jesus' coming would have been impossible, therefore, in the lifetime of Peter. Consequently, Peter could not be the person writing this letter.

Stop #4 3:14-16

Notice that in verse 3:16 Paul's letters are referred to as scripture! Paul's letters were not referred to as scripture until the end of the 1st century. In the first 60 years of the 1st century, the only scriptures of the Christians were the scriptures of the Jews. There was no New Testament in those years! This remark would seem to indicate that the writer of this letter is writing in the latter part of the 1st century.

2 Peter viewed as a writing containing some theological material

Stop #1 1:3-11

This passage is a very meaningful exposition of the Christian life. It is worthy of exploring it with the aid of a commentary. Note especially the message of verse eleven.

Stop #2 3:3-7

This passage provides support for those who may become disheartened that the day of the return of Jesus has not yet come. One must have patience and hope.

Stop #3 3:11-13

This passage counsels us to live lives of holiness and godliness while waiting for the day of God. Note also that it speaks of waiting for new heavens and a new earth which is an expression found also in Revelation.

This completes our investigation of the composition known as 2 Peter.

Exploring a possible literary relationship between Jude and 2 Peter

There is one further aspect of Jude and 2 Peter that remains to be explored. That is the possibility that there exists a literary relationship between them. Put another way, it is held by many scholars that either Jude borrowed from 2 Pater or that 2 Peter borrowed from Jude. Let us first examine the evidence which supports the position that a literary relationship exists between these two writings.

The most easily observed evidence for such a relationship is the existence of material in the two writings that is very close in both in wording and content. Consider the following:

Jude 4 = 2 Pet 2:1-3	Jude 11 = 2:15
Jude 6 = 2 Pet 2:4	Jude 12 = 2:13
Jude 7 = 2 Pet 2:6	Jude 12-13 = 2 Pet 2:17
Jude 8 = 2 Pet 2:10a	Jude 16 = 2 Pet 2:18
Jude 9 = 2 Pet 2:11	Jude 17 = 2 Pet 3:1-2

Jude 10 = 2Pet 2:12   Jude 18 = 2 Pet 3:3[215]

Another bit of evidence that borrowing was involved between these two writings is the presence in the text of rare Greek expressions in parallel passages of these writings. Consider the following six examples:

"blemishes" in Jude 12:2 and 2 Pet 2:13
"carouse together" in Jude 12 and 2 Pet 2 Pet 2:13
"waterless" in Jude 12-13 and 2 Pet 2:17
"loud boasts" or "bombast" in Jude 16 and 2 Pet 2:18
"scoffers" in Jude 18 and 2 Pet 3:3[216]

Several indications are available for deciding the question as to which way the borrowing took place. First, the order of the Old Testament events specified in Jude 5-7 is not in chronological order whereas they are in 2 Pet 2:4-10. It is more likely that 2 Peter borrowed from Jude and arranged them in their proper order than that the reverse would have transpired.

Also, 2 Pet 2:4-10 includes the theme of God's mercy to the righteous alongside the theme of condemnation toward the wicked. It is more likely that 2 Peter would have added the theme of God's mercy toward the righteous than that Jude would have deliberately have omitted it in his composition.

Finally, the mention of extracanonical writings (writings not included in the canon of the Bible) in Jude but not in 2 Peter argues in favor of the writer of 2 Peter being the borrower since it is more likely that a person would omit them rather than that someone would add them to his composition.

On the basis of these three observations the issue of who did the borrowing would seem to be decided in favor of the writer of 2 Peter.[217] That is, the writer of 2 Peter used the letter of Jude as a literary source.

This concludes our exploration and investigation of both Jude and 2 Peter and that is where the scholarly debate stands in the present day.

In conclusion

We have come to the end of our brief explorations in these concluding New Testament writings. It should be obvious that they present much to think about and they point to many problems that exist in Christianity and the world today. They are precious writings that should be read and studied along with the rest of the holy Bible!

---

[215] Daniel J. Harrington S.J., "Jude and 2 Peter" in *Sacra Pagina*, V. 15 (Collegeville, MN: The Liturgical Press, 2003), 162.

[216] Harrington, 162.

[217] Harrington, 162-163.

CHAPTER FORTY-four

THE HEART OF THE NEW TESTAMENT

Introduction

We have observed that the OT consists of 39 books (Protestant canon) or 46 books (Catholic canon) or 47 books (Eastern Orthodox canon) of a variety of literary types: historical narratives, prophetic collections, wisdom writings, folk tales and collections of psalms. It was noted that many of these writings came into being over long periods of time, in some cases more than a thousand years. Given the variety of types of writings and the very long historical periods over which they had been composed, it seemed improbable that there would be a heart. Nevertheless, we went in search of a heart and surprisingly we were successful. We discovered that the event of the Exodus and the making of a covenant at Sinai constituted the real heart of the OT Scriptures.

Now we turn our attention to the NT. It seems only natural to make our next goal that of answering the same two questions in regard to the NT that we just answered with regard to the OT. Does the NT have a heart? And if so, what is that heart? Our prospects of finding a heart would certainly seem to be much better than they were in the case of the OT. The period of time over which the NT was written is only some 75 years (50 - 125 CE) and the number of differing literary forms in which the NT is written is considerably less, containing only primarily gospels, history, letters and apocalyptic passages.

We found that the heart of the OT consisted of two parts: an event, the **Exodus,** and **the making of a covenant**. On the basis of symmetry, therefore, it would seem that in the New Testament we should expect to find, a heart consisting of two parts: an event and a related revelation of God – which not surprisingly indicates God once again offering the faithful a full relationship of love and life.

The Event at the Center

The event that lies at the center of the NT is not hard to find. We can begin to see what that important event was. Read **1 Corinthians 15:3-5**:

> For I handed on to you as of first importance what I in turn had received : that
> Christ died for our sins in accordance with the scriptures, and that he was buried,
> and that he was raised on the third day in accordance with the scriptures, and that
> he appeared to Cephas, then to the twelve. (NRSV)

Paul wrote this letter from Ephesus in about the year 56 CE. He says that he is handing a tradition on to the Corinthians that he received. This small piece dates, therefore, to a time prior to the time that Paul was writing. So it is very early!

See the parallelism here. Christ died (v3) and was buried (v4). How do we know that he had really and truly died? … because he was buried! He was raised to life (v4). How do we know that he truly was raised to life? … because he appeared to Cephas (Peter) and the Twelve (v5).

Here is the event that lies at the **heart of the NT -- the death and resurrection of Jesus Christ.** It is commonly held that the death and resurrection are not two separate events but rather two parts of the same event.

How did Jesus die? We probably all know that he died by crucifixion. This is plainly expressed in the Gospel of **Mark 15:25**: "It was nine in the morning when they crucified him." (NRSV) Or, as Paul describes it in **Galatians 3:1-2**: "You foolish Galatians! Who has bewitched you? It was before your eyes that Jesus Christ was publicly exhibited as crucified!" (NRSV). Or as it is expressed in the **Acts of the Apostles 10:39**: "They put him to death by hanging him on a tree." (NRSV)

But there is the important conclusion to Christ's death -- the resurrection. Thus, the full statement in **Acts 10:39** is: "They put him to death by hanging him on a tree; but God raised him on the third day and allowed him to appear …."(NRSV)

The Gospel and its Content

So we have found the **event** which lies at the heart of the NT -- **the death and resurrection of Jesus Christ.** But is there another part to what lies at the center of the NT? Does the center of the NT have two parts like the center of the OT does where the second part is integrally connected to the first? It does.

Look at **Mk 1:14-15:**

> Now after John was arrested, Jesus came to Galilee, proclaiming the good news of
> God, and saying, "The time is fulfilled, and the kingdom of God has come near;
> repent, and believe in the good news." (NRSV)

One of the principal things Jesus did was to go about **proclaiming** the good news (or gospel.) It was by proclaiming, or preaching, that Jesus went about seeking to gain followers or disciples.

Jesus sent out his disciples on a sort of "practice mission" to preach the gospel (see **Mk 6:7-13; Mt 10:5-15; Lk 9:1-6.**) He commissioned them to "make disciples of all nations"(**Mt 28:19**). Following Pentecost, the Twelve acted on the commission from Christ we see in Matthew, but powered by the Holy Spirit sent to them by the Lord. First, we see Peter preaching the gospel to all of the people who were in Jerusalem for the Feast of Pentecost:

> But Peter standing with the eleven, raised his voice and addressed them, "Men of
> Judea and all who live in Jerusalem, …. (**Acts 2:14**; NRSV)

So those who accepted his message were baptized, and that day about three thousand people were added. (**Acts 2:41**, NRSV)

(**Acts 2:43-47** gives a little summary of what went on within the community of believers following Pentecost).

Paul, after his conversion, preached the gospel. We see evidence for this in 1 Thessalonians, which dates to 50/51 CE and is the earliest writing contained in the NT:

You remember our labor and toil, brothers and sisters; we worked night and day so that we might not burden any of you while we proclaimed to you the gospel of God (**1 Thess 2:9**; NRSV).

…we had courage in our God to declare to you the gospel of God in spite of great opposition. (**1 Thess 2:2;** NRSV**)**

And, in Paul's first letter to the Corinthians we see:

When I came to you, brothers and sisters, I did not come proclaiming the mystery of God to you in lofty words or wisdom. (**1 Cor 2:1**; NRSV)

And there are numerous other examples to be found in Paul's writings.

We are prompted, therefore, to look for the other half of the heart of the NT in the **content of the proclamation of the gospel**. It was by accepting the gospel that the early Christians believed themselves to have been saved! Thus Paul states in 1 Corinthians:

Now I would remind you, brothers and sisters, of the good news that I proclaimed to you, which you in turn received, in which also you stand, through which also you are being saved, if you hold firmly to the message that I proclaimed to you …. (**1 Cor 15:1-2**; NRSV)

The significance of the content of the gospel is that, as Paul says, it was by means of belief in the gospel that the believers were being saved. And this is just as true today!

So let us take for our immediate task that of determining the content of the proclamation of the first Christians. In doing this let us make use of a very famous book, written by Charles H. Dodd: *The Apostolic Preaching and Its Developments.*[218] (In this regard, we keep firmly in mind the principle that, in the field of biblical studies, everything published a number of years ago is not necessarily outdated and everything that is newly written is not necessarily the best.)

---

[218] C.H. Dodd, *The Apostolic Preaching And Its Developments* (New York, NY: Harper & Row Publishers, 1964).

The Content of the Gospel as Revealed in the Letters of Paul

Dodd pointed out that two difficulties stand in the way of determining the content of the gospel from the letters of Paul:[219]

- ❑ In seeking to identify the proclamation in the letters of Paul we run the risk of finding Paul's distinctive gospel rather than finding what was common to most of the early Christian preachers.

- ❑ The letters themselves are not preaching but are addressed to people who are already Christians. The letters presuppose preaching. The letters deal with theological and ethical problems arising out of the attempt to live the Christian way of life.

Dodd said that the first of these difficulties could be removed by observing that Paul did not have a distinctive gospel. He based this assessment on **Galatians 2:2-10** where Paul states that he submitted his gospel to the leaders of the church in Jerusalem and they did not find any fault with it (v 6).[220]

Dodd concluded that the second of these two difficulties is overcome by carefully selecting the passages used to determine the content of the gospel. He basically used only two kinds of passages. First, he used those passages in the letters of Paul which were most likely to be bits of tradition that had been incorporated by Paul into his writings. Secondly, he argued that in Romans Paul is addressing a community which he did not found and had not previously visited and, therefore, when he referred to the data of the Christian faith he would have referred to those things which he believed his readers already knew.[221] Thus, Dodd draws on the following list of passages as the core content of the gospel (called the kerygma):

1. **1 Cor 15:3-5**
2. **Rom 1:1-4**
3. **Rom 8:31-34**
4. **1 Thess 1:9-10**
5. **Gal 1:1-4**
6. **2 Cor 4:5**
7. **2 Cor 5:10**
8. **1 Cor 4:5**
9. **Rom 10:8-9**
10. **Rom 14:7-10**
11. **Rom:2:16**

Let us proceed, therefore, to look at each of these passages carefully and see what we can learn from each about the content of the gospel.

---

[219] Dodd, 9.
[220] Dodd, 13.
[221] Dodd, 14.

1. **1 Cor 15:3-5**

    Jesus died for our sins in accordance with the Scriptures. He was buried.
    Jesus was raised and appeared to Cephas and to the Twelve.

2. **Rom 1:1-4**

    Jesus descended from David according to the flesh.
    Jesus was declared to be Son of God by resurrection from the dead.

3. **Rom 8:31-34**

    Jesus died for us all.
    Jesus died, was raised, is at the right hand of God and intercedes for us.

4. **1 Thess 9-10**

    Jesus was raised from the dead.
    He will come again from Heaven.
    He will rescue us from God's wrath.

5. **Gal 1:1-4**

    Jesus died for our sins to set us free from the present evil age according to the will of God
    our Father. He was raised from the dead.

6. **2 Cor 4:5**

    Jesus Christ is Lord.

7. **2 Cor 5:10**

    All of us must appear before the judgment seat of Christ.

8. **1 Cor 4:5**

    The Lord (Jesus Christ) will come again.

9. **Rom 10:8-9**

    Jesus is Lord.
    God raised him from the dead.

10. **Rom 14:7-10**

    Christ died and lived again.
    Christ is Lord of both the dead and the living.
    We will stand before the judgment seat of God.

11: **Rom 2:16**

    We will be judged by God through Jesus Christ.

If we put all of this together in a logical sequence we arrive at the following outline of the apostolic preaching as determined from the letters of Paul:[222]

---

[222] Dodd, 17.

- Jesus was descended from David according to the flesh (Rom 1:3)
- Jesus died for us all (Rom 8:32), for our sins, in accordance with the scriptures, to deliver us from this evil age (1 Cor 15:3; Gal 1:4)
- He was buried (1 Cor 15:4)
- He was raised (Rom 1:4) on the third day in accordance with the scriptures; he appeared to Cephas and to the Twelve (1 Cor 15:4-5)
- He is seated at the right hand of God (Rom 8:34), declared to be Son of God (Rom 1:4); he intercedes for us (Rom 8:34)
- And he is the Lord (Rom 10:9; 2 Cor 4:5) of the living and the dead (Rom 14:9)
- He will come again to judge us(Rom 2:16; 14:10; 2 Cor 5:10) and to save us from the wrath of God(1 Thess 1:10)

It is seen that this preaching is about Jesus Christ. It forms an important **Christology** (a study of who Christ was, is, and will be always).

The Content of the Gospel as Revealed in the Speeches of Peter

Paul's letters are the earliest writings of the NT and, therefore, are the **prime evidence for the early gospel.** The NT book, the Acts of the Apostles, is not as early as Paul's letters (perhaps 30 years later) but it speaks of the beginnings of the Christian community and, therefore, provides a possibility to be investigated. Let us now focus our attention on the speeches of Peter in Acts.

Dodd also contends reliability for Peter's speeches in the debate with those who claim that Luke composed the speeches and placed them in the mouth of Peter, as did ancient historians such as Thucydides when writing about heroes. Dodd proposes that the Book of Acts is validated by material from Aramaic-speaking Christians who lived in Jerusalem.[223]

Let us set for ourselves the task of seeking the apostolic preaching in the six speeches of Peter in Acts: **2:14-36; 2:38-39; 3:12-26; 4:8-12; 5:29-32 and 10:34-43**. We will do this in the same way as we did for the writings of Paul.

1. **Acts 2:14-36**
    The last days had dawned as foretold by the prophets. (vv16-21)
    Jesus of Nazareth deeds of power, wonders and signs. (v22)
    He was crucified according to the definite plan and foreknowledge of God (i.e. according to the scriptures). (v23 and v36)
    Jesus was raised up by God according to the scriptures (vv24-28); the Twelve are witnesses. (vv32)
    He is exalted at God's right hand and he poured out the Holy Spirit.
    God has made him both Lord and Messiah.

---

[223] Dodd, 20.

2. **Acts 2:38-39**

> Repent and be baptized every one of you in the name of Jesus Christ.
> So that your sins may be forgiven and you will receive the gift of the Holy Spirit.

3. **Acts 3:12-26**

> Jesus was killed (v15), according to the scriptures. (v18)
> God raised him from the dead.
> Repent and turn to God so that your sins may be wiped out. (v19)
> And so the God will send Jesus from heaven again. (v20-21)

4. **Acts 4:8-12**

> Jesus Christ of Nazareth was crucified and God raised him from the dead. (v10)
> There is no other name under heaven given to mortals by which we must be saved. (v12)

5. **Acts 5:29-32**

> Jesus was killed by being hung on a tree. (v30)
> God raised him up (v30) and exalted him at his right hand as leader and savior.   (v31)
> He will give repentance to Israel and forgiveness of sins. (v31)
> God will give the Holy Spirit to those who obey him. (v32)

6. **Acts 10:34-43**

> Jesus Christ is Lord of all. (v36)
> Jesus went about doing good and healing all who oppressed by the devil. (v38)
> He was put to death by hanging on a tree. (v39)
> God raised him on the third day and allowed him to appear. (v40)
> Jesus is the one ordained by God as judge of the living and the dead. (v42)
> Everyone who believes in him receives forgiveness of sins in his name. (v43)

This is what we learn from the six speeches in Acts. Let us now put what we have learned from the speeches in Acts into some reasonable order:[224]

- ♦ The last days are here, the Holy Spirit has been poured forth. (2:16-21)
- ♦ Jesus was crucified and died in accordance with the scriptures. (2:23; 3:15; 4:10; 5:30; 10:39)
- ♦ God raised him up (3:15; 4:10) on the third day (10:40) in accordance with the scriptures (2:24-32), and he appeared. (10:40-41)
- ♦ He is exalted at the right hand of God and has poured out the Holy Spirit. (2:33)
- ♦ God has made him both Lord and Messiah. (2:36; 10:36)
- ♦ He is ordained by God to judge the living and the dead. (10:42)
- ♦ Christ will come again. (3:20-21)

Comparison of the content of the gospel as determined from the speeches of Peter in Acts with what we learned from the letters of Paul shows that there is not a significant difference.

---

[224] Dodd, 21-23.

One element that appears here in Acts that does not appear in the passages we looked at in the letters of Paul is the **call for the people to repent and be baptized**, to receive the forgiveness of sins, and to receive the Holy Spirit (**Acts 2:38-39; 10:43**). The reason for this is simply that Paul was writing to people who already had been baptized whereas Peter is seeking to win new converts.

The Gospel Underlies the NT

The content of the gospel which we have discovered in the writings of Paul and in the speeches of Peter in Acts can be shown to underlie the whole NT. Indeed, Dodd goes so far as to point out that with all the diversity of the writings that make up the NT they are unified in their proclamation of the one gospel.[225] Let us consider two examples of this: 1 Peter and the Gospel of Mark.

Reading through **1 Peter,** the following elements of the gospel are to be found:

- Jesus died (**1:18-19; 2:18**) for our sins (**2:18**), in accordance with the scriptures (**1:11**)
- He was raised (**1:3, 21; 2:18,21**) in accordance with the scriptures (**1:11**)
- He is at the right hand of the Father (**2:22**)
- Jesus Christ is Lord (**1:3; 2:15**)
- Christ will come again (**1:7, 13; 5:4**)

Surely, this is quite close to being the core of the entire gospel.

Now let's read through **Acts 10:34-43** which is one of the passages we looked at when we determined the core of the gospel from Acts. Then, we can compare this passage in Acts with the entire Gospel of Mark. We will see that they parallel each other. This prompts one to propose that Mark was written as a fuller form of the proclamation of the early Christians. This could explain why Mark's gospel begins as it does: "The beginning of the Gospel of Jesus Christ, the Son of God." It is interesting to note that the consensus of scholars argue that the Gospel of Mark was written in the period 65-70 CE, and is, therefore, among the earliest writings in the NT.

Conclusion

We have found that the death and resurrection of Jesus lie at the heart of the NT. On closer examination we found that the heart actually consists of two parts: an event and a gospel (or good news). The event is the death and resurrection of Jesus the Christ. The gospel is the early proclamation of the Christians by which they sought to gain new converts to the Faith. Consider this: **Is not the life and death, resurrection and final coming again of Jesus evidence of a covenant of love with God, a love between God and humanity that will come to completion in and through Jesus?** We then have a mystical and remarkable unity of revelation between the heart of the OT and the heart of the NT!

---

[225] Dodd, 74.

344

CHAPTER FORTY-five

THE DIVINE TRINITY AT THE HEART OF THE SCRIPTURES

Introduction

At this point it is appropriate to seek the heart of the Scriptures in their entirety. Already we have successfully identified a heart of the OT and a heart of the New Testament. To seek for a heart of the Scriptures in their entirety, therefore, we need to seek for a third heart that contains both hearts of the OT and NT. But wait! This is awkward. In reality, there should only be one hear to a living entity, and so we need to revise our analysis and adjust our imagery. A body has two lungs. Let us take the two testaments, old and new, to be two lungs. Now it is proper to search for a heart of the whole Scriptures.

There is little need for a lengthy search. The heart of the Scriptures in their entirety is certainly God – the Divine Trinity!

The God of the Hebrew Scriptures (OT)

In the Hebrew Scriptures the reality (existence) of **God is the presupposition of all life.** We meet God in the very first verse of the first book of the OT (**Gen 1:1**) and God is still abiding with us in the last verse of the last book of the OT to be written (**Wisdom 19:22**)! **The question of God's existence is simply not questioned in the OT.**

The God of the OT completely transcends everything that is created. God is the creator of all that is; both the visible and the invisible. God created the heavens and the earth (**Gen 1:1**). It is God who has measured the waters in the hollow of his hand -- a metaphor of course (**Is 40:12-17**). It is God who sits above the circle of the earth and sees the earth's inhabitants to be like grasshoppers (**Is 40:22-23**). The sense of the **transcendent majesty** and power of God as Creator is also found in **Job: chapters 38-41**.

Because of this transcendence, God preexists and "sits above" the entire universe and is consequently hidden from mankind. God's transcendence and **"hidden-ness"** give rise to the prohibition against making images of God (**see Ex 20:4**) and to the belief that ordinarily no person can see God and live because God is in reality too powerful, too transcendent, too "other," too mystical … and so beyond us all (**Ex 19:21; 33:20; Jgs 6:22-23; Is 6:5**).

Our understanding is that this hidden God was revealed to Israel, such a firmly held belief in the OT! This self-revelation of God was given to the Israelites through the concrete events of their history. B.W. Anderson expresses the following:

> The OT has no systematic doctrine of God, for God is not an idea to be
> incorporated into a logical system or into a spiritual thought-world. It is therefore
> wrong to expect an answer to the question of the nature of God, if this means an

abstract analysis of what God is in himself – i.e. the attributes of his being. Just as persons are known in the context of relationship, so God's self is revealed in his historical relations with his people. He is the God of Abraham, Isaac and Jacob, not the god of speculative thought. He is known by what he has done, is doing, and will do – i.e. in the events of history. As the psalmist affirms:

> He made known his ways to Moses,
> His acts to the people of Israel. (Ps 1-3:7)

OT theology, then, is fundamentally historical theology. It is profoundly and radically historical, for it rests upon the witness that God's revelation takes the form of a history. Just as the power of poetry is lost when translated into prose, so the vitality of Israel's faith is lost when the dramatic story of God's actions and men's responses is converted into abstractions.[226]

Anderson also comments:

> …the central conviction of Israel's faith is that the eternal supra-mundane God enters into and acts in the temporal sphere of human existence.[227]

In this respect, the religious belief of Israel differs from the other religions of the Ancient Near East (ANE). Religions of antiquity took a number of different forms in the ANE, but often they were based only upon the belief that the divine powers were equivalent to powers in nature. Thus, Israel affirmed, in disagreement with the surrounding peoples, that divine reality is not encountered in nature but in historical experience. Importantly, the Israelites considered God to be the Lord **of** nature (not "in" or "revealed through") by virtue of being the creator of everything.

God revealed the Divine Name to Moses at the burning bush (**Ex 3:1-15**). God's revealed name in Hebrew is often called the *tetragrammaton*, a word with four Hebrew letters – *yod, heh, vav, heh* (a unique form of the verb "to be" encompassing all tenses!) The name which was revealed is **"YHWH"** is usually translated: "I am who am." The name, in reality, is a special name that appears nowhere else. It is a name that represents all forms of the verb "to be" conflated into one word (a unique word) which suggests that God is the Supreme "Being" and "Source of Life." Hebrew was originally written entirely with consonants so one has to add the vowels "a" and "e" to know that this name is "Yahweh." In revealing this name, God – as the eternal life-giving power – established a special relationship between himself and the Israelites. This interrelationship between God and people is present in the Song of Deborah (**Jgs Chapter 5**), which is the oldest poem of any length in the OT. It is explicitly expressed in **Ex 6:7, Jer 31:33,** and **Ezek 37:27**. Yahweh is the God of Israel and Israel is the people of God.

Israel's belief in Yahweh encompassed two features that seem to be mutually exclusive. On the one hand, Yahweh is the transcendent God, wholly beyond the full comprehension and understanding of humanity. On the other hand, Yahweh is present with the people. We see God commanding Moses to have the people build a sanctuary so that: "I may

---

[226] Bernhard W. Anderson: "God, OT View of" in *The Interpreter's Dictionary of the Bible*, Vol 2 (Nashville, TN: Abingdon Press, 1962), 418.

[227] Anderson, 423.

dwell among them." (**Ex 25:8**) We see Moses expressing the good fortune of Israel in having a God that is so near: "For what other great nation has a god so near to it as the LORD our God is whenever we call to him?" (Deut 4:7). The nearness of Yahweh to the people is symbolized in the Ark of the Covenant and later in the Temple in Jerusalem.

Just as we human beings show others about our inner selves through our inter-relationships and through our actions – so, too, God reveals traits through divine action in history and with the people of God. Through the experience of the Israelites it is seen that:[228]

1. **Yahweh is holy**
   Joshua states that God is a holy God (**Josh 24:19**). Both 1st Isaiah (**1:4: 5:19**) and 2nd Isaiah (**40:25; 41:14, 20**) call God the "Holy One of Israel. This holiness arises from the great difference between God's purity, on the one hand, and mankind's sinfulness on the other hand (See **Is 6:1-5; Pss 15; 24:3-6; Hab 1:12-13.**) **Ex 15:11** calls Yahweh: "majestic in holiness." It was the experience of Israel that Yahweh is One and Yahweh is holy.

2. **Yahweh abounds in steadfast love**
   In **Ex 34:6-7**, probably an ancient liturgical text, the LORD proclaims that the LORD abounds in steadfast love and faithfulness. It is frequently stated in the OT that Yahweh is distinguished by this trait. See for example: **Neh 9:17; Ps 86:15; 103:8; Joel 2:13;** and **Jonah 4:2**.

3. **Yahweh is a jealous God**
   The God of the Israelites was known to them to be a jealous God. This is attested to by the following passages: **Josh 24:19; Ex 20:5** and **34:14; Deut 6:14-15.** The term "jealous," like the other traits we have treated, is used analogically of God. Jealousy is the expression of God's will to be the God of the people of Israel. Because of this trait, the people of God were punished by God if they were attracted to the worship of other gods.

4. **The wrath of God**
   In situations when the faithful turn against the will of God, those who attack God and reject his love and care, the Hebrew and Greek words used in the Scriptures indicate a "boiling up," a heat of passion, and a resulting withdrawal of God's care. In human terms, it is seen as God's anger. However, the scriptures affirm that God is "slow to anger." The wrath of God is not a wild outburst of emotion but rather a "momentary" reaction to the failure of the Israelite community to obey the conditions of the covenant or the failure of individuals to follow the ways of the covenant. This can be understood in reference to God as a relational God, the "bridegroom of humanity." The relationship is broken and then God can draw back his gifts and cancel the action planned (see **Jer 18:7-10; Amos 7:1-6; and the Book of Jonah**). By the word "wrath" – in relation to God – is meant a passing phenomenon, not a permanent characteristic. The Hebrew word used for this refers to a strong, spontaneous

---

[228] Anderson, 424 – 428.

feeling in a human being and is then used analogically with regard to God. If God is a

loving and relational Being, the lover of the faithful, it is not hard to understand that when this depth of love and gifts are rejected that there may be a boiling reaction.

5. **Yahweh is a loving God**
   The love of God surpasses all human understanding but it is most like the love that a parent has for a child or that a man or woman has for a spouse. The presence of both strong, boiling passion and strong love in the same being seems impossible, but that this holds true for God, as the prophet Hosea attests
   (see Hos Chap 11.)

The oneness of God

It clearly says in **Exodus 20:2** that Yahweh is the God who brought the Israelites out of Egypt, out of the house of slavery, and, therefore, the Israelites are to have no other gods other than Yahweh. This obviously expresses the belief that within the community of Israel, Yahweh desires to be the **only God.**

It is apparent from **Exodus 15:11**, part of a very ancient song, that soon after the time of the Exodus the Israelites realized that Yahweh is unique regarding the ability to act within history. But it is probable that the faith of Israel at this early time was not always monotheistic in the true sense of the term, due to human doubt and questioning. The constant struggle of the Israelites with the problem of worshipping other gods tells us that more than likely many Israelites regarded Yahweh as one among many gods, no doubt the strongest god, but not convincingly the one and only God.

By the time of Jeremiah the belief of Israel had become more truly monotheistic. The great Confession of Judaism, the **Great Shema (Deut 6:4-9)**, which probably dates to the time of Josiah's reform in 621BCE, affirms that Yahweh is the only and unique God: "Hear, O Israel! The Lord is our God, the Lord alone!"

In the words of Bernhard Anderson:

> Israelite Monotheism comes to its finest expression in the prophecy
> of Second Isaiah. ...... Yahweh is God alone, unique and incomparable
> in wisdom, majesty, and power, the Lord of all human history and the
> creator of heaven and earth (Isa. 41:28-29; 42:17; 43:10-11; 44:7-8;
> 45:5-6, 14-17, 21-22; 46:1-2, 8-11; etc.)."

> ... the God who called Abraham from the East, who delivered his people from
> Egypt, who was on the verge of accomplishing a new exodus from Babylonian
> exile, is the sovereign who alone controls the destinies of the nations. The
> prophet ridicules the gods of the nations as man-made constructs because they
> have no power to act. [229]

---

[229] Anderson, 428.

As an example of the other gods not having the power to act, read the interesting story of Elijah and the prophets of Baal (**1 Kgs 18:1-39**).

The presence of God in the midst of the people

From the time of the exodus from Egypt until the beginning of the monarchy, the visible symbols of the presence of God with the people were the **Ark of the Covenant** and the **Tent of Meeting**. During his reign, King David brought the Ark to Jerusalem (see **2 Sam 6:1-19**). Sometime after, David realized that he himself was living in a house of cedar and the Ark of God rested in a tent. It was his deep desire to build a suitable house for God (**2 Sam 7:1-2**). But God's response is surprising (**2 Sam 7:4-17**). Indeed, it is Solomon who undertakes to build a house for God (**1 Kgs Chap 6**). From that time, the **temple in Jerusalem** became the visible symbol of the presence of God.

From the time of **Solomon (10th century BCE)** until the **destruction of Jerusalem by the Romans in 70 CE** one speaks of "the temple in Jerusalem." But during this long period the temple was rebuilt on two separate occasions. It was rebuilt the first time after the return from exile, the temple having been almost totally destroyed at the time of the beginning of the Babylonian captivity (587 BCE). King Herod undertook to almost completely rebuild the temple during his reign (37-4 BCE). Thus, it is common to use the following terminology for the temple:

1. The temple built by Solomon is called the "**Solomonic Temple**" or "First Temple" (1000 BCE – 587 BCE).
2. The temple rebuilt after the Exile is called the "**Second Temple**" (520 BCE – 70 CE).
3. The temple as rebuilt by King Herod is called the "**Herodian Temple**" (rebuilding began in 20 BCE and was completed sometime after Herod's death – The Gospel of John says it took 46 years)

There is necessarily some confusion here. Does one regard the building effort of Herod to constitute the building of an entirely new structure or as simply a rebuilding of that which already existed? There is no break in the character of Judaism at the time of the work of Herod. There is, however, such a break with the destruction of the temple in 70 CE. Thus, the Second Temple period effectively extended from 515 BCE through 70 CE.

The God of the Christian Scriptures (NT)

It is clear from the writings of the NT that Jesus and his followers all believed that the God of their day was the same as the God of the OT. Indeed, the writings of the OT were their Holy Scriptures. Thus, we find expressions of the same aspects of God that we find in the OT:

1. The **transcendence** of God (**1 Tim 1:17; 6:15-16; Rev 1:8; 4:8**)
2. God as **creator** (**Rom 11:36; 1 Cor 8:6; AA 4:24; 17:24; 1 Pet 4:19; Heb 1:2**)

3. God as the **one God** (**Jn 17:3; Rom 3:30; 1 Cor 8:4-6; Eph 4:4-6; 1 Tim 1:17; 2:5; Jas 2:19; Jude verse 25**)
4. God is the **"living God"** (**AA 14:15; 1 Thess 1:9** – and for the OT of this expression: **Jer 10:10; 23:36; Dan 6:26**)

In one important way, the experience of the one, only God was deepened for the followers of Jesus, quite different from that of the Israelites and the Jews of the Second Temple period. **The first Christians, both Jewish and Gentile people who put faith in Jeus, experienced the one God -- a Trinity!** They experienced God as the Father of Jesus Christ (**Lk 1:26-35; Rev 1:4-6**). They experienced Jesus as the Son of God (**Mk 1:1, 9-11; 9:2-8; 15:39; Heb 1:1-2**). They also experienced the living presence of the Holy Spirit (**AA 2:1-4; Jn 20:19-23**). Therefore, the One God of Life is now known through the Father, Jesus -- the Son of God, and the Holy Spirit of God.

Between the time of the Exodus and the time of the exile of the Israelites, there developed an ever-deepening understanding of what the meaning of the term "one God" really meant. The understanding moved from "one God," meaning one among many gods to an understanding that it meant "one, only God." Jesus revealed one God who relates to humanity and acts as: Father, Son and Holy Spirit. **The Christians came to believe in God as three "persons" without giving up their belief in "one, only God."** An explanation should be made about this word "persons." This is a term derived from Aristotelian philosophy that has a meaning referring to "identity." It does not infer that there were three "personalities," as we understand in our modern language. Therefore, God is known as "the Father," "the Son," and the "Holy Spirit" of God. This introduces the wonderful study of "Trinitarian theology."

In the OT, God is known as the creator. This way of describing God is expanded in the NT. In the NT, God retains the title of creator but God is also known as the One who "raises the dead" (**2 Cor 1:9**).

Another new feature of the NT concept of God is the use of the title "Father." This title is not unique to the NT (e.g. see **Is 63:16 and 64:8**). But it is Jesus in the NT who introduces his followers to the use of "Father" for God in a significant way. This is seen from the following: **1Thess 1:2; Gal 1:3; 2 Cor 1:2; Mt 6:9: Mk 11:26.**

In the NT, we find reference to the Holy Spirit in the Annunciation to Mary and at Pentecost. (**Mt 5:17**) We must remember though, that the Spirit of God was known in the OT, particularly in the Hebrew word *ruah,* which is used at the very beginning in Genesis 1:2! The term is used, for example in the Psalms: **Ps 31:5, Ps 51:11, and Ps 139:2.**

In conclusion, the same God is author of both the OT and the NT and, therefore, the Holy Scriptures, although containing many diverse writings on the human level, form a unity on a deeper level. The underlying unity of the Scriptures is revealed on the human level in two ways: 1) through prophecy and its fulfillment, and 2) through the common use of symbols. In both the OT and NT there are appointed people such as prophets and holy men and women and events that demonstrate the continuity of the OT and the NT. These symbols and factors all consistently show the active involvement of God in history which is ever continuing.

An example of the fulfillment of prophecy is Jeremiah's prophecy of a new covenant (**Jer 31:31-34**) and its fulfillment in the NT (**Lk 22:14-20; Heb 9:15**). (It should be noted that the covenant mentioned in Jeremiah is not destroyed but fulfilled, as Christ taught. Another example is God's promise of the Gospel and its fulfillment (**Rom 1:1-3**).

Revisiting the "How" of Inspiration

The Freedom of the Human Authors and Editors

On close examination, the writings of the Scriptures give evidence of the freedom of the human authors and editors to do their work in an entirely human way! We ask the question: how does the Divine Trinity reveal truths and love to humanity? Let us review the writings we have encountered all along in the Bible. In this regard consider the following observations:

❑ The writings of Scripture come to us in a number of basic literary forms. But these forms have been shown by scholars to be the same forms that we find in the societies which were contemporary with Israel and 1st century Christianity. We do not find any literary forms in Scripture that do not have their counterparts in writing outside the Bible.

❑ Many of the biblical writings, upon close examination, are found to be the result of rather long periods of composition involving a multiplicity of authors and editors, and there appears a continuity in the voice of God. Writings that come into being in this manner are said to have a literary history. Consider the following four cases:

  • **The Pentateuch -** Looking through the Pentateuch we found the following sorts of things: two sets of terminologies for places and peoples; two differing views of the nearness of God to mankind; three different literary styles; multiple accounts of events with conflicting details; contradictory etiologies; and conflicting statements on matters of significant theological importance. These sorts of inconsistencies are **not** what we would expect to find in a coherent literary composition penned by a single author. We found that these inconsistencies can be accounted for, however, on the assumption that the narrative of the Pentateuch is the result of combining four strands of tradition (they are denoted by J, E, P and D), each of which is itself a literary composite, plus the inclusion of a number of unconnected individual passages of larger and smaller extent (e.g. the Holiness Code of Ex 20:22-23:33). J and E, as we noted, stand for the name of God used in these traditions, i.e. Yahweh (J) and Elohim (E). The P tradition refers to the period of the priestly era. And D refers to the tradition of the Deuteronomist. The Pentateuch contains oral traditions dating to the time of Abraham (19th-17th centuries BCE) and involves the work of an editor(s) at the time of the exile (587-538 BCE.)
  • **Book of Isaiah** - The book begins, Is 1:1, with an introduction which states that it is a vision which Isaiah had concerning Judah and Jerusalem and we do

find that Is 1:13-20 is an oracle announcing the end of the kingdom of Judah if the people do not repent. But then we look at Is 40:1-5! This shows that Judah is in exile – this is sixth century BCE material whereas the Isaiah of 1:1 dates to the 8th century BCE. Furthermore, Is 66:1-6 depicts worship in the rebuilt temple and thus dates to the 4th or 5th centuries BCE. A detailed analysis of the book of Isaiah reveals the following structure, as described earlier:

- Chaps 1-39, less 24-27 and 34, 35 consist of oracles of Isaiah the prophet and date to the period 742-701 BCE.
- Chaps 40-55 date to the period of the end of the Exile (550-540 BCE) and contain the work of an unknown prophet, called "Second Isaiah.
- Chaps 56-66 are prophecies of another unknown prophet who is called "Third Isaiah." These prophecies date to sometime after the return from exile.

It is seen that the book of Isaiah has had a rather lengthy and complex literary history with more than one author and redactor.

- **Book of Proverbs -** Look at the book of Proverbs; one of the wisdom writings. The full title of the book reads: The Proverbs of Solomon *ben* David, King of Israel. **Verses 1:1, 10:1 and 25:1** specifically attribute the sayings to Solomon. But looking a bit more closely we see that **22:17 and 24:23** attribute some of the sayings to the "sages" and verse **30:1** attributes others to Agur. It is easily seen that the book of Proverbs contains, in addition to actual proverbs, the following: short warning passages, poems, moralizing couplets, acrostic verses, and a dialogue with a skeptic (**Ch 30**). Thus it becomes apparent that Proverbs has had a long literary history. Its connection with King Solomon is very tenuous and is, perhaps, one of honor.

- **The Synoptic Gospels -** Jesus lived his earthly life during the period 6B AD/CE – 30/33 AD/CE. Most scholars hold that the first gospel was written by Mark, in 65-70 AD/CE while Luke and Matthew were not written until sometime in the period 80-90 AD/CE. How did the memory of Jesus' earthly life get passed along and survive during the period before anything was written down? The answer to this is that it was carried by an oral tradition. Today, in the 20th century, we do not place much confidence in oral tradition; we prefer the written word. In the first century it was different. The people of the first and second centuries of the Common Era placed considerable confidence in oral traditions. A Christian writer in the early second century wrote that he believed the oral tradition much more than anything written. The Jews carried their Rabbinic tradition orally for centuries before it was written down in the Talmud. We can sketch the history of the traditions which lie behind the Synoptic gospels as follows:

  - **6 BCE to 30/33 CE -** The life of Jesus on earth. The gospel tradition is born; news of Jesus is passed by word of mouth.

- **30/33 to 65 CE** - The gospel tradition is passed along orally forming itself into units: pronouncement stories, miracle stories, and stories about Jesus. The parables and sayings of Jesus were remembered. Some development of the tradition took place to make it adapt to the changing times.

- **65 to70 CE** -Mark wrote his gospel, incorporating into it elements of the oral tradition. At the same time the oral tradition continued to develop.

- **70 to 80 CE** - The oral gospel tradition continued to develop. Mark's Gospel was circulated between the Christian communities.

- **80 to 90 CE** -Matthew and Luke wrote their gospels. Both Matthew and Luke used Mark as a written source, but they did so independently of each other. Both Matthew and Luke used another written source, called Q, which had probably been written during the previous period. In addition, it appears they also had their own sources. The oral tradition, however, continued on along with the written gospels.

So, the Synoptic gospels have a literary history themselves. It should be noted that the writings of the OT involve a period of more than 1000 years; the writings of the NT all fall within a period of 100-150 years.

- ❑ **Making use of sources** – Scholars today look for sources in the scriptural writings. The same phenomenon is found in the writings of Scripture. How do we tell when a source is being used in a scriptural writing? The most certain way is when the biblical author directly cites a source. Here are a couple of examples of this:

  - "The rest of Abijam's acts, with all that he did, are written in the book of chronicles of the kings of Judah" (1 Kgs 15:7; see also 15:23, 31).
  - "Now the rest of the acts of Jehu, and all the he did, and all his might, are they not written in the Book of the Chronicles of the Kings of Israel?" (2 Kgs 10:34)

  - Jude 9 (see that this book is short and has only verses, no chapters) sets forth a tradition from the Assumption of Moses, a non-canonical book. Jude 14-15 refers to the book of 1 Enoch, also a non-canonical book.

  - "Then was fulfilled what was said through Jeremiah the prophet…" (Mt 2:17 referencing Jer 31:15). See that the OT is source for the writers of the NT! We have treated this at some length.

- ❑ **The presence of inconsistencies** - Inconsistencies are to be found in the biblical text. Here are a few examples:

- Compare **Gen 7:2** and **7:15f.** Then compare **Gen 7:12** and **7:24**.
- Compare **1 Sam 10:1** and **12:16-18** – Is having a king a good thing for Israel?
- **Dan 5:1f** states that Belschazzar was the son of Nebuchadnezzar – in reality he was the son of Nabonidus, not Nebuchadnezzar.
- In **Mk 2:26,** Mark tells us that Abiathar was the high priest when David ate the consecrated loaves. But it states in **1 Sam 21:1-6** that it was Abimelech, Abiathar's father.
- In the gospel of John, Jesus cleanses the Temple at the beginning of his ministry; he does so at the end of his ministry in the gospel of Mark (see **Jn 2:13-22** and **Mk 11:15-18**).
- In **Mt 21:1-7** Jesus is seen riding into Jerusalem astride two animals! This is clearly a misinterpretation of **Zech 9:9** resulting from a lack of knowledge of parallelism in Hebrew poetry.

All of these things are to be seen in the texts of Scripture. They can all be explained on the basis of the assumption that Scripture is the result of the work of **human authors.** For example, the inconsistencies in the flood account in Genesis find their explanation by observing that a human editor has intertwined two separate accounts of the flood (namely, the J and P traditions of the Pentateuch.)

Conclusion

The above observations provide a strong basis for believing in the **freedom of the human authors of the Biblical writings.** This leaves us in a baffling situation. On the one hand, we hold that the Scriptures have God for their author and we strongly hold to this belief as a matter of faith. On the other hand there are strong reasons for believing in the freedom of the authors and editors of the Scriptures to do their work in an entirely human way. The resolution of this dilemma is found not by accepting one of the two possibilities and rejecting the other but by fully accepting **both** of the two possibilities! The Scriptures are both fully the word of God and fully the word of man. How can this be? This is truly a mystery but leads us all to understand that God is revealing himself in the words of human beings. God who is the Father, the Son, and the Holy Spirit is alive and breathing his invitation to relationship and love throughout the entire Bible!

CHAPTER FORTY-six

ATTAR OF SCRIPTURE

The word "attar" is defined in the dictionary as the fragrant essential oil extracted from the petals of flowers. Attar of roses, for example is a semisolid substance at ordinary temperatures, varying from pale yellow to pale red in color and having a sweet taste and fragrant odor.

Let us think of the Bible as being a flower with each book of the Bible being one of its petals. In terms of this image, one can ask the question: "Is it possible to extract the attar from this flower?"

Given our knowledge of the heterogeneous literary character of the biblical books and the complex literary histories of many of them, it is not immediately clear that it is meaningful to ask such a question. Given our knowledge of the nature of Scripture as the word of God and the word of mankind at the same time, truly being the incarnation of the word of God ... it is at once apparent that extracting the attar from this flower should be possible. We can consider the attar of Scripture to be the most precious substance that can ever be possessed: it is the fundamental substance of life!

One must be sure, however, when attempting to extract this essence from Scripture to include in the processing each and every one of the petals. Under no circumstances can one start with a certain number of the petals, excluding all of the remainder – as people are so frequently tempted to do.

Once having obtained the attar of Scripture, we can analyze its basic constituents and will find that it is composed of three distinct components:
- The message communicated by God through the words of human language.
- The message communicated to mankind through the events of salvation history.
- An underlying theme which permeates all of Scripture.
-

Let us consider each of these three constituents in turn.

Just as the beauty of a flower can be enhanced by proper illumination, so the beauty of Scripture is enhanced by the language which is used to express it. With this in mind, let us not confine ourselves to the use of a single translation. Let us rather abstract passages from a number of different translations in order to achieve the most appealing wording of a given passage. In this regard, let us use – for example - the *Jerusalem Bible* (JB), the *New American Bible* with Revised NT (NAB), the *New Revised Standard Version* (NRSV). the *New English Bible* (NEB), and the *Authorized King James Version* (KJV) and the *New Revised King James Version* (NKJV).

In the following passages, the JB version will be used unless otherwise stated ... to give an example of a beautifully translated version of the Bible that was originally translated into French and then subsequently into English.

The Message of the Words

First, through the words of Scripture we learn that there is one God and only one God:

> Thus says Yahweh, Israel's king,
> Yahweh Sabaoth, his redeemer:
> I am the first and I am the last;
> There is no God except me.
> (Is 44:6 JB)

This one God is neither wholly body nor part body and part spirit. God is wholly spirit:

> God is spirit,
> And those who worship
> Must worship in spirit and truth.
> (Jn 4:24 JB)

Secondly, we learn from the words of Scripture that this one God is a Trinity; the Father, his Son and the Holy Spirit. The individuality of the Father and the Son is clear from the words spoken by the Father at the time of the baptism of Jesus:

> And a voice came from heaven, 'You are my Son, the
> beloved; my favour rests on you.'
> (Mk 1:11 JB)

This is also apparent from the frequent references to God the Father in the discourses and prayers of Jesus, as for example:

> His answer to them was, 'My Father still goes on working,
> and I am at work, too.'
> (Jn 5:17 JB)

The individuality of the Holy Spirit is implied in Christ's promise that the Father will send the Holy Spirit to them after he (Christ) has left them:

> I have said these things to you
> while still with you;
> but the Paraclete, the Holy Spirit,
> whom the Father will send in my name,
> will teach you everything
> and remind you of all I have said to you.
> (Jn 14:25f JB)

Thirdly, the divinity of Jesus is clearly implied through the miracles he performed, the prophecies he made, and in the power to command the forces of nature and the powers of evil that he demonstrated. His divinity is also evident in his frequent use of phrases demonstrating that the Son is one with the Father. A most striking example of this the is time that the Apostle Philip made the statement: "Lord, show us the Father and then we shall be satisfied." Jesus responded:

> 'Have I been with you all this time, Philip, and you still do not know me?
> 'Anyone who has seen me has seen the Father,
> so how can you say, "Show us the Father"?
> (Jn 14:9 JB)

The divinity of the Holy Spirit is apparent from Peter's statement to Ananias concerning the latter's attempt to withhold a portion of the proceeds he received from the sale of some land from the Apostles (see Acts 5:1-6):

> Peter said, 'Ananias, how can Satan have so possessed you that
> you should lie to the Holy Spirit ….. You have been lying not to
> men, but to God.'
> (Acts 5:3-4 JB)

Fourthly, through the words of Scripture we learn that God is the creator of the universe. This truth is attested to in the very first verse of the Bible:

In the beginning God created the heaven and the earth (Gen 1:1, KJV)

It is stated again in one of the poems of Second Isaiah:

> 'I, Yahweh, have made all things,
> I alone spread out the heavens.
> When I hammered the earth into shape,
>   Who was with me?'
> (Is 44:24 JB)

Fifthly, from the words of Scripture we learn that God is the living God. God has not wound up the universe like a giant clock and then let it run on its own. God actively controls the events of human history. We find this truth expressed in the book of Psalms in the following way:

> For Yahweh, the Most High, is glorious,
> The great king over all the earth.
> He brings people under our yoke
> And nations under our feet
> (Ps 47:2-3 JB)

God is not only active in the affairs of nations, he is active in the lives of men and women:

> Yahweh guides a strong man's steps and keeps them firm;
> And takes pleasure in him.

When he trips he is not thrown sprawling,
Since Yahweh supports him by the hand.
(Ps 37:23 JB)

It is difficult for a person to comprehend the truth that God can view the world from heaven and at the same time see each one of us as an individual:

Yahweh is looks down from heaven
At the children of Adam.
To see if a single one is wise,
A single one seeks God.
(Ps 14:2 JB)

This truth is expressed in a somewhat different way in the following passage from the Wisdom of Ben Sira (Sirach):

Do not say, 'I shall hide from the Lord;
    Who is going to remember me up there?
I shall not be noticed among so many people;
    What am I in the immensity of creation?'
(Sir 16:17 JB)

Such are the thoughts of the person of little sense,
Stupid, misguided, cherishing his folly.
(Sir 16:23 JB)

We learn from the words of Scripture about the nature of mankind. We learn that a human being is the coalescence of an organic body and a spiritual soul:

Yahweh God shaped man from the soil of the ground and
blew the breath of life into his nostrils, and man became a
living being.
(Gen 2:7 JB)

Sixthly, we learn that the soul lives on after the death of the body, something we find expressed implicitly in the Gospel of Matthew and explicitly in the Gospel of John:

'Do not be afraid of those who kill the body but cannot kill
the soul; fear him rather who can destroy both body and soul
in hell.' (Mt 10:28 JB)
'In truth I tell you,
whoever listens to my words,
and believes in the one who sent me,
has eternal life;
without being brought to judgment
such a person has passed from death to life.' (Jn 5:24 JB)

Seventhly, we learn from the words of Scripture that a human being is created with free will:

> 'Today, I call heaven and earth to witness against you: I am
> offering you life or death, blessing or curse. Choose life,
> then, so that you and your descendants may live, in the love
> of Yahweh your God, obeying his voice, holding fast to him;
> for in this your life consists, ...'
> (Deut 30:19-20 JB)

and thus we also learn that a person is free to choose between accepting God or rejecting God:

> 'So now, fear Yahweh and serve him truly and sincerely; banish
> the gods whom your ancestors served beyond the River and in
> Egypt and serve Yahweh. But if serving Yahweh seems a bad thing
> to you, today you must make up your minds whom you do mean to
> serve, ...'
> (Josh 24:14-15 JB)

This was the challenge of Joshua to the Israelites during the time of the conquest of the Promised Land clearly shows.

Eighthly, through the words of Scripture we learn that God is the creator which is easily understood but that at the same time the creator is revealed through his creation. Scripture says that the hand of the creator is easily seen in what was created:

> Yes, naturally stupid are all who are unaware of God,
> And who, from good things seen, have not been able to discover Him-who-is,
> Or, by studying the works, have not recognized the artificer.
> (Wisdom 13:1 JB)

There is no excuse for a person who cannot discern the creator in the creation:

> Ever since the creation of the world his eternal power and divine
> nature, invisible though they are, have been understood and seen
> through the things he has made. So they are without excuse; ....
> (Rom 1:20 JB)

Ninthly, from the words of Scripture we learn that man is saved by faith in the gospel:

> For I am not ashamed of the gospel. It is the power of God for the salvation
> of everyone who believes: for the Jew first and then the Greek. (Rom 1:16,
> NAB / Rev NT)

The content of the gospel may be summarized as follows:

- Jesus was descended from David according to the flesh (Rom 1:3)
- Jesus died for us all (Rom 8:32), for our sins, in accordance with the scriptures, and to deliver us from this evil age (1 Cor 15:3; Gal 1:4)
- He was buried (1 Cor 15:4)
- He was raised (Rom 1:4) on the third day in accordance with the scriptures; he appeared to Cephas and to the Twelve (1 Cor 15:4-5)
- He is seated at the right hand of God (Rom 8:34), declared to be Son of God (Rom 1:4); he intercedes for us (Rom 8:34)
- And He is Lord (Rom 10:9; 2 Cor 4:5) of the living and the dead (Rom 14:9)
- He will come again to judge us (Rom 2:16; 14:10; 2 Cor 5:10) and to save us from the wrath of God (1 Thess 1:10)

We are saved by faith in the gospel, but faith cannot be separated from life. The gospel must be lived:

> For just as a body without a spirit is dead, so also faith without works is dead. (James 2:26 JB)

The Events of Salvation History

If God was a divinity who spoke to us only once in a while, and was content the rest of the time to sit back and watch us live out our lives, then all there would be to the Bible would be a communication of words from God to mankind. In actual fact, however, God is involved in all the events of human history in accordance with his will and, consequently, we can learn about God from the events of history as well. It is abundantly clear that God is active in world events. For example, we learn from the prophet Amos (8th century BCE):

> It was I who brought you up from Egypt
> and for forty years led you through the desert
> to take possession of the Amorite's country;
> I who raised up prophets from your sons
> And Nazirites from your young men.
> Israelites, is this not true?
> - declares Yahweh!
> (Amos 2:10-11 JB)

During the time of the Babylonian Exile in the 6th century BCE we find that the experience of God's chosen people explained in the following manner:

> You were sold to the nations,
> but not for extermination.
> You provoked God; and so were delivered to your enemies,
> Since you had angered your Creator
> by offering sacrifices to demons,
> and not to God.   (Baruch 4:6-7 JB)

History is not just an aimless series of events. It is progressing in accordance with a divine plan. We must accept the fact, however, that we cannot comprehend the plan of God without God's help:

> If you cannot sound the depths of the human heart
> Or unravel the arguments of the human mind,
> How can you fathom the God who made all things,
> Or sound his mind or unravel his purposes?
> (Judith 8:14 JB)

By virtue of the fact that we are living in the 21st century, it is easier for us to see God's plan for mankind because much of that plan has already come to pass. This plan is revealed to us through historical events that are identified and interpreted for us in the scriptures. From the historical summaries and other passages of the Scriptures, it is seen that the following nine events are of great significance.

❑ The call of Abraham and God's promise to him
> Yahweh said to Abram, 'leave your country, your kindred and your father's house, for a country which I shall show you; and I shall make you a great nation, I shall bless you and make your name famous; you are to be a blessing!
> (Gen 12:1-3 JB)

❑ The Exodus from Egypt
> …. and Yahweh brought us out of Egypt with mighty hand and outstretched arm, with great terror, and with signs and wonders.
> (Deut 26:8 JB)

❑ The conquest of the promised land
> "And now I have given you a country for which you have not toiled, towns you have not built, although you live in them, vineyards and olive groves you have not planted, although you eat their fruit."
> (Josh 24:13 JB)

❑ The establishment of the Davidic dynasty and God's promise to David
> He chose his servant David,
> and took him from the sheepfolds;
> from tending the nursing ewes he brought him
> to be the shepherd of his people Jacob,
> of Israel, his inheritance.
> With upright heart he tended them,
> And guided them with skillful hand.
> (Psalm 78: 70-72, NRSV)

> You said, "I have made a covenant with my chosen one,
> I have sworn to my servant David:

'I will establish your descendants forever,
and build your throne for all generations' "
(Ps 89: 3-4, NRSV)

❑   The deliverance of the Israelites from the Babylonian Exile (539 BCE)

In the first year of Cyrus king of Persia - to fulfill the word
of Yahweh that was spoken through Jeremiah - Yahweh
roused the spirit of Cyrus king of Persia to issue a
proclamation and to have it publicly displayed throughout
his Kingdom:
"Thus speaks Cyrus king of Persia, Yahweh the
God of Heaven, has given me all the kingdoms of
the earth; he has ordered me to build him a temple
in Jerusalem, in Judah. Whoever there is among you
of all his people, may his God be with him! Let him
go to Jerusalem in Judah to build the Temple of
Yahweh, the God of Israel…."
(Ezra 1:3 JB)

❑   The Incarnation (ca. 6 BCE)
The angel said to her, "Do not be afraid, Mary, for you have
found favor with God. And now, you will conceive in your
womb and bear a son, and you will name him Jesus."   (Lk
1:30-31, NRSV)

This is the gospel concerning God's Son who – in terms of human nature
was born a descendant of David, and who – in terms of the Spirit of
holiness, was designated Son of God in power by resurrection from the
dead: Jesus Christ, our Lord. See Rom 1:3-4.

❑   The Passion and death of Jesus Christ (30 CE)
Though they found nothing to justify his execution, they condemned
him and asked Pilate to have him put to death. When they had carried
out everything that scripture foretells about him they took him down
from the tree and buried him in a tomb.
(Acts 13:28-29 JB)
❑   The Resurrections of Jesus Christ
On the first day of the week, at the first sign of dawn, they went to
the tomb with the spices they had prepared. They found that the
stone had been rolled away from the tomb, but on entering they
could not find the body of the Lord Jesus. As they stood there
puzzled about this, two men in brilliant clothes suddenly appeared
at their side. Terrified, the women bowed their heads to the ground.
But the two said to them, 'Why look among the dead for someone
who is alive? He is not here; he has risen."

(Lk 24:1-6 JB)

❏ The Sending of the Holy Spirit
> When the day of Pentecost had come, they were all together
> in one place. And suddenly from heaven there came a sound
> like the rush of a violent wind, and it filled the entire house
> where they were sitting. Divided tongues, as of fire,
> appeared among them, and a tongue rested on each of them.
> All of them were filled with the Holy Spirit and began to
> speak in other languages, as the Spirit gave them ability.
> (Acts 2:1-4, NRSV)

❏ Christ Will Come Again
> "But in those days, after that suffering, the sun will be
> darkened, and the moon will not give its light, and the stars
> will be falling from heaven and the powers in the heavens
> will be shaken. Then they will see 'the Son of Man coming
> in clouds with great power and glory. (Mk 13:24-26,
> NRSV)

According to the scriptures these are nine significant events in the period of man's history from 1900 BCE to 150 CE (the tenth event is yet to come). If one consults a good encyclopedia or a history book and reads the section covering this same period of history, one only finds descriptions of such events as: the decline of Babylonia, the rise of the Assyrian Empire, the political growth of Carthage, and the unification of Italy under Rome. It is apparent from this observation that what is important to God is not what is important to mankind. God's ways are not mankind's ways. In the words of Jeremiah:

> .... but let those who boast boast in this, that they understand and know
> me, that I am the LORD; I act with steadfast love, justice, and
> righteousness in the earth, for in these things I delight, says the LORD.
> (Jer 9:24, NRSV)

God is Faithful in Fulfilling His Promises

The significant events revealed in Scripture teach us a very important lesson. If we look carefully at all but the last of the events specified above, we will find that each of these events was the fulfillment of a promise made before that event took place.

The call of Abraham initiates the process of mankind's salvation promised at the time of Adam and Eve when God says to the serpent:

> I will put enmity between you and the woman,
> And between your offspring and hers;
> He will strike at your head,
> While you strike at his heel.

363

(Gen 3:15, NAB)

The events of the Exodus and the Conquest were promised to Moses in the desert:

> Then the Lord said, "I have observed the misery of my people who
> are in Egypt; I have heard their cry on account of their taskmasters.
> Indeed, I know their sufferings, and I have come down to deliver
> them from the Egyptians, and to bring them up out of that land to a
> good and broad land flowing with milk and honey.... (Ex 3-8,
> NRSV)

The deliverance of the Israelites from the Babylonian captivity was promised through the prophet Ezekiel at the time that the exile began:

> Then he said to me, "Mortal, these bones are the whole house of
> Israel. They say, 'Our bones are dried up, and our hope is lost; we
> are cut off completely.' Therefore prophesy, and say to them, Thus
> says the Lord God: I am going to open your graves, and bring you
> up from your graves, O mt people; and I will bring you back to the
> land of Israel...." (Ezek 37:11-12, NRSV)

The passion, death and resurrection of Jesus were promised (in the sense of "foretold" since God acts in history, foretelling is equivalent to making a promise). Jesus foretold his death and resurrection to the Twelve while on the road to Jerusalem:

> He took the Twelve aside again and began to tell them what was to
> happen to him., saying, "See, we are going up to Jerusalem, and
> the Son of Man will be handed over to the chief priests and the
> scribes, and they will condemn him to death; then they will hand
> him over to the Gentiles; they will mock him, and spit upon him,
> and flog him, and kill him; and after three days he will rise again."
> (Ml 10:33-34, NRSV)

The incarnation is a very special event; one searches to find an explicit promise of this significant event. It is, however, prophetically stated in Isaiah 7:14 in a real or symbolic way: "therefore, the Lord himself will give you this sign: the virgin shall be with child, and bear a son, and shall name him Immanuel." (Isaiah 7:14 NAB) If we examine the OT carefully, we find the coming of Jesus, the circumstances of his life and death, the nature of his mission, and his resurrection are foretold – but only in perhaps veiled terms. When God sent his Son Jesus the expectations of Israel and of the Jews of the Second Temple period, concerning a promised savior were utterly dwarfed by the fulfillment! It is worthy of note that on the basis of Scripture it appears that it is characteristic of God that the fulfillment of his promises exceeds the scope of the promise itself.

The lesson here is that in each case a promise was made and in each case the promise was fulfilled and then some! God's promise that Jesus will come again to judge the living and the dead and God's promise that if we believe in the gospel then each one of us will have eternal life remain are promises to be fulfilled. On the basis of God's performance to date, we should not have one iota of doubt concerning the future fulfillment of these two promises. Our absolute guarantee of the fulfillment of these promises comes from century piled on century of God acting through human events **always** remaining faithful to the promises and the covenants that were made.

God's Great Love for Mankind

Through the events of salvation history we learn of God's great love for mankind. This love is made known to us in a number of different ways. First of all, it is revealed to us through the gratuitous nature of God's plan of salvation. The call of Abraham and the selection of the Hebrew people to be God's people was an act that was completely undeserved by Abraham and the Israelites. Thus, we read:

> Yahweh, you are the God who chose Abram. (Neh 9:7 JB)

> For by grace you have been saved through faith, and this is not from you; it is the
>
> gift of God; it is not from works, so that no one may boast. (Eph 2:8-9 NRSV)

God's great love for mankind is also revealed through his mercy and forgiveness in the face of repeated failures on the part of the chosen people to keep the covenant with God and to follow the commandments. The Israelites showed themselves to be unfaithful even while Moses was on Mt. Sinai receiving the commandments from God:

> So all the people took off the gold rings from their ears, and
> brought them to Aaron. He took the gold from them, formed it in a
> mold, and cast the image of a calf; and they said, "These are your
> gods, O Israel, who brought you up out of the land of Egypt!"
> (Ex 32:3-4. NRSV)

But God revealed his love by remaining faithful to his covenant with the people:

> "But you are a God ready to forgive, gracious and merciful, slow
> to anger and abounding in steadfast love, and you did not forsake
> them. Even when they had cast an image of a calf for themselves
> and said, "This is your God who brought you up out of Egypt,' and
> had committed great blasphemies, you in your great mercies did
> not forsake them in the wilderness ...." (Neh 9:17-19, NRSV)

In the days of the judges, a period lasting for over 200 years, the Israelites lived through a repeating cycle of sin, remedial punishment, repentance and forgiveness. Each time the Israelites were forgiven it was but a short time before they sinned again:

As soon as they had relief, they would go back to doing evil in
your sight. (Neh 9:28 NAB)

But as often as the Israelites were unfaithful, God would show his love by delivering them once
again:

....then again you abandoned them to the power of their enemies,
who crushed them. Then they cried out to you, and you heard them
from heaven and delivered them according to your mercy, many
times over.   (Neh 9:28, NAB)

After many years of repeated failures on the part of the Israelites to live up to the covenant with
God, God finally allowed them to experience terrible events – the destruction of Jerusalem and
the Babylonian captivity:

Many years you were patient with them, and warned them by your
spirit through your prophets; yet they would not listen. Therefore
you handed them over to the people of the lands. (Neh 9:30
NRSV)

But even through these events God showed his great mercy and love:

Nevertheless, in your great mercies you did not make an end of
them or forsake them, for you are a gracious and merciful God.
(Neh 9:31, NRSV)

Every human being is unfaithful to God's commandments in some way. Every person is a
sinner. This truth is made plain for all to see in an encounter of Christ with the scribes and
Pharisees while Jesus was teaching in the temple in Jerusalem:

The scribes and Pharisees brought a woman who had been caught in
adultery; and making her stand before all of them, they said to him,
"Teacher, this woman was caught in the very act of committing adultery.
Now in the law Moses commanded us to stone such women. Now what do
you say?" They said this to test him, so that they might have some charge
to bring against him. Jesus bent down and wrote with his finger on the
ground. When they kept on questioning him, he straightened up and said
to them, "Let anyone who is without sin be the first to throw a stone at
her." And once again he bent down and wrote on the ground. When they
heard it, they went away, one by one, beginning with the elders; and Jesus
was left alone with the woman standing before him.   (Jn 8:3-9 JB)

Abraham demonstrated his love of God by preparing to sacrifice Isaac, his only son, at
God's command (Gen Chap. 22). God has demonstrated his great love for mankind by allowing
the crucifixion of Jesus, God's only Son, on the cross. Because of this, all of us, although
undeserving, may be saved and have been offered the gift of eternal life:

366

"For God so loved the world that he gave his only Son, so that everyone who believes in him may not perish but may have eternal life." (Jn 3:16, NRSV)

The Underlying Theme

We have processed both the words of scripture and the events of salvation history for what they can tell us about God and ourselves. There remains just one more component of the attar of scripture to be processed – the single central theme. It should be possible to find such a theme given that the Bible was inspired, both OT and NT, by the one living God. That single central theme is **belief and discipleship.** We must believe in God and Jesus Christ and the Holy Spirit. We must live a life of discipleship which includes following the commandments, worshipping God and living with prayer, fasting and almsgiving.

We find this theme in the following places:
- In the life of Abraham – Abraham believed God and followed his command, and left his homeland.
- We find it in the life of Moses – he believed God and followed his command and led the Israelites out of Egypt.
- We find it in the Sinai covenant – God demanded of the Israelites that they believe in him as the one, only God and that they follow his commandments.
- We find this theme in the words of Jesus:
  "The man who has received my commands and obeys them – he it is who loves me; and he who loves me will be loved by my Father." (Jn 14:21, NEB)
- We find this theme again in Paul's letter to the Romans:
  Through him I received the privilege of a commission in his name to lead to faith and obedience men in all nations …. (Rom 1:5, NEB)
- We find this theme in Peter's address to the people in Cornelius' house:
  Then Peter began to speak to them: " I truly understand that God shows no partiality, but in every nation anyone who fears him[230] and does what is right is acceptable to him." (Acts 10:34, NRSV)

Attar of Scripture

We have now isolated the three components of which attar of Scripture is composed. From the flower that is Scripture, we have extracted the essence which comes from the words of Scripture, the essence that comes from the events of salvation history and the essence that comes

---

[230] The phrase "fear God" in OT usage means to have faith in God and to worship God. It is used by Peter here in this OT sense. It does not mean that we should fear God in the sense of being afraid, as we would fear going over a waterfall in canoe. See Psalm 15 in this regard – it is short but very interesting.

from the underlying theme of Scripture. We have only to mix these three components together to obtain that most precious of substances – the attar of Holy Scripture.

Consider for a moment the process of making attar of roses. The process begins by selecting the finest flowers; roses of the highest quality for making attar of roses are only found in the rose district of the Balkan Mountains, where the necessary conditions of soil and climate are found. Long experience has shown that the rose bushes yield their best blossoms in the third year of their growth and that they must be picked before the heat of the sun has a chance to fall on them. The blossoms must be distilled as soon as possible after they are picked as all of the processes active in the blossoms cease at the moment of picking. It is easily seen that the production of the highest quality attar of roses is based on many years of experience.

The situation is much the same with regard to attar of Scripture. The highest quality attar is only obtainable through long years of experience. Experience, in this application, means the thoughtful reading of the biblical text itself and the study of the various aspects about it.

Equally important, perhaps, is experience with living life. Just as one cannot fully plumb the depths of English literature if one has not lived life, so it is necessary to have real life experience in order to fathom the depths of the writings of Scripture. It is only on the basis of experience with life that we are able to draw from Scripture the full depth of its meaning. Because of this involvement with life, one person's attar will be somewhat different from that of a different person. One's efforts to improve the quality of his or her attar are, as a result, the work of a lifetime.

One final observation: when preparing attar of Scripture it is important to keep in mind that God communicates to each person through the Scriptures. We must, therefore, be prepared to look for this communication wherever God chooses to reveal. There may be times when God sees fit to communicate amid the noise of booming thunder as God did with Moses on Mt. Sinai:

> Now Mt. Sinai was wrapped in smoke, because the LORD had
> descended upon it in fire; the smoke went up like the smoke of a
> kiln, while the whole mountain shook violently. As the blast of the
> trumpet grew louder and louder, Moses would speak and God
> would answer him in thunder.
> (Ex 19:18-19, NRSV)

But there will be other times when God sees fit to communicate to a person in a quite different manner as he did in the case of the prophet Elijah:

> He (God) said, "Go out and stand on the mountain before the
> LORD, for the LORD is about to pass by." Now there was a great
> wind, so strong that it was splitting mountains and breaking rocks
> in pieces before the LORD, but the LORD was not in the wind;
> and after the wind an earthquake, but the LORD was not in the
> earthquake; and after the earthquake a fire, but the LORD was not
> in the fire; and after the fire a sound of sheer silence. When Elijah

heard it, he wrapped his face in his mantle and went out and stood
at the entrance of the cave. Then there came a voice to him ....
  (1 Kgs 19:11-13 JB)

If one were to refine and refine again the attar of Scripture in an effort to obtain the purest substance of all, one would find, after the refining process was completed, that the attar consisted of the following:

> The end of the matter; all has been heard. Fear God, and keep his
> commandments; for that is the whole duty of everyone.
> (Ecclesiastes 12:13, NRSV)

> He has told you, O mortal, what is good;
> And what does the LORD require of you
> But to do justice, and to love kindness,
> And to walk humbly with your God?   (Micah 6:8, NRSV)

***

A Thought in Conclusion

Encountering the Living God
... become a bible lover

Then the Lord said [to Elijah]*, "Go outside and stand on the mountain before the Lord; the Lord will be passing by." A strong and heavy wind was rending the mountain crushing rocks before the Lord – but the Lord was not in the wind. After the wind there was an earthquake – but the Lord was not in the earthquake. After the earthquake there was fire – but the Lord was not in the fire. After the fire there was a tiny whispering sound. When he heard this, Elijah hid his face in his cloak and went and stood at the mouth of the cave. 1 Kings 19: 11-13a
(Catholic Study Bible, 1990)*

Made in the
USA
Middletown, DE